THE CHANGING OF KNOWLEDGE
IN COMPOSITION

THE CHANGING OF KNOWLEDGE IN COMPOSITION

Contemporary Perspectives

Edited by

LANCE MASSEY
RICHARD C. GEBHARDT

UTAH STATE UNIVERSITY PRESS
Logan, Utah

Utah State University Press
Logan, Utah 84322-7800
© 2011 Utah State University Press

Manufactured in the United States of America
Cover design by Barbara Yale-Read

ISBN: 978-0-87421-820-6 (paper)
ISBN: 978-0-87421-821-3 (e-book)

Library of Congress Cataloging-in-Publication Data
The changing of knowledge in composition : contemporary perspectives / edited by Lance Massey,
Richard C. Gebhardt.
     p. cm.
   Includes bibliographical references and index.
   ISBN 978-0-87421-820-6 (pbk.) – ISBN 978-0-87421-821-3 (e-book)
   1. English language–Rhetoric–Study and teaching. 2. Report writing–Study and teaching (Higher)
I. Massey, Lance, 1969- II. Gebhardt, Richard C.
   PE1404.C473 2011
   808'.0420711–dc22
                         2011013070

CONTENTS

THE CHANGING OF KNOWLEDGE
IN COMPOSITION

INTRODUCTION
Making Knowledge in Composition Then, Now, and in the Future

Lance Massey
Richard C. Gebhardt

Two ideas motivated this project from the beginning of our collaboration on it. On one hand, we have worked to develop a book that revisits Stephen North's *The Making of Knowledge in Composition: Portrait of an Emerging Field* (*MKC*) nearly twenty-five years after its publication in 1987. On the other hand, we want to use this retrospective orientation as an occasion for trying to make sense of the ways knowledge making has (or hasn't) changed in the years since the publication of North's controversial and, by most accounts, influential book, and how it might change in the future. Consequently, this volume is not a *festschrift*, nor is it merely a critical reexamination of an aging canonical text. The call for chapter proposals, rather, invited "works that critically reassess such things as *MKC*'s influence/impact, rhetoric, aims, and values—with an eye toward using such reassessments to comment on the present and future of composition studies." A talented and diverse group of scholars responded to that call, allowing us to offer you a collection that uses North's book as a framing context within which to explore the methodological, theoretical, and institutional currents of composition's recent evolution and to anticipate future developments for the field.

And what better time for such a collection? Just as *MKC* was published at what was arguably a watershed moment in composition—the field's transition from an essentially modern to an essentially postmodern discipline (see Lance Massey's chapter in this volume)—we now find ourselves on the brink of what may become an equally paradigmatic shift, as we hear ever more calls to replace traditional composition and the pedagogical imperative that term has long implied with a writing studies model devoted to the study of writing as a fundamental tool of and force within all realms of human society.[1] By enacting the ambivalence inherent in such moments of transition—by, that is, proffering the postmodern epistemological argument that knowledge is made, not found, while choosing to do so in the monograph format for its decidedly modernist advantages of "coherence and breadth of vision" (5) and being the "product of a single consciousness" (5)—*MKC* became a flashpoint for enacting the disciplinary anxieties attendant to composition's transition into a postmodernist discipline. Indeed, even North's efforts to revive practitioner "lore" (the nonsystematic, informal knowledge of teachers who need help with Monday's lesson plan, not with analyzing standardized curricula as a form of panoptic discipline) were simultaneously lauded as a refreshingly "postdisciplinary" approach to teachers and teaching (Harkin 1989) and derided as "the imperialist's vision of the native" (i.e., teacher), which is "odious" and "untrue" (Bartholomae 1988, 225).

While we do not hope to set off any disciplinary melees, we see in this collection a deep ambivalence, running parallel to the ambivalence we find in *MKC,*

- as a project that both envisions composition retaining its commitment to broad-based, generalized writing instruction and sees it heading toward content-based vertical writing programs in departments and programs of writing studies,

- as a project that variously challenges and affirms composition's pedagogical heritage,

- and as a project that sounds both sanguine and pessimistic notes about composition's future as a discipline

We see in this collection, that is, all the signs that we again face a moment of precariousness in composition, poised to move not from

---

1.   See, for example, North's chapter 11 in this volume; see also Bazerman (2002), Cushman (1998), Foster (2007), and Miller (2005). We do not mean to imply that there have been no pedagogical arguments from within this writing studies sensibility. In fact, Douglas Downs and Elizabeth Wardle's "Teaching About Writing, Righting Misconceptions: (Re)Envisioning 'First Year Composition' as 'Introduction to Writing Studies,'" which is devoted exclusively to the problem of how to effectively teach writing in college, has been among the more talked-about publications in College Composition and Communication in recent years. We also do not mean the list of authors that begins this note to be exhaustive but, rather, representative. Virtually anybody who studies writing from a perspective informed by Actor-Network Theory, Activity Theory, or North American Genre Theory will implicitly or explicitly claim membership in this camp.

modern to postmodern but from process to postprocess, from a service-oriented field to a full-fledged research-driven discipline, even from being to nothingness, according to some of our field's more apocalyptic voices. Consequently, we anticipate that the meaning and import of the arguments found in this volume will be interpreted in as diverse a manner as those of *MKC* were. Moreover, it is precisely the space opened up by divergent readings of and responses to arguments in works like this one—a metadisciplinary text that indexes deep methodological and theoretical divides—that most directly allows us to engage in rigorous and spirited debate about who we are as a field and how we define our mission and work.[2] And this debate has only benefited by virtue of its taking *MKC* as a jumping-off point, because, as a map of the field itself, *MKC* provides an indispensable point of perspective against which to read the smaller maps contained in many of the following chapters and the larger project of orientation this volume embodies. Indeed, we relish the irony (or, depending on how you feel about such things, the propriety) of an edited collection being brought to bear on a work whose author justified its single-author form by noting that it would be the "product of a single consciousness."

In addition to the present disciplinary moment, unfortunately, we face deeply distressing economic and cultural moments as well. As of the latest revision of this introduction, the United States (and most of the rest of the globe) finds itself still struggling to emerge from its greatest financial crisis since the Great Depression. In the meantime, public support for higher education continues to decrease, the culture wars seem increasingly dominated by slash-and-burn argumentative tactics of politically-motivated, win-at-all-costs pundits and crusaders, and universities show no sign of ceasing—never mind reversing—the steady replacement of the tenured and tenurable professoriate by underpaid, overworked contingent labor. (To cut costs, in fact, our own institution has cut teaching and support staff, imposed a hiring freeze, and mounted a retirement-incentive program for faculty and staff. And our story is far from exceptional.)

---

2.   That such debate contributes to the health of the discipline is a matter of contention. In "Sp(l)itting Images: Back to the Future of (Rhetoric and?) Composition," Karen Kopelson (2008) laments compositionists' tendency to engage in "reflexive introspection" (773) or what C. Jan Swearingen calls "anxious definition and redefinition" (quoted in Kopelson, 774), worrying that such conversations keep us from exploring more important "theoretical and critical issues." We will respond to Kopelson's argument later in this introduction.

Needless to say, in this climate, the health of higher education in general and composition studies in particular is far from guaranteed. It is incumbent upon us to promote the important intellectual work we do, to work against inaccurate and dishonest representations of the ideas and aims of higher education, and to protect and, where possible, restore the dignity and reputation of our physical and intellectual labor. Part of doing these things, moreover, is maintaining as clear a sense as possible of our own disciplinary identities and how we fit into—or more to the point, how we *might* fit into, in some possible future—the larger academic, cultural, and economic ecologies of which we are a part. And while this volume does not cover every angle—were we to release our call again, we would specifically solicit treatments of gender and sexuality as they relate to *MKC*, and we would seek out discussions of technology as it has shaped composition research and practice since 1987—the plethora of angles it does cover offer a valuable closeup look at many of the fibers that make up the fabric of our discipline.

We also want to note here that we are aware of some compositionists' distaste for metadisciplinary projects like this one. A time-honored tradition in composition is to call for us to cease looking at and writing about ourselves and get on with the work at hand (as if determining what that work entailed were not itself a part of our work). In a recent *College Composition and Communication (CCC)* article, for example, Karen Kopelson worries that composition's penchant for such projects, "even when [they are] genial, rigorous, and provocative, is becoming at least wearisome and is actually what might prove deadly to our intellectual endeavors" (2008, 774). She goes on to note that "the costs are indeed high when self-scrutiny comes at the expense of taking up other critical concerns" (775). Such arguments, however, invariably exempt, or at least excuse, themselves from their own injunctions. As if she is a parent telling her children to "do as I say, not as I do," Kopelson notes "the deep irony" of her argument, "suggesting that we make a concerted and collective effort to release ourselves from the pattern represented" by her own work. Not only do we find such arguments unpersuasive,[3] but we also find projects of disciplinary "self-scrutiny," even at the "unrivaled" (775) levels to be found in composition (though they are still a small minority of the work being published in our journals and books), invigorating and challenging. We need only point to the essays in this

---

3.   How, for example, does one prove that such projects exist only "at the expense" of other concerns? Is scholarship really a zero sum game?

collection for evidence of that. Thus, what may seem to some like disciplinary self-absorption is, to us, the continuing of a healthy tradition of works in composition (Bloom, Daiker, and White 2003; Farris and Anson 1998; Olson 2002; Bloom, Daiker, and White 1997) that take a broad, encompassing look at ourselves in an effort to help us consciously build a discipline devoted to generating knowledge about writing and writing instruction and to making the local, regional, and national communities that sustain it more equitable places to live.

Scanning the table of contents gives a sense of the topics and approaches of the chapters that follow. Immediately following this introduction, Steve North's "Notes on the Origins of *The Making of Knowledge in Composition*" gives his personal reflections on the 1980s professional climate of composition and his university that led him to write the book he did. This personal perspective continues in part one, "Personal Responses," which includes pungently diverse perspectives on *MKC* and its significance by two scholars who studied the book and used it in their graduate courses almost as soon as it was published. Part two, "Working the Field," includes five chapters emphasizing knowledge-making communities since Steve North's book put "the making of knowledge" at the center of composition's scholarly professional agenda. Part three, "*MKC* and Education," includes three chapters that consider undergraduate writing instruction, the undergraduate writing major, and public educational issues in the context of *The Making of Knowledge in Composition*, as well as Steve North's view of the present and future place of composition in American higher education. In part four, "Disciplinary Identities, Disciplinary Challenges," five chapters illustrate and explore the disciplinary complexities and contradictions that have characterized composition's recent evolution.[4]

---

4.   Unlike the introductions of many edited collections, the discussion of chapters that follows introduces them not in the order in which they appear in the book but, rather, associatively as they relate to the discussion that unfolds here. Indeed, as will be clear, we do not hesitate to mention chapters more than once if they are relevant to different aspects of the discussion. This organizational choice was not made simply out of convenience, however. Rather, we recognize that tables of contents and the editorial decisions they reflect invariably fail—are indeed bound to fail—to capture the complexity and nuance with which authors treat their subjects. Specifically, the generalizations of the last few paragraphs hardly do justice to the authors' arguments about The Making of Knowledge in Composition, its place in composition's development, and the future of our field. As a result, we offer this associatively organized introduction as an implicit alternate table of contents. We invite you to do the same—to look through the abstracts, read the chapters, and find connections and associations of your own.

Part of the context of this book is the ongoing response to North's description of the field and judgments about the field's scholarship—quite a range of response, as is clear in chapters on the reception and citation of *MKC* by Lance Massey ("The (Dis)Order of Compositiion") and by Brad Lucas and Drew Loewe ("Coordinating Citations and the Cartography of Knowledge"), and parts of North's "Notes on the Origins of *The Making of Knowledge in Composition.*" For Ed White ("The Significance of *MKC* for Graduate Education"), North's book brought a major change in his graduate teaching because of North's willingness to ask probing questions and his assumption that "nothing and nobody were sacred or beyond questioning." North's "irreverent and questioning attitude toward his sources," White thinks, "is immensely valuable for graduate students to understand. They will be ready to see and examine the scholars as people rather like themselves, situated in a special vision of the world and working from a methodology that needs to be explicit and interrogated, for quotation from their work to be meaningful" (19). But as Lynn Bloom ("The World According to North") used *MKC* in graduate classes, she came to a very different view. After initially using North's innovative map of the hitherto unexplored territory of composition studies with graduate students, she came to believe there was *major terrain missing* from it (e.g., rhetoric, reading, style, theory, collaborative writing, writing in the disciplines, and issues of literacy, class and ethnicity). And, while White writes approvingly of North's energetic and personal tone, Bloom laments what she sees as his abrasive and confrontational style.

Given these divergent responses, as well as the controversy with which *MKC* was received for years after its publication, one might naturally assume—as we do—that *MKC* has been an influential work. It has certainly influenced White, and one might say it has influenced Bloom, too, though not, we suspect, in a way either North or Bloom might have hoped for. Yet, for all the sound and fury surrounding its reception, Smit concludes that *MKC* may have had an uncertain impact on the field of composition studies, and its influence may be in dispute. Still, Erica Frisicaro-Pawlowski ("Making Knowledge, Shaping History") suggests the book's influence on at least one strand of composition inquiry, finding that *MKC*'s efforts in linking notions of methodological-, historical-, and self-consciousness within an account of disciplinary formation anticipate subsequent developments in composition scholarship.

Despite *MKC*'s (apparent) influence, several chapters emphasize now-important subjects and approaches absent from *MKC* or about which North's judgments must be questioned in light of recent developments. Victor Villanueva ("Rhetoric, Racism, and the Remaking of Knowledge Making in Composition") notes that work about—and by— people of color is wholly absent in *MKC* and composition research of its day. Kelly Pender ("Philosophy(s) of Invention Twenty Years after *MKC*") thinks North underestimated the substance and importance of invention research in composition, but finds that recent invention research, most of which fits North's "philosophical" category, shows that North was right to be optimistic about the philosophical community. Though they see little about writing centers in *MKC*, Sarah Liggett, Keri Jordan, and Steve Price ("Makers of Knowledge in Writing Centers") find North's categories of research relevant to writing center research, for instance the writing center community's acceptance of multiple methodologies and affinity for philosophical inquiry. They conclude that writing center studies could benefit from sharper methodological awareness and from a reconsideration of practitioner inquiry. Similarly, Matthew Jackson notes that "the intersubjective pedagogical relationship between students and teacher is not discussed directly and in depth. The problem that arises from this absence, then, is that there is no allowance for serious consideration of an intersubjective pedagogical ethic that is necessary to a philosophy, not of knowledge making, but of *being and becoming* in composition" (168; italics in original).

As those chapters suggest, *The Changing of Knowledge in Composition* gives a complex sense of the field that has evolved—and is evolving still—since Stephen North's book was published in 1987. Even though *MKC* preceded developments in what have become known as undergraduate research and the writing major, for instance, Joyce Kinkead ("Undergraduate Researchers as Makers of Knowledge in Composition in the Writing Studies Major") sees much of relevance in North's book to future developments in the research component of the undergraduate writing major, especially in its emphasis on what North calls "practice as inquiry." Christine Hansen ("Are We There Yet? The Making of a Discipline in Composition") works with North's criteria for forming a discipline in composition to argue that the field had only mixed success in reaching disciplinary status, and that there have been few indicators that North's dream of methodological pluralism and egalitarianism has been realized. In contrast with Hansen's first point, David Smit ("*MKC* and the Future of Composition Studies 'Without Paradigm Hope'") argues that North's vision of the future of composition studies has, for all practical purposes, come true; that a type of scholarship distinctive to composition studies has evolved; and that the fragmented, postmodern, historicized composition studies about which North was ambivalent is something composition studies should embrace, even celebrate (219). In contrast to Hansen's second point about methodological pluralism, Bloom stresses the multiple approaches of our field, offering an "ambitious" but incomplete list of "research areas that emerged in the 1990s, among them collaborative writing, technology, multimedia, creative nonfiction, blurred and blended genres, assessment, writing in the disciplines or in particular disciplines, writing program administration, intellectual property, writing centers, contingent faculty, and writing in the extracurriculum, including issues of globalization, multilingualism, spirituality, and more" (37). And Patricia Webb Boyd ("Making Space in Composition Studies: Discursive Ecologies as Inquiry") argues that eco-composition and place-based research enact a diverse, multidisciplinary research paradigm that responds to Stephen North's call to recoup practice as inquiry as a valued methodology (308). Patricia Dunn ("Practice as Inquiry, Stephen North's Teaching, and Contemporary Public Policy") sees practice—especially the "exposing, naming, and analyzing" (195) of assumptions behind practice that North pursued in *MKC* and in his graduate teaching—as applicable to many public-policy controversies regarding teaching and testing that stem from fundamental differences in epistemological assumptions, which are rarely seriously examined. Unexplored assumptions regarding practice likewise concern Richard Fulkerson ("The Epistemic Paradoxes of 'Lore'"), who argues that lore, over the years since North wrote about it, has resisted defense or justification (because no one has been able to answer the question, "Under what conditions does a lore claim count as credible?") even though our leading empirical scholarship (ethnography) has become increasingly more lorelike. And Villanueva suggests that the field is developing in its inclusiveness, not only in the extent and centrality of race and gender, but also in the way narrative and personal writing are expanding the nature of knowledge making in composition.

Implicit in the authors' discussions of *MKC* and composition's evolution since 1987 are suggestions about the future of our field. Massey offers his analysis of composition's contemporary "identity crisis" as an effort at "clarifying our own vision of ourselves and the work we do so that we might better, and more self-consciously, define and redefine the discipline of composition in what are no doubt destined to be years, if not decades, of economic crises and public resistance" (311) to our work. Given such a seemingly tumultuous future, moreover, it is hard to imagine that race, class, and gender will relinquish their important places in composition or that personal and creative approaches will disappear from composition scholarship. Other subjects important to authors of this book also seem certain to remain concerns of our field, such as graduate education, historical and political considerations of composition's identity, tensions and/or synergies of practice and theory, composition's position within broad social issues, and (assuming continued interest and funding across higher education) writing centers, the writing major, and undergraduate research. Less settled in the chapters of this book seem issues of research diversity, the dominant methodologies that may develop, and the role of and respect for other research approaches.

Those are possibilities and questions, not predictions. Twenty years from now, how important will the topics emphasized in this book be— race, gender, invention, writing centers, graduate and undergraduate education, practice, the nature and formation of our discipline, and the like? Will we still feel the need to publish disciplinarily introspective volumes such as this one? How frequently (or rarely) will journal articles and books of that day utilize personal and narrative writing, place-based research, citation analysis, ethnography, replicable systematic research? With regard to such scholarly foci and approaches, will the extent or rate of change continue to match that implied by the authors writing here almost twenty-five years after Steven North described the field in *The Making of Knowledge in Composition?* We rather expect scholars writing in anticipation of North's fiftieth anniversary to see less change over a couple of decades than do the authors of this book, unless another book comes on the scene to attract and/or irritate scholars the way *MKC* did. Whether *MKC* will then be part of the scholarly and professional conversation—included in graduate syllabi and works-cited lists, for instance—is itself an intriguing question. We expect it to be, both as a representative of an ambitious effort to develop a view of the composition scholarship of its day and as part of—and stimulus to—the growth of our field over the decades that followed.

REFERENCES

Bartholomae, David. 1988. Review of *The making of knowledge in composition: Portrait of an emerging field*, by Stephen M. North. *Rhetoric Review* 6: 224-28.

Bazerman, Charles. 2002. The case for writing studies as a major discipline. In Olson, 32–38.

Bloom, Lynn Z., Donald A. Daiker, and Edward M. White, eds. 1997. *Composition in the 21ˢᵗ century: Crisis and change.* Carbondale: Southern Illinois University Press.

———. 2003. *Composition studies in the new millennium: Rereading the past, rewriting the future.* Carbondale: Southern Illinois University Press.

Cushman, Ellen. 2003. Vertical writing programs in departments of rhetoric and writing. In Bloom, Daiker, and White, 121–29.

Downs, Douglas, and Elizabeth M. Wardle. 2007. Teaching about writing, righting misconceptions: (Re)envisioning "first year composition" as "introduction to writing studies." *CCC* 58: 552–84.

Farris, Christine, and Chris M. Anson. 1998. *Under construction: Working at the intersections of composition theory, research, and practice.* Logan: Utah State University Press.

Foster, Helen. 2007. *Networked process: Dissolving boundaries of process and post-process.* West Lafayette, IN: Parlor.

Harkin, Patricia. 1991. The postdisciplinary politics of lore. In *Contending with words: Composition and rhetoric in a postmodern age,* edited by Patricia Harkin and John Schilb, 124–38. New York: MLA.

Kopelson, Karen. (2008). Sp(l)itting images; or, Back to future of (rhetoric and?) composition. *CCC* 59: 750–80.

Miller, Susan. 2002. Writing studies as a mode of inquiry. In Olson, 41–54.

North, Stephen. 1988. *The making of knowledge in composition: Portrait of an emerging field.* Portsmouth: Boynton/Cook.

Olson, Gary, ed. 2002. *Rhetoric and composition as intellectual work.* Carbondale: Southern Illinois University Press.

NOTES ON THE ORIGINS OF *THE MAKING OF KNOWLEDGE IN COMPOSITION*

Stephen M. North

Reading the essays Lance Massey and Rick Gebhardt have assembled here has led me to reflect—not, to be sure, for the first time—on why a debut book by an untenured writing center director should have caused the kind of stir *MKC* unquestionably did, or enough of one that we are still discussing it. One part of the answer, I think, is that my professional concerns and anxieties, which account for so much of what the book is about, resonated with a great many other people in composition. The other— a minor but crucial corollary, and not as tongue-in-cheek as it probably sounds—is that unlike most other people in composition, I had to write a book early in my career, and it couldn't be about writing centers.

I don't think there's anything particularly contentious about the first claim. From the mid-1970s through the mid-1980s, composition underwent what passes in U.S. higher education for amazingly rapid change, a veritable overnight process of professionalization: upgrades of existing and the emergence of new refereed journals; serious access to public and private funding for both research and pedagogical innovation; the beginnings of graduate education beyond the traditional practicum; and, most materially significant, a substantial increase in the number of full-time, tenure-track positions. Inevitably, though, these changes— these unprecedented opportunities—provoked parallel and unprecedented anxieties. What would it take to publish in these new venues, or to compete for these grants? What was a graduate course in composition supposed to look like? What would these new tenure-track positions entail, exactly, and what would it take to land one . . . and keep it? And the big question, in some sense lurking beneath all the others: What exactly *was* composition, and did it—did we—really constitute a legitimate professional and disciplinary enterprise? Did we, in short, really belong in the academy?

And my own professional trajectory was very much of a piece with these developments. Certainly I benefited enormously from the opportunities. Consider: when I enrolled as a doctoral student at Albany for the 1975–1976 academic year, the English department had never hired a faculty member in composition. Its forty-section-per-term composition course was overseen by a director, but that was an assigned duty, not an academic specialization. However—fatefully, I daresay—at the end of that year, the university brought in John Gerber, longtime chair of English at Iowa and first chair of the Conference on College Composition and Communication (CCCC), to lead the department in rebuilding after a series of setbacks. By fall 1977, Gerber had hired the department's first-ever director of writing, a fiction writer with a strong interest in composition (who would direct my dissertation), followed in fall 1978 by its first tenured associate professor of composition (Lee Odell). And shortly after that, in 1980, the department conducted its first-ever search for a junior hire in composition, which led to my appointment as assistant professor and director of the writing center. I wouldn't be surprised if it was the first time in the history of U.S. higher education that a doctoral-granting English department had devoted a tenure-track line to hiring a writing center director; and it may still be the only time when such a department did all that *and* hired one of its own graduates.

All that good fortune notwithstanding, though, the position also came with a full share of the aforementioned anxieties. Certainly I understood—and felt acutely—the pressure for grants and publications: I had been at Albany long enough, in fact, to see more than a couple of candidates, including highly regarded teachers, denied tenure for having too little of both. I also learned immediately the challenges that making composition a subject for formal graduate education posed: from 1981 to 1986, the department never had more than two composition faculty, so there was never a time when I wasn't engaged with the attendant duties: offering graduate courses, serving on dissertation committees, and so on. Last but far from least, I understood—especially as the local candidate—how many other departmental priorities had been slighted in creating this new emphasis on writing in general, and therefore how much skepticism, and even hostility, some of my colleagues felt toward the whole thing. So while it was exciting to be part of an ascendant group, it was not without its perils.

Still, I was managing to channel those anxieties in what I believe even now were useful ways: administering a rapidly expanding writing center, developing grant proposals for research on tutoring, cofounding (with

Lil Brannon, then of NYU) a journal for writing center scholarship—and, of course, writing about all of these things in conference papers and journal articles. All things being equal, in other words, these sorts of activities would have been as much of an expression of or response to composition's broader disciplinary and professional anxieties as I ever would have offered.

But things did not, of course, stay equal, which brings me back to the second part of my answer about why *MKC* should have caused a stir: I had to write a book, and it couldn't be about writing centers. In 1984, I met with our new department chair (Gerber having retired the year before) on the occasion of my first contract renewal. He explained, kindly but candidly, that while this writing center work I'd been doing was all very well, if I hoped to be ready for a tenure decision in a few years I would need to produce, like my untenured counterparts in Victorian literature and Shakespeare, a scholarly monograph—which was to say, as I understood it then and now, not a teacherly monograph (e.g., a book on training tutors), nor an administrative one (theory and practice of writing centers), nor (God forbid) a textbook. No: a scholarly monograph from a respectable press about . . . well, about whatever it was that people in composition wrote scholarly monographs on.

Talk about—excuse the family vernacular—an oh-shit moment. I'm certain my book plans prior to that meeting were vague, but I'm equally certain they revolved, in all their vagueness, around writing centers. How could they not? That was, in a very real sense, all I *knew*. For while I may have been, as I noted in *MKC*, a member of the first generation to claim professional certification in composition—in my case, on the strength of a dissertation about writing centers—my actual coursework in the field had consisted of a practicum on the teaching of writing and litera-ture taught by an American studies professor; and a single independent study, with an English education professor, focused on Aristotle's *Rhetoric* and the professor's high- school composition text.

And let's face it: even if I had taken a fuller slate of formal courses, it's not as though my chair's invocation of scholarly monographs in compo-sition conjured up a clear tradition or a ready set of alternatives to my obscurely imagined book about writing centers. Yes, there were mono-graphs to consider—although not, in 1984, so very many—but most of them had not been written for anything my English department was likely to have accepted as a "scholarly" audience (*Writing without Teachers*, say, or *Errors and Expectations*); and those that had been either posed serious methodological obstacles (Emig's *The Composing Processes of Twelfth Graders* would be a hard sell even now), or else were so far beyond my capacity (e.g., Kinneavy's *A Theory of Discourse*) as to make book writing seem impossible altogether. I don't remember exactly how the plan I ended up following actually took shape except that, as I explain in *MKC*'s preface, I was deeply concerned about having failed a doctoral student on a qualifying examination because he had been unable to explain how composition made sense as a field—and had been unable, I knew, because I had failed to explain it to him. And then, at about the same time, I read Robert Connors's "Composition and Science," which somehow led me to Diesing's study, which in turn gave me the framework I needed to write a book on a subject that, at least compared to writing centers, I really knew very little about. Or put it this way: I spent the next two years composing an account of composition that was also (a) my first systematic education in the field and (b) the key credential in my bid for tenure and promotion in the kind of unit—an English department—that my account would end up casting as composition's hostile host.

All of which is by way of reiterating my opening assertion: that *MKC* ended up resonating as powerfully in its time not simply because it was a product of my particular experience of composition's widely shared professional and disciplinary anxieties—everything we write is that—but because it was, as a function of my peculiar situation, an outsized expression of and response to those anxieties. Certainly that is how I have come to understand the sheer magnitude of the book's initial reception. The February 1989 issue of *College Composition and Communicaton* (*CCC*), for instance, featured three simultaneous reviews—an unprecedented clustering, and a weighty one, at that: the authors were James Raymond, then editor of *College English*; Richard Lloyd-Jones, a past chair of both CCCC and the National Council of Teachers of English (NCTE); and Richard Larson, immediate past editor of *CCC* itself. William Irmscher, another former *CCC* editor, reviewed it in the *Harvard Educational Review*. David Bartholomae in *Rhetoric Review*. And why did such senior scholars pay this kind of attention in such high-powered venues to a writer only a few years removed from graduate school? Because, to recast my refrain in slightly different terms, for a brief but very intense moment, my individual trajectory coincided to an unusual degree with that of the larger composition enterprise; and it did so in a form—a big, fat, single-author book—that served, for both trajectories, as a powerful emblem of legitimacy. Small wonder the reviews were so mixed: this was, if I might push the scatological rhetoric a little further, something of an oh-shit moment for the field, too.

PART ONE

Personal Responses to
The Making of Knowledge in Composition

1

THE SIGNIFICANCE OF NORTH'S *THE MAKING OF KNOWLEDGE IN COMPOSITION* FOR GRADUATE EDUCATION

Edward M. White

I was among the handful of English faculty teaching a graduate course in writing research when Stephen M. North's *The Making of Knowledge in Composition: Portrait of an Emerging Field* (*MKC*) appeared in 1987. Before it became available, I used two books for the course, the only ones that seemed to me appropriate: the survey of research produced by Richard Braddock, Richard Lloyd-Jones, and Lowell Shoer twenty-four years earlier (1963), and the collection of essays on writing research edited by Charles Cooper and Lee Odell in 1978. Neither book was really satisfactory. The Braddock, Lloyd-Jones, and Shoer book was hard headed and comprehensive for its time but had one huge drawback: it defined research as only empirical, statistically based research; none other was worthy of the term. Cooper and Odell had a more expansive view of research, yet the book was a series of discrete essays of varying quality and perspective. I adopted the views of both texts, teaching an incoherent and statistically oriented course. In common with the accepted truths of the day, I mocked teacher knowledge as a kind of superstition, although I presented isolated studies, including success narratives, as examples of approved research. I am embarrassed at the course I taught, as I look back at it, and I hope it did not do too much damage to the students in it.

Like most of us in those remote days establishing, unawares, the "new" field of composition studies, I was reasonably qualified to teach the course, and my enthusiasm for it may in part have compensated for my ignorance about the burgeoning research about to flower everywhere in the field. (I was also painfully ignorant of rhetoric, a word never, I think, mentioned in my graduate studies of English and American literature. That large lacuna was widely shared, most obviously by North.)

I had published a number of articles on the teaching of writing, had become rather an authority on writing assessment (the first edition of my *Teaching and Assessing Writing* appeared in 1985, just too late for North to include) and I had edited two composition textbooks for W.W. Norton. But I had no real understanding of the varieties and methodologies of writing research. I accepted the division of such research into "quantitative" and "qualitative" categories, with its reductive dichotomy, and I struggled with a vague understanding of what constituted knowledge in our field. I remember Jim Gray, founder of the then Bay Area Writing Project, inviting me to present a survey of what we knew about writing and writing instruction to the second group of Project Fellows. When I asked him why he didn't do that himself, he scowled and said, "Everyone thinks I'm an expert, but I don't know anything about that stuff. Now you, you know what you're talking about." I didn't have the confidence to confess my own ignorance, so I did the best I could. I can't recall a word I said, but the presentation was well received, so I suppose I knew a tad more than the others in the room.

I also remember asking Rich Haswell, who was teaching a course in writing research then at Washington State University, how he structured it. He replied glumly that he spent the first half of the term teaching statistics to the literature graduates in his class and that that approach was a recipe for disaster. He asked me what I did. After I told him, we both shook our heads in silence; we knew enough to know that what we were doing wasn't good enough. Steve Witte was more positive; he was certain that statistics were the basis of any serious research and, indeed, argued that position until his untimely death. But I, perhaps because I saw myself as a writer first and a scholar second, was not convinced. I was and am at heart a storyteller and I was not about to give away the power of narrative in practice, though I had done so in theory. But storytelling is hardly a curriculum and not even I could call it research.

Into this world burst North's book, which I immediately saw as transforming the teaching I had been doing. The copy I first read sits on my desk as I write now, held together by a rubber band as it slowly disintegrates, with my precious pencil notations in the generous margins of almost every page. I immediately saw the book as the center of my course in writing research. For the first time, we had a book with basic concepts and procedures at its core to hold the course together, itself unified by a powerful narrative presence—an energetic and personal tone that still takes some readers by surprise. But, in addition, the book in time began to change the way I wrote and read, so powerful was its analysis of methodology. As years went by, it began to change my other courses, most notably the graduate seminar in literary theory I taught for composition/rhetoric graduate students; I'll get back to that course later. As years went by, competing books began to appear and I tried them, but none of them filled the need the way *MKC* did, and I always returned to it. I don't mean to imply that the book became a sacred text. Indeed, part of its value for students as time passed was for them to notice what it omitted as the field of rhetoric and composition developed. By the time the book was ten years old, I began urging North to do a revision, an update. But he shuddered at the very thought, maintaining that the book was of its time and done. Maybe he was right. It is hard to imagine the scholar today who could master the vast world of writing research as he did over twenty years ago. Besides, what made his book so important was its basic attitude and methodology, not its inclusiveness. So it is to his attitude toward research that we now turn.

THE NORTH POLE

The power of North's approach to research lay in his willingness to ask probing questions. Nothing and nobody were sacred or beyond questioning. With a kind of foolhardy fearlessness, he accused Robert Connors of inconsistency, Flower and Hayes of misusing protocols, and Steve Witte of pedantry and a lack of awareness of his own methodology, a tactic not calculated to win him friends. "Where does that guy get off," Witte said to me angrily, shortly after the book appeared, "attacking his betters?" I didn't need to ask just who his betters were. North had mercilessly deconstructed Witte's prize-winning 1983 *CCC* essay, "Topical Structure and Revision: An Exploratory Study," in *MKC*. Typically, North began his examination of the essay most respectfully, but his ironic tendency broke out before the first sentence was completed: "The essay is an important piece of Researcher work . . . (and incidentally the most heavily documented article in the history of the journal)" (339).

North's irreverent and questioning attitude toward his sources—the biggest guns in the field at the time he was writing—is immensely valuable for graduate students to understand. While undergraduates have trouble using sources well, generally because of their lack of context in the field and a lack of clarity about their own ideas, graduate students have a different problem: an excessive respect and even awe at the scholarly community they are seeking to join, particularly if some of these scholars are their teachers. Though those who were subject to his sharp analyses have never seen it this way, North is never merely ironic or deflating, though he is occasionally both of these. He simply expects the major scholars to be held to the highest standards of consistency and he makes clear again and again just what these standards are. He also knows, as the baseball proverb has it, that even the best pitchers put their pants on one leg at a time. Graduate students paying close attention to North will not be tempted to drop quotations from scholars into their own writing as if they were truths. They will be ready to see and examine the scholars as people rather like themselves, situated in a special vision of the world and working from a methodology that needs to be explicit and interrogated for the quotation to be meaningful.

North adapted from his social-science sources his pattern of interrogating the assumptions behind the various methodologies he described. What, he repeatedly asks, is the kind of world the researcher sees as suitable for his or her particular kind of research? Empirical research, for instance, with its demand for replicability and for convincing data, needs a stable and predictable universe, suitable enough for astronomy and chemistry, perhaps, but maybe not quite the world of teaching and learning writing. Again and again, he pursues the thinking about thinking that some psychologists call *metacognition*, though he avoids using the term. And everywhere he tests the particular vision of the world assumed by a research methodology according to the reality of his own world, one, again for instance, in which his eight o'clock class is quite different from his three o'clock class.

Whenever North encountered pride, inconsistency, pedantry, or unjustified claims, and he encountered them often, he pounced and left his mark. Just how deep those wounds were surprised him, and indeed me, since I emerged unscathed and found his style a clean breath of fresh air in a field clouded by too much jargon and pretension. In 1992, when two colleagues and I were putting together the program for the 1993 writing-program administrators conference (the papers were published in 1996 by Southern Illinois University Press as Bloom, Daiker, and White, eds., *Composition in the Twenty-First Century*), I asked North to be half of the session on writing research in the twenty-first century. He agreed. Then I sought another researcher for the panel. No dice. Almost everyone I spoke to refused to share the podium with North. Finally, University of California professor Sarah Freedman agreed, but only if she could be the first speaker. The session went well enough, but the question period afterwards evinced considerable hostility toward North from the large audience. He has clearly paid a price for his originality and critical perspective on the field.

Perhaps that price has been his retreat into the comparative safety of administrative work and less provocative writing, and his decision not to follow the virtuoso performance of *MKC* with anything of like power. To be sure, if this collection of essays were about North, instead of his most compelling book, we would have to see his work at the National Council of Teachers of English, where he spent five years as acquisitions editor, and his *Refiguring the Ph.D. in English Studies*, as substantial critical and creative contributions to the field. But the unique power of *MKC* has not been matched by North or approached by anyone else. The North pole has turned out to be a lonely place and one such journey may be enough even for the most intrepid explorer.

DEFINING WORLDS

When North sets out to examine a research methodology, he does not begin with method. Instead he begins with the reality taken for granted by the methodology. As I said above, unless the world is orderly enough to be consistent, to follow its own laws of mathematics and chemistry, scientific study, including empirical research in composition, makes no sense. (North calls those doing empirical research "experimentalists," not the only idiosyncratic usage in the book.) If no generalizations can hold, a methodology aimed at generating and confirming, or disconfirming, generalizations will be of no use in the making of knowledge. North is not presumptuous enough to question whether that vision of the world (or any other) is accurate or not as an epistemological fact; he is perfectly willing to grant any researcher his or her vision of the world, however it may differ from his own. But once you make clear what world you are assuming, you had better stick to it. Thus the empiricist or the formalist (the confusing term he uses for those trying to diagram and chart the writing process) may make their charts and compile their data, but when their conclusions impinge on what teachers know from their practice, the method often breaks down. Practitioners inhabit the house of lore, not the statistical package for the social sciences, and their suspicions of generalizations and descriptions that do not match their experience are not only, or merely, personal quirks. As North the writing teacher is quick to remind us, they live in a different world and their world is far from neat or orderly.

When Yvonna S. Guba and Egon G. Lincoln set out to describe what they called fourth-generation evaluation (1989), they tried to distinguish the perceptions of reality of different research procedures according to a chronological scheme, strongly implying steady progress across the centuries toward better and more responsible methodologies. Although they do not cite North, they also argue that the lens through which one looks helps determine what one sees. North does not try for any such hierarchy or idea of progress. He merely demands that the researcher understand and articulate the world assumed by the method employed, and that the conclusions not go beyond the data or the argument; it turns out that such a demand is "merely" the hardest criterion for most composition research of substance to meet. Thus when Robert Connors, North's example of a historian, concludes his historic survey of the concept of "modes of discourse" with an injunction to teachers to avoid them in instruction, or when Linda Flower, North's primary formalist, protests that the model she and John Hayes developed of the mind in the process of writing is not intended to describe all possible rhetorical situations, they are rejecting North's strictures. As well they might, since every researcher hopes for findings with large ramifications, not the narrow ones dictated by method. But in the end, we must conclude, it does no service to research to allow it to bend its own rules and to imagine that what takes place in the world of a particular research study will necessarily happen in other worlds as well.

THE CATEGORIES

Although North protested that his eight categories were not intended to be inclusive—and surely every reader then and now has come up with important omissions—the structure of the book gives them a kind of authority beyond the disclaimer. He called them "clusters" and "rough groupings," rather than definitive patterns of inquiry, "not *the* eight modes of the field" (6). They are not intended to prescribe the official lines of inquiry for the field. And they certainly do not define the researchers. As I taught the book, I had no difficulty coming up with work of my own that fit pretty well in each of North's categories. But what made the categories important was not their different characteristics. It was his underlying defining method: they were distinguished according to the questions they asked. "The Practitioners . . . want to know What do we do? the Scholars . . . try to discover What does it mean? and the Researchers . . . ask What happened (or happens)?" (3).

I found this way of looking at research—according to the questions behind the research—to be a most useful way of helping my graduate students see what different kinds of researchers were up to. I don't mean to suggest that this approach was new. I remember from my graduate work in literature differences in literary periods being defined by questions, or at least by metaphors for questions: seventeenth-century scientists shifting attention from *why* natural phenomena occurred to *how* they occurred; the romantic writers changing the conception of art from a mirror to a lamp; and so on. Yet this focus on the questions behind research is a powerful teaching tool for apprentice researchers. What, I have come to ask in the opening class session, is the single indispensable component of any research project? The students look puzzled. "MLA style?" one will hazard. "A good bibliography," another will say. Finally the most thoughtful student will say quietly, "A good research question." And that response leads to why researchers keep at their projects: the itch of a question that needs to be scratched. The question, and its assumptions about the world, then lead to a methodology and, often but not always, to a hypothesis. And the ability to generate interesting hypotheses is a major goal of graduate education.

Nonetheless, North's categories are troubling, not merely because they leave too much out (such as feminism and rhetoric) but because they are sometimes misleading. In the early 1990s, I sent a post to North about his use of the term *formalists* to describe researchers like Flower and Hayes, who draw up working models of the writing process. Since many, perhaps most, of our graduate students come to us from an English major heavy in literary studies, they know formalism, if they know any theory at all, as close reading of texts. They are not likely to know its European roots, but they will know its American version in the old New Criticism, still the dominant methodology for teaching literature in the schools and many colleges. North defended his use of the term, explaining both his usage and its connection, in his mind, to literary formalism:

As for the collision with literary formalisms, yes, I was aware of it. As I explained (I think) in the book, I was working from Paul Diesing's book on Patterns of Discovery in the Social Sciences, and that was his term. And I guess I would also suggest that in fact the formalist tendencies in literary studies actually have much the same roots: i.e., that they arose out of the field's longstanding desire to claim a method (and an object of study for that method) that was as systematic and "rigorous" as what the math and science folk seemed to claim (and that seemed then as now to be favored in the academy). So I can live with the confusions, and in fact would invite readers to work further into the connections between a formalist "model" of reading and a cognitive formalist "model" of writing. [Here, and below, I am quoting from informal email exchanges with North, with his permission granted by personal correspondence, May 20, 2008.]

I haven't seen anyone rise to that challenge, perhaps due to the precipitous fall of literary formalism among theorists, and I continue to find the connection a bit forced. But this passage, informal and casual in the way of email, also reveals North's way of thinking, inviting others (with great cordiality) to consider origins, roots, basic questions.

When North calls teacher researchers "practitioners," he also stirs up unwelcome problems. Despite his strong effort to distinguish teachers as teachers from teachers doing research as teachers, many graduate students, particularly new teaching assistants, take his view to be disparaging or even demeaning. After all, teachers believe in "lore," that rambling structure filled with contradictory rooms and outdated intellectual furniture, and are basically committed to whatever might work on Monday morning. One of my tasks as a graduate seminar teacher is to point out that North was the first major researcher to take teacher research seriously and to maintain his standing as a teacher (see Dunn, this volume, for an account of North's teaching). His underlying critique of empirical research is that its world is not his world, where what works on Monday morning may well not work on Monday afternoon, for reasons beyond knowing. But the teachers who now fill our research seminars have become supersensitive to slurs and, despite the pride of placement North gives to practitioner research, they do not feel he is one of them and sufficiently respectful of the jobs they do. Would another name have helped? Probably, but I can't come up with a better one.

My graduate students, sensitized to methodologies, inevitably ask about North's own method, particularly after reading David Bartholomae's slighting reference in his early review of the book in *Rhetoric Review* to "North's sociology or anthropology or history of composition" (1988, 228). Early in 1997, I sent an email to North, working in Finland at the time, forwarding the student question. Here is his reply, again in the informal discourse of email:

> How would I classify my own method? This one gets asked a lot. In fact, I asked it in the book itself, and even answered it (somewhere in the beginning), but nobody has ever seemed satisfied with that. If I were to classify it now, I suppose I'd call it a hermeneutical study. After all, I worked exclusively

with texts and textual interpretation, even when I was invoking social con-texts. On the other hand, it has elements of what people do now in variously conceived cultural studies stuff, as well. Frankly, I think the reason I get asked this—and not, say, Susan Miller about Textual Carnivals or Lester Faigley about Fragments of Rationality, say, is that I am—or my narrator is—such a bug about everyone else's method, right? About methodological integrity? But my study was, by definition, meta-methodological in that sense: i.e., it was not—could not be—a study from within. Hence it might be called (fol-lowing Patty Harkin) a post-disciplinary method; or, following people like Jim Raymond, say, a rhetorical study (with rhetoric conceived as the study of the discursive practices of other disciplines). Hidden in the question, too, I sense, are questions like Who the hell do you think you are? or maybe, OK, but where exactly do YOU stand? Me, I think I answer those questions quite clearly: that's why the flippin' manuscript ran over 600 pages.

The question about North's method is far from trivial or easy to answer, as other essays in this collection demonstrate. For me, the answer would lie somewhere in the realm of ethos, where personal nar-rative blends with epistemological rigor. As I write these words, I realize that has always been my goal as a writer as well, as I demonstrate in the essay you are now reading.

EVERY DIRECTION FROM TRUE NORTH IS SOUTH

North's introduction of the Diesing pattern of thought to English fac-ulty has been powerful, as reflected in much graduate teaching and scholarship. When I was confronted with the daunting task of teaching a one-term course on literary theory to graduate students in a composi-tion program, it worked very well indeed. I sought to group theoretical approaches according to the questions they sought to answer and the world-views they expressed. Thus a grouping I called Moral Approaches generally asked questions about the effects of reading on human behav-ior and envisioned a world in which reading could have a powerful influence on that behavior. This common thread allowed us to connect Aristotle to Sir Philip Sidney to Samuel Johnson to T.S. Eliot and move on to issues of censorship and the contents of school libraries. Again, psychological approaches tend to focus on three kinds of psyches: those of the author, of the more or less fictional characters in literary works, and of the reader or audience. The root question for such approaches has to do with examining these various psyches and their interplay with text to determine meaning. Again, the inner world of psychological approaches contrasts sharply with social approaches, asking about the interaction of a text with society through research in history, Marxism, or various kinds of cultural studies. And so on. I am not claiming originality in these (representative) groupings—various texts were available that used some or all of them—but rather that looking closely at assumptions and underlying questions gave coherence and meaning to a vast subject defined by apparently idiosyncratic approaches. And this is a core pedagogical problem for graduate courses.

In common with my graduate students, my close attention to North also had a direct effect on my scholarly writing. For instance, when I began writing the essay that became "The Opening of the Modern Era of Writing Assessment: A Narrative" in 2001, I was working with *MKC* in class. As I began revising a simple narrative into a historical document, I kept North's descriptions of the best historical research at hand. A narrative is fine, even good fun, but a historical narrative, based on new information, is in quest of the meaning of events, their causes and implications, as well as the events themselves. I feel quite sure that all those using *MKC* in their graduate classes also wrote somewhat differently themselves as a result of the experience. I might also hazard a view of the essay you are now reading, if anyone has gotten this far, not only as a chronicle of one admiring reader using a particularly valuable book for graduate education, but also as a representative case study of how important scholarship has wide-ranging effects on our profession.

A PERSONAL CONCLUSION

During the 1990s, North and I happened to be using each other's books in graduate courses: he was asking his students to read my book on writing programs (1989) and I was using his *MKC*. Though we did not know each other well—and still do not—we developed an interesting crosslink. We exchanged term papers, each reading those from the other's class, commenting on and, in some cases, actually grading them. I have a handwritten cover note from North from one of these exchanges, in which he mentions the "pretty extensive" replies he wrote to each student. Extensive indeed they were, warm and witty as well. But the note he sent to the entire class left an unforgettable impression: "Hope these comments are of some use! And please, one of you, decide to supplant that damn book. After 10 years, it's time for it to be (sup)planted. Take care."

Over ten more years more have gone by since then and "that damn book" looks better than ever. I suspect that it will not be supplanted.

REFERENCES

Bartholomae, David. 1988. Making knowledge/making composition. *Rhetoric Review* 6 224–230.

Bloom, Lynn Z., Donald Daiker, and Edward M. White, eds. 1996. *Composition in the twenty-first century: Crisis and change.* Carbondale: Southern Illinois University Press.

Braddock, Richard, Richard Lloyd-Jones, and Lowell Schoer. 1963. *Research in written composition.* Urbana, IL: National Council of Teachers of English.

Cooper, Charles, and Lee Odell, eds. 1978. *Research on composing: Points of departure.* Urbana, IL: National Council of Teachers of English.

Guba, Egon G., and Yvonna Lincoln. 1989. *Fourth generation evaluation.* Newbury Park, CA: Sage.

North, Stephen. 1988. *The making of knowledge in composition: Portrait of an emerging field.* Portsmouth: Boynton/Cook.

White, Edward M. 1985. *Teaching and assessing writing.* San Francisco: Jossey-Bass.

———. 1989. *Developing successful college writing programs.* San Francisco: Jossey-Bass.

———. January 2001. The opening of the modern era of writing assessment: A narrative. *College English* 63 (3): 306–320.

Witte, Stephen P. "Topical structure and revision: An exploratory study." *CCC* 34: 313–41.

2

THE WORLD ACCORDING TO
NORTH—AND BEYOND
The Changing Geography of Composition Studies

Lynn Z. Bloom

Mapmakers control our view of the world—if we let them. Too often
we forget the arbitrary nature of the configuration, its underlying intellectual, political, and linguistic constructs. The Mercator projection of
1569 strategically locates Western Europe in a central and dominant
position in the world, thereby giving the tiny British Isles the visual and
political prominence they warranted at the time, and relegating whole
continents down under the equator to a point beneath the Western
chauvinist gaze. Likewise, Saul Steinberg's "View of the World from 9th
Avenue," the *New Yorker*'s widely reproduced cover of March 29, 1976,
shows a richly detailed Manhattan reaching from Ninth Avenue to the
Hudson River, occupying half the page. Beyond that, the football-field
flatland stretches from the barren Jersey shore clear to the west coast,
one quarter the size of the urban foreground. The Pacific Ocean,
from this intentionally myopic perspective, is only twice as wide as the
Hudson; China, Japan, and Russia are mere blips on the far horizon.

In a comparable vein, Stephen North's *The Making of Knowledge in
Composition* proffers a map of the hitherto virgin territory of composition (today we might call it composition studies), one young man's
window on a brave new world. Before I explain how North sets out to
go where no man (I use the term advisedly) had ever trod, let me map
the territory of my own essay that follows. In the first section, "A Fine
Romance," I'll tell you the story of my early infatuation with this stranger
who strode into town, intriguingly different from the predictable locals,
innovative, arrogant, tight lipped, unsmiling, rigidly uncompromising.
Then, in "Reality Check," I'll tell you how this tale, too, inexorably followed the conventional masterplot, after I had taken a good hard look at

what this intruder had to offer. In the conclusion, "D-i-v-o-r-c-e," I anato-
mize the departure of the newcomer—now all too familiar—in this case
booted out, leaving behind the heroine, sadder but wiser. What began in
romance ended, as extravagant passions often do, in gimlet-eyed analysis, a return to reason. You can identify the making of knowledge in this
essay as a combination of a case history, textual analysis, critical reading,
pedagogical philosophy, intellectual and disciplinary history and projection, stylistic analysis, a statement of professional ethics, and oh yes, professional autobiography—just the usual eclectic mix of methods that has
characterized my scholarly writing for the past fifteen years.

STAGE ONE: A FINE ROMANCE

It was a stretch for a single grad course to cover the research territory
even in the years before there was much territory to be covered. As
a newcomer teaching research in composition to new graduate students seven years before North swaggered into town, I had been badly
burned, as I have confessed in "Subverting the Academic Masterplot"
(1998), by my innocence of the ways of research-as-it-is-conducted-in-
schools-of-education—mostly quantitative at the time, in contrast to the
qualitative research I knew and loved. I was further flummoxed by the
concept of *ethnographic research* in composition, for Shirley Brice Heath
had not yet published her work, and its terminology and parameters
were uncharted.

As the scars gradually blanched from blood-red to ashen, I clung
to safe texts as if professional survival for teacher and students alike
depended on the reliable and trusty guides. My research course was
anchored with the canonical research classics of the time, Emig's *The
Composing Processes of Twelfth Graders* (1971), Shaughnessy's *Errors and
Expectations* (1977), Ed White's *Teaching and Assessing Writing* (1985).
By then, Elliott Mishler's eye-opening common sense call for "Meaning
in Context: Is There Any Other Kind?" (1979) had paved the way
for Heath's most welcome *Ways with Words* (1983), a ten-year study of
the meaning of literacy in multiple life contexts. Graves's *Rhetoric and
Composition: A Sourcebook for Teachers and Writers* (1990) included excellent
research articles, as did Tate and Corbett's *The Writing Teacher's Sourcebook*
(1981), and Tate's *Teaching Composition: Ten Bibliographical Essays* (1976)
provided the bibliographic underpinning. These books addressed such
topics as invention, structure and form in nonfiction prose, style, modes
of discourse, basic writing, linguistics, dialects, and more. All of these

works were carefully constructed, thoroughly researched, respectful of disciplinary norms, polite to colleagues, intellectually engaging, and unostentatious in tone and claims even when they unveiled exciting new research methods and opened up totally new vistas. If composition teachers or researchers wanted to know the lay of the land on a given topic we could just look it up.

Then, it must have been in 1987, Ed White met me for lunch at the Conference on College Composition and Communicaton (CCCC) bearing a pristine copy of *The Making of Knowledge in Composition*, aquiver with excitement as he examined North's bold demarcation of the territory from the perspective of a cultural anthropologist, unfamiliar if not alien to his target audience. Amaz'd from our peak in Darien, we noted that North adopted a social-science perspective, rather than the one we humanists, trained as literary critics (along with linguistics, the only game in town for English doctoral students of a certain age at Harvard—Ed— and Michigan—myself) knew and loved. North's bold new approach and terminology was adopted from the research of Paul Diesing, a political scientist at SUNY-Buffalo studying communities as a participant-observer, but never—from that day to this—a member of the composition studies community. Diesing's concepts enabled North to reconfigure the world as he knew it in or around 1987. He simultaneously took the stance as an insider, a member of whatever community he was looking at, and as an outsider as well. This dual perspective allowed North to maintain not only critical detachment, but at times to address his material with the quasidivine disparagement characteristic of the nineteenth-century British travelers' supercilious commentary on their colonial outposts. In the spirit of Fanny Trollope's *Domestic Manners of the Americans*, North appears to share her view that "on first touching the soil of a new land, of a new continent, of a new world, it is impossible not to feel considerable excitement and deep interest in almost every object that excites us" (1947, 7). But this pleasure is quickly undercut by the realities of the new context: "Let no one who wishes to receive agreeable impressions of American manners commence their travels in a Mississippi steam boat . . . I would infinitely prefer sharing the apartment of a party of well conditioned pigs to the being confined to its cabin [sic]" (16).

North divided the emergent composition world into eight categories whose labels I bought immediately, although the researchers themselves didn't use either this terminology or North's categorization scheme. First came *The Scholars*, including *Historians*, *Philosophers*, and *Critics*;

then *The Researchers,* populated by *Experimentalists, Clinicians, Formalists,* and *Ethnographers.* These terms sounded so right, so smart. But even at infatuation's first blush I balked at calling teachers *The Practitioners.* My husband, a social psychologist, had long used this social–science label to identify social workers and therapists. I was—and to this day remain—a *teacher,* not a practitioner of teaching; if writing teachers summoned a "practitioner," who would come (I personally envision a personal trainer)? Moreover, I was then, and remain, a *writer,* a practitioner of a different sort, although it took writing this essay for me to realize that in North, "writer" is generally prefaced by "student."

Nevertheless, because *MKC* was so new, so innovative, so wide ranging, and yes, so insouciantly arrogant, its initial appeal was undeniable, the call of the wild that led not only Ed and me but many composition studies professors across the nation to assign it to new TAs in the late 1980s and early 1990s to introduce them to the lay of the land.[1] (Lauer and Asher's 1988 *Composition Research: Empirical Designs,* the main alternative, seemed too mathematically oriented for English department grad students.) The SUNY-Albany website, which as of 2001 identified *MKC* as "required reading in virtually every graduate writing program in the country," would lead readers to believe this *MKC* was still a staple of everyone's grad syllabus at the beginning of the twenty-first century. This was surely an overstatement, since most of North's research matrix had been superseded by the mid 1990s. Unfortunately, my attempts to assess the current state of North's work via queries on the Writing Program Administrator (WPA) listserv—Have you ever taught *MKC?* If so, in what course(s)? When? Why did you choose this book? And (if relevant), why did you stop?—have elicited too few replies to generalize from—an ineffective research method, alas.

At first blush *The Making of Knowledge in Composition* looked astonishingly comprehensive. For North (or anyone) to examine an entire field—or several fields, depending on how one wants to carve up the terrain—from the perspective of research methodology rather than topic reversed the familiar perspective of figure and ground. Foregrounding the research methodology emphasizes how the researcher goes about designing the research in order to find answers to questions large and small, general (and perhaps vague and open ended) or specific and circumscribed, important or trivial. Refocusing the question from *what*

---

1.   See reviews by James Raymond and Richard Lloyd-Jones in the February 1989 issue of College Composition and Communication.

to *how* meant that North had to remap the entire field, as conceived of from his vantage point in the mid 1980s. To perform this herculean task he had to have a sophisticated understanding of research methodology as well as an extensive knowledge of multiple topics and issues in an ever-widening field. Although—as I shall discuss later—there are a number of significant omissions, North chose a broad rather than a narrow view of the field, and multiple rather than single illustrations of a particular research method or issue.

North's criticism blew in like a brash north wind on a cozy Grandma Moses landscape. He chose to represent the development of modern composition studies in terms of researchers' aggressive conflicts over territory, for the "power and prestige that go with being able to say what constitutes knowledge." The World According to North is a rerun of the Wild West, "a kind of methodological land-rush" conducted by "group after group of [ruthless] investigators, each equipped with some different mode of inquiry" scrambling "to stake their claim to a portion of what they have perceived as virgin territory," and trampling "roughshod over the claims of previous inquirers" by ignoring, discounting, or ridiculing the knowledge of the "'indigenous' population," practitioners (a.k.a. teachers) (3–4).

This is not the World of Composition Studies as I knew it during its formative decades, nor the World as I know it now. I fell in love with the composition community—if such a freewheeling assemblage of folks in the late sixties could be called a community—from the moment I set foot at my first CCCC meeting. The people I met, numbers of them movers and shapers in this newly configured world, became instant friends. Risk takers all, often renegades from the disciplinary constraints of the Modern Language Association (MLA), these people were and remain friends and colleagues, sharing ideas, ways to move the profession along, plans to help students and each other, with excitement and good will; the profession's Girl Scouts, Boy Scouts, and Johnny Appleseeds. The collective sense is that the territory remains full of wide open spaces with lots of land for one and all, and many rooms in The House of Lore. From the outset I never bought North's concept or his aggressive language; if my colleagues have been guilty of land grabs, they've concealed their territoriality well. In retrospect, I should have stopped with page four of *MKC*, but the book was so intriguingly audacious that I persevered.

For North to map such a vast, evolving, and amorphous territory using his particular categorical scheme, expressed in harshly vivid language (styled by Leona Helmsley rather than Brooke Astor), required supreme confidence that he (and he alone—there were no collaborators on this project) could do the job quickly enough to publish *MKC* in time for his tenure review. Because *MKC* provides a critical evaluation of the research methods and reception of many of the projects (such as awards and other indications of professional esteem, but rarely censure), his chosen method also involved, though it didn't require, considerable chutzpah. North, this self-designated judge—and jury—arrogated the right to override a host of others' previous judgments of a given work— dissertation directors, editors, publishers, professional award commit- tees. That he was often right, in a genteel disciplinary culture commit- ted to praise rather than scathing criticism, was at first read refreshing, though unsettling in its churning of the waters of polite discourse. (It later came to seem like a scorched-earth scholarship.)

A characteristic case in point is North's acerbic analysis of Janet Emig's canonical, foundational, award-winning *The Composing Processes of Twelfth Graders*. North introduces Emig's work as a "technically innovative," quot- ing Earl Buxton, "'expedition into new territory, an investigation of the writing *process*,' a powerful, pioneering influence on subsequent research" (197). Emig asked eight students "to do three pieces of writing for her" during summer vacation; two "composed aloud with Emig present" while she tape recorded them, prompting them to explain connections between their thinking and their writing (or not writing) (211). Lynn, Emig's pri- mary subject, produced "some 567 words of prose composed on two very unusual occasions over a period of about three hours, supplemented by an account of the composing of 86 words of poetry . . . and an hour-long background interview that included questions about 10 or 15 pieces of other writing" (211). On the basis of this evidence, Emig made a variety of claims about *The Composing Processes of Twelfth Graders*.

The praise with which North began (significantly, not even in his own words, but another's) is soon eclipsed by his characteristic mode of analysis, which translates into attacks on the research design, execu- tion, results, claims, misguided judgments of those who evaluate it or model their own work on it; and how well (usually badly) the research fits North's designated category—in Emig's case, clinical. Emig, claims North, has chosen an unclear research design unaligned with either cli- nicians or experimentalists (North's labels). Emig's "uneasiness with her method" (199), considering her work "a subsidiary, second-class kind of inquiry" (200), obviates any claim to "any substantial methodological authority" (199). For, says North, "There is no treatment, no really tested or even testable hypotheses, no framing of a problem in paradigmatic terms" (200). By creating an arbitrary, artificial experimental setting—out of school, with an investigator (Emig herself) who was not their teacher—Emig's research, full of "methodological waffling" (202), was "too intrusive, too context-irreverent" (202) to be ethnographic, too idiosyncratic, intuitive, and improvisatory to be replicable, and consequently not very viable as either an experimental or clinical study. Here North characteristically sets up a straw category (in this case, two or three) and then blames the researcher because her work doesn't fit—a vehement case of blame-the-victim.

North does not (and, I think, cannot) offer evidence that Emig, in fulfillment of his overriding metaphor, is toting a six gun and trying to blast rivals off the turf; in fact, her generous example provides a model for others' work. Nevertheless, he asserts that despite its flaws, the clinical approach has an advantage for the researcher in its "marketability," because the "satisfyingly full portraits" of its subjects permit an "extraordinary, almost instant impact, on the field" (205). Practitioners (i.e., teachers) can "easily" translate the characters and the findings into "lore," and take them to their hearts—and classrooms (206).

The clinical knowledge that practitioners are embracing, however, is "the result of a bad compromise, an impure method birthing a bastard knowledge." It is therefore "bound to be unreliable." Poor misguided souls; the practitioners are tricked by Emig's grandiose title and her "amazingly ambitious and freewheeling" (227) interpretations into believing that the evidence from Lynn represents *The Composing Processes of [Millions of] Twelfth Graders*. In fact, says North, this "snapshot study of Lynn," augmented with "bus station biographies" of the seven other twelfth graders in the study, should more accurately have been titled *The Composing Processes of Eight Twelfth Graders*, with *Processes* modified to *Process* because the essentially one-shot research had "no longitudinal dimension" (206–12). That is true. Nevertheless, what North chooses to identify as a pitifully shrunken universe of discourse could have been redeemed by different labeling: had he considered Emig's work an augmented case study rather than a diminished and highly flawed clinical investigation it could have shone as brilliantly in *MKC* as it did for decades in the wider professional firmament.

Immediately following this painfully detailed, largely negative assessment of Emig, North, in a comparable vein, examines the writing process dissertation research and related publications by Sondra Perl, Nancy Sommers, Cynthia Selfe, and Sharon Pianko. He accurately observes that composing aloud depends heavily on the researchers' interpretations of surface "behavior"—"moving jaw and tongue, eyes and hands, making sounds" (and silence—"The writer doesn't say 'I'm searching long term memory now'") as reflective of textual features. However, because despite elaborate coding schemes such interpretations remain highly subjective and variable, "composing aloud still [after fifteen years] presents Clinical investigators with serious problems in terms of validity and reliability. . . . further evidence of the Clinical community's retarded growth" (224–25). There is more, but you get the drift; clinicians, with their "technical eclecticism" (218), will grasp at any observable "complex phenomenon" that occurs when people are writing, "whose various layers . . . can be peeled off by a variety of techniques for investigative purposes, and then re-layered to form a communal knowledge. Hence their freedom to poke and prod subjects," in Naziesque fashion, "to make them compose when and where and how they want" (219). North's most helpful concluding suggestion is that such research be expanded, in depth and in longitude, to provide portraits of individual student writers as "whole, complex people," "each drawn with the acute sensitivity Emig shows in her portrait of Lynn, but with steadily improving sources of data, and within a gradually richer canonical framework" (237).

Yes, it was unfair for North to slot a researcher such as Emig into a category of his own contrivance and then to criticize her for not accommodating his strictures rather than following her own plan.[2] Yes, his death-by-metaphor language was abrasive, sometimes unwarranted ("methodological land-rush"), at other times ("bus station biographies") compelling in its mode of repellent dismissiveness. Much of the time he was right: Emig's method, despite her impersonal, quasiscientific language, was seriously flawed and ultimately impressionistic; her claims grandiose; her reputation overstated by a cadre of admirers and copycats. Reading North was like listening to gossip, demeaning to the listener as well as to the perpetrator, but at times irresistible. I must admit that I was fascinated by North's nitpicking discovery of imperfections, whether large or microscopic, and his nattering nuances of negativism.

---

2.   See also Richard Larson's 1989 review of North , which I deliberately avoided rereading until I had finished writing this essay.

STAGE TWO: REALITY CHECK

The syllabi of yesteryear tell me that I taught *MKC* in a master's/doc-
toral level course in rhetorical theory and composition research at
the University of Connecticut from 1990 to 1994—and that it occu-
pied three weeks in a syllabus that now exhausts me (though it did
not faze my students) just to read the titles of the core works. These
included the following: significant segments of Bizzell and Herzberg's
The Rhetorical Tradition (1992)—classical, medieval, eighteenth and
nineteenth century, right on up to Bakhtin, Burke, Foucault, Derrida,
Cixous, Anzaldúa, and Gates; Robert Scholes's *Textual Power* (1985)
for its application of literary theory to the teaching of English ("Our
job is not to produce 'readings' for our students but to give them the
tools for producing their own," [24]); Jane Tompkins's *Reader Response
Criticism*, for ways of reading *From Formalism to Post Structuralism* (1980);
Clifford Geertz's *Works and Lives* (1988) for analyses of the power and
authority of four anthropologists' compelling, competing literary styles,
augmented by Susan J. Leonardi's succulent "Summer Pasta, Lobster a
la Riseholme, and Key Lime Pie"—the darling of *PMLA* in 1989; Mike
Rose's earthshaking *Lives on the Boundary* (1989), for its utterly grip-
ping mix of autobiography, ethnography, case history, writing-process
research, institutional analysis, social commentary, educational philosophy, literacy auto/biographies, creative nonfiction—and cheerleading.
Whatever nastiness North's negativity may have engendered was more
than counteracted by the plethora of other voices in this dialogue—
lively, emphatic, encouraging, occasionally shrill.

In the second year I used it, it was apparent that *MKC* was creating problems for the students because the studies North subjected to
analysis were aging or already out of date. Thus to fill in the ever-widening lacunae I was discovering in North's map of the research territory, in 1992, the year it was published, I augmented *MKC* with Gesa
Kirsch and Patricia Sullivan's *Methods and Methodology in Composition
Research*. Sullivan's interpretation of "Feminism and Methodology
in Composition Studies," Thomas Huckin's "Context-Sensitive Text
Analysis," and Thomas Newkirk's "Narrative Roots of the Case Study"
not only provided new perspectives, but a welcome level of civility in
language and manner of analysis.

These essays, and others in Kirsch and Sullivan's book, took issue
with the dominant research claim, promulgated not only by *MKC* but
by Lauer and Asher's *Composition Research: Empirical Designs* (1988), that

scientific knowledge registered "objectively and dispassionately reality as it is . . . value neutral and hence gender neutral as well " (Sullivan 1992, 56). Disinterested detachment is not possible, argued Sullivan, speaking for feminist scholars in general: "The realities recorded and reported via so-called objectivist methodologies are always versions of a reality that is subject to revision; reality 'as it is' is always someone's perception . . . always a situated perspective" affected by the "researcher's own race, class, culture, and gender assumptions" (56). In the same volume Kirsch examined "Methodological Pluralism," a concept that could have allayed much of North's fretting about blurred methods, had his categorization scheme accommodated the actual messiness of the way much humanistic research actually operates rather than insisting on methodological purity. And Duane Roen and Robert K. Mittan collaborated on issues of "Collaborative Scholarship in Composition," a research orientation North overlooks even while indexing categories of researchers as "Experimental community," "Historian community," "Practitioner community."

The areas addressed by the other books in the course I taught reveal major terrain missing from North's map, which seems very focused on topics dear to schools of education. Omitted are such topics as *classical and modern rhetoric, reading, style,* applications of *theory*—literary, pedagogical—to practice (none of the italicized words or their derivatives are in North's index). That way be not monsters, as the explorer's ship approached the edge of the known universe, but feminists and others dealing with ethical and political issues; real-world writers (Donald Murray's *A Writer Teaches Writing* (1968), Tom Wolfe's *The New Journalism* (1973), and related works); autobiographers such as Maxine Hong Kingston, *Woman Warrior* (1975), and Richard Rodriguez, *Hunger of Memory* (1982), who along with Mike Rose incorporated analyses of literacy, class, and ethnicity; rhetoricians; linguists; genre theorists and others concerned with reading; essayists galore. All of these topics were of particular interest in the 1970s and early 1980s, when North was working on his book. Even my ambitious list couldn't cover all of the major research areas that emerged in the 1990s, among them collaborative writing, technology, multimedia, creative nonfiction, blurred and blended genres, assessment, writing in the disciplines or in particular disciplines, writing program administration, intellectual property, writing centers, contingent faculty, and writing in the extracurriculum, including issues of globalization, multilingualism, spirituality, and more.

By1994 *MKC* was simply too outdated to use for a research overview, so I dropped it. Since then I have used Christine Farris and Chris Anson's *Under Construction: Working at the Intersections of Composition Theory, Research, and Practice* (1998); Lisa Ede's *On Writing Research: The Braddock Essays 1975–1998* (1999); and my own (with Daiker and White) *Composition Studies in the New Millennium* (2003). Next at bat will be Gesa Kirsch and Liz Rohan's *Beyond the Archives: Research as a Lived Process* (2008).

The many titles above illustrate how any field, emerging or established, continues to grow and change, and the rapidity with which composition studies explored new territory. The limitless, greatly reconfigured world of composition studies at the beginning of the twenty-first century seems light years away from North's 1987 map, with the addition of new terms and changing interpretations of familiar ones: *rhetoric* (as in Cheryl Glenn's *Unspoken: The Rhetoric of Silence* [2004]; Krista Ratcliffe's *Rhetorical Listening* [2005]; Barbara Couture and Thomas Kent's *The Private, the Public, and the Published: Reconciling Private Lives and Public Rhetoric* [2004]; and John Schilb's *Rhetorical Refusals* [2007]); *humanities* in Kurt Spellmeyer's *Arts of Living* (2003); *writing program administration* in McLeod et al.'s *WAC for the New Millennium* (2001) and Brown and Enos's *The Writing Program Administrator's Resource* (2002); *human rights* as addressed by Ellen Cushman's *The Struggle and the Tools* (1998) and Richard Miller's *Writing at the End of the World* (2005); *technology* intertwined with *law, ethics, politics, public debate, privacy,* and *internet usage* as in Vicinus and Eisner's *Originality, Imitation, Plagiarism* (2008); comparable dimensions of *teaching and writing in a traumatized world,* as in Thomas Deans's *Writing Partnerships* (2000) and Shane Borrowman's *Trauma and the Teaching of Writing* (2005).

Besides these striking abysses and lacunae in the landscape that indicate that this world indeed is out of joint, North's take-no-prisoners approach and language seem more to abuse his subject than enlighten it. North's complaints about fuzzy or flawed methodology cast progressively more doubts on his categorization system, rather than on the research he is analyzing. Categories of research and researchers, neatly labeled, make discussion of the subject manageable, but too often arbitrary and unreal. For in my experience and that of researchers I've talked with over the past year (an informal way to provide anecdotal evidence for this essay, unreplicable but in my view totally valid), all good research begins with a good question. This leads to more good questions, and still more. Then the researcher figures out the best way to answer these, often involving multiple methods. Pragmatism trumps methodological purity (a colleague calls this "methodological opportunism"); composition studies researchers generally do not choose North's labels (say formalists or clinicians) and most would not restrict themselves to such a categorization system.

Would North have written a conceptually clearer, less querulous book if he had focused on the nature of the questions researchers ask, rather than on their methodology? Indeed, while harping insistently on methodological "impurities," North often fails to get at the heart of the important questions researchers are asking. Characteristic is his dismissal of Shirley Brice Heath's *Ways With Words* (1983), on which he spends only a single paragraph, writing it off with a faint praise ("the focus is not as narrow as usual," 287) while ignoring the scope, depth, innovative methodology (including ten years' immersion, participation in, recording of, and interpreting dual and interrelated cultures and a host of subcultures, embedding a wide range of speaking and writing in context), and humane analysis that have made the work an enduring classic and won Heath a MacArthur. If North had concentrated on the big picture—on major, groundbreaking research by scholars of distinction such as Heath—instead of spending pages and pages picking at flaws in dissertations such as those of Perl, Sommers, and Pianko (among others), which are by definition learning opportunities for novices, *MKC* might have been more generous—and more enduring.

STAGE THREE: D-I-V-O-R-C-E

Since North and I parted ways I have really never looked back from that day until I agreed to write a chapter for *The Changing of Knowledge in Composition*. As far as I know, this severance has been without emotion on both sides.

However, when I reexamine the subject I uncover many regrets. Anyone can make a mistake once, but to have used *MKC* for four years is three too many. I regret having been seduced too early and too long by a book with so many flaws, among them scope, selection of evidence, point of view, language, and method of analysis. I prefer always to concentrate on the positive features of others' work; how else can one be a cheerleader for grad students being initiated into the profession one loves? Thus I regret teaching a book that obliged me to provide a thoroughgoing critique of North's categorization system, as well of as his choice of victims, and ultimately to turn against him his very own complaints about flaws

in research design and execution, his lamentations over researchers' dis-
loyalty to a particular method, his preoccupation with minutiae that led
him to overlook interesting and fundamental questions. For instance,
instead of belaboring minor problems in composition-process research,
why didn't North address the illogical, unnatural use of composing aloud
as a way of investigating how people write? What, if any, correspondence
exists between speaking and writing? How trustworthy can researchers'
claims about the writing process (or processes) be if they are based on
oral, rather than written, composition? Because so much goes on in writing that is never consciously articulated (matters of audience, genre form
and convention, usage norms and preferences, and on and on) how
closely can any investigation of writing, by any means, oral or written,
accurately represent the process? By focusing on the small stuff, North
scarcely attended to these—and other—very big questions.

I also regret that I was initially so respectful of North's rigidly delineated categories that I did not sooner bring to bear in teaching *MKC* my
in-the-trenches understanding of how I myself do research. When, during the second year of using *MKC*, I drew more extensively on my firsthand knowledge, I was able to see how complicated the research process
is, how difficult it is to try to unbraid its interwoven strands, even in the
interests of sorting out the individual techniques; and how misleading it
is to examine each in isolation without allowing for their integrated use.
I'm not the Queen of Eclecticism; I believe that's how most composition
studies researchers work most of the time.[3]

---

3.   One case in point will suffice to illustrate a complex of mixed methodologies, discovered pragmatically at the outset of my research career. My dissertation, "How Literary
Biographers Use Their Subjects' Works: A Study of Biographical Method, 1865–
1962," asked, "How do literary biographers use their subjects' works?" To discover the
answer(s) involved examining how biographers constructed their subjects and constructed their texts. The dissertation was therefore a study of reading, of the nature
of evidence, of the methodology and rhetoric employed in using that evidence. It
was also a study of the rhetorical conventions and parameters of a scarcely examined
genre of nonfiction prose. It was a study of rhetorical arrangement—including the
selection, nature, and organization of evidence; and of emphases and omissions
(aha—gaps!). It was a study of personae, of both the primary authors and the biographers, and thus a study of style—particularly syntax, vocabulary, and tone. It was
a study of critical response to the authors' primary texts over four centuries. The
dissertation also included quantitative as well as qualitative analysis, highly unusual
for a literature dissertation at that time or at any time, for in it I examined how often
biographers used each subject's works in particular ways and presented the results in
tables, to the astonishment of my committee. The tables, in fact, signaled an affinity
with the scientific method, an inductive process common in those composition studies from the 1960s to the present that deal with numbers of things (students, papers,
errors, words in T-units), including the twenty thousand-item database of essays in

Were North to heed his own advice and replicate his study with a new map of the ever-evolving new world of twenty-first century composition studies, would I use a nouveau *MKC*? For me to use a revised, revived—and perforce greatly expanded—*MKC*, either for my own information or for teaching, North would have to make some major changes. He'd have to focus on major research rather than on dissertations. He'd need to ask big and therefore significant questions, and stop sweating the small stuff. He'd need to sheathe tooth and claw, eschew the savage metaphors, however arresting, and address his human subjects—colleagues nationwide, major and aspiring contributors to the contemporary terrain, with greater sympathy, more courtesy. I'm not asking for North to replace his John Wayne stance with Mister Rogers; Sir Edmund Hillary would be my companion to climb the next Everest.

REFERENCES

Bizzell, Patricia and Bruce Herzberg, eds. 1992. *The rhetorical tradition: Readings from classical times to the present.* Boston: Bedford.

Bloom, Lynn Z. 1963. How literary biographers use their subjects' works: A study of biographical method, 1865–1962. PhD diss., University of Michigan.

———. The essay canon. 1999. *College English* 61: 401–30.

———. Subverting the academic masterplot. 1998. In *Composition studies as a creative art,* 130–40. Logan: Utah State University Press.

Bloom, Lynn Z., Donald A. Daiker, and Edward M. White, eds. 2003. *Composition studies in the new millennium: Rereading the past, rewriting the future.* Carbondale, IL: Southern Illinois University Press.

Borrowman, Shane, ed. 2005. *Trauma and the teaching of writing.* Albany: State University of New York Press.

Brown, Stuart C., and Theresa Enos, eds. 2002. *The writing program administrator's resource: A guide to reflective institutional practice.* Mahwah, NJ: Erlbaum.

Couture, Barbara, and Thomas Kent. 2004. *The private, the public, and the published: Reconciling private lives and public rhetoric.* Logan: Utah State University Press.

Cushman, Ellen. 1998. *The struggle and the tools: Oral and literate strategies in an inner city community.* Albany: State University of New York Press.

Deans, Thomas. 2000. *Writing partnerships: Service-learning in composition.* Urbana, IL: National Council of Teachers of English.

Ede, Lisa, ed. 1999. *On writing research: The Braddock essays 1975–1998.* Boston: Bedford/ St. Martin's.

Emig, Janet. 1971. *The composing processes of twelfth graders.* Research Report 13. Urbana, IL: National Council of Teachers of English.

Farris, Christine, and Chris M. Anson, eds. 1998. *Under construction: Working at the intersections of composition theory, research, and practice.* Logan: Utah State University Press.

Geertz, Clifford. 1988. *Works and lives: The anthropologist as author.* Stanford: Stanford University Press.

Glenn, Cheryl. 2004. *Unspoken: A rhetoric of silence.* Carbondale: Southern Illinois University Press.

---

textbooks I have assembled to study "The Essay Canon" (1999).

Graves, Richard L., ed. 1990. *Rhetoric and composition: A sourcebook for teachers and writers.* Upper Montclair, NJ: Boynton/Cook.

Heath, Shirley Brice. 1983. *Ways with words: Language, life and work in communities and classrooms.* Cambridge: Cambridge University Press.

Huckin, Thomas. 1992. Context-sensitive text analysis. In Kirsch and Sullivan, 84–104.

Kingston, Maxine Hong. 1975. *Woman warrior: Memories of a girlhood among ghosts.* New York: Vintage.

Kirsch, Gesa. 1992. Methodological pluralism. In Kirsch and Sullivan, 247–69.

Kirsch, Gesa, and Liz Rohan, eds. 2008. *Beyond the archives: Research as a lived process.* Carbondale: Southern Illinois University Press.

Kirsch, Gesa, and Patricia A. Sullivan, eds. 1992. *Methods and methodology in composition research.* Carbondale: Southern Illinois University Press.

Lauer, Janice M., and J. William Asher. 1988. *Composition research: Empirical designs.* New York: Oxford University Press.

Larson, Richard. 1989 Review of *The making of knowledge in composition. CCC* 40: 95–98.

Leonardi, Susan J. 1989. "Recipes for reading: Summer pasta, lobster à la Riseholme, and key lime pie." *PMLA* 104: 340–47.

Lloyd-Jones, Richard. 1989. Review of *The making of knowledge in composition. CCC* 40: 98–100.

Miller, Richard. 2005. *Writing at the end of the world.* Pittsburgh: University of Pittsburgh Press.

Mishler, Elliott. 1979. Meaning in context: Is there any other kind? *Harvard Educational Review* 49: 1–19.

McLeod, Susan H., Eric Miraglia, Margot Soven, and Christopher Thaiss, eds. 2001. *WAC for the new millennium: Strategies for continuing writing-across-the-curriculum programs.* Urbana, IL: National Council of Teachers of English.

Murray, Donald. 1968. *A Writer teaches writing: A practical method of teaching composition.* Boston: Houghton.

Newkirk, Thomas. 1992. Narrative roots of the case study. In Kirsch and Sullivan, 130–53.

North, Stephen M. 1987. *The making of knowledge in composition: Portrait of an emerging field.* Upper Montclair, NJ: Boynton.

Ratcliffe, Krista. 2005. *Rhetorical listening: Identification, gender, whiteness.* Carbondale: Southern Illinois University Press.

Raymond, James. 1989. Review of *The making of knowledge in composition. CCC* 40: 93–95.

Rodriguez, Richard. 1982. *Hunger of memory: The education of Richard Rodriguez.* New York: Godine.

Roen, Duane, and Robert K. Mittan. 1992. Collaborative scholarship in composition. In Kirsch and Sullivan, 287–313.

Rose, Mike. 1989. *Lives on the boundary: The struggles and achievements of America's underprepared.* New York: Free Press.

Schilb, John. 2007. *Rhetorical refusals: Defying audiences' expectations.* Carbondale: Southern Illinois University Press.

Scholes, Robert. 1985. *Textual power: Literary theory and the teaching of English.* New Haven: Yale University Press.

Shaughnessy, Mina. 1977. *Errors and expectations: A guide for the teacher of basic writing.* New York: Oxford University Press.

Spellmeyer, Kurt. 2003. *Arts of living: Reinventing the humanities for the twenty-first century.* Albany: State University of New York Press.

Sullivan, Patricia. 1992. Feminism and methodology in composition studies. In Kirsch and Sullivan, 37–61.

Tate, Gary, ed. 1976. *Teaching composition: Ten bibliographical essays.* Fort Worth: Texas Christian University Press.

Tate, Gary, and Edward P.J. Corbett. 1981. *The writing teacher's sourcebook.* New York: Oxford University Press.

Tompkins, Jane, ed. 1980. *Reader response criticism: From formalism to post structuralism.* Baltimore: Johns Hopkins University Press.

Trollope, Frances. 1947. *Domestic manners of the Americans.* 1947. Edited by Donald Smalley. New York: Knopf.

Vicinus, Martha, and Caroline Eisner, eds. 2008. *Originality, imitation, plagiarism.* Ann Arbor: University of Michigan Press.

White, Edward M. 1985. *Teaching and assessing writing.* San Francisco: Jossey-Bass.

Wolfe, Tom. 1973. The new journalism. In *The new journalism,* edited by Tom Wolfe and E.W. Johnson, 3–52. New York: Harper.

PART TWO

Working the Field: Knowledge-Making Communities Since
The Making of Knowledge in Composition

3
THE EPISTEMIC PARADOXES OF "LORE"
From The Making of Knowledge in Composition to the Present (Almost)

Richard Fulkerson

Some lore is just plain false.
Mary Sue MacNealy

Crossword Clue: folk wisdom
Solution: lore

In *The Making of Knowledge in Composition* (*MKC*) Stephen North defined one of the eight types of "knowledge making" in the discipline as "lore," "the accumulated body of traditions, practices, and beliefs in terms of which Practitioners understand how writing is done, learned, and taught" (1987, 22). Nor must a piece of lore actually be "traditional": "literally anything can become part of lore. The only requirement for entry is that the idea, notion, practice, or whatever be nominated: some member of the community must claim that it worked, or seemed to work, or might work" (24).

I once had a colleague, call her Bonni, who was frustrated that students didn't learn from the Harbrace-style marking symbols that she spent hours placing in the margins of their papers, even though she required them to "look up" and then "correct" their errors. One semester, Bonni told me that she had figured out a way to get the students to pay attention to her marks and the handbook rules their papers had violated: in addition to looking up the error symbol and correcting the textual offense, she was making them copy down and hand in the relevant handbook rule—five times (this was pre-word processing). Presumably the repetition would make them actually aware of the nature of their violation and of the real grammar or punctuation rule, and thus (also presumably) reduce their tendency to make such errors in the future.

Bonni's decision to have her students copy handbook rules five times over, as bizarre as the practice might seem to some composition- ists, myself included, qualifies as composition lore, as North defined it, and thus as "knowledge"—or at least as a candidate for knowledge. One of the more basic problems about lore is that it is often impossible to distinguish among three potential meanings of the term: (1) lore as knowledge, (2) lore as a hypothesis to be considered as a candidate for inclusion in the field's body of knowledge, and (3) lore as a *way* of making knowledge. That is, lore as conclusion, possibility, or method. In what follows, I hope context will generally indicate which meaning I have in mind.

Now Bonni's story of lore is pretty trivial. As far as I know, Bonni didn't publish her "finding" anywhere except over lunch, and I don't know how long she kept her practice up. But we are all probably familiar with our own Bonnis, and with some of their more public lorisms. These range from the now-common view that a teacher should not use red ink in responding to student papers because of cultural associations of red with blood, stop signs, and adultery, to the still widely prevalent view that the teaching of for- mal traditional grammar (Latinate parts of speech, parts of the sentence, etc.) will drastically improve the quality of student prose. I recently read an article in a National Council of Teachers of English (NCTE)-refereed journal that argues that using cartoons can help students understand the Toulmin model of argument, which will in turn improve their writing. Naturally, the author uses as support her own classroom (Brunk-Chavez 2004). Since this CTW (cartoon/Toulmin/writing improvement) finding has been refereed and published, does it constitute knowledge about com- position? Presumably North would have to say it does. As I hope to show in this chapter, the epistemological question about lore claims, which was vexing when North invented the concept of lore as a way of making knowl- edge, despite a number of serious scholarly elaborations, both modernist and postmodernist, has become even more problematic now. In addition, as composition's major research models have shifted in the last decade or so, the concept of knowledge as an outgrowth of personal experience (nar- rative knowledge) has become more troubling still.

THE EPISTEMIC PARADOX OF LORE: OVERVIEW

The idea of lore as knowledge was problematic from the first. In a scath- ing review of North's book, David Bartholomae more or less presented the two extremes:

> On the one hand he [North] is arguing that teachers deserve a status equiv-
> alent to that of researchers and that we must make room for story-telling
> and anecdote as legitimate ways of knowing about writing and the teaching
> of writing.
> At the same time, he talks about teachers through a grid determined by a
> tired and corrupt "anthropological" way of speaking: They (the teachers/the
> others) belong to an oral culture, they can talk but not write or think, they
> deal in a "mythic kind of truth," they can barely rise above the specifics of
> daily life ("the muddled details of workaday experience"), they go to confer-
> ences the way we go to the movies, for escape and to be entertained. This is
> the imperialist's representation of the native, and it is odious and, as always,
> untrue. It undermines the argument of the text—that we should pay honor-
> able attention to teachers. (1998, 225)

So for Bartholomae, North says that practitioners should be accepted
as serious knowledge makers but simultaneously treats them as a primitive culture under the observing gaze of the compositionist as cultural
imperialist. Practitioners are knowledge makers through their narratives—but not really.

Most reviewers, however, praised North for actually recognizing
the contributions of practitioners to the making of knowledge: James
Raymond noted in his glowing review that "North's discussion of practitioner lore is especially valuable because he does not demean it" (1989,
93). However, Raymond went on to suggest that lumping together as
"practitioners" ordinary classroom teachers and publishing authors like
Peter Elbow, James McCrimmon, and Ken Macrorie is to "miss one of the
essential paradoxes of our field" (94): "practice, even practice expressed
in a textbook, can be a theoretical statement" (94). In his review, Lloyd-
Jones also complained of the unwieldiness of the category: "To have
only one practitioner category tempts one to attribute to the method
the failings of those who use the method badly" (99). Such a remark
highlights the epistemic paradox that surrounds lore like a cocoon. If
it is possible to use the "method" of lore (telling classroom anecdotes)
"badly," how are receivers of lore claims to assess bad uses of anecdotes
from good ones? (More on this below and throughout.)

A decade later, *lore* had become an entry in Babin and Harrison's
reference guide *Contemporary Composition Studies: A Guide to Theorists and
Terms*, where the authors write, "North does not use the term [lore]
negatively, but uses it to represent often valuable, experience-based

knowledge" (1999, 198). (The term does not, however, appear in Theresa Enos's 1996 *Encyclopedia of Rhetoric and Composition*.)

When it comes to North on lore, often, as with Bartholomae and Raymond, different readers seem to be reading different texts.

NORTH'S PARADOXICAL AMBIVALENCE

My own reading is that North himself was ambivalent about the epistemological status of practitioner lore. To map our field, he had to have some category into which the work of writers like Elbow, Shaughnessy, Macrorie, Rose, and a host of other publishing practitioners would fit. Hence came lore. And although North would subject individual published works of lore to the same, often acerbic, commentary used in other sections of *MKC*, the category *per se* would have to be presented as valuable, as a legitimate way of "making knowledge," that is, of making credible truth claims about the reality of teaching writing. Yet from the initial definition onward, a careful reading shows the ambivalence of the presentation, an ambivalence that might explain why Raymond found that North "does not demean" practitioners, and why Karen Spear described the book as "a plea for the restoration of practice as a means of inquiry and lore as a viable source of knowledge" (1989, 207), while Bartholomae saw North as presenting an imperialist's view of "natives."

North treats practitioner knowledge primarily in two sections of *MKC*. The initial treatment is chapter 2, "The Practitioners" (21–55). But he returns to the subject several times in his concluding chapters (e.g., 331, 337, 371–72, and 378).

Let me work through some of the textual evidence of what I am calling North's ambivalence on lore. The paradox of "valuing and demeaning" appears early: "Judged against non-lore standards, Practitioners are bound to seem consistently undiscriminating, illogical, and sloppy" (27). Now if one reads carefully it is probably clear that North implies that judging lore by nonlore standards inappropriate; still, the phrasing of "consistently undiscriminating, illogical and sloppy" at the climax of the sentence seems to have more heft than the easily unnoticed qualifier.

Soon, in describing the written texts of practitioners, North remarks that the traditional defenses of the teaching of literacy are "a kind of propaganda, one means by which to propagate the 'faith' of literacy" (31). And even the more "liberal" presentations such as Elbow's are "no less propaganda" (31). Since "propaganda," usually not defined with any care, nevertheless carries the valence of a "devil word," North's characterization here is certainly not flattering.

As he begins to introduce the prototypical structure of practitioner research (lore as method), North remarks that "practitioners are not all that methodologically self conscious" (36) and in a practitioner voice, "If I try something and say it works for me, that's the end of it. Nobody else has to try it to be accepted as part of lore" (36). Terms like "not . . . methodologically self conscious" certainly don't sound like ringing endorsements. And if the only validation lore requires is someone saying "It works for me," then why should it be dignified by the term *knowledge* in the first place? Doesn't knowledge have to have some sort of evidentiary or test validation? And for practitioners, "problems are usually not formulated with any great clarity or precision early on" (38). Which makes practitioner lore seem the work of people bumbling around, being both unclear and imprecise. Later, after using the phrases "habitually impatient" and "relatively cavalier" (40), North allows that "this description of Practitioners' patterns of inquiry may not seem particularly flattering" (40). Indeed! North proceeds to discuss the work of Mina Shaughnessy and Ken Macrorie, plus an anecdote of his own about working with a single graduate student; presumably these are to be the "flattering" examples of lore (40–42). After them, North remarks, "The House of Lore may be rambling, but it's basically very sound" (44), which affirmation comes as a rather distinct surprise.

Later he asks, "How do they know what they are looking for? How do they know when they've found it?" (45). And the answer is "I don't think Practitioners *do* know, in any exact way, what they are looking for by way of solutions" (45). So to "impatient" and "cavalier," we seem to be able to add "unaware" to the description of practitioners as they engage in "trial and error" (45) knowledge making. And to close the discussion North says, "When Practitioners report on their inquiry in writing, they tend to misrepresent both its nature and authority. . . . They look more and more like bad scholars" (54).

Much later in the text, in his retrospective commentary, North says that as a result of the revolution in composition, "lore and Practitioner inquiry have been, for most official purposes, anyway, effectively discredited. It is now a second-class sort of knowledge rapidly approaching the status of superstition" (328). Even more damning, perhaps, is that "Practitioners' apparent willingness to retain, on the one hand, what seem to be unenlightened, not to say primitive, beliefs and methods, and to ignore or distort, on the other, the new information they are given, smacks less of simple ignorance than of plain old intractability" (329). Again the negatively valenced words jump out as a damning analysis: "primitive," "unenlightened," "ignore or distort," and "intractability," while one probably overlooks the early adjective "apparent" and the verb "seem." Actually, however, I have taken the quotation out of context to emphasize its critical tone. The entire quoted sentence is prefaced by an introductory "From the point of view of the purveyors of this new knowledge, anyway . . . ." That phrase can, perhaps should, be read as a warning that North does not share this view of practitioners, one that is held (only?) by the unnamed disrespectful purveyors of new knowledge.

It might have been a lot simpler, less controversial, and clearer if North had not tried to include practitioner lore as any sort of knowledge, and had foregone the quaint and memorable metaphor of the "House of Lore." But that wouldn't have been possible because it would mean also eliminating the powerful and highly regarded projects of major writers who actually work as lorists, such as Elbow, Shaughnessy, Macrorie, and Moffett. What North needed but could not find or develop was some fair way of distinguishing credible lore from incredible. In his paradigm for lore (36), North includes a step of "testing solution in practice" (which is the essence of lore), and then a "validation" stage (prior to "dissemination"). But in contrast to all the chapters on other types of knowledge, in "The Practitioners" North does not devote a section heading to this validation stage. He has a combination section on "Testing a Solution in Practice: Implementation and Evaluation" (46–50), then jumps to "Dissemination" (51–55). Making any distinction between credible lore and not-so-credible lore isn't an option if there is no test and if nothing can ever be rejected or discarded (27). North, moreover, is well aware of this situation: "As problematic as implementing solutions can be, though, evaluating them is even tougher" (47), and although various causes exist for the "general erosion in Practitioner authority . . . none of them will have a more central role in accounting for the decline of Practitioner knowledge than this matter of evaluation" (50).

ONTOLOGICAL DIMENSIONS OF THE PARADOX

The debate over lore is actually as much about how our field views "reality" (the ontological question) as it is about how we come to know "reality" (the epistemic question). Lore's ontological status also makes it difficult to credit it as reliable knowledge. Let me see if I can explain what

I mean by that. As North uses the term, *lore* includes or implies not just narrative reports, but also causal claims deriving from the narrative(s); indeed, in its fullest formulation, lore also includes procedural recommendations, or "ought-statements:" "teachers ought not to use red ink," "teachers ought to use peer-response groups," "teachers ought to have their students engage in cultural critique." Not all lore recommendations are quite so baldly put; many are phrased as causal evaluations: "freewriting works," or "having students copy handbook rules repeatedly works." Of course, what "works" is what we should be doing. However, these evaluative causal claims and any resultant ought statements, whether stated, implied, or inferred, are fundamentally grounded in experiential narrative: as North says, if a teacher somewhere says that she or he has experience of a procedure "working," then that statement becomes part of the house of lore. Even if the originator of the lore restricts any transmission of it to the purely narrative account, and thus can't be criticized for drawing ungrounded inferences, readers are likely to do the work. As Powell remarks, "Lore . . . dramatizes—a distinction that transfers interpretive agency to the listener, the reader of the lore." The "lorist" can tell her or his story, which readers can bring to their own places, "not as a narrative template to lay atop it, nor as a rational analysis to test it against, but as some more-or-less useful perspectives that might cohere around your own problems and priorities" (2000, 12).

In other words, lore consists of two fundamentally different sorts of verbal material, what Bruner has called "Narrative and Paradigmatic modes of thought" (quoted in Murphy 1989, 470). The two do not mix tidily, as I will attempt to illustrate by turning now to treatments of lore by scholars following up on North.

BEYOND NORTH: MODERNIST VIEWS OF THE EPISTEMIC PARADOX

After North, a number of scholars attempted to rehabilitate lore (the personal-narrative-based method) as a credible way to make knowledge. The attempts have largely been unsuccessful I think, not because of the scholars' inadequacies but because of the intractable nature of the epistemological problem of lore itself. From a modernist perspective, a claim that "X works" and "you should do X" could not be satisfactorily grounded in personal experience and observation. Such claims require careful research design, objective data gathering, replication, critical assessment by outsiders, not to mention the tricky move from *is* to *ought*." A good modernist would call such claims "merely" anecdotal, and they would not get by either journal referees or reviewers for a scholarly press. In a writing across the curriculum (WAC) context, Michael Charlton has discussed the frequent response from science faculty when an English teacher uses a personal narrative about teaching writing: "That's Just a Story" (2007). (Ironically, Charlton's claim that science faculty do commonly have that attitude is itself a piece of lore.) As Bruce Horner puts it, "The knowledge constituting lore doesn't stand up to the usual criteria for achieving status as disciplinary knowledge." Thus he reads North as saying that "in the end . . . it seems the lore produced by Practitioner Inquiry just won't cut it as knowledge, and so they had better retrain" (2000, 378).[1] Lisa Ede, remarking on lore *en passant*, describes it as "teaching that in critical ways remains inadequately theorized" (2004, 116).

The key question about lore is Does it work? Which seems to mean that there is good lore (which works) and bad lore (which doesn't), or real lore and phony lore. Consider the possibility that various lore claims exist on some sort of modernist continuum, ranging from the purely flaky recipe swapping all teachers engage in to a thoroughly imagined, investigated, philosophized-about analysis that seems to have complete credibility but is still founded in personal narrative. After all, none of North's categories automatically produces knowledge. Lore, like scholarship or experimentation, is the *method* of proceeding, not the outcome. That's why for each way of making knowledge, North must include a validation stage. Any method can be ill used and produce "findings" on the flaky end of that spectrum. (Although when North says that literally anything can become lore as long as someone somewhere testifies that it worked, he sort of undercuts the idea that there could be any assessment of lore claims.)

But how are readers or the discipline to decide where a given candidate for lore-based knowledge should fall? Since there seems no rational (logical, paradigmatic, argument-based) way to distinguish between good (trustworthy, well-grounded, dependable) and bad lore (such as Bonni's requiring her students to copy the handbook rules multiple times), all lore is dubious, and the entire house of lore seems not to merit being described as knowledge at all. In short the category, although necessary to North's taxonomy, is essentially unhelpful.

Not that modernist scholars have ignored this epistemic paradox.

---

1.   See North, 372

Several have suggested ways to assess lore claims while staying within a modernist paradigm. As I noted above, the attempts seem to me to be largely circular and self defeating. For instance, without mentioning North or lore, Candace Spigelman (2004) attempts to develop principles for evaluating teacher narratives in *Personally Speaking: Experience as Evidence in Academic Discourse*. She accepts the postmodern/feminist critique that "traditional standards of evidence function oppressively" (96), but she nevertheless argues that "*although we must choose carefully our methods for securing confidence in our evidence, we cannot discount the need to do this particular kind of work*" (96; italics in original). The latter remark accounts for my discussing her within a modernist rather than a postmodernist framework. Part of her reasoning is that "if we don't find a way to submit personal evidence to rigorous examination, we surrender to critics who discount it as merely subjective and therefore inadequate for academic purposes" (98). She proceeds to do a careful reading of two narrative articles from *Teaching English in the Two-Year College*, both on the vexed topic of teacher response to student writing. She concludes that, although each piece has narrative probability, one is superior to the other in "fidelity" (102), by which she seems to mean that the causal links it proposes (between one sort of teacher commentary and certain results) simply square better with common sense and with other published scholarship. I find her move surprising because it is so modernist. While she builds her case in favor of one narrative over the other effectively, she largely leaves untouched the issue of how to evaluate lore when there isn't scholarship" to compare it to.[2] Far from rehabilitating lore, Spigelman's line of argument actually privileges empirical (i.e., quantitative) research as the standard, making lore as a method epistemologically impotent.

Cindy Johanek presents a related analysis in *Composing Research: A Contextualist Paradigm for Rhetoric and Composition*, in which she argues that "a Contextualist Theory of Epistemic Justification draws us to an analysis of context: *what* do I want to know? *Why* do I need to know it? *How* can I frame my question in a way it can be answered?" (2000, 104). For her, framing our research questions contextually leads to multimodal inquiry. Hence lore (as personal narrative) can be one feature of a broader inquiry. She rejects North's "methodological egalitarianism," calling it the "I'm OK, you're OK" approach to knowledge making, which she

---

2.   See also Spigelman 2001.

compares to a multiracial neighborhood in which the several groups of "neighbors" have agreed not to interact (108). As far as distinguishing lore$_A$ (credible) from lore$_B$ (flaky) is concerned, requesting multimodality in research is of no help because it presupposes that knowledge will be based in systematic (planned) research using several sorts of data, not solely experiential narratives. In Johanek's contextualist paradigm, there is no room for lore (i.e., experienced-based claims).

So a modernist analysis of lore simply runs into the intractable problem that you can't derive credible procedural knowledge from personal experience because generalizing from the experience isn't reliable: what *happened* isn't the same as *what happens* or as *what ought to happen.* Claims have to be judged against a reality.[3]

BEYOND NORTH: POSTMODERNIST VIEW(S) OF THE EPISTEMIC PARADOX

But composition now claims to be postmodern, meaning that "modern"

---

3. After North invoked the term lore, its use expanded in several ways that are only tangentially related to his work (at best). Most significant is the Teacher Lore Project run by William Schubert, an education professor at the University of Illinois at Chicago. It was begun as an archive of case studies of teachers in all fields and at all levels in 1985 (Varnado 1998). Its mission, according to the UIC website, is to "give greater credibility to the learning teachers have acquired from their experience. Insights and understandings from interviews, stories, autobiographies, biographies, and observations are used as a basis for preservice and inservice teacher education." (http:// ness2.uic.edu/UI-Service/programs/UIC118.html) (See Schubert 1990; Schubert and Ayers 1992.)

   In addition, two English doctoral dissertations have centered on lore. Varnado used the concepts as developed by Schubert in an ethnographic case study of three English teachers from the same high school. Sherry Cook Stanforth (1999) used folklore theory to study certain common patterns of lore among graduate teaching assistants and undergraduate students at the University of Cincinnati. Instead of treating the oral lore she recorded as knowledge of any sort, she treated it as myth and identified patterns within it that seemed to reveal the culture of composition teachers. For Stanforth, the epistemological issue isn't whether claims such as those about the effects of using red ink are true, but whether the culture of English teachers believes them. In a sense hers is a second- order study of selected lore. Her work was ethnography within her own university culture, so no generalizing is possible, although in my judgment, any English teacher will immediately recognize the myths she identifies, such as the myth of teaching as a war with students or that of the student from hell.

   There is even an online journal entitled Lore: Rhetoric, Writing and Culture produced by the rhetoric and writing studies department at San Diego State University, which began publishing in 2001 and published Vol. 6.2 in May of 2008. (http:// www-rohan.sdsu.edu/dept/drwswebb/lore/lore.html) Its web page refers directly to North's definition of lore, but an examination of all the tables of contents suggests that it publishes the same sort of wide range of scholarship and criticism that any journal about college composition or rhetoric would.

(empiricist, rationalist, positivist, scientific, scientistic—choose your term) epistemologies are outmoded because all seek "foundational" knowledge of an "external reality," whereas both knowledge and reality are social constructs).[4] Such a perspective seems to open up a possibility for personal narrative to be an acceptable basis for at least some sort of intersubjective knowledge claim.

Does that mean that teacher narratives leading to causal claims and resulting procedural recommendations no longer must meet rigorous standards of "proof" of the sort that assumes the existence of an external reality? Does just anything go? Well, no, not exactly. Even to postmodernists, much practitioner knowledge is still highly suspect. Assess it we must, but we must eschew even those traditional quasiscientific standards of judging. Such a move makes it that much more problematic to distinguish $lore_A$ from $lore_B$. But at least lore is not automatically out by the rules of the game. So, in postmodern thinking, when is a narrative claim to be considered well grounded?

Let's look at three postmodern theorists who have noted the problem and taken steps toward resolving it. Louise Phelps offers the following analysis based fundamentally in Schon's concept of reflection:

> Although at various points North pictures lore as private and idiosyncratic knowledge, coming close to identifying it with anything that works for any practitioner, he cannot seriously mean that, for he consistently describes lore as communally produced and publicly shared. He could not do otherwise, since to call it "knowledge" (especially, knowledge in a discipline) implies that lore makes a public claim on others for attention, belief or appropriation. . . . Behaviors, beliefs, and experiences do not count as knowledge just because teachers have them in common; they are *lore* rather than simply common practices by virtue of symbolic expressions and exchanges that turn personal acts into publicly accessible terms for conceiving and acting in new situations. Moreover, this process is selective over time. Lore is experience that has been expressed, circulated, imitated, sustained and confirmed by repetition, achieving canonical status as "common sense" through its range of cultural distribution and its staying power. (1991, 869)

Such an analysis attempts to recoup lore as a valued form of knowledge essentially by denying that North could have meant what he plainly said. Phelps clearly does not agree with North that "literally anything can become lore" or that lore can never be removed from the house,

---

4.   See Massey, this volume, for a discussion of modernism and postmodernism in composition and *MKC*.

but her move requires both changing what North said and then supply-
ing an epistemological grounding to distinguish lore, which earns the
status of knowledge, from mere "behaviors, beliefs, and experiences."
When lore is made public and endures, it becomes validated and she
will elevate it to the status of an "art" (1991, 874), which is a "higher
level of lore." (Shades of Plato's "Gorgias"!) Needless to say, such a move
doesn't resolve the problem. "Cultural distribution" and "staying power"
have little relationship to whether a classroom practice is justified or not.
In fact, Phelps's analysis seems only a short remove from "We've always
done it that way!" (Or, more charitably, it describes a rather traditional
dialectical winnowing among varying public claims—essentially the
same modernist point Spigelman makes.)

Elizabeth Rankin recognized the epistemological problem with lore
and focused it admirably: "But how do we *know* 'what works'? And what
does that *mean* anyway? For example, at what point does my declaration
that writing groups 'work' in the classroom leave the domain of hollow
assertion and enter the realm of 'knowledge'?" (1990, 261).

Like Phelps, Rankin attempts to distinguish two varieties of North's
lore: "True practitioner knowledge—as opposed to what he calls
'lore'—is essentially no different in structure from scholarship or
research . . . practitioners share with scholars and researchers the
same method of validating their claims to knowledge" (1990, 263). She
explains that puzzling remark by identifying what she calls "codes of
authority:" "If we listen more closely to practitioner narratives, and listen to ourselves listening in, we can begin to interpret those codes of
authority and understand what we mean when we recognize as knowledge a particular practitioner's claim" (265). She identifies these "codes
of authority" as experience, enlightenment, skepticism, altruism, and
modest claims (266). Presumably if a piece of practitioner assertion
meets these five, it can be called "knowledge." Then we can distinguish
"mere assertions" from "responsible claims to knowledge" (266). Now
no one would deny that in relationship to any claims about what works
in classrooms it would be important for the practitioner (or researcher)
to be experienced, to be enlightened (whatever that might mean), to be
skeptical, to have the good of others at heart (altruism), and to keep the
claims within modest range. But all of that still begs the question of what
good such a litmus test does, since it would actually rule out almost no
procedural claim made by any composition teacher about what works or
has worked. Bonni's handbook rule copying and Brunk-Chavez's CTW

proposal seem to fit (unless as a reader *I* judge either teacher to be "unenlightened").

Patricia Harkin discussed lore in three articles (1989, 1991a, 1991b), which makes her the reigning expert on postmodern views of lore. Probably her most thorough explication came in "The Postdisciplinary Politics of Lore" (1991b). Harkin argues (citing Stanley Fish) that in our postmodern/postdisciplinary world "there can be no such thing as 'knowledge' (at least, as foundationalists understand it) to contribute to" (132). Once that card is played, the frequent critiques of lore as a type of "knowledge," of course, become nonsensical. At that point "informed intuition" (128), like Mina Shaughnessy's work, becomes just as strong a candidate for "knowledge" as the most rigorous of quantitative findings. But Harkin is careful to make the same point as Phelps and Rankin, that there must nevertheless be distinctions made between "real" lore and mere classroom whim, even though there is no such thing as "knowledge:" "I certainly do not advocate . . . mindless, antitheoretical pluralism. Nor do I recommend practitioners' tendency to operate uncritically in terms of dualisms like correct versus incorrect, or process versus product. *We should not accept lore uncritically*" (1991b, 135; italics added).

So (again), how to assess nominations for lore? Harkin proposes a new sort of composition conference in which practitioners would present videotapes of teachers (presumably including themselves) engaging in practices they want to propose as lore/knowledge. To assess the lore proposals critically, a panel of "theorists, representatives of disciplinary ways of knowing, experienced in thinking through the implications of a practice" (1991b, 137) would be on hand to discuss the video sequences (plus the usual audience questions and comments). As I revise this chapter in November of 2008, I can't help thinking of some CNN panel observing a speech of Sarah Palin or Barack Obama prior to offering their "expert" commentary. Says Harkin, "Our problem is nothing less than getting the academy to change its understanding of knowledge production. We need to denaturalize lore to the point at which the institution, having been made aware of it, can learn to value it" (135). So narrative claims are to be "settled" by a discussion of outside expert observers—a combination of authority, tradition, and consensus.

THE PARADOX OF EMPIRICISM AND LORE IN A POSTMODERN WORLD; OR, THE COLLAPSE OF RESEARCH INTO LORE

When leaving the editorship of *Research in the Teaching of English*, after

two three-year terms, Smagorinsky and Smith noted that "the vast majority of papers submitted during our editorship have employed qualitative
methods" (2003, 418). The dominant empirical work now is either case
study or onsite ethnography, and researchers are careful to specify that
their work is a snapshot of what occurred at a given place and time, as
perceived by one (or sometimes a few) observers, and thus is not generalizable. Its status as "knowledge" is somewhat peculiar in that it is limited to narrative knowledge of past events, events that are fully situated
and thus unique.

The situation is incredibly ironic. Nonquantitative research now dom-
inates the journal that was created to be a venue for publishing precisely
rigorous empirical research in order to counter the field's "alchemical"
reliance on guesswork and speculation. Although contemporary empirical research, being qualitative, resists making either value judgment or
procedural recommendation, it *shares* with lore the fundamentally narrative and observational grounding for its work. That is, both lorists and
ethnographers mostly tell stories.

One might think, then, that the standards governing the acceptability
of ethnography and case study in the social sciences and in composition
(standards which are themselves controversial) would be equally applicable to lore and thus could help resolve the question of how to assess
lore-based claims. But not so. And that was part of North's basic point:
if a report meets the criteria for satisfactory qualitative research, then it
is either clinician knowledge or ethnography. If it doesn't rise to those
standards, even under postmodern assumptions, then it's lore—whether
it's the work of Mina Shaughnessy or my friend Bonni. So is lore just
bad ethnography/case study? If so, attempts to distinguish among lore
claims on the basis of quality are predoomed.

Shortly after North's work appeared, Richard Murphy attempted to
explain crucial differences between lore and qualitative studies, while
preserving the value of each: "We need to distinguish such stories [lore]
from case study. However much a case depends on rich description and
narration, its meaning is propositional, a statement of abstract generalization. . . . The meaning of the stories we tell ourselves about our
lives and work, on the other hand, is aesthetic. . . . The meaning of the
stories I think we should tell and value lies in their forceful representation of the experience of teaching and learning, in their believability, in
their memorability. Case study aspires to science. Stories of teaching and
learning aspire to poetry. (1989, 470)

Maybe Murphy is correct that teacher narratives should be considered aesthetically and read as poetry. That might at least explain why I love reading teacher narratives, even though I try to avoid drawing propositional conclusions. If we accept Murphy's perspective, then lore could just as well be powerful fiction, a fully aesthetic textual experience. Murphy's analysis "saves" lore by removing it from the realm of knowledge making. Ironically, though, I also love reading case studies and ethnographies, still without drawing propositional conclusions. But I always end up asking myself, What have I learned?

Contra Murphy, it is no longer granted, if indeed it ever was, that the meaning of case study (and ethnography) is "propositional" or "a statement of abstract generalization," Bruner's paradigmatic thinking. Yet as mentioned, the bulk of research submitted to and published in our preeminent empirical journal, the sort of research in fact that now wins the Braddock Award pretty regularly, is case study/ethnography. In other words, qualitative and narrative based. If lore does not equal bad ethnography/case study, then does it make sense to say that ethnography and case study is lore done well? For me, such a scholarly "collapse into lore" raises serious red flags. North was worried that the field of composition would pull itself apart because of the conflicts among its various knowledge-making communities. I am more concerned that the field's future is endangered by its totalizing embrace of lore done well.

REFERENCES

Babin, Edith, and Kimberly Harrison. 1999. *Contemporary composition studies: A guide to theorists and terms.* Westport: Greenwood.

Bartholomae, David. 1988. Review of *The making of knowledge in composition: Portrait of an emerging field*, by Stephen M. North. *Rhetoric Review* 6: 224–228.

Brunk-Chavez, Beth. 2004. What's so funny about Stephen Toulmin? Using cartoons to teach the Toulmin analysis. *TETYC* 32 (2): 179–185.

Charlton, Michael. 2007. That's just a story: Academic genres and teaching anecdotes in writing-across-the-curriculum projects. *The WAC Journal* 18: 19–29.

Ede, Lisa. 2004. *Situating composition: Composition studies and the politics of location.* Carbondale: Southern Illinois University Press.

Enos, Theresa, ed. 1996. *Encyclopedia of rhetoric and composition.* New York: Garland.

Harkin, Patricia. 1989. Bringing lore to light. *Pre/Text* 10 (1–2): 55–67.

———. 1991a. Hyperscholarship and the curriculum. *Rhetoric Review* 10 (1): 70–90.

———. 1991b. Postdisciplinary politics of lore. In *Contending with words: Composition and rhetoric in a postmodern age*, edited by John Schilb and Patricia Harkin, 124–38. New York: Modern Language Association.

Horner, Bruce. 2000. Tradition and professionalization: Reconceiving work in composition. *CCC* 51 (3): 96–128.

Johanek, Cindy. 2000. *Composing research: A contextualist paradigm for rhetoric and composition.*

Logan: Utah State University Press.

Lloyd-Jones, Richard. 1989. Review of *The making of knowledge in composition: Portrait of an emerging field*, by Stephen M. North. *CCC* 40: 98–100.

MacNealy, Mary Sue. 1999. *Strategies for Empirical Research in Writing*. Needham Heights, MA: Allyn & Bacon.

Murphy, Richard J., Jr. 1989. On stories and scholarship. *CCC* 40 (4): 466–72.

North, Stephen M. 1987. *The making of knowledge in composition: Portrait of an emerging field*. Upper Montclair, NJ: Boynton/Cook.

Phelps, Louise Wetherbee. 1991. Practical wisdom and the geography of knowledge in composition. *College English* 53 (8): 863–885.

Powell, Douglas Reichert. 2000. The story of the story *is* the story: Placing the blunder narrative. In *Blundering for a change: Errors and expectations in critical pedagogy*, edited by John Paul Tassoni and William H. Thelin. Portsmouth: Boynton/Cook.

Rankin, Elizabeth. 1990. Taking practitioner inquiry seriously: An argument with Stephen North. *Rhetoric Review* 8 (2): 260–267.

Raymond, James C. 1989. Review of *The making of knowledge in composition: Portrait of an emerging field*, by Stephen M. North. *CCC* 40: 93–95.

Schubert, William. 1990. Acknowledging teachers' experiential knowledge: Reports from the Teacher Lore Project. *Kappa Delta Pi Record* 26: 99–100.

Schubert, William, and William Ayers, eds. 1992. *Teacher lore: Learning from our own experience*. New York: Longman.

Smagorinsky, Peter, and Michael Smith. 2003. Introduction to Reconsidering research in the teaching of English. *RTE* 37: 417–424.

Spear, Karen. 1989. Review of *The making of knowledge in composition: Portrait of an emerging field*, by Stephen M. North. *JAC* 9: 205–208.

Spigelman, Candace. 2001. Argument and evidence in the case of the personal. *College English* 64 (1): 63–87.

———. 2004. *Personally speaking: Experience as evidence in academic discourse*. Carbondale: Southern Illinois University Press.

Stanforth, Sherry Cook. 1999. "Talk isn't cheap:" Writing lore and valuation in university culture. PhD diss., University of Cincinnati.

Varnado, Beverly Bratton. 1998. Informing the practice of high school English teachers with teacher lore, reflective practice and a culture of inquiry. PhD diss., University of South Carolina. Ann Arbor, MI: UMI Microform 9841777.

4

PHILOSOPHIES OF INVENTION TWENTY YEARS AFTER *THE MAKING OF KNOWLEDGE IN COMPOSITION*

Kelly Pender

In the preface to his 2003 *Where Writing Begins*, Michael Carter uses Stephen North's not-entirely-approving description of philosophical inquiry in *The Making of Knowledge in Composition* (*MKC*) (1987) as a kind of disclaimer—as a way to fess up to the methodological shortcomings of his argument before he begins making it. Carter admits, for instance, that he has "foraged far and wide" into theology, astrophysics, ancient Greek philosophy, dialectical theory, and scientific chaos theory for the premises of his argument (xv–xvi). He counts himself among the "accidental philosophers," who, as North explained, try to solve a practical problem only to find themselves more concerned with its underlying presuppositions (xv; North, 101). And finally, Carter pleads guilty to preaching, that is, to pushing his philosophical investigation of invention into philosophical reformism by offering it as a guide to action (xvi; North 111). "I am interested in reforming the way we conceive of writing and the teaching of writing," Carter confesses. "I think there is a lot at stake here" (xvi).

What's interesting about these weaknesses of philosophical inquiry—foraging, low methodological self-awareness, and proselytizing—is the fact that North described them (and others) in *The Making of Knowledge in Composition* sixteen years before Carter published *Where Writing Begins*. Moreover, while North admitted that these weaknesses made it difficult for him to characterize the methodological community of composition philosophers, he also expressed optimism about that community's future. "I am convinced," he wrote, "that somewhere within this welter of arguing voices, a genuine dialectic and a real Philosophical community are taking shape" (92). The obvious question raised by Carter's preface, then, is *have they?* Have a "genuine dialectic" and a "real community" of composition philosophers emerged in the way that North anticipated

they would when he wrote *MKC* nearly twenty-five years ago? Has philosophical inquiry achieved the "more coherent future" he hoped for? If
so, how? What changes have occurred? And if not, why? Are some weaknesses just too difficult for composition philosophers to overcome?

These are, of course, huge questions—ones that cannot be conclusively answered here because, among other reasons, the body of philosophical research in composition is just too extensive. To provide some
tentative answers, then, I will look at one small segment of that large
corpus: philosophical research on invention. Initially, this might seem
like a strange move since, as North made clear in the penultimate chapter of *MKC*, his expectations for the future of invention research were
not very high. Criticizing what he referred to as Richard Young's call for
an "investigative assault" on invention in order to "unlock its secrets,"
North argued that the term's only meaning came from the incompatible methodologies used to carry out that assault and gain disciplinary
power. Thus he worried that come "accumulation time," this meaning
would reveal more about the field's "inter-methodological tensions"
than it would about invention itself (339).

However, North also argued that as long as composition was subject to
the "fairly strict methodological homogeneity" exerted by literature within
the English department, its four researcher methods (experimental, clinical, formal, and ethnographic) would "be driven away," leaving the three
scholarly methods (historical, philosophical, and critical) to predominate
(367). I would argue that this shift in composition has been nowhere
more apparent than in invention research. As even a cursory review of the
literature reveals, most of the compositionists and rhetoricians who study
invention today do so with scholarly methods, and of those methods, the
most common is philosophical.[1] It makes sense, then, to look to invention, a place where the philosophical community has become dominant,
in order to reflect on the state of philosophical method. Importantly, such
reflection also gives us an opportunity to see what invention is becoming
in light of the "methodological homogeneity" that North foresaw.

WHAT IS PHILOSOPHICAL INQUIRY?

Because its subject matter could come from virtually any area of composition studies, North argued that we should understand philosophical

---

1.   Janice Lauer and Janet Atwill reach the same conclusion in the introduction to their
      edited collection, Perspectives on Rhetorical Invention (2003, xi). However, they use
      the word theory to describe the kind of inquiry North described as "philosophical" in
      order to avoid the implication that creating knowledge is a philosophical (as opposed
      to rhetorical) enterprise.

inquiry in terms of its method, dialectic (96). He described philosophical method as dialectical for two reasons: (1) its individual arguments move inferentially from premises to conclusion and (2) they interact with each other dialogically, creating "free-ranging, never-ending debate[s]" (96). Although he admitted that at their best, these philosophical debates could look "like a series of endless, ill-connected arguments," North defended their value for the field, arguing that they were good ways of framing fundamental problems and of understanding the preconditions for solving those problems (97).

But, as I indicated earlier, when North wrote *MKC*, he thought that most of composition's philosophical debates were *not* operating at their best. Reversing that trend, he suggested, would require a number of changes, including, most importantly, a rise in philosophers' methodological self-awareness. To be fair, North criticized all composition researchers for low methodological self-awareness, warning that their unreflectiveness was resulting in a body of composition knowledge that lacked "any clear coherence or methodological integrity" (3). In the case of philosophical inquiry, he was particularly concerned with "the urge to proselytize," that is, the tendency among philosophers to cross the line between analyzing some set of assumptions and advocating them as *the* set of assumptions (91). Philosophical inquiry can do the former, North argued, but it cannot do the latter. To improve the quality of their work, he believed that composition philosophers would have to realize that philosophical positions should not be used "as a means to political and pedagogical influence" (111, 115)

North also believed that to improve their work composition philosophers would have to become better foragers. "Foraging" is the term he used ("mostly without disparagement") to describe the activity of moving outside the field of composition in order to find premises to serve as the foundations of philosophical arguments about writing (102). While North seemed willing to accept the necessity of this activity for a field as young as composition, he hoped that as the field matured, its philosophers would become more aware of the assumptions that foraged premises bring with them. He also hoped they would stop treating foraged premises as unassailable facts. According to the rules of dialectic, all premises are up for debate, no matter what discipline they come from. To treat them otherwise, North argued, was to inhibit the very dialogue that good philosophical inquiry seeks to create (105).

Another threat to this dialogue, according to North, was how members of the philosophical community actually responded to each other

(99). Obviously, response is what keeps a dialectic moving, each argument forcing positions to be defined more precisely and more synthetically over time (111). But for North, that process of redefinition was *not* tantamount to a process of replacement or usurpation. In other words, progress in philosophical inquiry shouldn't (and maybe couldn't) happen through "the steady weeding out of mistaken world views," no matter how confident an investigator was in the superiority of new knowledge over old knowledge (97). When *MKC* was published, however, many philosophical arguments in composition had failed to generate productive responses (97). Although North didn't attribute this failure to any one cause, he did cite some contributing factors, noting for instance that many compositionists were visitors to the philosophical community whose one or two contributions weren't enough to help it develop a "cumulative heritage" (92). Of those who did stay permanently, North suggested that more than a few were power-hungry zealots who liked the sound of their own voice too much to hear what other philosophers were saying (92). Such a negative characterization leaves little reason to wonder why a writer like Carter—that is, a writer who explicitly identifies his methodology as philosophical—would feel the need to do some disclaiming in the preface to his book. Simply put, his method (philosophical inquiry) and his topic (invention) probably wouldn't have been North's idea of a winning combination sixteen years ago.

WHAT HAPPENED TO INVENTION?

As Janice Lauer observed in her 2002 "Rhetorical Invention: The Diaspora" (and as North's work predicted), after the 1980s, compositionists weren't exactly lining up to answer the question, *What is invention?* Research on the subject didn't necessarily die, she explained, but instead became "implicit [and] fragmented" as it moved into other areas of inquiry, such as writing in the disciplines, cultural studies, and genre studies (2). Although Lauer didn't speculate about why scholars were less frequently and less directly studying invention, I think we can attribute this change, at least in part, to a perceived impasse between the neoclassicist work that inaugurated so much new research in the 1960s and 1970s and the postmodernist work that followed it in the late 1980s, 1990s, and early 2000s.[2] Whereas the former sought to reinstate

---

2.   Janet Atwill and Janice Lauer make a similar point when they argue that political critiques of empirical research methods stifled research on invention (Introduction 2003, xiv–xv).

invention as the intellectual core of rhetoric by studying its processes and making them teachable, the latter rejected those goals by rejecting the theories of language, knowledge, and subjectivity on which they rested. If, for instance, the neoclassicist position was based on the thesis that researchers could investigate the writing process in order to develop heuristics for gaining control over invention, the postmodernist position was based on the antithesis that writing was not an identifiable, generalizable process that could be investigated by a researcher-subject and then taught to others.

Describing the work that actually comprises these positions in the starkly oppositional terms of thesis/antithesis is, of course, an act of oversimplification. In a way, though, that's the point: no matter how nuanced some of this scholarship actually was, it created a sense of theoretical stalemate that, for a period of time, discouraged explicit research on invention. In this section of the chapter, I will describe some of this work, using North's critique of philosophical inquiry to help explain how it created the perception of an impasse. I will then turn to new philosophical work on invention to demonstrate how some rhetoricians have tried to move beyond that perception. It is important to note that my goal here is not to provide a comprehensive account of this scholarship but rather, as I indicated earlier, to reflect on the state of invention and the research methodology most commonly used to study it.

Theses/Antitheses

The story of invention's demise after the classical period is so ingrained in our disciplinary identity that it does not warrant a detailed retelling here. Highlights (or lowlights, rather) include the assimilation of invention into biblical hermeneutics and the transference of the commonplaces from rhetoric to logic during the medieval period. During the Renaissance, Peter Ramus's decision to move invention from rhetoric to logic and Francis Bacon's rejection of rhetorical reasoning in favor of scientific method further deprived rhetoric of its epistemic roles. This inventionless view of rhetoric persisted through the eighteenth and nineteenth centuries, eventually culminating in the formalistic, arrangement-driven rhetoric that was retrospectively dubbed "current-traditional."

What's important about this narrative, at least for my purposes here, isn't its historical accuracy (which rightfully has been challenged by a number of scholars since the neoclassicists) but rather the fact that it set the stage for the mid-twentieth-century effort to return invention to rhetoric and, therefore, rhetoric to the academy.[3] From the perspective of an assistant professor whose PhD is from a twenty-eight-year-old rhetoric program and who teaches in a new rhetoric program at a major research university, this effort appears to have been successful.[4] But I know that success isn't the result of an uncritical acceptance of everything the neoclassicists said about invention. Far from it. Scholars working with postmodern theory challenged (occasionally to the point of rejecting) some of the neoclassicists' most fundamental claims about writing and invention.[5] Especially controversial were the three claims I discuss below: (1) writing is a process of discovery; (2) invention should be understood and taught as a techne; and (3) deliberate control of invention yields better results than habit or chance.

Neoclassicist Claim One: Writing is a Process of Discovery

To understand writing as a process is, in the most basic sense, to understand it as a recursive combination of three stages: prewriting, writing, and rewriting. In this basic understanding, invention is equated with prewriting, a period of discovery that happens *before* writing and rewriting. Characterized by discrete, causally linked stages, Gordon Rohman's model of the writing process identified prewriting as the thinking that takes place prior to writing in order to discover the "writing idea" and prepare it for "the words and the page" (1965, 106).[6] However, others like Janet Emig, Maxine Hairston, and Donald Murray identified the whole writing process, not just the initial stage of prewriting, with discovery. Hence the 1980s-era mantra that writing *is* discovery or that, as James McCrimmon put it in his tellingly titled essay, "Writing as a Way of Knowing," "We write in order to understand—to figure out what we want to say" (1985, 4). The claim that writing is a process of

---

3. See, for example, Charles Paine's The Resistant Writer (1999) and Sue Carter Simmons's "Constructing Writers: Barrett Wendell's Pedagogy at Harvard" (1995).

4. I realize, of course, that this is not an unqualified success.

5. I want to stress that the works I review here are examples of neoclassicist and postmodernist positions. I think they are representative examples, but they should be read as examples nonetheless. Also, my use of the labels neoclassicist and postmodernist inevitably suggests that all work on invention fit into one camp or another and that there were no disagreements within camps. This is, of course, not true.

6. While Rohman did identify prewriting with thinking, he promoted certain kinds of writing as ways of engaging in that thinking. So the line between thinking and writing in his notion of prewriting isn't as clear as he depicts it.

discovery, then, asserts two things about writing: that it happens in discernible, repeatable stages, and that by moving through these stages, writers discover their ideas and intentions.

Despite (or maybe because of) the fact that these assertions were treated as disciplinary truisms during the 1980s, a number of scholars began articulating a postprocess understanding of writing late in that decade. Associated most directly with the work of Thomas Kent, postprocess theory rejected the claim that writing is a process of discovery on the grounds that (1) it is a radically situated activity and (2) it is a fundamentally interpretive act. Understanding writing as radically situated, according to Kent, meant understanding that it happens at such specific historical moments and in such specific relations that no process theory could usefully describe it (1999, 2). To shore up this claim, Kent turned to Donald Davidson's concepts of prior and passing theories. Everyone enters a communicative situation with prior theories, that is, beliefs about how others use language. These prior theories allow communication to begin but, because no two interlocutors share prior theories, they have to create passing theories to actually decode each other's language. As Kent explained, Davidson refers to these theories as "passing" because they don't exist long enough to be codified for reuse in other situations (5).

Kent again relied on Davidson, in addition to Jacques Derrida, to explain why writing is fundamentally interpretive. Although Davidson and Derrida come from different philosophical traditions, Kent explained, they both believe that because of the split between signifier and signified, there is no way to predict the effect of a sign in the world. More specifically, they both believe that no "identifiable conventional element exists that links a written sign to its context, because a context can never be absolutely determinable" (1993, 28, 32). Using this claim as his major premise, Kent argued that writing must start with the writer's effort to interpret her interlocutor's code and match it to her own (26). He thus concluded that it is not the writer's inventive act of discovering her intentions or subject matter but rather the "hermeneutic guesswork" she does in order to interpret another's code that constitutes the fundamental element of writing (26–27).

Neoclassicist Claim Two: Invention Should Be Understood and Taught as a Techne

A—if not *the*—major task of the neoclassicists was to support the claim that invention could be studied and taught. In fact, the label *neoclassicist* came from Richard Young's use of the Aristotelian under-standing of *techne* to distinguish this claim from the supposedly neoro-mantic position that invention was unteachable. As Young explained in "Arts, Crafts, Gifts, and Knacks," neoclassicists followed Aristotle in contrasting *techne* with knack: whereas those who have a knack rely on repeated experience to achieve results, those with a *techne* rely on con-scious, directed action (1980, 56). Thus the latter can explain their process and teach it others, but the former cannot. In order to teach the art of invention, Young and others recommended the use of heu-ristics, open-ended questions or operations designed to guide inquiry toward new insights. While some turned to rhetorical theory or their own writing processes to create heuristics, rhetoricians like Janice Lauer urged scholars to investigate possibilities in other disciplines, particularly work in psychology on creative problem solving. This sug-gestion to move outside of the humanities garnered criticism from scholars like Ann Berthoff, who worried that importing work from the social sciences would make writing too technical and scientific (1971, 238). Lauer responded by arguing, among other things, that Berthoff's fears were based on the misperception that all work on problem solv-ing was rigidly scientific (1972, 99).[7]

Berthoff, however, was not the only rhetorician to criticize neoclassi-cist efforts to make invention teachable through heuristics. In the same year that *MKC* came out (1987), Lynn Worsham published her essay "The Question Concerning Invention." And, in contrast to Berthoff's critique, Worsham's argument generated no direct response. In part, this lack of response had to be the result of the depth of Worsham's critique. Whereas Berthoff took aim mainly at *where* rhetoricians for-aged in order to understand and teach invention, Worsham took aim at the neoclassicist concept of *techne* upon which those efforts to understand and teach invention were based. Or, more specifically, she took aim at the theory of subjectivity operating within that concept of *techne*. Unlike the original Greek notion of *techne*, in which causal-ity is understood as the complex combination of all four Aristotelian causes, the neoclassicist version, according to Worsham, reduces cau-sality to the *causa efficiens*, that is, to the action of an independent

7.   North excerpted Lauer and Berthoff's now-famous debate over heuristics in his chapter on philosophical inquiry, calling it a "representative" example of the "move-ment—and the vigor, too—[that] dialectical confrontation can take on" (107, 111).

subject who brings products into being to achieve predetermined goals (207).[8] Relying on the work of Martin Heidegger, Worsham maintained that such a reduction is symptomatic of a kind of "technological thinking" in which the human being sees itself as a subject whose primary task is the control and regulation of all resources (205).

Worsham argued that in the case of writing this control and regulation turn what should be an experience of radical questioning and defamiliarization (1987, 233) into one of "retrieving or creating meaning" and "impos[ing] order and arrangement on data" (211). Despite their goal of helping writers break free from "a stereotypic past that wants to be retrieved" (Young 1980, 59), Worsham believed that heuristics produced "pre-selected answer[s]" before any "genuine questioning" could take place (13). What neoclassicists don't realize, she wrote, is the possibility that the form of subjectivity operating within their understanding of invention, "may itself be, at this point in our collective history, *the* fundamental stereotypic response to the world" (235; italics in original).

Neoclassicist Claim Three: Deliberate Control of Invention through Heuristics Yields Better Results than Habit or Chance

The neoclassicist effort to return invention to rhetoric was fueled not only by disciplinary ambitions but also by very real dissatisfaction with life in the composition classroom. Tired of reading student papers that did little more than "flourish a trite opinion," teachers hoped heuristics could help students discover the kind of original insight capable of giving their writing a purpose beyond completing an assignment (Jennings 1968, 192). To make these discoveries, rhetoricians like Young argued that students would need to move beyond their habitual ways of thinking; thus he and others recommended heuristics designed to help writers view subjects from multiple perspectives, such as the tagmemic procedure (1980, 59).

Equally important to the discovery of insight, however, was the need

---

8.   According to Aristotle, there are four kinds of causality (note that cause is not an exact interpretation of the ancient Greek *aition*, so we should not understand causality strictly in terms of cause and effect but more generally as "being responsible for" or "as an explanation of"): (1) the material cause, a thing's matter; (2) the formal cause, a thing's form; (3) the efficient cause, the producer of the change that results in the thing; and (4) the final cause, a thing's purpose. Worsham argued that the neoclassical version of techne recognizes only the efficient cause (i.e., the writer) and ignores the other three. See Aristotle's Physics II.3 and Metaphysics V.2 for his treatment of the four causes.

to remove students from their dependence on chance. To rely on chance, after all, is to have less control over writing. And as critics like Worsham demonstrated, neoclassicists wanted nothing if not more control over the writing process.[9] But the aim of that control wasn't, as some believe, to steer writing myopically toward a predetermined end; rather it was to avoid the same pitfalls associated with an overreliance on habit, namely, reiterating a stale position instead of saying something new. We can see this objective clearly in E.M. Jennings's 1968 essay, "A Paradigm of Discovery." After describing his heuristic for creating new associations by juxtaposing unrelated contexts, Jennings argued that "what appears to be random movement through the maze [of contexts]" is very much conditioned and biased by our experiences and "hidden presumptions" (196–98). And if writers didn't consciously try to understand and control that "random" movement, he warned, their writing would remain in "the rut of familiarity" (192). Perhaps ironically, then, Jennings wanted writers to have more control over chance so that they could be more surprised by their discoveries.

In his 1987 essay, "Invention, Serendipity, Catastrophe, and a Unified, Ironic Theory of Change," Victor Vitanza took issue with this attempt to control chance, arguing that heuristics, particularly those designed to help students solve problems, represented a "conceptually closed" approach to invention (136–37). As soon as a writer commits herself to a problem, he explained, she has eliminated many inventional possibilities since that problem will have a finite number of solutions. Moreover, because those solutions are predetermined by the problem, Vitanza argued, any change that comes about through this kind of invention is teleological. In other words, the ends of that change "are made present through its forms" (136). In order to have a more open and balanced approach to invention, then, Vitanza advocated complementary theories of chance that "openly favor an anachronistic and sophistic bias" (134).

Vitanza sharpened this contrast between chance and heuristics in

---

9.   Worsham cites the especially telling example from the introduction to Young, Becker, and Pike's Rhetoric: Discovery and Change when they write that "the book's structure is a consequence of our belief that the discipline of rhetoric is primarily concerned with the control of a process. Mastering rhetoric means not only mastering a theory of how and why one communicates but mastering the process of communication as well" (quoted in Worsham 1987, 211). This kind of language is present in other key neoclassicist texts, such as Young's "Arts, Crafts, Gifts, and Knacks" (1980).

his 2000 "From Heuristics to Aleatory Procedures" by aligning heuristics with Georges Bataille's concept of the restricted economy and
aleatory procedures with his concept of the general economy (186).[10]
As a product of the restricted economy, Vitanza argued, heuristics generate meaning through a negative process of definition in which what
something *is* is determined by what it is not (186). And they do this in
accordance with Aristotle's three laws of logic: the law of identity, the
law of noncontradiction, and the law of the excluded middle. Aleatory
procedures, on the other hand, invent by embracing the third alternatives or "monsters of thought" that are excluded by the strict "logical
categorization" at work in heuristics (186, 193). Thus they provide a
more open, more ethical approach to invention by allowing to us to
"create whole new worlds of writing that have heretofore been forbid-
den from us" (191).

Syntheses

Short reviews like these cannot help but to oversimplify the positions
they represent. There just isn't space within the pages of a book chapter
to describe the nuances and exceptions that complicate this historical
narrative about invention. Yet even in a book devoted entirely to this narrative, the impasse between neoclassicist and postmodernist approaches
to invention would be obvious. If neoclassicists worked zealously to
replace the inventionless rhetoric of current-traditionalism, then postmodernists worked just as zealously to replace the process-oriented,
techne-centric invention of neoclassicism. But as North tried to demonstrate, replacement—or as he put it, the "steady weeding out of mistaken
world views"—should not be the motor of dialectic because it inhibits
the field's ability to develop more refined positions (97).[11] Moreover,
and perhaps more importantly, it obscures the fact that philosophical

---

10. Bataille develops these two concepts in "The Notion of Expenditure" (1985) and
    in his three-volume The Accursed Share (1989). Generally speaking, the restricted
    economy, which dominates human life, is based on production and measures value
    in terms of utility. The general economy, however, is based on the notion of nonpro-
    ductive expenditures and excess. Although Bataille distinguishes between these two
    economies, and even promotes the general economy over the restricted economy,
    he sees them as inseparable, the latter being just a moment or phase in the former
    (1989, 37–43;1985, 129).

11. Janet Atwill and Janice Lauer make a similar claim, arguing that in the case of
    invention, the intensity of postmodern critiques "inhibit[ed] the kind of cumulative
    research that helps a field of study develop and mature" (Introduction 2003, xvi).

debate never ends, that it never "breaks through to some Truth." (111). Yet this is precisely what happened to debates about invention: each side had the truth, and so there was nothing to talk about. Explicit conversation about invention all but died.

Within the past five or six years, however, a handful of rhetoricians have been trying to rekindle that conversation. And, for the most part, they've done so by creating some kind of synthesis out of the oppositional positions of the neoclassicists and postmodernists. Importantly, this isn't to say that every scholar who has recently written about invention has consciously sought the middle ground or a perfectly balanced compromise. To the contrary, some of this work remains quite polemical. Yet in each case, there's an acknowledgment—occasionally explicit, more often implicit—that while each side may have had *some* truth about invention, neither had *the* truth. Usually more tentative in their claims, these rhetoricians (who are all engaged in philosophical inquiry) seem to share the neoclassicist conviction that invention is essential to rhetoric and its institutional status while realizing, as North did, that the neoclassicist program for securing that status was not entirely tenable. Thus they have all foraged in new domains, looking for the premises they need to articulate new ways of understanding invention in rhetoric and composition today. In the remainder of this essay, I will review some of this work by explaining how its authors have responded to the postmodernist counterclaims that came out of the clash with neoclassicism. This will allow us to see not only what invention is becoming in light of the methodological homogeneity that North predicted but also how the dialectic of philosophical inquiry has moved in this area of study. I will conclude by considering the implications of this movement for the philosophical community in general.

Postmodernist Counterclaim One: Writing is a Radically Situated Act of Interpretation

This counterclaim turns the first neoclassicist claim on its head, rejecting both of its key elements: that writing is a process of discernible, repeatable stages and that it is fundamentally characterized by the writer's discovery of his intentions and subject matter. However, by virtue of the fact that new work on invention still uses the word *invention*, we can assume that this second element, the emphasis on discovery, has not been replaced by an emphasis on interpretation. This does *not* mean, of course, that rhetoricians aren't studying hermeneutics. Plenty are. But, for the most part, those who have recently written about invention are still invested in the idea that, at its core, writing is a creative act.[12] Of this recent work, Janet Atwill's 2006 "Bodies and Art" probably offers the most synthetic position. Drawing on the work of Pierre Bourdieu, Atwill argues that an art (or *techne*) is created when the tacit elements of a culture's "structuring structures" are challenged by instability and heterogeneity (168). In other words, an art becomes necessary when outsiders must learn explicitly what a culture's insiders have learned by habit.[13] And to do that, they must be able to interpret or "decode" its naturalized social practice (169). Thus Atwill concludes that if having critical perspective means "recognizing the contingent character of cultural conventions and identities," then art should be understood as a means of invention *and* as an enabler of cultural critique (165, 169).

Interestingly, those rhetoricians still invested in the idea that writing is fundamentally creative have reunderstood "creative" in ways that challenge the first element of the neoclassicist claim (that writing is a process of discernible, repeatable stages) without explicitly embracing the postprocess alternative (that it is too radically situated for any codification whatsoever). Take, for instance, Debra Hawhee's 2002 essay, "Kairotic Encounters." For reasons that I will explain below, Hawhee turns to classical rhetoric and continental philosophy to formulate the concept of *invention-in-the-middle*, which she describes as a kind of kairotic event that "always occurs on the spur of the moment, as a response to the forces at work in a particular encounter." Such a notion, she argues, moves invention away from "rhetorical beginnings, with specific 'ends' in sight . . . toward notions of discursive movements, the inbetweeness of rhetoric" (18). This shift, in turn, requires a "reshaping of rhetoric itself," one that maintains the five canons but replaces the idea that they are related linearly (invention, *then* style, *then* arrangement, and so on) with the idea that they "cluster around 'ands,' held in tension and enacted only through movements—or turns—of discourse." As

---

12. I don't want to imply a binary here between invention and hermeneutics since some who study hermeneutics do so in order to understand the processes of invention a particular rhetor used. In addition, there are scholars like Steven Mailloux who argue that rhetoric (understood as production) and interpretation "are practical forms of the same human activity" since rhetoric depends on interpretation and interpretation is expressed through rhetoric. "Hermeneutics is the rhetoric of establishing meaning," he explains in Reception Histories, "and rhetoric is the hermeneutics of problematic linguistic situations" (4).

13. Atwill makes similar arguments in her 1995 "Refiguring Rhetoric as an Art," which she cowrote with Janice Lauer, and in her 1998 Rhetoric Reclaimed.

Hawhee points out, while this replacement challenges "programmatic approaches to discourse production," it does not invalidate the usefulness of invention as rhetorical concept (32).

Like Hawhee, Michael Carter understands invention as an event that happens in the "between spaces" of an encounter. However, his path to this understanding isn't quite the same as hers. Troubled by the pervasiveness of instrumental definitions of writing, Carter wants to define writing as a form of creativity that is valuable for itself rather than for the discovery, knowledge, or insight it produces. To do this, he turns to the Greek term *arche*, an ontological conception of beginning characterized by the juxtaposition of contradictory forces, such as the known and unknown, the finite and infinite (2003, 55). Carter then uses dialectical theory and process philosophy to distinguish the creativity of archeological beginnings from that of the creator tradition, arguing that while the latter is monolithic and unilateral, the former is multilateral and "utterly collaborative," each moment understood as a threshold that presents an opportunity for newness and change (131,138). It is within this archeological form of creativity that Carter finds intrinsic value: "Because creation is ongoing and (dis)continuous, creativity itself is the chief source of the good, intrinsic to the ever renewable creative moment, in and for itself, and available to all entities of the universe" (138). It is also within this form of creativity that Carter finds the intrinsic value of writing, an event through which we not only participate in archeological beginnings but also become highly aware of that participation.[14]

As Carter points out, many scholars have described good writing as the juxtaposition of contradictory forces, but none have argued that its intrinsic value lies in this juxtaposition. Moreover, none have used that argument to reunderstand invention in ways more commensurate with postmodern theory. Typically associated with the effort to generate "ready answers" through heuristics, invention has suffered from "an anemic and externalized conception of creativity," according to Carter (2003, 140). When understood from the perspective of archeological creativity, however, it becomes a "threshold event" that places everything into question by bringing the known into contact with the unknown (140–42). And once this happens, he concludes, we should no longer think of invention as the "step in a procedure" that initiates writing but rather as the creativity inherent in writing itself (142). Like Hawhee's,

---

14. See chapter 6, "Defining Writing," for Carter's argument that writing participates in archeological beginnings.

then, Carter's reconceptualization of invention responds to the first postmodernist counterclaim by pushing rhetoric away from a process model but not necessarily into a postprocess one.

Postmodernist Counterclaim Two: Invention Should Be Understood and Taught as an Experience of Questioning That Is Not Based on the Subject/ Object Split of Technological Thinking

Carter's reconceptualization of invention is also a response to this second counterclaim. His argument that invention is "marked by disruption, discontinuity, [and] disorientation" clearly echoes Worsham's emphasis on questioning and defamiliarization.[15] In addition, both he and Hawhee are motivated by the critique of subjectivity that drives Worsham's argument. Hawhee, for instance, develops her concept of "invention-in-the-middle" as a way to move beyond those concepts that "posit an active, sovereign subject who sets out to either 'find' or 'create' discursive stuff" (2002, 16). Thus she argues that "I invent" should be understood according to the middle voice of ancient Greek to mean "I invent and am invented by myself and others (in each encounter)" (17). Carter is after a similar effect, claiming that the multilateral flow of archeological creativity erases "the division between creator-subject and created object" (2003, 131).

Byron Hawk's 2007 *Counter-History of Composition* also responds to Worsham's critique of subjectivity, accepting its basic premises while pushing it in a more posthumanist direction. Like Worsham, Hawk draws on Heidegger to challenge the idea that *techne* can be used by a subject to control language and achieve predetermined ends. But whereas Worsham contrasts the experience of controlling language to one in which writers are "owned and possessed and appropriated by it" (1987, 227), Hawk contrasts it to one in which writers, language, and all the elements of a particular environment are "co-responsible" in the creation of new products, techniques, and possibilities (2007, 176). Relying on theories of posthumanism, vitalism, and complexity, Hawk maintains that a writer's agency, that is, her ability to create something with language, emerges not from her will but rather from the ways in which the elements of her situation "strive to be played out to completion." "A

---

15. Both Worsham's and Carter's emphasis on questioning, defamiliarization, and disorientation actually echoes the earlier emphasis on dissonance we find in some neoclassicist work on invention. See especially Janice Lauer's "Writing for Insight" (1987) and "The Rhetorical Approach: Stages of Writing and Strategies for Writers" (1980).

human might have an internal, psychological, or intellectual motive" he argues, "but a huge variety of cultural, linguistic, and material factors help create and enact that motive" (126). Thus any creation we might attribute to a writer is really an expression of the "larger ecological reality" in which she operates (165). Hawk then applies this argument to *techne*, concluding that it functions *not* by giving the writer the knowledge she needs to create predetermined products but rather by locating her in an ecology "in ways that reveal the potential for invention, especially the invention of new techniques" (206).

Postmodernist Counterclaim Three: Deliberate Control of Invention through Heuristics Limits Invention by Excluding Chance

Although he does not promote or develop aleatory procedures as an alternative to heuristics, Hawk does share Vitanza's conviction that deliberate control of invention is limiting. That limitation, however, stems more from the exclusion of habit than chance. Because the goal of heuristics is to help a writer "find a pre-designed something," Hawk argues, they are by nature rational and mind-centered (2007, 102, 208). In other words, they are too focused on discursive thought to take into account the complex contexts in and through which that thought happens (103, 249). What this exclusionary focus leaves out, he explains, are "the ambient, unconscious, habitual elements of invention that emerge out of the complex technological systems that human bodies inhabit today" (169). The key to a more "open-ended" invention, then, is to develop heuristics out of these complex contexts that will allow writers to "map points of intervention, insertion, or connection" (201). As Hawk points out, this kind of invention is aimed more toward designing specific occasions for writing than giving writers "generic, mental strategies that [can] function unproblematically in any classroom situation" (249).

Like Hawk, Louise Wetherbee Phelps applies elements of complexity theory to invention, arguing in her 2002 essay "Institutional Invention" that in order to reinvent higher education we need "a concept of creation or discovery as a holistic feature of cultural systems" (72). One reason the field hasn't yet developed such a concept, she explains, is that even in social constructivist theories of invention, the creativity of individuals has been separated from the "culture that does or does not support or respond to them." In other words, we've failed to see the individual as "part of the system of creativity" (73). According to complexity theory, however, innovation emerges not from the ideas or actions of individuals but instead from tension that exists when a system is on the edge of orderliness and chaos (78, 81). Although Phelps does not use complexity theory *because* she wants to challenge the role of deliberate control in invention, it does have this effect. Following Stuart Kauffman's argument in *At Home in the Universe* (1995), for example, she argues that systemic complexity "escapes mindful human control and planning" (Phelps, 79). What's interesting about Phelps's argument, though, is that she recognizes the difference between being "locally wise" and "globally wise" (79). While the latter is impossible in a complex system, the former is not. For her, then, the issue surrounding deliberate control isn't whether it's good or bad—which is to say, inventive or limiting—but instead the levels at which it can and cannot be effectively applied.

TOWARD A POSTDIALECTICAL PHILOSOPHY OF INVENTION

If it were "accumulation time," that is, if the philosophical community were to convene in order to say what it knows about invention, chances are that there would be no consensus. In other words, it would be difficult to merge recent work on invention into some kind of coherent philosophy. But I think it would be equally difficult to defend North's claim that the term "serves as little more than a general rubric" under which unrelated pieces of research are gathered (339). In part, this is because those pieces of research are now methodologically related. But there's another, more important reason, one that I think North overlooked because he was so intent on showing how new research in composition had disenfranchised its founding community, the practitioners (317). As I explained earlier, North thought there wasn't much to invention research other than a desire among investigators to "unlock its secrets" and replace composition lore with disciplinary knowledge (337–39). While it's certainly true that those investigators studied invention because they thought it could make composition more legitimate, it's also true that they studied invention because they thought it could make writing more rewarding. When current-traditional pedagogy ignored invention, they argued, it ignored the very thing that made writing valuable: its ability to produce knowledge, solve problems, and generate insight. Yes, these are all instrumental values, but they are values nonetheless. And the term *invention* was used primarily as a way to name them, not simply to unite research around a "topically identified problem" (339).

Although only Carter's book discusses invention explicitly in terms of value, I would argue that the thread connecting all of the work reviewed here is a shared sense that the value of writing lies in invention, even when invention is reunderstood as interpretation. If we look at the debate between the neoclassicists and postmodernists from this perspective, we can see that it has suffered from some of the problems of philosophical inquiry because, as Carter noted, so much is at stake in arguments about value. When we look at this new work on invention from the same perspective, however, we see that while a lot is still at stake, these methodological problems have been mitigated by the effort to reach synthesis. For instance, scholars have been less interested in replacing old knowledge than they have been in building upon or modifying it. I pointed out this shift in Hawhee's and Carter's responses to the process/postprocess debate, but it is also true for Hawk's modification of Worsham's critique of subjectivity and Phelps's effort to push rhetorical invention toward institutional invention. In each case, these investigators have built their arguments on premises foraged from areas like complexity theory, network theory, and ecology—all of which stress the mutual constitution of opposition positions rather than their differences. In addition, writers like Carter and Hawk have managed to extend their philosophical arguments to pedagogy without yoking them to specific practices the way others did, particularly the neoclassicists. Carter, of course, confesses that he uses his philosophical position to lead reform, but I think even North would read this confession as a sign of increasing methodological awareness, not just ongoing methodological weakness.

It would seem, then, that if we used philosophical work on invention as a test case, we could conclude that philosophical inquiry is on its way to the "more coherent future" North anticipated. No, it's not perfect, but the dialectic appears to be doing its job, forcing composition philosophers to create more synthetic, more self-aware positions over time. This is a nice conclusion, one that I think has obvious merit. But, according to John Muckelbauer, it has some problems, too. Muckelbauer addresses what he calls the "problem of change" in his 2008 *The Future of Invention*, arguing that despite all of the effort in our field to create improvement through change, no one has really considered the troubling implications of how that change happens (3–5). As Muckelbauer points out, change almost always occurs dialectically, that is, by "overcoming or negating particular others—outdated concepts, oppressive social structures, limited subjectivities, or simply undesirable propositions" (4). The problem here (besides the ethical issue of negating others) is that this kind of change maintains binary thinking, such as the binaries of same/different and traditional/innovative. Not even the change that occurs through synthesis is exempt from this charge, Muckelbauer contends, because any attempt to exist in the space between two poles inevitably assumes and affirms the existence of those poles (9). No matter how the content of our positions changes, then, it is still "the product of the monotonous, complex repetition of dialectical change" (10). Thus we might summarize Muckelbauer's rather complicated argument about dialectic with a very simple cliché: *the more things change, the more they stay the same.*

Although North could not have anticipated Muckelbauer's critique of dialectic (it relies on theory that simply was not part of our disciplinary conversation in the 1980s), I want to use it to reflect on his cautiously optimistic predictions about the philosophical community. On the one hand, it presents a clear challenge to North's faith in "the restorative powers of a long-term commitment to dialectic" to compensate for the weaknesses of philosophical inquiry (111). Regardless of how long the "back and forth of argument and counter-argument" goes on about a particular topic in the philosophical community, the change it produces will be dialectical change (106). And so we have to question its ability to achieve real progress, both in our understanding of the topics it addresses and in itself. But, on the other hand, Muckelbauer's argument is a product of precisely the dialectical movement he critiques. And it illustrates nothing if not Muckelbauer's very high methodological self-awareness. In this sense, then, it is a perfect example of the kind of progress North hoped for. Exactly where this contradiction leaves philosophical inquiry, I'm not sure. But I do think North was right to predict that "a real Philosophical community" would emerge in composition. I just don't think he saw one emerging around work on invention, and I don't think he could have foreseen the degree to which that emergence would challenge the most fundamental feature of philosophical inquiry—dialectic.

REFERENCES

Atwill, Janet M.. 1998. *Rhetoric reclaimed: Aristotle and the liberal arts tradition.* Ithaca, NY: Cornell University Press.
———. 2006. Bodies and art. *Rhetoric Society Quarterly* 36: 165–170.

Atwill, Janet M., and Janice M. Lauer. 1995. Refiguring rhetoric as an art: Aristotle's concept of *techne*. In *discourse studies in honor of James L. Kinneavy*, edited by Rosalind J. Gabin, 25–40. Potomac, MD: Scripta Humanistica.

———. 2002. Introduction to Atwill and Lauer, xi–xxi.

———, eds. 2002. *Perspectives on rhetorical invention*. Knoxville: University of Tennessee Press.

Bataille, Georges. 1985. The notion of expenditure. In *Visions of excess: Selected writings 1927–1939*. Translated by Allan Stoekl. Minneapolis: University of Minnesota Press. 116–29.

———. 1989. Vol. 1 of *The accursed share*. Translated by Robert Hurley. New York: Zone Books.

Berthoff, Ann. 1971. The problem of problem solving. *CCC* 22: 237–42.

Carter, Michael P. 2003. *Where writing begins: A postmodern reconstruction*. Carbondale: Southern Illinois University Press.

Hawhee, Debra. 2002. Kairotic encounters. In Atwill and Lauer, 16–35.

Hawk, Byron. 2007. *A counter-history of composition: Toward methodologies of complexity*. Pittsburgh, PA: University of Pittsburgh Press.

Jennings, E.M. 1968. A paradigm for discovery. *CCC* 19: 192–200.

Kaufmann, Stuart. 1995. *At home in the universe: The search for the laws of self-organization and complexity*. New York: Oxford University Press.

Kent, Thomas. 1993. *Paralogic rhetoric: A theory of communicative interaction*. Lewisburg, PA: Bucknell University Press.

———. 1999. Introduction to *Post-process theory: Beyond the writing-process paradigm*, edited by Thomas Kent, 1–6. Carbondale: Southern Illinois University Press.

Lauer, Janice M. 1972. Response to Ann E. Berthoff. *CCC* 23: 208–10.

———. 1980. The rhetorical approach: Stages of writing and strategies for writers. In *Eight approaches to teaching composition*, edited by Timothy Donovan and Ben W. McClelland, 53–64. Urbana, IL: National Council of Teachers of English.

Mailloux, Steven. 1998. *Reception histories: rhetoric, pragmatism, and American cultural politics*. Ithaca, NY: Cornell University Press.

———. 1987. *Writing for insight*. In *Conversations in composition, proceedings of New Dimensions in Writing: The first Merrimack College Conference on Composition Instruction*, edited by Albert C. DeCiccio and Michael J. Rossi, 1–6. North Andover, MA: Merrimack College.

———.2002. Rhetorical invention: The diaspora. In Atwill and Lauer, 1–15.

McCrimmon, James M. 1985. Writing as a way of knowing. In Graves, 3–11.

Muckelbauer, John. 2008. *The future of invention: Rhetoric, postmodernism, and the problem of change*. Albany: State University of New York Press.

Murray, Donald. 1985. Teach writing as a process not product. In Graves, 89–92.

North, Stephen. 1987. *The making of knowledge in composition: Portrait of an emerging field*. Portsmouth, NH: Boynton/Cook Publishers.

Paine, Charles. 1999. *The resistant writer: Rhetoric as immunity, 1850 to the present*. Albany: State University of New York Press.

Phelps, Louise Wetherbee. 2002. Institutional invention: (How) is it possible? In Atwill and Lauer, 64–95.

Rohman, Gordon D. 1965. Pre-writing: The stage of discovery in the writing process. *CCC* 16: 106–12.

Simmons, Sue Carter. 1995. Constructing writers: Barrett Wendell's pedagogy at Harvard. *CCC* 46: 327–52.

Vitanza, Victor. 1987. Invention, serendipity, catastrophe, and a unified, ironic theory of change: The two master and two mistress tropes, with attendant offspring. In *Visions of rhetoric: History, theory, and criticism*, edited by Charles Kneupper, 132–45. Arlington,

TX: Rhetoric Society of America.

———. 2000. From heuristics to aleatory procedures; Or toward writing the accident. In *Inventing a discipline*, edited by Maureen Daly Goggin, 185–206. Urbana, IL: National Council of Teachers of English.

Worsham, Lynn. 1987. The question concerning invention: Hermeneutics and the genesis of writing. *PRE/TEXT* 8: 197–244.

Young, Richard E. 1980. Arts, crafts, gifts, and knacks: Some disharmonies in the new rhetoric. In *Reinventing the rhetorical tradition*, edited by Ian Pringle and Avia Freedman, 53–60. Conway, AK: L and S Books.

Young, Richard, Alton Becker, and Kenneth Pike. 1970. *Rhetoric: Discovery and change.* New York: Harcourt, Brace, and World.

5

MAKING KNOWLEDGE, SHAPING HISTORY

Critical Consciousness and the Historical Impulse in Composition Studies

Erica Frisicaro-Pawlowski

As the essays in this volume attest, Stephen North's *The Making of Knowledge in Composition: Portrait of an Emerging Field* (*MKC*), published in 1987, is a landmark text in composition, a comprehensive record of key developments, communities, and epistemologies relevant to understanding the field as a field. Yet nearly twenty-five years after its publication, its proper classification within the corpus of disciplinary work produced prior to 1990 is somewhat difficult. North's text is most commonly defined as an overview of research methods in composition, as in Richard Lloyd-Jones's 1989 review of the text published in *College Composition and Communication* (*CCC*). In the same volume, James Raymond defines its purposes as twofold: as "an indispensable reference work" and as a "critical survey" (93). Similarly, *An Introduction to Composition Studies* identifies the text as a categorical investigation of composition research and practice (Lindemann and Tate 1991, 18), as a bibliographic resource (76), and as a social-scientific classification of composition scholarship (99).

However, I wish to focus on the historical impulse evident within *MKC*—the foundational assumption grounding North's work that composition is a unique professional entity with distinct roots and communities traceable through various stages of development. Working from North's characterization of historical inquiry "as a cycle of interpretation and reinterpretation" (71), what is the value of *MKC* in examining the emergence of practices, definitions, and events that have shaped what composition is now?

In this chapter, I argue that in attempting to bind what North defines as "critical consciousness" (preface) to a record of the field's scholarly development, *MKC* sheds light on the ways in which history, community, and personal belief shape composition's records of its own development—lessons that have fueled disciplinary inquiry over the past twenty years and honed the ends and aims of the historical impulse in more contemporary accounts of the discipline. First, I reread *MKC* as a history, calling attention to the relationship between historical and critical consciousness shaped within it, as well as the problems the text poses in attempting to construct a consistent account of the field's development. In the next two sections, I demonstrate how North's difficulties in reconstructing composition "as the product of a single consciousness" (5) may have influenced the shape of historical scholarship since the publication of *MKC*, leading to a more focused historical vision for the field. And the final section examines broad patterns in recent histories to evaluate the nature of the historical impulse in composition, and to speculate about how North's vision of critical consciousness remains relevant to contemporary scholarship.

REPRESENTING HISTORY: THE NATURE OF INQUIRY IN *MKC*

In considering how we might recast North's account as a history, the purpose defined in his introduction to *MKC* proves noteworthy. The first line of the text indicates the primary subject of the work is "how knowledge is made in the field that has come to be called Composition" (1); however, North then indicates his study describes the "modes of inquiry" that have given rise to composition scholarship, illuminating a secondary aim linked with historical vision: "The book's central purpose, then, is to describe these modes, and *to account for the emergence of these communities in Composition*" (2; italics added). While the first statement raises questions about what methods shape knowledge in the field, the second raises questions of why such methods "emerged"— how they gained prominence through social networks. The former are questions of fact, of observation about what happens when one sets out to create disciplinary knowledge; the latter are questions North characterizes as those of history, of reflections upon the question "'What has Composition been that it is what it is now?'" (72).

Further, *MKC* calls attention to what exactly is at stake in posing such questions. In asserting "how these techniques and their results come to *mean* for any particular investigation—is not inherent in the techniques themselves, but a function of community standards" (2), the scope of North's work extends beyond an account of what has happened (how knowledge emerged in the field) or what happens (how knowledge is

shaped in the field) in formulating disciplinary knowledge. North's queries also call us to consider the *subject* of composition and *its subjects*: to
create a more socially conscious account of the field's actors *and* actions.
Throughout *MKC*, North connects the nature of research practices to
the nature of community, highlighting both modes of inquiry and the
process of disciplinary formation simultaneously.

As such, *MKC* is distinctly historical: it defines methods that mark the
field's boundaries; it delineates relationships between methodological
communities, tracing their origins and assumptions; and it advocates for
both methodological and historical awareness as crucial to the growth
of the field. What ultimately distinguishes the text, however, are North's
efforts in crafting a scholarly ethos that models an *emergent* awareness
of discipline-specific methods, discourse communities, and beliefs as
the field takes shape. Though North's attempts to offer a portrayal of
"the portrait of Composition *as a whole . . .* as a product of a single consciousness" (5) have opened the text to a good deal of criticism, they
also represent an important development. In linking formative notions
of methodological consciousness, historical consciousness, and self-consciousness, North's approach to understanding composition from an
individual, developing, yet situated subject position anticipates subsequent developments in disciplinary scholarship.

In order to further explore the relationships between North's position as author/researcher and the objects of historical inquiry in *MKC*,
it is essential to examine how the text constructs an ethos appropriate
for a wide-ranging survey of the field's development. Undeniably, the
methodological integrity of *MKC* is perhaps too reliant upon North's
individual interpretation of composition's traditions of inquiry. Yet his
approach also serves a central aim at the heart of the historical impulse
in composition: it establishes a comprehensive vision of the field as
a distinct and orderly academic formation, one grounded in intellectual histories that can be both observed subjectively and weighed
objectively by disciplinary insiders and outsiders. The introduction
includes a brief section that proves illuminating in this regard. North
defines his work as akin to participant observation, describing the influence of Paul Diesing's *Patterns of Discovery in the Social Sciences* on *MKC*.
While he is "inclined to take a similar position" to Diesing's, North tai-
lors his approach by bringing his personal experience to the fore in
describing his framework for investigation: "Having conceived of these
various [methodological] communities as constituting the 'society'
of Composition, and of each method—each mode of inquiry—as the

subculture of one or another of them, I have tried here to make sense of what I have seen and done in my ten years of 'living among' the people of Composition" (4). Here, North establishes his narrative authority as aligned with that of an outside scientific authority.

While it should be noted that North's approach was likely influenced by the prevalence of empirical studies in composition common during this period, the association with Diesing seems, in retrospect, conflicted. These tensions become all the more prohibitive when, a few lines later, North indicates that he intends "to provide that image of the whole [field] myself, to account for what I saw from the particular vantage of insider/outsider, participant/observer" (5). *MKC* thus establishes a tremendously complicated vision of the development of the field: one in which North is responsible for reconstructing representations of each community, its individual history, and its organizational principles as based on "insider" texts, observing and classifying each through an "outsider's" consciousness, and, through a "single consciousness," attempting to relate, compare, and classify the relationships within each community, as well as within the whole of composition. Despite the longing for a single consciousness through which to map the field and chart its history evident in the introductory material, *MKC* instead invokes a patchwork of narrative perspectives, a network of angles through which the historical impulse might be said to navigate in representing knowledge formation within composition.

The account that follows, while privileging informative ends in tracing the development of the field, thus begins to chart a course through disciplinary history that invokes "deliberate and critical consciousness" (preface) as a force imperative to the field's development—and this force, in turn, comes to provide a sort of narrative center to the text. While this concept has been deployed in numerous ways in composition scholarship over the years, I define critical consciousness and its relevance to disciplinary history in somewhat general terms: as the impulse to craft purposeful, transparent, and ethically self-aware records of the field's development. Because North presents a record of the field that calls attention to processes that determine *identification of* key landmarks and knowledge-making activities in the discipline, as well as the critical processes that help to determine *identification with* such disciplinary activities, *MKC* marks a unique achievement in this regard. Further, the concept of critical consciousness that guides North's overview of the field's development, as described in the preface to the account, is less political or polemical than reflective:

This is a book I have written for myself. The blind enthusiasm and naïve faith that were mine as a new recruit to Composition will no longer serve. The development of further commitment, of a mature loyalty, requires a new perspective—one based on a broader and deeper knowledge, yes, but even more on a deliberate and critical consciousness. This book represents my search for that perspective. It is a search that I have found, and that I believe many readers will find, often painful; it just plain isn't easy to look hard at what you believe, and to discover the very narrow limits of what you know.

The notions of critical consciousness deployed in this statement indicate that, for North, recalling the development of the field through its records of knowledge-making activities is ultimately necessary not just to defining what the field is, but who *we* are—what it means to not only practice composition, but also to identify with the field in deliberate, self-conscious ways.

In this sense, *MKC*'s construction of history is not ultimately centered on method, but on membership—on how disciplinary inclusion is shaped by available networks for making and sharing knowledge. Notably, in describing his aims, North indicates that critical consciousness grows out of the scholar's examination of not what is known, but what is believed; indeed, it is in considering one's own beliefs that one "discover[s] the very limits of what you know." This notion of critical consciousness implies that the historical impulse is best deployed in the service of personal location within the discipline, rather than in the service of locating the discipline in relation to others. *MKC* is therefore quite distinct from other histories written during this period, which tended to downplay individual consciousness and highlight what can be called disciplinary consciousness—the location of the field in relation to other institutional or scholarly formations.[1]

North does not neglect the importance of critical consciousness to disciplinary integrity entirely, however. In her article "Composition as a

---

1.   It is important to note the paucity of full-length histories of composition studies prior to the publication of *MKC* in 1987. Texts most relevant to tracing disciplinary history before 1987 included Arthur Applebee's Tradition and Reform in the Teaching of English: A History (1974); James Berlin's Writing Instruction in American Colleges (1984) and Rhetoric and Reality: Writing Instruction in American Colleges 1900–1985 (published one month prior to the release of North's text in March 1987); and Albert Kitzhaber's dissertation "Rhetoric in American Colleges, 1850–1900" (not published as a book until 1990). As these titles indicate, such scholarship represents a pattern in disciplinary history that troubled North—what he called "an allegiance to something outside of Composition" (64): literature, in the case of Applebee, and rhetoric, in the case of Berlin and Kitzhaber. North's work attempts to treat composition as a disciplinary entity influenced by, but not reliant upon, rhetorical practice or literary study. As such, it represents perhaps the first history of its kind.

Postdisciplinary Formation," Susan Brown Carlton notes that North's "professional commitment to historicizing composition as a knowledge-making activity suggests that he wants to see composition studies flourish and sees disciplinarity as a mechanism for securing its future within the university" (1995, 78). What is not as clear, however, is how North would encourage the field's constituents to shape its futures in what he might call deliberate and critically self-conscious ways. Instead, he tends to provide fragmented notions of what disciplinary consciousness entails among his descriptions of methodological communities. In his section on the historians, for instance, North links critical self-consciousness to the healthy practice of dialectic: "The greater critical self-consciousness of the second generation will likely lead to a more powerful dialectic" (86). In the section on the philosophers, consciousness is linked to reflexive practices of deliberation:

> This wide-ranging search for a foundation, for some first principles, seems to have become both more self-conscious and more reflexive. . . . The writers who have served as the core of the community . . . as well as some members of a very articulate second-generation—have become more careful and more critical about what contributions from elsewhere might entail; and, at the same time, turned their attention inward." (95)

Finally, North associates critical consciousness with the capacity to evaluate principles of methodology that guide each mode of inquiry, citing a lack of discernment as one of the problems among experimentalists: "The Experimental community has been a deeply troubled one. That the work of novice investigators, and work so seriously troubled at that, should be held up as work to be emulated, is surely evidence of that claim" (190).

There is a central factor connecting these characterizations: in each, individual and communal self-consciousness develops out of a historical awareness, whether that stems from disputing the claims of predecessors to create new possibilities for the field's futures (in the case of the historians), from revisiting the ideas of others to apply them to new sites or practices in the field (in the case of the philosophers), or from learning from the mistakes of previous studies (in the case of the experimentalists). For North, it seems, the historical impulse is the very essence of critical consciousness in composition, and one that should best inform the everyday work of both individuals and communities.

Since the publication of *MKC*—and particularly since the political turn in the field took shape in the 1990s—critical consciousness has remained a prominent goal in composition scholarship and practice.

As such, North's frequent references to the rising consciousness of generations yet to come seem appropriate. While recent accounts of the field's development can be said to utilize more critically and politically self-conscious strategies for positioning the scholar in relation to their object of study, however, what is not as clear is whether subsequent histories have the same scope and singular vision North advocates as essential to the creation of critically conscious scholarship. In reflecting back upon the continued significance of *MKC* on the anniversary of its publication, it is crucial to consider to what purposes composition scholars have deployed disciplinary history over the past twenty-five years, as well as how they have enacted, positioned, and promoted the notion of critical consciousness in tracing the development of the field.

COMPOSITION HISTORY SINCE 1987—A BRIEF SKETCH

It is commonly noted that composition scholarship proliferated in the years following the publication of *MKC*, and bibliographic records confirm the advancement of historical studies of composition during this period. In compiling records gleaned from the *CCCC Bibliography of Composition and Rhetoric, The MLA International Bibliography, The Bedford Bibliography for Teachers of Writing* (Bizzell and Herzberg 2004), and catalogs of major university and professional presses, I found that nearly one hundred accounts of disciplinary history were printed between 1987 and 2007, representing nearly all areas of interest within the field.[22] For example, among the seventy titles grouped under the heading "History of Rhetoric and Education" published between 1906 and 2002, *The Bedford Bibliography* indicates over half, forty-five out of seventy, were published after 1987.

When one looks more closely at the nature of the histories produced within this time frame, many accounts included in the field's bibliographic data remain largely interested in linking composition to either

---

2.   Conducting bibliographic research in composition has been a challenge nearly since its inception, due to the absence of established, consistently updated, and comprehensive bibliographic publications (see Scott 1986 and Lindemann 2002). The Bedford Bibliography, last published in 2004, is not a comprehensive list of publications, as its full title implies. The CCCC Executive Committee ended production of The CCCC Bibliography in 1999, and the last print edition appeared in 1995. Since 2000, composition publications have been included in The MLA International Bibliography; however, more formalized, discipline-specific bibliographic efforts are currently lacking. Partial online bibliographies (such as at CompPile.org or those maintained by individuals) have served as informal reference guides, though their reliability, currency, and consistency cannot match those offered by the CCCC.

the classical tradition or to research in rhetorical theory. For instance, works such as *Nineteenth-Century Rhetoric in North America* (Johnson 1991) or *The Formation of College English: Rhetoric and Belles Lettres in the British Cultural Provinces,* (Miller 1997) served to widen readers' understanding of the cultural and historical contexts from which composition stems, yet they speak of composition instruction as an outgrowth or extension of rhetorical instruction. It is clear, however, that *MKC* advocated new approaches to historical scholarship which could distinguish composition as an institutional practice different from rhetorical education, as "there could be no Composition—academic field, capital 'C'—before, say, 1958" (North, 9). North linked this tendency to connect composition and classical rhetoric to the struggle for status within English departments, and felt such approaches perpetuated misperceptions about the field:

> As new modes of inquiry compete for power in Composition, they need to prove themselves, and a chief means for doing so is to demonstrate their ties to some already legitimate academic enterprise. One such enterprise—and one that sells particularly well . . . is Rhetoric. Whereas Composition is conceived of pretty narrowly, usually as 'mere' practice, Rhetoric is not only the crown of the classical trivium, but can arguably claim a tradition as deep and rich, maybe deeper and richer, than poetics. . . . It stands as a more legitimate intellectual enterprise than just plain Composition. (64–5)

MKC thus characterizes rhetorical history in composition as aligned with a quest for disciplinary legitimation, rather than disciplinary self-awareness, and his insistence on considering composition as a distinct (and distinctly) academic field "emerging" around 1963 is central to creating what he would deem a critically conscious account of its development.

In the years following 1987, the notion of disciplinary consciousness prominent within the field changed shape—a shift that, in retrospect, validates North's inclination to separate work in rhetoric from work in composition. In their article, "Making Use of the Nineteenth Century: The Writings of Robert Connors and Recent Histories of Rhetoric and Composition," Lyneé Lewis Gaillet and Thomas Miller indicate that "by the early 1990s . . . a more-politicized view of the historical constraints that define composition" became commonplace (2001, 149). While Gaillet and Miller attribute this shift to the histories of James Berlin, in particular, North's interest in illuminating how composition practices are shaped by their unique institutional position also speaks to the prescience of his vision.

It is then somewhat disheartening to observe that of the historical works published between 1987 and 2000, a fairly limited number represent extensive studies of composition as an institutional entity largely independent from rhetoric.[3] Only a handful of full-length studies written from what North might deem a "singular perspective" were published during this important period: *Origins of Composition Studies in the American College: A Documentary History, 187–1925* (Brereton 1995); *A Teaching Subject: Composition Since 1966* (Harris 1996); *Fencing with Words: A History of Writing Instruction at Amherst College during the Era of Theodore Baird, 1938–1966* (Varnum 1996); *The Resistant Writer: Rhetoric as Immunity, 1850 to the Present* (Paine 1999); and *The Young Composers: Composition's Beginnings in 19th Century Schools* (Schultz 1999). The relative dearth of full-length histories that trace the development of composition as a unique institutional construct is particularly disappointing, in light of the potential for criticism offered in the wake of the political turn burgeoning in this period.

From 2000 and 2007, these trends in publication appear to have continued. Full-length monographs on composition history published by major presses[4] include *Practicing Writing: The Postwar Discourse of Freshman English* (Masters 2004) and *A Counter-History of Composition: Toward Methodologies of Complexity* (Hawk 2007). In recent years, in-depth studies of archival materials and institutional practices have become more prominent than general overviews of the field's history, including *Authoring a Discipline: Scholarly Journals and the Post-World War II Emergence of Rhetoric and Composition* (Goggin 2000); *On a Scale: A Social History of Writing Assessment in America* (Elliot 2005); and *Archives of Instruction: Nineteenth-Century Rhetorics, Readers, and Composition Books in the United*

---

3.   Determining which texts to include within this category is challenging, considering the complementary work performed by historians of rhetoric and historians of composition. In this survey, I have limited inclusion to those texts dealing with composition as an institutional formation different from rhetoric—those North might deem appropriate to tracing the tradition of what he calls "new composition" (17). To that end, I have excluded texts like Rhetoric and Reality: Writing Instruction in American Colleges, 1900–1985 (Berlin 1987) and Composition-Rhetoric: Backgrounds, Theory, and Pedagogy (Connors 1997), as they are just as interested in tracing the development of rhetorical education as in tracing the development of composition as a field. I have also excluded texts that seek to historicize particular areas or sites within the field (for example, histories of writing centers, assessment, or writing program administration) and highlighted those interested in tracing the history "of Composition as a whole" to use North's emphasis.

4.   In compiling this overview, I consulted catalogs of major composition presses (among them SUNY, University of Pittsburgh, Southern Illinois University, NCTE, and Heinemann), as well as the current edition of the MLA International Bibliography online database.

States (Carr, Carr, and Schultz 2005). Considering the proliferation of composition scholarship since the early 1990s, however, these works represent a minute percentage of total publications in the field.

Weighing such evidence, it may seem as if the historical impulse in composition studies has diminished over time. A decline in the publication of full-length monographs tracing disciplinary history over the last ten years can be attributed to a number of factors: disciplinary history may currently be perceived as less valuable than other forms of scholarship; historical methodology may have become more complex, challenging, or time consuming as the field has developed; the impulse to historicize the field as a whole may have waned in light of its continued growth and strength. But I am inclined to believe that none of these factors is entirely true. Instead, if we reenvision how the historical impulse is woven into the nature of critically conscious work in contemporary composition scholarship, we find that the work of historical reflection is increasingly not confined to a specific community of historians, but is now more dispersed across the entire community of knowledge makers in the field. Shifts in how compositionists envision our relationship with history and in how we enact critical consciousness have influenced the current shape of historical scholarship; and retracing how these relationships have evolved since the publication of *MKC* allows us not only to measure the consequences of this shift, but also to reenvision the role of historical consciousness in the ongoing achievements of the discipline.

REENVISIONING HISTORICAL HORIZONS: 1990–2000

If we take papers from the first Watson Conference in Composition (collected in Rosner, Boehm, and Journet 1998) as accurately representing attitudes toward historical scholarship in the 1990s, concerns regarding the status of historical knowledge in composition were emerging by mid-decade. For example, in his essay "Composition History and Disciplinarity," Robert Connors indicates that the field's "movement toward disciplinarity may be a movement away from the human meaning of what we do" (1998, 16). Connors's concern stems from a perception that new generations of composition scholars lack historical consciousness, and his work reminds us that "without an understanding of history, a field of action has no memory, and without memory it cannot measure movement outside of the realm of a narrow, incremental present" (4). Similar impressions were shared by others who feared that as the first generation of compositionists retired from the public life of the discipline, new generations of scholars would lose a lived sense of disciplinary history.

However, in her contribution "Paths Not Taken: Recovering History as Alternative Future," Louise Phelps takes a different approach, reflecting upon the late 1980s as a period crucial to the maturation of the discipline. In particular, she makes a case for looking back on 1988 as a benchmark in the professionalization of the field, as "emblematic of a certain historical moment . . . representing a choice point or branching of paths. This is something like how we have imagined 1963 as a partly historical and partly fictionalized, symbolic point of origin for the modern professionalized field" (1998, 41). This moment framed an ideological choice between the impulse to employ historical consciousness in service of disciplinary ethics, or to develop other methods of scholarship, such as theory and cognitive research, crucial to the professionalization of composition. In 1988, according to Phelps, "a relationship with the future was chosen over a connection with the past." While acknowledging that her own reflection is composed in 1996, an era in which the field is "developing more deeply historicized representations of its own identity," with "historical studies burgeoning," she also speaks of a failure to mark the moral significance of this choice. Citing Robert Connors's participation in a symposium entitled "What Are We Doing as a Research Community?" at the 1988 Conference on College Composition and Communication (CCCC), Phelps highlights links between history and critical consciousness, indicating that Connors "presented historical knowledge as a precondition not only for defining the field (self-understanding), but also for making wise choices in our personal actions as writers or teachers and for deciding where the field should go as a research discipline" (40). Like North and Connors before her, Phelps advocates historical inquiry as fundamental to deliberative reflection.

How might we weigh Phelps's observations in light of North's advocacy of critical consciousness? And how should her work be interpreted as an outgrowth of its own historical moment? Clearly, Phelps argues against a retreat from disciplinary efforts to employ historical knowledge in critically conscious ways. At the same time, scholarship that placed critical consciousness at the forefront of the field flowered throughout the 1990s. For example, Patricia Bizzell's collection Academic Discourse and Critical Consciousness presents an extended study of the importance of this concept in composition practice. In the introduction to her work, Bizzell links her initial understanding of this concept to Freire: "'Critical Consciousness,' a term I learned from the work of Paolo Freire, once meant for me an awareness of the injustices of social inequality in America, coupled with a commitment to rectifying those injustices" (1992, 3). This political interpretation of critically conscious disciplinary work was pervasive, particularly in pedagogies designed to "guide them [students] toward a more critically interactive relationship with their school experience" (7).

Looking closely at the work of Freire, we see that critical consciousness is not only fundamental to practical application, but also to intellectual endeavors. In *Education for Critical Consciousness*, the understanding of temporality—of one's location in relation to history—is a crucial element: "Men relate to their world in a critical way. They apprehend the objective data of their reality (as well as the ties that link one datum to the other) through reflection. . . . And in the act of critical perception, men discover their own temporality. Transcending a single dimension, they reach back to yesterday, recognize today, and come upon tomorrow" (Freire 1974, 3). In Freire's vision of education, reflection and recollection are intricately tied to this awareness of one's temporal location. Reflection "implies invention and reinvention. It claims from each person a critical reflection on the very act of knowing. It must be a reflection which recognizes the knowing process" (10; Bizzell, 137). In this vision of critical consciousness, history itself becomes a way of knowing, a way of reinventing the intellectual enterprise.

Similarly, in *MKC*, critical consciousness is seen as a primary aim of historical scholarship and the notions of community and disciplinarity shaped by it. Yet, in looking back at the forms of history that fell into favor from 1990 to 2000, we find fewer studies of how composition as a whole enacts ways of knowing (particular "knowing processes" to use Freire's term), and more regarding the artifacts of composition practice. So, for example, archival studies by Brereton (*Origins* 1995), Varnum (*Fencing with Words* 1996), and Schultz (*Young Composers* 1999) sought to analyze the nature of teaching practices in use throughout American classrooms over time. Such work opened up new historical vistas as the decade progressed, promoting scholarship "more attentive to specific historical contexts, trends, and figures" (Gaillet and Miller 2001, 150). In turning to more meticulous and hence more focused archival work, composition historians applied their efforts to more functional purposes, in terms of consciousness building: namely, to creating more methodologically self-conscious records of disciplinary development.

Archivists seek, whenever possible, to work not from impressions but artifacts. The type of reconstructive historical vision required of such work entails acts of interpretation similar to those required within other approaches to history, yet it poses fundamentally different questions than other forms of historical scholarship.

North's key historical questions involve reflection on professional identity: "'What has composition been that it is what it is now?'—or, in its more pointed form, 'Who have we been that we are who we are now?'" (72). Within *MKC*, questions of history are posed in order to seek the soul of the field; yet these questions are derived from intensely subjective experiences of disciplinarity. Critical consciousness hence lies in the *ends* of such historical work, as it creates greater awareness of what it means to belong to a discipline—a community of compositionists.

On the other hand, inquiry into the field modeled by archival historians begins with methodological identification: What do we *have* that can help us to understand who we have been and who we are now? And how do we read such objects against the backdrop of disciplinary history? Such questions lead to less sweeping conclusions, focusing the historical gaze more intently on disciplinary locations—particular institutions, events, and artifacts—rather than the experience of disciplinarity writ large. To that end, critical consciousness in recent histories has served as a tool for engaging in the acts of vision and reconstruction that comprise scholarly inquiry, residing not primarily in the ends, but the means of historical investigation.

THE ENDS OF DISCIPLINARY HISTORY: FURTHER NOTES ON "FUTURES"

Since 2000, three patterns of historical scholarship emergent within the 1990s have remained consistent. First, creating disciplinary histories of the field as a whole, in the fashion of *MKC*, is still generally eschewed, and the historical gaze continues to be focused more intently upon specific aspects of the discipline. So, while the past decade's historical scholarship has provided us with more varied historical accounts of publication forums and patterns in the field (Goggin 2000) and the development of formalized writing assessment (Elliot 2005), comprehensive accounts of the origins, configuration, and growth of the field "as a whole" have fallen out of favor.

Second, and central to understanding the direction of the historical impulse in relation to North's vision of critical consciousness, more recent accounts of the field's development seem less driven by what we might call a personal politics of location and more compelled by a sense of disciplinary placement. For example, accounts by Thomas Masters (2004) and Steven Mailloux (2006) trace the distinct discursive and institutional patterns of representation that characterize the development of composition, rather than seeking to locate the position of individual subjects in relation to the field.

Third, objects of study—including textbooks, testimonials, curricular designs, and so forth—continue to form the primary locus of the contemporary historical impulse. The field's historians are more likely to use the material, measurable artifacts of composition as their data, rather than less tangible forms of evidence: testimonials and first-person accounts of disciplinary developments, or even previous interpretations of disciplinary origins

To evaluate the current shape of the historical impulse in composition, it is helpful to recall once again North's questions regarding the uses of history as a means of boosting critical consciousness: "'Who have we been that we are who we are now?'" (72). In retracing the trajectory of the historical impulse, I have sought to consider the first half of this critical lens: what disciplinary history has entailed since the publication of *MKC*. But what of who we are now? What follows is speculative inquiry—results of reading the contemporary landscape of composition scholarship against the backdrop of history, a tentative examination of "the limits of what we know" about the nature of historical scholarship in the field.

In considering the first pattern in contemporary disciplinary history, it seems feasible that both practical and critical concerns have led to the scarcity of sweeping overviews of the development of composition as a whole. The publication of full-length, single-authored monographs is a difficult achievement, and the kind of depth and breadth of historical research required to produce a comprehensive account of such vast terrain may thus appear less attractive—if not unworkable—to contemporary scholars.

Publication trends also illuminate a more positive outlook for historical studies of composition when article-length and edited collections on the history of the field are taken into account. So, for example, when notable contributions such as "History in the Spaces Left: African-American Presence and Narratives of Composition Studies" (Royster and Williams 1999), "Process and Post-Process: a Discursive History" (Matsuda 2003), or the edited collection *Research on Composition: Multiple Perspectives on Two Decades of Change* (Smagorinsky 2006) are included within the corpus of historical work from the last decade, the historical impulse appears quite strong. Where North envisioned a critical, conscious utilization of the dialectic among a tightly-knit community of historians in his overview of disciplinary futures, it can be said that historical dialogue has expanded over time, and has been dispersed among a wider circle of investigators.

The second pattern evident among recent publications proves historians continue to devise new methods for connecting historical accounts to discipline-specific contexts. Rather than mapping for readers visions of the discipline as a whole, contemporary historical scholars often choose to illuminate particular disciplinary locations: the classroom, the curriculum, the individual institution. This development should not be interpreted as a growing myopia, but instead as an outgrowth of the success and vitality of composition studies. The limits of the field are constantly being redrawn, contested, and revised as a result of its growth. And when a field has so many areas of specialization, when it influences so many sites and subjects, this refinement of the historical gaze seems a natural and ethical response. One of the central features of critical consciousness North sought from the recollection of the field's history was a sense of identity in community, a way for the historian to find a particular standpoint to speak from. Given the current nature of the discipline, then, a singular historical gaze is insufficient. Instead, we might best envision not a unitary historical impulse driving contemporary composition, but a historical impulse channeled through a multiplicity of visions, each with its own limitations and advantages in relation to the whole.

This proliferation of perspectives then fuels the third pattern evident among disciplinary histories—that which reveals a trend toward the study of material, archival data in composition. This last pattern appears somewhat puzzling, in light of developments in other disciplinary arenas. In "Writing the Discipline: a Generic History of English Studies," Jessica Yood argues that in examining disciplinary discourse from the past thirty years, one can see that a "new kind of writing—self-conscious, reflective prose—is creating a new 'life form' in academic culture" (2003, 526), a new genre of professional writing in which first-person references to critical reflection are frequently highlighted. Indeed, Yood cites *MKC*, along with Scholes's *The Rise and Fall of English* and Gerald Graff's *Beyond the Culture Wars*, as examples of a new consciousness that developed in the late 1980s and early 1990s. This genre, according to

Yood, "has created a new kind of scholar—one who searches for deep relations and connections between systematic ways of knowing and experiential realizations of knowledge" (538). By nature, however, archival methodology defers the experiential, shifting the field of historical inquiry to the quantifiable, the readily observable, the material. How then are we to interpret this trend, when read in relation to those Yood traces in English studies as a whole?

Arguably, this final pattern may mark a significant shift in the connection between critical consciousness and the role of historical inquiry—a shift that turns on the very role of the historian in shaping composition's past, present, and future. As composition has attained a more lasting, more empowered position within institutional settings, so it has attained a more stable sense of its own identity. While critical consciousness once served North and other pioneers in the field as a means of anchoring individual identity to a developing sense of community, current trends operate in an inverse fashion, in that disciplinary consciousness serves as a means for shaping individual identities within various locations comprising the discipline.

For example, one of the defining features of *MKC* is North's struggle to articulate his location within the field—indeed, it is never exactly clear where North might place himself within his classification of disciplinary identities. Finally settling on the role of participant-observer, his work attempts to encompass or bridge multiple subject positions frequently in tension with one another. For today's scholars, roles designating where one enters into the intellectual life of the discipline are more clearly cut. Is one a theorist or a researcher? Does one work predominantly with issues of writing and technology, or with issues of basic writing? For many contemporary compositionists, where one stands is not only a product of relentless introspection—of looking hard at "the limits of what you know"—but of where one is located in relation to a network of institutional sites for writing that fall under the influence of composition. If we take as a given North's assumption that methods of knowledge making (and hence consciousness raising) gain their currency and relevance as "a function of community standards," once common values and practices have been established within a disciplinary location, the force of those assumptions drives inclusion to a degree that we are only beginning now to understand. That is not to say that today's scholars are less critically conscious than their predecessors, nor that they are driven by "blind enthusiasm and naïve faith" in their participation in the discipline, to use North's terms. Instead, what it means to create critically conscious historical work in composition has shifted in a direction that *MKC* first advocated twenty-five years ago, as it entails greater recognition of methodological ethics—and the standards driving them—that North sought to advocate.

In his final chapter, North also cautions us to resist the complacency that may stem from strict allegiance to methodological communities, citing what he calls "Diesing's law: "communication and co-operation occur primarily within the boundaries of a method, not within a field," (365). Because critical consciousness causes us to interrogate the nature of such inclusion—to probe and revise the very limits of our knowledge and our beliefs—it can, in fact, serve to mitigate the power of custom that often comes with community. Arguably, critical consciousness now is made evident in a range of scholarly practices, in the elaboration of the steps one takes in evaluating such practices, and, most importantly, in the ways in which a scholar overtly situates herself in relation to the web of those practices, politics, and perspectives that give shape to inquiry in composition. Recent histories model critical awareness in their attention to disciplinary contexts and locations, demonstrating the importance of history to critical reflection, and keeping the historical impulse very much at the forefront of disciplinary consciousness.

REFERENCES

Applebee, Arthur N. 1974. *Tradition and reform in the teaching of English: A history.* Urbana, IL: National Council of Teachers of English.

Berlin, James. 1984. *Writing instruction in nineteenth-century American colleges.* Carbondale: Southern Illinois University Press.

———. 1987. *Rhetoric and reality: Writing in American colleges, 1900–1985.* Carbondale: Southern Illinois University Press.

Bizzell, Patricia. 1992. *Academic discourse and critical consciousness.* Pittsburgh: University of Pittsburgh Press.

Bizzell, Patricia and Bruce Herzberg. 2004. *The Bedford bibliography for teachers of writing.* 6th ed. Boston: Bedford/St. Martin's.

Brereton, John. 1995. *Origins of composition studies in the American college: A documentary history, 1875–1925.* Pittsburgh, PA: University of Pittsburgh Press.

Carlton, Susan Brown. 1995. Composition as a post-disciplinary formation. *Rhetoric Review* 14: 78–87.

Carr, Jean Ferguson, Stephen Carr and Lucille Schultz. 2005. *Archives of instruction: Nineteenth-century rhetorics, readers, and composition books in the United States.* Carbondale: Southern Illinois University Press.

Connors, Robert J. 1998. *Composition-rhetoric: Backgrounds, theory, and pedagogy.* Pittsburgh: University of Pittsburgh Press.

———. 1998. *Composition history and disciplinarity.* In Rosner, Boehm, and Journet.

Elliot, Norbert. 2005. *On a scale: A social history of writing assessment in America.* New York: Peter Lang.

Freire, Paolo. 1974. *Education for critical consciousness.* New York: Continuum Publishing Company.

Gaillet, Lyneé Lewis, and Thomas P. Miller. 2001. Making use of the nineteenth century: The writings of Robert Connors and recent histories of rhetoric and composition. *Rhetoric Review* 20: 147–157.

Goggin, Maureen. 2000. *Authoring a discipline: Scholarly journals and the post-world War II emergence of rhetoric and composition.* Mahwah: Lawrence Erlbaum Associates.

Harris, Joseph. 1996. *A teaching subject: Composition since 1966.* Upper Saddle River, NJ: Prentice Hall.

Hawk, Byron. 2007. *A Counter-history of composition: Toward methodologies of complexity.* Pittsburgh, PA: University of Pittsburgh Press.

Johnson, Nan. 1991. *Nineteenth-century rhetoric in North America.* Carbondale: Southern Illinois University Press.

Kitzhaber, Albert. 1990. *Rhetoric in American colleges, 1850–1900.* Dallas: Southern Methodist University Press.

Lindemann, Erika. 2002. Early bibliographic work in composition studies. *Profession:* 151–157.

Lindemann, Erika, and Gary Tate. 1991. *An introduction to composition studies.* New York: Oxford University Press.

Lloyd-Jones, Richard. 1989. *Review of The making of knowledge in composition: Portrait of an emerging field,* by Stephen North. *CCC* 40: 98–100.

Mailloux, Stephen. 2006. *Disciplinary identities: Rhetorical paths of English, speech, and composition.* New York: Modern Language Association.

Masters, Thomas. 2004. *Practicing writing: The postwar discourse of freshman English.* Pittsburgh, PA: University of Pittsburgh Press.

Matsuda, Paul Kei. 2003. Process and post-process: A discursive history. *Journal of Second Language Writing* 12: 65–83.

Miller, Thomas. 1997. *The formation of college English: Rhetoric and belles lettres in the British cultural provinces.* Pittsburgh: University of Pittsburgh Press.

North, Stephen M. 1987. *The making of knowledge in composition: Portrait of an emerging field.* Boynton/Cook Heinemann.

Paine, Charles. 1999. *The resistant writer: Rhetoric as immunity, 1850–Present.* Albany: State University of New York Press.

Phelps, Louise Wetherbee. 1998. *Paths not taken: Recovering history as alternative future.* In Rosner, Boehm, and Journet.

Raymond, James. 1989. Review of the making of knowledge in composition: Portrait of an emerging field, by Stephen North. *CCC* 40: 93–96.

Rosner, Mary, Beth Boehm, and Debra Journet, eds. 1998. *History, reflection, and narrative: The professionalization of composition 1963–1983.* Greenwich: Ablex.

Royster, Jacqueline Jones, and Jean C. Williams. 1999. History in the spaces left: African American presence and narratives of composition studies. *CCC* 50: 563–584.

Schultz, Lucille. 1999. *The young composers: Composition's beginnings in 19ᵗʰ century schools.* Carbondale: Southern Illinois University Press.

Scott, Patrick. 1986. Bibliographical problems in research on composition. *CCC* 37: 167–177.

Smagorinsky, Peter, ed. 2006. *Research on composition: Multiple perspectives on two decades of change.* New York: Teacher's College Press.

Varnum, Robin. 1996. *Fencing with words: A history of writing instruction at Amherst College during the era of Theodore Baird, 1938–1966.* Urbana: National Council of Teachers of English.

Yood, Jessica. 2003. Writing the discipline: A generic history of English studies. *College English* 65: 526–540.

6

MAKERS OF KNOWLEDGE IN WRITING CENTERS
Practitioners, Scholars, and Researchers at Work

Sarah Liggett
Kerri Jordan
Steve Price

Stephen M. North's greatest impact on writing center literature is not *The Making of Knowledge in Composition: Portrait of an Emerging Field (MKC)*, published in 1987. Rather it is his 1984 *College English* article, "The Idea of a Writing Center," which explains the purposes and workings of writing centers to faculty and administrators not directly involved with them. Grateful that North, viewed then by many as the "leader and spokesperson for writing center work" (Gillam 2002a, xix), had argued so passionately about the importance of writing centers, few writing center folks may recall that he concludes by urging writing center professionals to investigate "the dynamics of the tutorial," taking our knowledge beyond practitioners' anecdotes, to understand more fully how one talks about writing. North acknowledges that many writing center professionals have "neither the time, the training, nor the status to undertake any serious research" (1984, 444). Thus, his article targets a market for the forthcoming *MKC*, a text with potential to educate the writing center community on the kinds of inquiry by which to build a more solid knowledge base for writing centers.

If North's article encouraged its readers to imagine that writing centers could become "the centers of consciousness about writing on campuses" (1984, 446), the opening sections in *MKC* may well have deflated any sense of importance.[1] North discusses writing centers at length only

---

1. North addresses this quote in particular in his follow-up essay, "Revisiting 'The Idea of a Writing Center,'" which appeared a decade later in The Writing Center Journal. He acknowledges that the earlier article may have been a "romantic idealization" (1994, 9) and that writing centers at best are likely to be an "institutional conscience, that small nagging voice that ostensibly reminds the institution of its duties regarding writing" (15).

in chapter 2, as a site for practitioner inquiry, the mode that receives his harshest criticism. In the bulk of *MKC*, North outlines methodologies that could "replace practice as the . . . dominant mode of inquiry," describing a shift that had begun to transform composition (lowercase, writing course) to Composition (uppercase, academic field) (1987, 15). Scholars and researchers "*make* knowledge; Practitioners apply it" (21). Practitioners are "Composition's rank and file" whose main concern is "what to *do* about the teaching of writing"; they draw upon "*lore*: the accumulated body of traditions, practices, and beliefs in terms of which Practitioners understand how writing is done, learned, and taught" (22). Because its properties are problematic—"anything can become part of lore, nothing can ever be dropped from it," and practitioners adapt lore to fit their needs (24–25)— it is clear why "the academic reflex to hold lore in low regard represents a serious problem in Composition" (55). Most readers will gladly move on, hoping to find in the methodological communities of scholars and researchers a more engaging way to work, and perhaps a group of colleagues with more intellectual cachet.

The questions at hand, then, are these: Through what modes of inquiry has writing center knowledge expanded since the publication of *MKC?* How closely have authors followed North's outlines for conducting inquiry and to what ends? What new modes of inquiry have emerged? What do our findings suggest about knowledge making in writing center work? To answer these questions, we conduct a hermeneutical inquiry and go to work as critics.

CRITICS AT WORK: ARTICULATING QUESTIONS AND SELECTING TEXTS

At the empirical stage in our inquiry, we selected, assembled, and validated as texts for analyses those articles that earned their authors Outstanding Scholarship Awards presented annually since 1985 by the International Writing Centers Association (IWCA).[2] Ironically, the first

---

2. The IWCA website lists six criteria for its scholarship award: the publication addresses one or more issues of long-term interest to writing center administrators, theorists, and/or practitioners; discusses theories, practices, or policies that contribute to a richer understanding of writing center theory and practice; shows sensitivity toward the situated contexts of writing centers; significantly contributes to writing center scholarship and research; strongly represents writing center scholarship and research; and embodies the qualities of compelling and meaningful writing. Our study is comparable to Ede's critical work in On Writing Research: The Braddock Essays 1975–1998. Ede explains, "Awards for outstanding scholarly research are another accouterment of traditional disciplinarity, . . . suggesting as they do that a

article to win was North's "Idea of a Writing Center." Although a more extensive review of writing center literature might provide a somewhat different picture of knowledge making in writing centers, we assume these texts represent new knowledge that the writing center community has found valuable, first having been peer reviewed for publication and then recognized by an awards committee of peers.[3] Another reason for selecting the award-winning articles for our canon is that North was coeditor, with Lil Brannon, when *The Writing Center Journal* was first published in 1980. In their call for papers, the editors request "essays that are primarily theoretical"; "articles that connect theory with practice"; and "essays that draw upon experience . . . to offer insights and advice" (Brannon 1980, 2–3). Here seeds were sown to reap articles based on scholarship, research, and practitioner inquiry. We were curious to see what the writing center community grew.

At the interpretive stage, our primary means of analysis is to identify the authors' mode or modes of inquiry, testing the ability of North's classifications to map the terrain of writing center investigations. We then seek to articulate patterns evidenced through our analysis, interpreting what the award-winning articles suggest about the nature of knowledge making in writing center work and about the significance of North's modes of inquiry for writing center contexts. Our participation in the "Communal Dialectic" (North 1987, 120) is evident on several levels, as well. Working collaboratively, we refine our interpretations through a scholarly dialectic among ourselves and the authors whose articles we study. We also position our voices alongside additional key publications that allow us to contextualize and further explain our interpretations.

---

field has a developed a body of research and that such research can be evaluated by a group of 'objective' experts" (1999, 11). She observes that composition needed to signify its development of a research program, and that the "Braddock Award and the essays it honors bear the mark of that need. " (11–12). A decade later the National Writing Centers Association (which became the IWCA) established its own Outstanding Scholarship Awards, undoubtedly for a similar purpose. Gillam has also analyzed the award-winning articles from 1985–2001 in "The Call to Research: Early Representations of Writing Center Research" (2002). Whereas she regards the articles as primarily theoretical, we apply North's modes of inquiry from *MKC* and look for distinctions among them.

3.   In validating the award-winning articles, we wanted to avoid what North describes as those "texts that are atypical of the types they purportedly represent" (1987, 122). The 1989 winner, "Computers, Computers, Computers," is a special edition of The Writing Center Journal edited by Jeanette Harris and Joyce Kinkead. Unique among award winners, it is not the work of one person or even a team. Despite its collective usefulness, we eliminated it from our study because of our focus on individual articles deemed it independently worthy of the award.

Finally, by disseminating our work in this collection, we invite our readers to join the conversation.

"AND THE WINNER IS": SEEKING METHODOLOGICAL PATTERNS IN AWARD-WINNING ARTICLES

Coding the articles according to North's classifications proved challenging—much like pounding square pegs in round holes. Indeed, even North's article does not fit a single category. "The Idea of a Writing Center" is certainly practitioner based, but North speaks mainly as a philosopher, arguing for a process approach and an expressivist pedagogy. Actually, few of the authors work consistently or exclusively within a discreet methodological community as North envisions. In addition, some articles, such as Neal Lerner's multimodal project, "Writing Center Assessment: Searching for the 'Proof' of Our Effectiveness," defy North's classifications, a phenomenon variously attributable to post-*MKC* methodological developments or to differences in how North and an author conceptualize a mode or modes of inquiry.

Coding the texts was difficult partly because we debated whether to treat North's outlines as prescriptive formulas for conducting modes of inquiry or as descriptive patterns for suggesting ways knowledge is made in composition. North himself sometimes waivers. While he cautions that his outlines are "suggestive . . . not definitive," he is often emphatic about what a particular mode of inquiry can or cannot do. For example, hermeneutical inquiry "cannot be instrumental; in neither its theoretical nor applied form can it tell anyone what to do," while "Ethnographic knowledge cannot *accumulate* in the same way as other Researcher knowledge" (1987, 131, 276). So while the process of inquiry may diverge sometimes from North's outline, the limits of a particular methodology—the kinds of authority and knowledge a practitioner, scholar or researcher can claim—are more strictly defined. Therefore, as we coded the articles, we assumed that the authors had "put together the best design possible under the circumstances" (177), but we also observed whether the authors' claims stayed within methodological boundaries.

Our analysis of the articles' methodologies offers a snapshot of writing center scholarship and research from 1985 to 2007. In short, the articles reflect a group of practitioners generally embracing multimodal inquiry to articulate what writing centers do and are or might become. As detailed below, the winners are, in North's terms, most often scholars;

their inquiry is frequently philosophical or historical, occasionally critical, and often some combination. Though the writing center community has experienced periodic calls to research, which Gillam chronicles
(2002b), researcher inquiry as North conceives it is rare among the winners, and full-fledged practitioner inquiry is markedly absent.

Not until the 2008 winning article did we identify the study that
comes closest to practitioner inquiry. Renee Brown and colleagues
investigate Turnitin, a for-profit, web-based system designed to detect
plagiarism. Their work questions the ethics, legality, accuracy, and pedagogical limitations of the service. Here truly is a "new problem" needing
"a new solution" (North 1987, 43). But like several articles that follow
North's initial steps for practitioner inquiry—"Identifying a Problem,"
"Searching for Cause(s)," and "Searching for Possible Solutions"—it
too stops short of testing and validation of proposed solutions (a point
to which we will return). While North concedes that investigators may
"change the order of these steps, vary their relative importance, or drop
some altogether" (36), we feel strongly that testing and validations of
solutions are critical to exemplary practitioner inquiry. Yet, what we find
most often among the award winners are aborted and/or redirected
practitioner inquiry, rather than the completion of North's steps.

Practitioners' voices, however, do permeate the collection. Most of
the articles are laced with, if not built around, practitioners' experiential knowledge, and the authors' affinities for narrative and anecdote
give a lore-like feel even to some articles that clearly move beyond lore.
Neither the frequency of practical content nor the practitioner's voice
and style, of course, comes as a surprise: both have long been appealing
to writing center audiences.

Our initial codings, then, were complicated by the multimodal quality
of many articles. Two strategies enabled us to code more productively.
First, because it was not represented among our articles, we eliminated
practitioner inquiry as North conceives it from our list of classifications.
Next, because we agreed that the articles are virtually all practitioner
based, to varying degrees, we accepted practitioner qualities as a given.
Rather than trying to sort the practitioners from the "others," we could
focus on how practitioner qualities affect work across modes of inquiry.

The Scholars

Scholars (philosophers, historians, and critics) dominate as winners
through 2008, following the pattern in composition in which North

contends that philosophers make up the "second largest" group, out-numbered only by practitioners (1987, 91). Half of the winners oper-ate from a strongly philosophical stance with several others—including some researchers—waxing philosophical to varying degrees. The chart below lists the articles that most clearly reflect North's three modes of scholar inquiry. In addition to the predominant mode, we indicate other prevalent modes of inquiry where appropriate. In the sections that follow, we discuss selected articles to highlight features of the vari-ous modes.

The Scholars

Philosophers	1985	Stephen North	The Idea of a Writing Center
	1987	Edward Lotto	The Writer's Subject is Sometimes a Fiction
	1988	John Trimbur	Peer Tutoring: A Contradiction in Terms?
	1990	Richard Behm	Ethical Issues in Peer Tutoring: A Defense of Collaborative Learning
	1990	Lisa Ede (also historian)	Writing as a Social Process: A Theoretical Foundation for Writing Centers?
	1991	Lex Runciman (also historian)	Defining Ourselves: Do We Really Want to Use the Word Tutor?
	1992	Alice Gillam	Writing Center Ecology: A Bakhtinian Perspective
	1992	Muriel Harris	Solutions and Trade-offs in Writing Center Administration
	1994	Michael Pemberton	Writing Lab Newsletter Ethics Column
	1998	Nancy Maloney Grimm (also historian)	The Regulatory Role of the Writing Center: Coming to Terms with a Loss of Innocence
	2005	Margaret Weaver	Censoring What Tutors' Clothing 'Says': First Amendment Rights/ Writes Within Tutorial Space
	2007	Bonnie Devet, Susan Orr, Margo Blythman, and Cecilia Bishop	Peering Across the Pond: The Role of Students in Developing Other Students' Writing in the US and UK
	2008	Michael Mattison	Someone to Watch Over Me: Reflections and Authority in the Writing Center

Historians	1997	Peter Carino (also philosopher)	Open Admissions and the Construction of Writing Center History: A Tale of Three Models
	1999	Neal Lerner	Drill Pads, Teaching Machines, and Programmed Texts: Origins of Instructional Technology in Writing Centers
	2000	Elizabeth Boquet (also philosopher)	"Our Little Secret": A History of Writing Centers, Pre- to Post-Open Admissions
	2001	Neal Lerner	Confessions of a First-Time Writing Center Director
Critics	1995	Christina Murphy (also historian)	The Writing Center and Social Constructionist Theory
	1996	Peter Carino (also historian)	Theorizing the Writing Center: An Uneasy Task

Philosophers

According to *MKC*, the philosopher's hallmark is the use of "foraged knowledge" (105): "The Composition Philosopher makes a foray into some field outside Composition itself, works to reach some degree of expertise in it, then returns ready to work out an argument about the nature of doing, learning, or teaching writing" (102). Because not all writing center philosophers are composition philosophers, where else do writing- center philosophers forage? Some venture into fields such as education (Behm), critical theory (Lotto, Gillam, Grimm, Mattison), and constitutional law (Weaver); others engage in more introspective explorations, within writing center scholarship, the writing center community, or/and the author him or herself (Trimbur, Runciman, Pemberton, and Harris). Because the winning philosophical articles emphasize to varying degrees the practitioners' experiential knowledge, we imagine them along a philosopher-practitioner continuum. At one end is Ede's scholarly borrowing from social construction theory in composition; at the other is Pemberton's blog-like Ethics Column and its casual style and requests for audience responses (a kind of foray into practitioner lore). Somewhere in between are philosophers such as Harris, Trimbur, Runciman, Lotto, and Mattison. For instance, Lotto first acts more as a philosopher, building on Walter Ong's work (1975) in rhetorical theory and literary studies ("The Writer's Audience is Always a Fiction") to make a similar claim about a writer's "subject." He subsequently shifts into practitioner mode, turning to writing center experiences and offering examples and applications of how to help writers create their subjects.

Herein lies a danger. Philosophers overstep their methodological boundaries when they offer an agenda for reform, yet writers in this category can easily fall prey to this temptation. The limitation of the philosophers addressing a writing center audience is that their practical impact should be restricted. Philosophical inquiry, North insists, "does not lead to action" since "it deals not with things in the world, hands on, directly—like Practitioners, or Experimental Researchers, or even Historians—but with the operations of reason". According to North, the "nature of philosophical knowledge" is "the great debate," which, rather than leading to action, brings about "the dialectical opposition of competing inferential systems" (1987, 96). Devet and her coauthors model this dialectic. Their article returns, in part, to issues raised by Trimbur and Runciman regarding the nature of peer tutoring as they explore the importability of the American peer-tutoring model for writing centers to the United Kingdom. They do so by juxtaposing Devet's understanding of the American model alongside her colleagues' reflections on the arguably more hierarchical paradigms. Following the award announcement, Devet describes how Orr, Blythman, and Bishop "interrogate [the American] model without rejecting it, leaving readers to assess its appropriateness for their own institutional contexts" (2006, 8). While philosophers can "trace a premises-to-conclusion line of reasoning" (North 1987, 96)—one that might explain two views of tutoring, for example—they cannot, based on their mode of inquiry, declare which is better. Instead, they would be more loyal to their methodology to indicate implications for their work or suggest avenues for further inquiry (105).

Historians and Critics

North's historians "work to provide a coherent past for the field" (1987, 59). They engage in two main stages of inquiry—the Empirical Stage and the Interpretive Stage—as they identify and gather relevant artifacts to create a new narrative (71). His critics follow a similar pattern but ultimately focus more on interpretation of a body of texts (120). Among the award winners, historical inquiry appears second in frequency to, and often in connection with, the philosophical. Several philosophers incorporate historical elements in their work, and vice versa, and our two critics, Murphy and Carino (Theorizing), also write with an historical slant. Just as we noted a philosopher-practitioner continuum, we note a philosopher-historian continuum as well: Runciman, Ede, and Grimm, for example, offer strongly philosophical work with historical elements interwoven; Carino (Open Admissions) and Boquet work as historians but shift into philosophical speculation about their findings; and Lerner (both articles) works most exclusively as an historian.

Lerner's 1998 article, "Drill Pads, Teaching Machines, and Programmed Texts: Origins of Instructional Technology in Writing Centers," exemplifies North's historical inquiry. Examining the emerging trend of using programmed materials in writing centers, Lerner follows North's empirical strategies by gathering a wide range of texts (from journals, colleges, and universities as far back as 1895) that illustrate how instructional technology has supplemented writing instruction. His analysis shows how unprepared students are repeatedly cast as the cause of "messy instruction" (1998, 130) and are routinely sent to work with programmed texts, despite little evidence of effectiveness (134).

In contrast, in "Open Admissions and the Construction of Writing Center History: A Tale of Three Models," Carino overtly engages other narratives and dissenting voices: indeed, he uses his historical research to argue philosophically for their necessity. Making a case for and implementing a "cultural model of writing center history," Carino follows a carefully articulated research strategy involving, in part, "thick descriptions" of key texts (1996, 3). He accordingly demonstrates how the cultural model might "deconstruct oversimplified notions of the 1970s writing center as either a remedial supplement or the home of the brave, through recognizing instances of both incarnations" (10). While Carino diverges from North's model—in particular, he seems more interested in in-depth reading of selected texts rather than in pattern seeking—he does operate within the spirit of North's "Communal Dialectic" (1987, 71) by engaging with a variety of narratives.

Also with historical leanings, but working overwhelmingly as critics, are Murphy in "The Writing Center and Social Constructionist Theory" and Carino in "Theorizing the Writing Center: An Uneasy Task." Both select their texts for analysis in connection with historical trends: Murphy's work is rooted in the social constructivist literature, especially in composition, and Carino's in the "several attempts" over the preceding "twelve years . . . to construct a comprehensive theory to define writing centers and explain what they do" (1995, 124). Neither critic makes clear her or his method of textual analysis, but the emphasis on textual interpretation is obvious. Murphy reads at least in part with an eye toward whether theoretical articles evidence practical applicability for the writing center, and

Carino sets as his goal the investigation of "tensions" faced by writing centers "in terms of how [those tensions] both drive and undermine a representative sampling of past and recent attempts at theorizing the writing center as an institution and a set of practices" (125).

Whether or not the writing center community consciously acknowledges being influenced by North's book or his early call for papers for *The Writing Center Journal*, they have followed his dictates to venture beyond practitioner inquiry as seen in the winners' scholarly work. The trends are clear. Of the first twelve winners, nine are philosophers. In 1995 and 1996, the winners were critics; from 1997 to 2001, four out of five worked as historians. The seeds of intellectual curiosity have germinated into distinct varieties of scholarly inquiry.

The Researchers

In comparison to the scholars, the researchers are a very small group: two teams working somewhat as experimentalists, a hand full of clinicians of sorts, no formalists, and an ethnographer. Their respective articles are listed below:

The Researchers

Experimentalists	2002	Valerie Balester and James C. McDonald	A View of Status and Working Conditions: Relations Between Writing Program and Writing Center Directors
	2007	Jo Ann Griffin, Daniel Keller, Iswari P. Pandey, Anne-Marie Pendersen, and Carolyn Skinner	Local Practices, National Consequences: Surveying and (Re)Constructing Writing Center Identities
Clinicians	1993	Meg Woolbright	The Politics of Tutoring: Feminism Within the Patriarchy
	2003	Sharon Thomas, Julie Bevins, and Mary Ann Crawford (also philosophers)	The Portfolio Project: Sharing Our Stories
	2006	Anne Ellen Geller (also philosopher)	Tick-Tock, Next: Finding Epochal Time in the Writing Center
Ethnographers	1993	Anne DiPardo (also philosopher)	Whispers of Coming and Going: Lessons from Fannie

Experimentalists

Given the rejection of positivistic research in composition shortly after *MKC* was published, the lack of true or even pre- or quasi-experimental studies among the writing center articles is not surprising. The two experimentalist teams (Griffin and colleagues and Balester and McDonald) hold tenuous positions in North's thinking because both mainly use surveys, a research methodology in which he finds little value. North describes the survey "as a tool, a technique—and one to be used, most often, not to make a contribution to a knowledge-making community, but to gain political leverage." For North, surveys as a mode of inquiry "[do] not warrant full treatment" in *MKC* because "no community of inquirers, united by their loyalty to this methodology, has emerged" (139–40).

In contrast to North's depiction of survey methodology, both experimentalist teams conduct their research with clear goals and research questions in mind, and they establish specific, intentional research strategies. For example, in "Local Practices, National Consequences: Surveying and (Re)Constructing Writing Center Identities," Griffin and coauthors analyze the Writing Centers Research Project (WCRP) National Survey with the "long-term goal . . . to establish benchmark data about writing centers nationwide that writing center directors can use to justify, reinforce, and improve their own practices" (2006, 3–4). The authors counter North's concerns with surveys as they explain the uses of survey data: "National surveys, and the WCRP survey in particular, are different from other sources of information . . . in part due to the form the information takes (quantitative) and the uses to which the information is put (providing 'hard numbers' to academic administrators to justify particular change)." Interpreting their data, the authors describe national trends and elevate their discussion further by showing that "a dialectical tension exists in which the national influences the local, and vice versa" (6). The team is quantitatively savvy, providing a model for articulating data-driven conclusions. That two articles have won IWCA awards signals that the writing center community has valued and learned from well conducted surveys, confirming that *MKC* presents "*some*, not *the*, modes of Researcher inquiry" (North 1987, 140).

Clinicians and Ethnographers

In contrast to Experimentalists who generalize their findings, clinicians are concerned with "particularization: data collected is valuable precisely for what it reveals about individuals" (North 1987, 137). How clinicians learn about individuals varies widely; North calls their approaches "technical eclecticism" (218). Interviews, surveys, conference transcripts, video-taped conferences—whatever the strategies, the goal is to gather comprehensive data from which to create a picture (205). While replication is not an issue in a study that focuses on the individual, readers must still know the motivating research questions or problems, details of the design, and methods for collecting and interpreting data to understand how the clinician draws conclusions (207). Clinician Woolbright's study, "The Politics of Tutoring: Feminism Within the Patriarchy," makes clear her research agenda—"to learn more about what it is we do when we talk to students about their writing" (1993, 18) and to determine whether a tutor's espoused feminist values are evident in her conferencing—as well as her methodology, which involves recording and analyzing a series of conferences and conducting interviews with the tutor.

Ethnographer DiPardo crafts an engaging account of her subjects, studying how one student/tutor relationship is complicated by unresolved crosscultural tensions and shifts in conferencing pedagogy (1992). In DiPardo's article, space constraints limit what she can include about her methodology as she extracts a coherent narrative from her dissertation. As North warns, "ethnography's fictions obviously don't lend themselves" to "the format and length of researcher journal articles" (1987, 313). DiPardo's work nonetheless adheres to North's conception of ethnographic inquiry: "a methodological celebration of the individual consciousness as a source of meaning" and "a kind of collaboration whereby the life of the community finds articulation via the phenomenal experience, and the words, of a single individual" (139).

It is not surprising that researchers constitute a smaller group than scholars, given North's reminder that "the rise to power of Researcher modes of inquiry has been a very gradual affair" (1987, 135). Of more interest is the overlap between the two groups. North acknowledges that "the methodological boundaries of any community . . . can blur at the edges" (272), and we see evidence of such blurring in the tools and intents of the award winners. Scholars and researchers alike, for example, employ case studies, surveys, and interviews; similarly, both groups have among them those who offer more pointed recommendations than seem justifiable given their evidence and methodologies, an issue which leads us to wonder whether the desire for positivist knowledge lingers even in the absence of positivist research methods. But as critics, our goal is to seek and interpret patterns, and it is to these patterns that we now turn.

WHAT THE CRITICS LEARNED: ACCOUNTING FOR THE PATTERNS

As we account for the methodological patterns in the winning articles, we remind ourselves that "in neither its theoretical nor applied form can [Hermeneutical inquiry] tell anyone what to do" (North 1987, 131). So to keep us off our soap boxes, we list again the questions that initially shaped our study: Through what modes of inquiry has writing center knowledge expanded since the publication of *MKC*? How closely have authors adhered to North's outlines for conducting inquiry and to what ends? What new modes of inquiry have emerged? What do our findings suggest about knowledge making in writing center work? To these we add another: How well does North's *MKC* guide the development and critique of modes of inquiry in writing center studies?

Through what modes of inquiry has writing center knowledge expanded since the publication of MKC? North's predictions about the frequency of the modes of inquiry in composition do not quite hold true for writing center studies. In 1987, he believed that practitioners would form the largest methodological community but that only 10 percent of their work would actually qualify as practitioner inquiry (34), and he predicted that philosophers would be the second-largest group. Our study reflects a similar pattern in writing center work except that no work qualified fully as practitioner inquiry, at least not if we value testing and validation before dissemination. Furthermore, what North did not foresee in the mid-1980s is that the experimentalists, whose methodology had been "the dominant mode of formal educational research in this country over the past 75 years" (141), would soon lose favor in composition. The only experimentalists in our study investigate through surveys; no one conducted a hypothesis-driven experiment. Nor did any researchers emerge as formalists, probably because the highly contextualized nature of one-on-one conferencing makes it hard to imagine modeling writing center interactions. Recent winners have, however, worked as clinicians, with case studies and ethnographies remaining popular methodologies.

That the winners work in six of North's eight modes indicates that the writing center-community values a range of methodologies. Appreciative of colleagues who find time to conduct formal studies and write about them, the community has so far avoided the scenario that North imagines in his "Futures" chapter where composition "is gradually pulling itself apart" over "methodological differences—disagreements over how knowledge is made, what knowledge can be" (464, 465).

How closely have authors followed North's outlines for conducting inquiry and to what ends? Only because North concedes that the outlines for each mode of inquiry need not be followed strictly were we able to code some articles. At times, North's steps helped us spot problems with the designs of studies. North observes that "Methodological differentiation—indeed, even methodological self-consciousness—has come to Composition in general only very slowly" (1987, 136). The same is true for writing center work. At times the writing center community has experienced the same problem that North claims beset the rapidly emerging field of composition from the 1960s to the early 1980s: the "growth of methodological awareness has not kept pace with this scramble for the power and prestige that go with being able to say what constitutes knowledge. Investigators often seem unreflective about their own mode of inquiry . . . [and] are wont to claim more for their work than they can or should" (3).

While the writing center community embraces methodological pluralism, it frequently lacks methodological awareness. Several authors in our study appear to operate with less carefully planned or defined strategies—or at least not to articulate them fully. For example, when an author uses a commonly accepted method, such as the case study, without adequately describing key characteristics or without making certain that the methods serve the goals for the project, the reader must speculate about the work involved. Gillam, for instance, puts a brief but pronounced emphasis on what she calls a "case study" excerpt (1991, 5) as a springboard to theorize about *what might have happened* had the tutor implemented strategies based on Bakhtinian philosophies. Because she offers little about the hows and whys of her case study and because she fictionalizes how the tutor *might* have behaved differently, we wonder how she defines *case study* and what makes her approach appropriate to her purposes.

Occasionally, authors make their methodology clear but fail to answer their research questions. For example, clinicians Thomas, Bevins, and Crawford promise to report on their longitudinal study of "the culture of writing at [their] university from the perspective of . . . the students" (2002, 150). However, they shift focus to analyze student writing through the lenses of cultural studies after having "begun to understand more deeply the politics of writing and writing centers and the kinds of conversations that can make change possible" (166). They justify their reason for refocusing their work: "Such conversations rely less on the information of 'findings' that research can provide (although those are certainly valuable) and more on valuing the stories that students share with us" (166). We would have liked to learn about the findings too since longitudinal studies are seldom conducted in writing research.

Other times authors' research methods are overshadowed by the narratives through which they convey their findings. Geller, for example, tells a detailed story about how three tutors experience time in the writing center. However, she omits important information about her research strategy and decision-making processes. For example, we know that her quotations come from interviews, but we do not learn what questions she asked. Furthermore, her conclusion makes a strong causal statement: "When writing center tutors, and the student writers at their sides, can shift their concerns from the unyielding demands of clock time to the fluidity and possibility of epochal time, they create space for tutor and student alike to think, to imagine, to experiment, to collaborate, to build a relationship, and to learn" (2005, 9). We wonder how and whether her *research* conclusively supports that claim.

Our criticisms of these articles (we are acting as critics, after all) are not meant to imply that we did not learn from them; we did. But we could have learned more. Methodological clarity is important not only for evaluating the soundness of a study but also for educating readers about *how knowledge is created* in writing center studies. As Balester and McDonald report, only 57 percent of the writing center administrators who completed their survey identified composition as their area of specialization, whereas 39 percent indicated professional preparation in literary studies (2001, 64), graduate programs that are less likely to teach research methodologies other than textual studies.

What new modes of inquiry have emerged? Our analysis of the articles reveals no new modes of inquiry, although some investigators report multimodal studies. The strongest example is Lerner's 2003 contribution, "Writing Center Assessment: Searching for the 'Proof' of Our Effectiveness." He works as an historian, examining texts from as early as 1939 that illustrate the writing center community's interest in and "uneasiness with evaluation research" (2003, 58–59); he acts as a critic, drawing on a range of authors, including Cindy Johanek,[4] Grimm, and North; he edges toward being an experimentalist, demonstrating to

---

4.   Lerner's use of Johanek's work (2000) is fitting, since it advocates for multimodal research that incorporates quantitative methods; Johanek also expresses concern with the anecdotal trend in composition scholarship.

his writing center audience how to develop "a framework for research on writing center effects" (64); and he acts as a practitioner, offering encouragement that we can "assess our work in ways that we feel are meaningful and useful" (73). His multimodal approach is effective, providing practitioners with the means for implementing local assessment. A three-time award winner, Lerner typifies the contributor North has in mind when he writes that "the Practitioner community must depend on those members who stay in the field long enough, under reasonably favorable conditions, and with sufficient motivation, to keep making their practice inquiry" (1987, 35).

This sort of program assessment, a combination of quantitative and qualitative methods, is probably the most frequent and certainly one of most important types of investigations that writing center administrators routinely conduct, as Lerner reminds us (2003, 61, 73). Because program assessment is an important issue in composition as well, we suspect that if North were writing *MKC* today, he would have much more to say about it, the multimodal approach it requires, and its relationship to practice, scholarship, and research.

What do our findings suggest about knowledge making in writing center work? Our study confirms that there are distinct ways of making knowledge: different problems require different kinds of investigations, and different kinds of investigations create different kinds of knowledge. To ignore these differences is to compromise the soundness of an investigation. A "heightened methodological consciousness," says North, means understanding "limits of the authority" that various modes "can claim . . . and work[ing] within them. In that direction, and not in any sort of methodological masquerade, lies the basis for a genuine credibility" (1987, 55).

The trends in the articles suggest that the writing center community in the last two decades may have concentrated its epistemic endeavors on scholarship and research at the expense of practitioner inquiry. What motivates this action is beyond the scope of our critical inquiry, but our readings and analysis suggest possible catalysts: editors' calls for papers that privilege scholarship and research over practice, the publication of *MKC* and other influential books about research on writing, a mimicked response to what was happening in composition, or a desire to move up the academic pecking order. We would not want to see, as North rightly predicts for composition, further attempts to distance writing center work from practice (1987, 368). By favoring the inquiry of scholars and researchers over that of practitioners, we will ignore many important questions about writing and writers.

Given that the writing center community is practitioner based, practitioner inquiry is critical to its mission. How best to reestablish the value of practitioner inquiry is a topic for serious dialogue within the writing center community; indeed, the discussion has already begun (Gillam 2002b). Yet practitioner work is not the same as practitioner inquiry, and many questions remain about how to conduct it, especially: what are the functions of testing and validation in practitioner inquiry, and how are these steps to be undertaken? These questions puzzle North as well. In regards to "testing" the effectiveness of our writing pedagogies, he recommends "textual and non-textual indicators," with few specifics (1987, 49). And although "Validation" is a separate step in his process of practitioner inquiry, he omits it in his discussion. Many articles with strong practitioner voices arrive at solutions that are more often local than global in application, heavily dependent upon the individual and context. Does the writing center community expect more of practitioner inquiry? If so, how might the work of scholars and researchers aid the work of practitioners? Are multimodal studies to be expected? And, how do we keep *multimodal* from translating into *haphazard*?

How well does North's MKC guide the development and critique of modes of inquiry in writing center studies? This question we can answer from personal experience, and here an anecdote seems fitting. Throughout our collaboration, North's guidelines for hermeneutical inquiry kept us true to the methodology. More than once, we cautioned each other, "you can't say this based on the articles." His procedural lists and critical examination of articles served as ready reference points against which to analyze and evaluate the methods and contributions of this knowledge-making community. Although North's outlines are meant to be descriptive rather than prescriptive, authors who featured their inquiry processes improved the clarity of their articles. Whether the writing center community follows North's processes or Janice M. Lauer and J. William Asher's checklists for empirical designs (1988) or Mary Sue MacNealy's strategies (1999), the end results are likely to be more complete, informative, reflective investigations.

AN INVITATION TO THE COMMUNAL DIALOGUE

Reflecting on our critical investigation of the award-winning articles, we must ask what we have gained and what knowledge we have contributed to the writing center community. Certainly, collaboration on this article has enabled a deeper understanding of the methodologies used by authors who have been honored by our professional organization; likewise, we hope our readers benefit from our analysis and interpretation. We also have a better understanding of North's landmark book. We conclude, however, that much work remains in comprehending how the writing center community creates knowledge. Conducted through hundreds of emails and track changes on multiple drafts, our dialectic is finished . . . until we hear from our wider audience about how they think meaning is or should be made in writing center studies. For it is ultimately in the subsequent dialogue as it challenges or extends the conversation that a critical inquiry makes knowledge.

REFERENCES

Balester, Valerie, and James C. McDonald. 2001. A view of status and working conditions: Relations between writing program and writing center directors. *WPA: Writing Program Administration* 24 (3): 59–82.

Behm, Richard. 1989. Ethical issues in peer tutoring: A defense of collaborative learning. *The Writing Center Journal* 10 (1): 3–13.

Boquet, Elizabeth H. 1999. "Our little secret": A history of writing centers, pre- to post-open admissions. *CCC* 50 (3): 463–82.

Brannon, Lil, and Stephen North. 1980. From the editors. *The Writing Center Journal* 1 (1): 1–3.

Brown, Renee, Brian Fallon, Jessica Lott, Elizabeth Matthews, and Elizabeth Mintie. 2007. Taking on Turnitin: Tutors advocating change. *The Writing Center Journal* 27 (1): 7–28.

Carino, Peter. 1995. Theorizing the writing center: An uneasy task. *Dialogue: A Journal for Composition Specialists* 2 (1): 23–37.

———. 1996. Open admissions and the construction of writing center history: A tale of three models. *The Writing Center Journal* 17 (1): 30–49.

Devet, Bonnie. 2007. Summary of chapter by Devet. *International Writing Center Association Update* 8 (1): 8, 9.

Devet, Bonnie, Susan Orr, Margo Blythman, and Cecilia Bishop. 2006. Peering across the pond: The role of students in developing other students' writing in the US and UK. In *Teaching academic writing in UK higher education: Theories, practices and models*, edited by Lisa Ganobcsik-Williams. New York: Palgrave Macmillan.

DiPardo, Anne. 1992. "Whispers of coming and going": Lessons from Fannie. *The Writing Center Journal* 12 (2): 125–145.

Ede, Lisa. 1989. Writing as a social process: A theoretical foundation for writing centers. *The Writing Center Journal* 9 (2): 3–15.

———, ed. 1999. *On writing research: The Braddock essays, 1975–1998*. Boston: Bedford/St. Martin's.

Geller, Anne Ellen. 2005. Tick-tock, next: Finding epochal time in the writing center. *The Writing Center Journal* 25 (1): 5–24.

Gillam, Alice M. 1991. Writing center ecology: A Bakhtinian perspective. *The Writing Center Journal* 11 (2): 3–13.

———. 2002a. Introduction to Gillespie, Gillam, Brown, and Stay.

———. 2002b. The call to research: Early representations of writing center research. In Gillespie, Gillam, Brown, and Stay.

Gillespie, Paula, Alice Gillam, Lady Falls Brown, and Byron Stay, eds. 2002. *Writing center research: Extending the conversation.* Mahwah: Lawrence Erlbaum.

Griffin, Jo Ann, Daniel Keller, Iswari P. Pandey, Anne-Marie Pedersen, and Carolyn Skinner. 2006. Local practices, national consequences: Surveying and (re)constructing writing center identities. *The Writing Center Journal* 26 (2): 3–21.

Grimm, Nancy. 1996. The regulatory role of the writing center: Coming to terms with a loss of innocence. *The Writing Center Journal* 17 (1): 5–30.

Harris, Jeanne, and Joyce Kinkead, eds. 1987. Computers, computers, computers. Special issue, *The Writing Center Journal* 8 (1).

Harris, Muriel. 1991. Solutions and trade-offs in writing center administration. *The Writing Center Journal* 12 (1): 63–80.

International Writing Centers Association. About IWCA: Awards: Criteria for the IWCA scholarship awards. http://writingcenters.org/awards.htm.

Johanek, Cindy. 2000. *Composing research: A contextualist paradigm for rhetoric and composition.* Logan: Utah State University Press.

Lauer, Janice M., and J. William Asher. 1988. *Composition research: Empirical designs.* New York: Oxford University Press.

Lerner, Neal. 1998. Drill pads, teaching machines, and programmed texts: Origins of instructional technology in writing centers. In *Wiring the writing center,* edited by Eric H. Hobson. Logan: Utah State University Press.

———. 2000. Confessions of a first-time writing center director. *The Writing Center Journal* 21 (1): 29–48.

———. 2003. Writing center assessment: Searching for the "proof" of our effectiveness. In *The center will hold: Critical perspectives on writing center scholarship,* edited by Michael A. Pemberton and Joyce Kinkead. Logan: Utah State University Press.

Lotto, Edward. 1985. The writer's audience is sometimes a fiction. *The Writing Center Journal* 5 (2) and 6 (1): 15–21.

MacNealy, Mary Sue. 1999. *Strategies for empirical research in writing.* Boston: Allyn and Bacon.

Mattison, Michael. 2007. Someone to watch over me: Reflection and authority in the writing center. *The Writing Center Journal* 27 (1):29–51.

Murphy, Christina. 1994. The writing center and social constructionist theory. In *Intersections: Theory–practice in the writing center,* edited by Joan A. Mullin and Ray Wallace. Urbana, IL: National Council of Teachers of English

North, Stephen M. 1984. The idea of a writing center. *College English* 46 (5): 433–446.

———. 1987. *The making of knowledge in composition: Portrait of an emerging Field.* Portsmouth: Heinemann.

———. 1994. Revisiting "The idea of a writing center." *The Writing Center Journal* 15 (1): 7–19.

Ong, Walter J. 1975. The writer's audience is always a fiction. *PMLA* 90: 9–21.

Pemberton, Michael. 1993-1994. Writing center ethics. *The Writing Lab Newsletter* 17:5, 17:710, 18:2, 18:47.

Runciman, Lex. 1990. Defining ourselves: Do we really want to use the word tutor? *The Writing Center Journal* 11 (1): 27–35.

Thomas, Sharon, Julie Bevins, and Mary Ann Crawford. 2002. The portfolio project: Sharing our stories. In Gillespie, Gillam, Brown, and Stay.

Trimbur, John. 1987. Peer tutoring: A contradiction in terms? *The Writing Center Journal* 7 (2): 21–29.

Weaver, Margaret. 2004. Censoring what tutors' clothing "Says": First amendment rights/ writes within tutorial space. *The Writing Center Journal* 24 (2): 19–36.

Woolbright, Meg. 1993. The politics of tutoring: Feminism within the patriarchy. *Writing Center Journal* 13 (1): 16–31.

7

RHETORIC, RACISM, AND THE REMAKING OF KNOWLEDGE-MAKING IN COMPOSITION

Victor Villanueva

1987. The year after the PhD in English with an emphasis in rhetoric and composition. There weren't many of us who could make the claim to a rhet and comp degree. Most of us, like Stephen North says, had been trained in literary studies (116). Me too. But I could claim rhetoric and composition—and an empirical study for a dissertation, a reluctant clinician.

1987. Two years as an assistant prof, about to change institutions. One real publication under the belt, about writing processes, a reluctant practitioner, at least reluctant to write about distinctions between "writing as a process" and "writing as processes." A bit silly, in retrospect.

1987. A year for taxonomies. Berlin's second. North. Flipping folks into slots. Anne Berthoff, the new rhetorician for Berlin, the new rhetorician who quotes Aristotle's four causes for basic writers (1982) and advocates I.A. Richards and his philosophy of rhetoric, Richards, the writer of basal readers. Maybe not so new. North decides that Berthoff is not a rhetorician at all, that she showed at best no interest in rhetoric (64). There are problems with taxonomies, when it's people being taxonomized. Never cut-and-dried, an essence; some taxonomies forgotten.

The Making of Knowledge in Composition (*MKC*) was causing quite a stir. There was no being a young professional in composition and not reading the book. I read it. Felt good about my training, that I was familiar with most of the references. Tried to fit myself into the taxonomy: surely a practitioner (since one can't be a compositionist and not practice composing and teaching composing). I wanted to be a historian, the rhetoric kind, though like I'll make clearer, I would now say a rhetorician, the global-historical kind, some of which analyzes through rhetoric, some of which historicizes through rhetoric. And I reckon I had been an experimentalist. Twice. Yet I was none of it, not then. I wasn't troubled, really, that the likes of me weren't there. North was seeking to explain research methods, with the people intended as illustrations of methods. And folks of color were implicit in those examples: the students that Shaughnessy, Perl, Sommers, Graves looked at, worried about, studied, tried to help. But that they were in fact students of color seems only implicit, never fully developed.

It would be a full decade before Ralph Cintron (1997) would so beautifully point out that ethnography is itself inherently rhetorical, weaving narrative within his observations, never pretending to be the outsider, the detached observer. But North, whatever his tendencies against the positivists reflected throughout *MKC*, and despite his insightful analyses of underlying assumptions of the various camps he lays out, nevertheless never quite gets there, gets to the realization that there are biases at play—in the whole notion of research where people and art are concerned—never gets to acknowledge, or maybe even realize, the biases in his gaze. Many (maybe most) of the practitioners and experimenters and critics are women in *MKC*, though the idea that gender would then become a part of the observations isn't there.[1] And none—not one—of the many people he cites is a person of color (assuming a later twentieth-century definition of an American of color: Black, Latino, American Indian, Asian American, a distinction I make because Matsuhashi is Matsuhashi by marriage, later returning to Feldman, and Jewish-as-color is complicated in America, as Deborah Holdstein and David Bleich point out in *Personal Effects* (2001), where they also point out—again—that objective research just ain't possible in comp).

This is significant, that the studies that look at people of color are observations through white folks' eyes. That is how Shaughnessy could ask what had gone wrong in her students writing, and what could she do about it" (North, 40). These are questions North never questions: the presumption that something is wrong with the students, rather, say, than asking about the social conditions, the educational conditions, the linguistic complexities that range far beyond simple orality-literacy distinctions that obtained for the Black and Puerto Rican students Shaughnessy faced; rather than asking how it is that the good-hearted literature professor, Shaughnessy, can assume the power to fix the real what-had-gone-wrong. That's quite a blind spot. 1987. Who were Perl's "unskilled writers"? We can only guess who the students were by the school in South Bronx named after a Puerto Rican educator and

---

1.   For more on this, see Kirsch (1999).

revolutionary (Eugenio María deHostos y Bonilla). Sommers's Boston students? Graves's Brooklyn students? And why was Heath never questioned about living among the Roadville but never among the Trackton and how that would affect observations? It's the later twentieth century at the time of this writing, civil rights movements and the like already written into the history. Yet structural racism remains, the women not quite acknowledged, the people of color, when acknowledged, acknowledged only as victims.

I know that in some sense these are not faults in North. He's looking at research methods. And he's conscribed by a field—composition. His writing predates the criticisms of ethnography provided by bell hooks (1990) or Linda Tuhiwai Smith (1999) and others of color, particularly indigenous peoples. And conscribed by a field, he would not discuss Smitherman (1977) or Roseann Dueñas González (1983), as active as they were in composition studies during the same decade that North observes. Smitherman and González are linguists. And maybe, in his choosing to stay focused on compositionists, he can't discuss William Labov (though Heath and Scribner and Cole do turn up in *MKC*, the linguistic anthropologist and the two psychologists, more white folks studying those of color; one tires of being a subject and a specimen). Labov's great (even if obvious in retrospect) contribution to language research methodology was his pointing out that the cultural and racialized makeup of the researcher affects the research outcome. Bringing Black researchers into Harlem provided the insight that speakers of what we now term African American Language did not suffer from a verbal deficit as the white researchers had found.[2]

Still, even though Smitherman's field was linguistics, her *Talkin and Testifyin* (1977) had been around for a while and it stood in contrast against—including methodologically—Shaughnessy, as Joseph Harris points out (1997, 80–83). And Charlotte Brooks's *Tapping Potential* (1985), published by the National Council of Teachers of English (NCTE), contained a virtual who's who of Black compositionists, (including four chairs of the Conference on College Composition and Communication), experimentalists and practitioners, that could have complemented Perl and Graves.

This is the nature of structural racism, when believing oneself not a bigot allows one to ignore the bigotry that nevertheless obtains. North

---

2.   For more on this, see Villanueva (1993, 1–11)

was a victim of his time, a time when a consciousness of women was rising, and one would think unavoidable in our field, yet with the constructions of women remaining quiet in composition, for the most part. Perl even simply identifies herself as the "researcher," as North points out (214), gender-neutered, as North apparently failed to notice, since his distinction was between "researcher" and "teacher," not among researcher, teacher, woman. And people of color were only the disaffected, the student-victims. Those who had transcended victim status, as in being a part of the composition community, were not even recognized.

A Puerto Rican Girl's Sentimental Education

Your daughter didn't pass
the English reading test in second grade.
Left back like a donkey
or another number on
the red, white and blue
statistical roster.

Mrs. Rivera,
the Section 8 projects
breed social dilemmas

or was it

Mrs. Hernandez,
My roster tells me your name is Fernandez.

Systematic, elementary school
oppression, hippie teachers, granola breaks
in the classroom.

A low-income prodigy child
caught in the American cross fire,
between SATs and insular-community vocabulary.
Mami and Papi told me to pray in Spanish
read the Scriptures, mi niña.

Memories choke my throat,
stuttering in English, crying
into my grammar textbook.

Mental deficits, developmental crises
and bowlegged walks to the school nurse.

Take the reading test over,
at the psychiatrist's office.
Diagnosis: psychedelic, psycholinguistic
genius survives the warring factions
of cultural schizophrenia.

Like Charlie Brown vs. Cantinflas
Like the Beatles vs. Menudo.
Like myself divided into myself
Like I'm a movie in subtitles.

Now my mind's tied up.
Hostage in a desert of hope and opportunity.
Dyslexic like Albert Einstein and
prolific like Cervantes's ego in prison.

In 1982, in "The Winds of Change," Maxine Hairston demonstrated that composition studies was undergoing a paradigm shift. *Process* was the term she focused on, but it was those students of Shaughnessy that led her to believe that a shift in how we think about writing was taking place. Later, she would be upset about the shift, as it turned to the more overtly political. But she was right that something was happening. What I would like to suggest in this part of this chapter, however, is that it wasn't only the students of color and from poverty who would mark the shift away from composition's ways of making knowledge. It would also be the scholars of color, recognizing the personal, recognizing the primacy of rhetoric.

North's book arrived during this time of transition, not only the shift to process that Hairston noted, but the move away from what he calls formalism to what would be called social construction. North sensed it, this change. It was there, in his negative appraisal of the formalists and the clinicians, in his separating out the ethnographers, in his even wishing to claim being a metaphorical ethnographer of metaphorical communities in creating the book (4–5), even if the folks of color in the community were overlooked. The move to ethnography marked the move away from the scientific surety of cognitive explanations for what writers do.

And with social construction came the consciousness that women, gays, lesbians, and people of color would be constructed differently from, say, Janet Emig's "Lynn," the white woman of talent and promise who formed the basis of our understanding what writers do when writing (1971). If we are socially constructed, then how we construct texts, how we would regard language, what we would do with language, would also be socially constructed, tied to context, tied to the experiential.

Writing at about the same time as North, Keith Gilyard is at pains to explain the experiential in research-like terms, calling on E.W. Eisner's "On the Differences Between Scientific and Artistic Approaches to Qualitative Research," which appeared in *Educational Research* in 1981:

> In artistic approaches to research, the cannons of test reliability and sampling do not apply. While one might consider or question a writer's or film producer's reliability, there is no formalized set of procedures to measure writer reliability; one doesn't really want the mean view of four writers' observations about the mental hospital in Oregon, which served as the subject-matter for Ken Kesey's play [*One Flew Over The Cuckoo's Nest*]. One simply wants Ken Kesey's view. Its validity, if that is the appropriate term, is to be determined by our view of its credibility, and not by reducing his work to some average by using only that portion that it shares with the views of others. Validity in the arts is the product of the persuasiveness of a personal vision; its utility is determined by the extent to which it informs. There is no test of statistical significance, no measure of construct validity in artistically rendered research. What one seeks is illumination and penetration. The proof of the pudding is the way in which it shapes our conception of the world or some aspect of it. (quoted in Gilyard 1991, 12)

Eisner and others in educational research were making a case for research-as-rhetoric: persuasion, the credibility of the writer (ethos), time and place (kairos). That argument for those of us in composition would be most forcefully made by people of color. Although people of color were not the only ones making the shift to "artistically rendered research" (thinking here of Mike Rose as a popular mixed-genre, critical autobiographer of the later 1980s), it would be the writers of color who, by placing rhetorical strategies over scientistic ones, would feel compelled to underscore the continuing racism in our society and implicitly point to the continuing racism in what we do. People of color, addressing assimilation, addressing code switching, addressing forgotten histories, helping to change, instrumental in the change, in how we go about making knowledge in composition.

What Candice Spigelman would call "personal academic discourse" had not yet made its entry into composition studies, not really, during the years that North was compiling *MKC*. My own first attempt came out the same year as his book. The voice that those in English studies was hearing, the personal voice, belonged to Richard Rodriguez, his *Hunger of Memory*.

> Carol says that if it weren't for Richard Rodriguez, I wouldn't have had a career. She tells friends that I couldn't go into the bookstore in the U-District, see a copy of *Hunger of Memory* and not break into a tirade. And it was during another tirade at the NCTE national convention in 1985 or 1986 that my Latina friends encouraged me to write about Rodriguez's speech, the speech delivered to the NCTE audience to a standing ovation. The only real way to explain my aggravation was to point to differences in context, the assimilationist pull of the immigrant versus the assimilation-denied of the person of color, to explain and narrate what Linda Flower would many years later call an "intercultural rhetoric" (2003).[3]
>
> But that wasn't the whole of it, my aggravation with Rodriguez. It was the *pobrecito* mentality in the narrative that troubled me, the sorrowful ethos, the melancholy. I had been deeply moved by Hélène Cixous's call for a feminine rhetoric (1976), a woman's rhetorical muscularity (intended neither as masculine nor oxymoronic, a woman's muscularity). What would a Latino and Latina dignified, respectful rhetoric look like?

We are still arguing about the legitimacy of the critical autobiography in composition studies. This is ironic. We continue not to believe our own legitimacy, not even, really, to accept the genealogy we constructed. Berlin, Miller, and North himself make it clear that composition studies really did arise as its own discipline, but in seeking legitimacy composition tied itself to an older, revered discipline—rhetoric. The precedents were there in Kenneth Burke and Alexander Bain before him. For North, those who turn to rhetoric are the scholars and the historians. And the scholars and historians really are filling out the picture. Cheryl Glenn (1997), Susan Jarratt (1991), Andrea Lunsford (1995), Joy Ritchie and Kate Ronald (2001), among many others, are telling us of women rhetoricians and what those women rhetoricians can tell us about writing today. Jacqueline Jones Royster and Jean C. Williams (1999) write about African American women rhetoricians of the nineteenth century. Keith Gilyard (2003) and Adam Banks (2005) and David Holmes (2007) tell of African

---

3.   For my complete response, see Villanueva 1987.

American rhetoricians from slavery to the present day—including implications for composition. Damián Baca (2008) tells of pre-Columbian
rhetoric in Mesoamerica. And I have written about and continue to write
about the clash of rhetorics between AmerIndian rhetorics and those of
the Europeans (1999). Malea Powell (2002) and Scott Lyons (2000) on
American Indians. Morris Young (2004) on Asian Americans.

It was Kenneth Burke who claimed that the work of rhetoric had been
divided among the new sciences, and as he makes most explicitly clear
in *Language as Symbolic Action*, rhetoric would be reinvigorated by rein-
corporating the concepts of the new sciences with dialectic, poetic, and
rhetoric (1966, 306–07). Racism has flourished under the scientific paradigm—from the creation of the "races" by Blumenbach (1969) in the
late eighteenth century to scientifically proven verbal deficits in African
Americans. People of color would be skeptical but also recognize the rhetorical power in science. Keith Gilyard moved from narrative to linguistic
analysis in alternating chapters of his *Voices of the Self* (1991). My *Bootstraps*
(1993) explicitly combined ethnography, poetics, and rhetoric. Now,
Eduardo Bonilla-Silva describes the ways in which college students and
others continue to betray racist conceptions through their talk (2006).
His method arises from Erving Goffman's framing (1974), essentially
looking at rhetorical tropes displayed through narrative. Elliot Mishler—
who is cited in the Kantor reference in North (274)—argued persuasively
in 1979 in the *Harvard Educational Review* that the scientific methods of
the natural sciences cannot apply to education or to the social sciences.
Mishler, the social psychologist, now argues for the centrality of narrative
in his field (2000). There is even narrative-based medicine (Greenhalgh
and Hurwitz 1999). Deirdre McCloskey (1994, 1998) has argued in a
number of books that the economic sciences actually conduct their business through narrative, through storytelling, through rhetoric, and she
supports her case in part by pointing to our own rhetorical canonical
genealogy: rhetoricians like Adam Smith, John Locke, Hobbes. The sciences are turning to the paradigm that was most forcefully introduced to
composition and rhetoric by the people of color. We debate rather than
assume our rightful place, as the ones who can talk about language and
literacy narrative and rhetoric as well as the social scientists once talked
about chi factors and null hypotheses, recognizing that *ceteris paribus* as
the key assumption of the sciences is the one assumption that cannot
obtain for people within social contexts, with political and economic constraints, with bounded up ideological contradictions.

When I was a graduate student, William Irmscher told me that if I wanted to do empirical analyses of writing processes I should go to the college of education or to psychology. Yet it was 1983, and the coin of the realm in rhetoric and composition was research. I didn't want to offend Irmscher, but how else to write about composing? Besides, I knew, even then, that this "research" wasn't quite legitimate. I had never seen a failed educational research project, where the hypothesis proved wrong. Happens in the sciences. So I knew that even though there was an element of mystery to "research," it wasn't really science at all. It was production design: setting up the situation to demonstrate (rather than to prove) what the "researcher" believed. And the result was rhetoric: finding for any given case the available scientistic means of persuasion. Tried one more empirical research study as an assistant prof. Then decided to practice what I preached—writing and rhetoric—and leave science to the scientists. Our work is the word.

Part of a poem by Pablo Neruda
(translated by Alastair Reid)

The word
was born in the blood,
grew in the dark body, beating,
and took flight through the lips and the mouth.

Farther away and nearer
still, still it came
from dead fathers and from wandering races,
from lands which had turned to stone,
lands weary of their poor tribes,
for when grief took to the roads
the people set out and arrived
and married new land and water
to grow their words again.
And so this is the inheritance;
this is the wavelength which connects us
with dead men and the dawning
of new beings not yet come to light.

So Linda Flower, once our straw formalist, was right when she argued Burke's case, that sheer speculation isn't enough, that we need ways to test what it is we believe in our theory (1989). But the postformalist in Flower defines this testing in a way that is our own. Read the opening narrative to her recent article in *College Composition and Communication*:

> When blacks and whites of goodwill in my city gather to talk about significant issues, they face hard questions, such as why don't black youth find meaning-ful work? or what would it mean to carry out a police-enforced youth curfew in the black community? And in these moments, the desire for intercultural dialogue is often matched by a sense of the distance between the ways we rep-resent those issues. Hoping for a collaboratively constructed understanding, we instead encounter an unarticulated chasm. For behind the words we use in common lie strikingly different life experiences that instantiate a concept (such as *police-enforced*) with different flesh and blood realities. (2003, 38)

Referring to many of the writers I have alluded to here, Flower argues for an intercultural rhetoric of inquiry that allows for racialized, encul-turated, ideologically realized, situated knowledge making. And in so arguing, she is acknowledging that what we do is rhetoric and writing, and that all those scientific models of making knowledge described by North are myopic:

> We stand within a history that has alternately marginalized and ignored the knowledge of the powerless and then (when we must listen) domesticated and assimilated that experience into mainstream and middle class schemas. As academics we stand in a profession more accustomed to speak "for others" than listening to their unanticipated, resistant meanings. (2003, 38)

And if those meanings are resistant, then they are not quite so pow-erless as even this very sensitive argument from Flower would suggest. Even as Flower rightly tries to compensate for the scientific paradigm that had driven her—and the entire profession—she remains at least partially tied to what Carl Gutierrez-Jones (2001) in discussing cultural race theory calls "the rhetoric of injury." We have been attempting to be heard since before Dr. Diego Alavarez Chanca, Christopher Columbus's physician, first sought to record his transactions with the Taínos of the Caribbean, the first misnamed "Indians" (Wagenheim and Jiménez deW-agenheim 2002). And those trying to be heard include those who rose from one notion of powerlessness, the poor and ghettoized, to another, the successful academics who were nevertheless ignored in those early days of composition during its need for scientific legitimacy.

Flower (2003) is right, arguing for much the same as Krista Ratcliffe does (2006), that there must be a rhetoric of listening, real listening, as we enter real dialectical processes with the whole of humanity. The men and women of color who pulled this profession into the world of personal academic discourse, of storytelling mixed with evidence of various other sorts, have been pointing to what so many others see, that understanding humanity's humanity can best be attained through telling our own stories of ourselves. This is our "science," not to be relegated to the scholars resisting composition's ties to literature in English departments, not to be relegated to the historians who are tied to a rhetoric that rises Adam-like out of Athens and then Rome, inevitably tied to the story of European expansion, when we would all of us have had our own rhetorics. We are *homo rhetoricus, homo retórico.*

[Woman is, and] Man is
the symbol-using (symbol-making, symbol-misusing) animal
inventor of the negative (or moralized by the negative)
separated from his natural condition by instruments of his own
    making
goaded by the spirit of hierarchy (or moved by the sense of order)
and rotten with perfection. (Burke 1966, 16)

In 1987, Stephen North was blinded to the works—even scientific-like works—of people of color, a reluctant victim of the myth that there could be an objective discourse and an objective method, failing to recognize the powerful influences of the ideological, the unspoken belief that people of color do not do science.[4] Today, he would no doubt acknowledge not just ethnography but the symbolist ethnography of a Clifford Geertz (1973) and, likely, the rhetorical ethnography of a Ralph Cintron (1997). And he would likely acknowledge the artistically rendered research of personal academic discourse. And I would hope he would recognize the current work on the rhetorics historically tied to people of color.

REFERENCES

Baca, Damián. 2008. *Mestiz@ scripts, digital migrations, and the territories of writing.* New York: Palgrave-Macmillan.

Banks, Adam. 2005. *Race, rhetoric, and technology: Searching for higher ground.* Philadelphia: Lawrence Erlbaum.

Berthoff. 1982. *Forming/thinking/writing: The composing imagination.* Portsmouth: Boynton/ Cook.

---

4.   For more on this, see Banks (2005).

Blumenbach, Johann Friedrich. 1969. *On the natural varieties of mankind: De generis humani varietate nativa*. New York: Bergman.

Bonilla-Silva, Eduardo. 2006. *Racism without racists: Color-blind racism and the persistence of racial inequality in the United States*. 2nd ed. Lanham, MD: Rowman and Littlefield.

Brooks, Charlotte K. 1985. *Tapping potential: English and language arts for the black learner*. Urbana, IL: National Council of Teachers of English.

Burke, Kenneth. 1966. *Language as symbolic action: Essays on life, literature, and method*. Berkeley: University of California Press.

Cintron, Ralph. 1997. *Angels' town: Chero ways, gang life, and rhetorics of the everyday*. Boston: Beacon.

Cixous Hélène. 1976. The laugh of the medusa. Translated by Keith Cohen and Paula Cohen. *Signs* 1 875–93.

Emig, Janet. 1971. *The composing process of twelfth graders*. Urbana, IL: National Council of Teachers of English

Flower, Linda. 1989. Cognition, context, and theory building. *CCC* : 282–311.

———. 2003. Talking across difference: Intercultural rhetoric and the search for situated knowledge. *CCC*: 38–68.

Geertz, Clifford. 1973. *The interpretation of cultures*. New York: Harper Collins.

Gilyard, Keith. 2003. *Liberation memories: The rhetoric and poetics of John Oliver Killens*. Detroit: Wayne State University Press.

———. 1991. *Voices of the self: A study of language competence*. Detroit: Wayne State University Press.

Glenn, Cheryl. 1997. *Rhetoric retold: Regendering the tradition from antiquity through the Renaissance*. Carbondale: Southern Illinois University Press.

Goffman, Erving. 1974. *Frame analysis: An essay on the organization of experience*. London: Harper and Row.

Gonzalez, Roseann Dueñas. 1983. *Copy, combine, and compose: Controlling composition*. New York: Wadsworth.

Greenhalgh, Trisha, and Brian Hurwitz. 1999. Narrative based medicine: Why study narrative? *BMJ*: 48–50.

Gutierrez-Jones, Carl. 2001. *Critical race narratives: A study of race, rhetoric, and injury*. New York: New York University Press.

Hairston, Maxine. 1982. The winds of change: Thomas Kuhn and the revolution in the teaching of writing. *CCC* 33: 76–88.

Harris, Joseph D. 1997. *A teaching subject: Composition since 1966*. Upper Saddle River, NJ: Prentice Hall.

Holdstein, Deborah H., and David Bleich. 2001. *Personal effects: The social character of scholarly writing*. Logan: Utah State University Press.

Holmes, David G. 2007. *Revisiting racialized voice: African American ethos in language and literature*. Carbondale: Southern Illinois University Press.

hooks, bell. 1990. *Yearning: Race, gender, and cultural politics*. Boston: South End.

Jarratt, Susan. 1991. *Rereading the sophists: Classical rhetoric refigured*. Carbondale: Southern Illinois University Press.

Kirsch, Gesa. 1999. *Ethical dilemmas in feminist research: The politics of location, interpretation, and publication*. Albany: State University of New York Press.

Logan, Shirley Wilson. 1999. *"We are coming": The persuasive discourse of nineteenth-century black women*. Carbondale: Southern Illinois University Press.

Lunsford, Andrea A., ed. 1995. *Reclaiming Rhetorica: Women in the rhetorical tradition*. Pittsburgh, PA: University of Pittsburgh Press.

Lyons, Richard Scott. 2000. Rhetorical sovereignty: What do American Indians want from writing? *CCC*: 447–68.

McCloskey, Deirdre. 1994. *Knowledge and persuasion in economics*. Cambridge: Cambridge University Press.

————. 1998. *The rhetoric of economics.* 2nd ed. Madison: University of Wisconsin Press.

Mishler, Elliot G. 1979. Meaning in context: Is there any other kind? *Harvard Education Review* 49: 1–19.

————. 2000. *Storylines: Craftartists' narratives of identity.* Cambridge, MA: Harvard University Press.

Neruda, Pablo. 2003. The Word. In *The poetry of Pablo Neruda,* edited by Ilan Stavans, 621–22. Translated by Alastair Reid. New York: Farrar, Strauss and Giroux

North, Stephen M. 1987. *The making of knowledge in composition: Portrait of an emerging field.* Portsmouth: Boynton/Cook.

Powell, Malea. 2002. Rhetorics of survivance: How American Indians use writing. *CCC*: 396–434.

Ratcliffe, Krista. 2006. *Rhetorical listening: Identification, gender, whiteness.* Carbondale: Southern Illinois University Press.

Ritchie, Joy, and Kate Ronald. 2001. *Available means: An anthology of women's rhetoric.* Pittsburgh, PA: Pittsburgh University Press.

Rodriguez, Richard. 1982. *Hunger of memory: The education of Richard Rodriguez.* New York: Bantam.

Rose, Mike. 1989. *Lives on the boundary.* New York: Free Press.

Royster, Jacqueline Jones, and Jean C. Williams. 1999. "History in the Spaces Left: African American Presence and Narratives of Composition Studies." *CCC* 50: 563–84.

Smith, Linda Tuhiwai. 1999. *Decolonizing methodologies: Research and indigenous peoples.* London: Zed and Dunedin.

Smitherman, Geneva. 1977. *Talkin and testifyin: The language of black America.* Boston: Houghton Mifflin.

Spigelman, Candace. 2004. *Personally speaking: Experience as evidence in academic discourse.* Carbondale: Southern Illinois University Press.

Vega, Johanna. 1994. A Puerto Rican Girl's Sentimental Journey. In *Cool salsa: Bilingual poems on growing up Latino in the United States,* ed. Lori M. Carlson, 12-13. New York: Fawcett Juniper.

Villanueva, Victor. 1987. Whose voice is it anyway? Rodriguez' speech in retrospect. *English Journal* 76: 17–21.

————. 1993. *Bootstraps: From an American academic of color.* Urbana, IL: National Council of Teachers of English.

————. 1999. On the rhetoric and precedents of racism. *CCC*: 645–62.

Wagenheim, Karl, and Olga Jiménez deWagenheim. 2002. *The Puerto Ricans: A documentary history.* Expanded ed. Princeton: Markus Wiener.

Young, Morris. 2004. *Minor re/visions: Asian American literacy narratives as a rhetoric of citizenship.* Carbondale: Southern Illinois University Press.

PART THREE

The Making of Knowledge in Composition
and Education: Undergraduate, Graduate, and Beyond

8

UNDERGRADUATE RESEARCHERS AS MAKERS OF KNOWLEDGE IN COMPOSITION IN THE WRITING STUDIES MAJOR

Joyce Kinkead

How can we account for these fresh and startling voices?

North, 121

North's milestone volume, published in 1987, endorses the work of Bruffee and Macrorie, who propose that students within writing courses and writing programs "have more right to textual authority than has been traditionally afforded them" (118). North calls for textual authority for students *within* writing courses and courses such as introduction to philosophy, in which he analyzed three students' writing over the course of a term. His research question? "How can we account for these fresh and startling voices?" Twenty-five years on from the publication of *The Making of Knowledge in Composition: Portrait of an Emerging Field* (*MKC*), the "fresh and startling voices" include not only those students writing in the philosophy class that he explicates in his chapter on "The Critics," but also those in the new writing studies major. In this chapter, I call not only for the textual authority of students who choose to major in writing studies but the acknowledgement that students can and do join us as makers of knowledge. A new brand of student writer-scholars represents early versions of ourselves—compositionists in training. These young researchers increasingly are finding ways into the profession at the undergraduate level, many of them through relatively recent degree programs in writing. Composition studies, no longer "emerging," is instead *evolving*. North did not and probably could not envision the emergence of majors in writing studies nor students as makers of knowledge in composition studies, but his volume certainly anticipates the new major.

Undergraduate research, termed "the pedagogy for the 21st century" in a Joint Statement of Principles composed by the Council on Undergraduate Research and National Conferences on Undergraduate Research (2005; 2005), has experienced tremendous growth over the last twenty years. Unfortunately, the movement has been slow to gain ground in composition studies. In fact, Dotterer (2002) notes that "humanities departments have been the slowest to participate" (83) in this "shift in how scholarship is practiced in a broad range of disciplines" (83).

A definition of *undergraduate research* may be helpful at this juncture. According to the Council on Undergraduate Research (CUR), "Undergraduate research is an inquiry or investigation conducted by an undergraduate that makes an original, intellectual, or creative contribution to the field" (About the council). In terms of composition studies, North characterizes *practice as inquiry* (one way in which scholars make knowledge) in this way: researchers identify a problem, search for causes and then possible solutions, test solutions in practice, validate, and disseminate (36). Students engaged in undergraduate research in writing thus begin by identifying and acquiring methodology appropriate to the discipline. This may be done through modeling and direct instruction. But teaching *about* methodology lays only the foundation. Undergraduate researchers, working with a faculty mentor, must develop a concrete problem to investigate—the researchable question that, when studied, fills a gap in the profession's knowledge base. This phase also calls for a review of literature germane to the study. The student then carries out the project, and finally, the results of the study are shared with peers and/or disseminated to a professional audience. This last step, dissemination, is too often absent, a step that North calls a crucial element of inquiry.

The importance of dissemination was brought home to me shortly after the publication of *MKC*. In my own teaching, particularly a seminar designed for students employed as tutors in a writing-across-the-curriculum program, I came to believe that meaningful, authentic writing assignments, as advocated by Walter Loban (1976), are essential to students' growth and professional development. At the time, I could not have articulated that I was becoming an advocate for undergraduate research. Collaboratively, the students and I developed case studies to be used in future seminars. By the end of the project, we felt that these cases were applicable not only to our group but to tutors at other institutions. Thus, these studies became the basis for "Situations and Solutions in Writing-Across-the-Curriculum Tutoring" (1995) published in the *Writing Lab Newsletter* (*WLN*), a collaborative essay written by the nine of us. (I am mindful that I am using the term *case studies* in the same generic way that Janet Emig did in her landmark study, as North notes in his chapter on "The Clinicians.")

Our essay came more than a decade after Muriel Harris issued a call for tutors to join in the professional conversation. The *Writing Lab Newsletter* featured for the first time in 1984 the Tutor's Column, to "encourage them [tutors] to add their voices to the conversation." In other words, undergraduates were invited to join the community of writing center scholars in *making knowledge*. As Pemberton (2003) notes, the Tutor's Corner in *WLN* has contributed to the "growth of the writing center field" (34). One of the many students published in *WLN* as a result of authentic writing in my course was Matt Babcock. His "Leggo My Ego" appeared in 1996, a combination of what North might describe as both philosophizing and proselytizing (91). A couple of years later, Matt reported that his essay was part of a course reader in his graduate seminar at an eastern university. As he put it, "There I was, a student in a course in which my writing was part of our reading assignments. Did that make me feel like something special!" Matt's experience contributed to my own growing conviction that meaningful writing, paired with dissemination, is essential to students' initiation into the club of composition scholars.

Undergraduate research is central to the exploration and mastery of a field of study. Elgren and Hensel (2006) report that programs that include undergraduate research "promote greater exposure to the primary literature; create opportunities to articulate and test hypotheses and intellectual models; and encourage students to contextualize and communicate objectives, approaches, analyses, and conclusions" (4). Students in the writing major deserve the same access to research as students in other fields have experienced. An understanding of the national movement in undergraduate research can inform the new major.

UNDERGRADUATE RESEARCH AS A NATIONAL MOVEMENT

If undergraduate research in writing studies is playing catch-up to degree programs in which undergraduate research has been an integral part, what is it that was missed and why? The national undergraduate research movement precedes even North's *MKC*. Two main organizations, CUR and NCUR, have led the way in the undergraduate research movement.

The former, the Council on Undergraduate Research (CUR), established in 1978 by a group of chemists from private liberal arts colleges, is largely a faculty-based organization. CUR believes that "faculty members enhance their teaching and contribution to society by remaining active in research and by involving undergraduates in research" (About the council). The organization is governed by councilors elected in subject-specific disciplines. Councilors who come from writing studies have gravitated to the social sciences division, but with the new humanities division, that may change. (The tension that exists between social sciences and humanities in relationship to writing studies will be addressed shortly.)

CUR's biennial national conference for its three thousand members features topics such as research ethics, dissemination venues for student research, and interdisciplinary research. Special workshops and institutes on topics such as grant writing are also sponsored by the organization. The *CUR Quarterly* features articles focusing on undergraduate research, generally by faculty authors. Some articles focusing on the humanities (Bost 1992–93; DeVries 2001; McDorman 2004; Rogers 2003; Uffelman 1995) have appeared, but as yet there have not been any focusing on writing studies with the notable exception of Grobman (2007). Finally, CUR also publishes books such as the ambitious compilation of successful practices, *Developing and Sustaining a Research-Supportive Curriculum* (Karukstis and Elgren 2007).

Although frequently confused with CUR, the National Conferences on Undergraduate Research (NCUR) is quite different, an annual conference where undergraduates present their research, scholarship, and creative products. Attended by about two thousand students, NCUR provides plenary sessions as well as poster sessions, oral presentations, and performances. Its mission is to "promote undergraduate research, scholarship, and creative activity done in partnership with faculty or other mentors as a vital component of higher education" (What is NCUR?). A modest set of sessions is reserved for the Faculty and Administrative Network (FAN), where faculty members make presentations about undergraduate research, typically during the lunch hour so faculty do not miss their students' presentations. Founded in 1987, NCUR sought to provide a professional venue for students to present their work. CUR and NCUR worked together to produce the *Joint Statement of Principles in Support of Undergraduate Research, Scholarship, and Creative Activities* (2005) that reads something like a Declaration of Independence. That collaboration anticipated a joining of the two organizations—CUR and NCUR—in 2010.

This document has much to say to compositionists who might wonder why we should care about undergraduate research, but its words will also sound quite familiar in many ways. They are principles similar to those embodied in documents generated by the Conference on College Composition and Communication (CCCC), such as *Students' Rights to Their Own Language*. And, certainly, the bedrock statements here echo North's concern for authority of text. As new writing studies majors are integrated into the curriculum of departments of English or rhetoric, the *Joint Statement* can inform their structure and being.

The *Joint Statement* posits that inquiry-based learning anticipates a "major shift in how scholarship is practiced in the academy" as undergraduate research combines "two historic poles of a professional dichotomy"—teaching and research—"into one integrated pedagogy and system of performance" (Council 2005; National 2005). The goal of the *Joint Statement* and its authors is to embrace a curricular reform movement that partners students and faculty in collaborative relationships. These collaborative partnerships have the possibility of producing new discoveries and applications. Additionally, students improve skills such as analysis, teamwork, problem solving, time management, leadership, and communication. Their self-confidence is strengthened as well as their understanding of research integrity and ethics.

The intangible results from close relationships between mentor and student have been noted in higher education literature (e.g., Involvement in Learning; Light 2004). While assessment of undergraduate research is still in the early stages, studies have demonstrated that students gain experience in specific skills such as making use of primary literature and communicating results (Kardash 2000). They also tend to persist to degree completion (Nagda et al., 1998) and pursue graduate education at high rates (Hathaway, Nagda, and Gregerman 2002). As alumni, they retrospectively report higher gains than comparison groups in skills such as carrying out research, acquiring information, and speaking effectively (Bauer and Bennett 2003). And, while it has not yet been linked, it is highly likely that alumni who engaged in hands-on learning and one-on-one collaboration with faculty mentors that connected them to the institution are more likely to donate to the institution, both in time and money.

Students who engage in undergraduate research usually get a much better idea of what it will be like to work in the field postbaccalaureate. Career clarification as a result of such an experience may result in increased passion or even rejection of the course of study. From my own experience of overseeing a campus-wide undergraduate research program, I've noticed this clarification of career goals several times. An international research experience for one student led her to begin to refocus her major coursework to prepare for medical school; through her social-sciences research on immigration patterns of Latin and South America, she determined that health practice and policy could have a positive impact, and she wanted to be involved in that effort. Another student noted that although she originally thought she was interested in animal science from a microscopic perspective, after looking at so many cell cultures, it became clear that she really preferred a social scientist's viewpoint. For others, work in the field or lab confirms their interest in and understanding of the subject; David, a biology major, told me that he was taught a particular concept via the textbook, a classroom lecture, and the class lab, but it was only when he was dissecting a mouse brain in his research lab placement that the concept truly clicked for him. It is the power of such experiences to enhance teaching and learning that have made passionate advocates out of so many faculty members across the nation.

But back to the national movement. A third important organization advocating for undergraduate research in the academy is the Reinvention Center, which grew out of the benchmark Boyer Commission Report (1998) Reinventing Undergraduate Education: A Blueprint for America's Research Universities. Although directed at research universities, the report offers ten points to improve undergraduate education that could be applied to any institution. A prime one is "to make research-based learning the standard." As the report notes, "Undergraduate education . . . requires renewed emphasis on a point strongly made by John Dewey almost a century ago: learning is based on discovery guided by mentoring rather than on the transmission of information. Inherent in inquiry-based learning is an element of reciprocity: faculty can learn from students as students are learning from faculty" (23).

The Reinvention Center offers on its expansive website resources on undergraduate education overall. Undergraduate research in the humanities—although not yet in writing studies specifically—is addressed through spotlight features and listings of exemplary programs. The Center, which originated on the SUNY-Stony Brook campus but recently moved to the University of Miami in Florida, also hosts a biennial national conference and more frequent regional meetings, targeting in particular those administrative leaders who oversee undergraduate education.

The undergraduate research imperative is evidenced in these three leading organizations; however, its roots lie further back in time to the 1950s when the United States responded to the Sputnik challenge by increasing funding to support instruction in science and mathematics, what came to be known as the STEM areas: science, technology, engineering, and mathematics. Research-rich environments for students in various academic settings grew out of this campaign and gained ground, particularly in the 1990s, as the value of inquiry-based learning became increasingly evident. For instances, Project Kaleidoscope, a national group aimed at improving instruction in STEM areas, arose from conversations with the National Academy of Sciences in 1993.

So where is writing studies in this national movement? One of the logical places to look for participation by students doing undergraduate research in writing studies is NCUR, which has a twenty-year history. An analysis of the annual programs for NCUR reveals that over those two decades, only forty-one abstracts could be identified as belonging to composition and rhetoric.[1] In contrast, students presenting in categories classified as English, literary studies, creative writing, or linguistics greatly outnumbered students doing research in writing. For many of the NCUR annual conferences, no presentations focused on rhetoric and composition research. A typical number of presentations for literature, on the other hand, comes in at several dozen in the early years and one hundred or more in NCUR's second decade.

Confirming our earlier assertion that tutoring lends itself to practice as inquiry, several of the NCUR abstracts focus on tutoring. In 1988, at the second NCUR, Daniel Schultz of the University of Minnesota-Twin Cities examined common grammatical problems found in student papers in introductory writing classes; Sheila Martin of Arkansas Tech University looked at "The Effects of Peer Editing on Student Writing." In 1991, Peter Gray of the University of San Diego talked about his experiences as a writing assistant in an engineering classroom and the conflict he found between discourse communities. Michelle Szpara in 1993 explored the "institutional history of serving ESL students at Penn State"

---

1.   I am indebted to Jessica Wallace, an undergraduate at the University of North Carolina-Asheville, for analyzing the NCUR archives and compiling data that is cited here.

and made recommendations for the campus writing center. John Bean's mentee, Jennifer Ching, explored in 1994 "Personality Type Preferences and the Conduct of Writing Center Sessions." These sessions would have been familiar to North, who began his academic career in writing centers and, with Lil Brannon, who created *The Writing Center Journal*. Not only do these NCUR presentations draw on practice as inquiry common in writing centers but also on historical and case study methodologies.

Other NCUR presentations were classified as education because they applied to K–12 instruction. At the 10th Annual NCUR in 1996, Adrienne Hollifield of UNC-Asheville shared the results of her study on "The Effects of Storytelling on the Quality of Narrative Composition of Ninth-Grade Students." Reading achievement and its positive correlation to content-related writing was the topic of a 2005 presentation by Emily Wells from Hendrix College entitled "Teacher Instruction Utilizing the Reciprocal Nature of Reading and Writing." In 2007, another student from Hendrix, Kristy Chambers, addressed how parental involvement assists in success in reading and writing. These students utilized clinical and ethnographic approaches.

Mentors for papers in the rhetoric and composition section include recognizable names in the profession: Andrea Lunsford, John Bean, Larry Reynolds, and Joseph Moxley. Clearly, as Heidi Estrem noted in her introduction to the 2007 special issue of *Composition Studies*, there are students with whom we compositionists want to work and collaborate.

RESEARCH IN THE NEW WRITING STUDIES MAJOR

A significant shift is occurring in the study of writing by undergraduates, evidenced, in part, by the growing number of institutions that offer a major in writing. The CCCC Committee on the Major in Rhetoric and Composition developed an initial list of some forty such degree programs, increased as of this writing to more than fifty. Attention to the writing major has been championed by Kathleen Yancey, who, as chair of CCCC, authorized the Committee on the Writing Major. Yancey, a compositionist who is also keenly aware of national trends and issues, noted the gap between lower-division writing courses and graduate programs in rhetoric and composition, the "in-between" spaces that cried out for a major in writing, in her 2004 CCCC chair's address. Heidi Estrem credits the chair's address for inspiring her institution to undertake the creation of a writing major so that she and colleagues could have "access" to students whom they "wanted to teach." Their goal?

"They could emphasize the "disciplinary traditions and research practices of composition and rhetoric [that had] remained underemphasized for students" (2007, 11).

Degree programs in technical and professional writing, which most likely have the longest track record among majors in writing, provide a very marketable degree for students desiring employment following the baccalaureate. (Likewise, creative writing has a lengthy record; however, less can be said about its practical applicability.) Technical and professional writing courses, no doubt, began as service courses offered by English departments but for other departments' majors. The faculty teaching these courses must have realized that their own students in English could benefit from a degree path in this area. As composition studies has evolved, so has the new writing major. Employability of these graduates stands in stark contrast to the oft satirized English major, who is fondly lampooned in Garrison Keillor's weekly radio show *A Prairie Home Companion*: "English majors have all the qualities women look for—intelligence, curiosity, a sense of adventure, and excellent punctuation" (2005).

In 2002, Bazerman made "The Case for Writing Studies as a Major Discipline": "Inquiry into skills, practices, objects, and consequences of reading and writing is the concern of only a few people, fragmented across university disciplines, with no serious home of its own" (32). Graduate programs in rhetoric and composition are relatively young, perhaps thirty to forty years in existence, with new programs still being created. The writing studies major is even younger, hardly mature in its curriculum.

What should the curriculum in writing studies contain? Certainly *MKC* provides a blueprint, but the list of writing majors compiled by the CCCC Committee on the Writing Major is diverse in terms of classes offered. On some campuses, it is a cluster of courses cobbled together from existing resources, building on the traditional core of classes in literary studies. North himself pondered in the last section of *MKC* whether or not "composition [can] really muster enough coherence to justify an autonomous academic existence" (374). Rightly so. Kelly Lowe warns in the special issue of *Composition Studies* on the writing major that such cobbling together without concordant faculty and staff can result in a major not "done right" (2007, 97). Others have noted that undergraduates may be more interested in creative writing than in rhetoric and composition. And, we have already mentioned that coherent programs in technical and professional writing have proved popular with students. Writing majors listed on the Writing Majors at a Glance website include courses as wide-ranging as the journalistic news writing at Briar Cliff to Arizona State's Principles of Visual Communication. To be sure, the amorphous nature of writing leads to challenges in designing a curriculum. While a course such as Drake University's Reading and Writing Sexuality might not appear consistently in other degree programs, it's more likely that its Writing, Literacy, and Schooling would, just as Bazerman suggests that "the teaching of writing is all about education and education's place in making and remaking lives and society" (2006, 12). It would make sense that a writing studies curriculum also include courses on the history of writing, particularly classical rhetoric. Let me focus here, though, on the one course I see as essential to a major in writing studies: research methodology.

An analysis of the curricula for the writing degree indicates that research methodology classes are not automatically included. This oversight is problematic. For some time on my own campus, I have noted that students who undertake graduate studies in the field of composition tend to be unaware of and inexperienced in the very modes of inquiry that North explicates in *MKC*. The ability to define a researchable question seems unpracticed. It is quite clear that the students have not developed a fluency in research methodology appropriate to composition studies. Had they experience in such modes of inquiry at the undergraduate level—as majors in literary studies do—they would be better prepared to undertake graduate work in the field. As Willison and O'Regan (2007) note, students move on a continuum "from knowledge new to the learner to knowledge new to humankind, moving from the commonly known, to the commonly not known, to the totally unknown" (394).

Such a course introduces students to the methods of inquiry in the discipline and also addresses the crucial question of why we should do research. North's *MKC*, written to provide a "logical hierarchy of knowledge in the field" (iv), provides a good foundation. Three excellent more recent books summarize inquiry in the field: Bazerman's 2007 *Handbook of Writing Research*; Smagorinsky's 2006 *Research on Composition: Multiple Perspectives on Two Decades of Change*; and MacArthur, Graham, and Fitzgerald's 2006 *Handbook of Writing Research*. These volumes build on the earlier benchmark works of Braddock, Lloyd-Jones, and Schoer's 1963 *Research in Written Communication* and Hillocks' 1986 *Research on Written Composition*.

Multiple ways to organize a research methodology class exist. Landmark studies that illuminate and exemplify various approaches could provide the basis of the course, but it would also need to address traditions as well as techniques for gathering information. First, landmark studies. A logical starting point is Janet Emig's *The Composing Processes of Twelfth Graders* (1971), case study research that is easily accessible. North calls it "the most influential piece of Researcher work ever published" (135), a statement that holds true even twenty-five years later. The case study approach allows for a researchable question to be addressed by defining the problem or question, the site, the subject(s), the scope in terms of time and size, and the method. It also quickly gets at the ways in which a researcher gathers information: interviews (group interviews, focus groups, individuals); observations; videotaping; audiotaping; researcher logs or field notes; interest surveys or surveys in general; pre and posttests; counting (e.g., time spent on task; number of conferences; types of services requested).

Strategies for Empirical Research in Writing (1998) by Mary Sue MacNealy offers helpful methodological chapters on approaches such as "Focus Groups" and "Surveys.". Quite naturally, issues concerning responsible conduct of research (RCR) will arise as the case study is all about human subjects, which necessitates approval by an Institutional Review Board (IRB). *On Being a Scientist: Responsible Conduct in Research* and *ORI Introduction to the Responsible Conduct of Research* (the latter authored by Nicholas Steneck, a professor emeritus of history at the University of Michigan), offer information on the fundamentals of research misconduct, human and animal research, data management, conflict of interest, collaboration, mentoring, authorship, and peer review. Schneider's "Ethical Research and Pedagogical Gaps" provides a rationale for research integrity in its discussion of CCCC's *Guidelines for the Ethical Treatment of Students and Student Writing in Composition Studies.* Although North defines research that involves human subjects, little, if any, space is devoted to the topic of human subjects and the ethical issues involved. Undergraduate researchers involved in research now would be required to become much more familiar with IRB standards.

Other landmark studies are accessible through Ede's *On Writing Research,* the helpful compilation of Braddock Award-winning essays that offers examples of historical inquiry, as in Connors's "The Rise and Fall of the Modes of Discourse" (1981), and of formalist and clinical (North's terms) studies, such as those conducted by Flower and Hayes (1977), and Sommers (1980), respectively.

Yet another approach to a research methodology course is to organize it by the *traditions* on which it draws, many of these exemplified in *MKC*, the first volume to undertake how "knowledge is made in field" (1). The *historical* approach, exemplified by Connors's (1981) and Fitzgerald's (2001) Braddock essays, for instance, offers insights into how the teaching of writing has changed, using documents and other artifacts from the past to develop explanations. Historians may draw on personal accounts as the researcher looks at autobiography, biography, and oral histories. Writing studies draws liberally from anthropology, particularly ethnographic research in which the researcher wishes to describe the culture of a particular group, often as a participant-observer. Another social science, sociology, lends its interest in social and economic class, gender, ethnicity, and stratification. Cognitive science that addresses the way people think and write is particularly evident in the work of Flower and Hayes (1977). For those interested in policy and practice, the case study can offer evidence that contributes to innovation and intervention. A *linguistic* approach may focus on discourse analysis. Drawing on the *rhetorical* tradition as Young, Becker, and Pike did in their groundbreaking work on invention (1970) illuminates how classical rhetoric still influences writing. A *process* approach focuses on how people write, as Flower and Hayes did so notably in several works on the act of writing. Conversely, a *developmental* approach on how people learn to write is exemplified in the work of James Britton and Arthur Applebee. *Cultural* studies situate writing in its community as illustrated by the research of Shirley Brice Heath (1983) and Anne Dyson (1984), to name just two. *Instructional* approaches focus on how we teach writing and its outcomes, studies that Hillocks (1986) enumerates. Finally, *philosophical* approaches—North's term again—address the nature of writing as scholars of writing, well, philosophize. A later volume, Lancy's *Qualitative Research in Education: An Introduction to the Major Traditions* (1993), provides not only useful information on these traditions, often with illustrations from research in writing, but also has a helpful chapter to students on framing a research proposal and writing a thesis.

While I have suggested various approaches to the organization of the course, I must also acknowledge that these frameworks may be false in practice. Researchers often draw on multiple perspectives and multiple traditions to conduct their research. We have addressed, for instance, the tension that exists between humanistic inquiry and social-sciences research, but a research project may be enhanced by a combination of them. Durst argues in his analysis of Braddock Award essays that "human-istically-grounded inquiry" makes significant contributions to the field, but the award has typically gone to empirical research that uses quantita-tive and/or qualitative methods (1991, 58). And, ironically, after Durst's essay, the awards did turn toward more humanistic, nonempirical works. Frankly, it does not have to be an either/or matter. A richness of meth-odological inquiry is to be welcomed. Although North worried about this lack of clear-cut divisions among research methodologies when com-position was an emerging field, it is to be applauded in a more mature approach to making knowledge. The other issue North addresses, though, is the researcher who does not have "heightened methodological consciousness" (370). In effect, some researchers are so married to their own methodological approaches that they do not or would not engage in "methodological egalitarianism" (371). To fail to introduce undergradu-ates to the multiple and complex approaches to making knowledge in writing studies would be a failure of the profession.

No methodology class is worth its salt though if students are not actu-ally engaging in research in some way. As Schneider (2006) notes, it's time to "shift our perspective of student writing from exercises at the barre to performances of real work" (72). She sees students as "up-and-coming colleagues" (86). Research is a time-consuming process, which suggests that a methodology course might very well extend over an academic year. Students need to try on various ways to look at a ques-tion or problem. No doubt they have questions about writing or writ-ing processes that can be situated in the literature and then explored through a proposal. Or, the research project may be one designed by the teacher. For instance, in a semester-based course that I taught, stu-dents took on a large-scale assessment of writing on campus, analyzing more than 700 syllabi.[2]

UNDERGRADUATES AS MAKERS OF KNOWLEDGE

Undergraduates *are* producing knowledge for the field in some read-ily identifiable places. The excellent refereed journal *Young Scholars in Writing*, founded by Laurie Grobman and the late Candace Spigelman in 2003, is "dedicated to publishing research articles written by undergrad-uates in a wide variety of disciplines associated with writing and rheto-ric" (University of Missouri). Its authors could be categorized by North's

---

2.   For more on this, see Grobman and Kinkead (2010).

chapters on the various modes of inquiry: historian, critic, philosopher, and ethnographer. A couple of titles will illustrate: "Institutional Change and the University of Wisconsin-Madison Writing Fellows Program" (Corroy 2003); "The Visible Rhetoric and Composition of Invisible Antebellum Female Seminary Students: Clay Seminary, Liberty, Missouri, 1855–1865" (Petrillo 2004). Amy Robillard (2006) suggests that this journal "functions as evidence that students are able and willing to contribute to composition studies' disciplinary knowledge about writing and rhetoric" (262). Likewise, *The Writing Center Journal* has featured undergraduate authors, particularly the excellent "Taking on Turnitin: Tutors Advocating Change" by Brown et al. (2007).

Another viable outlet for undergraduate researchers—albeit one that is quite focused in a specific area—is the National Conference on Peer Tutoring in Writing (NCPTW), which has for more than two decades offered "peer tutors the opportunity to contribute in professional and scholarly ways to the larger writing center community." NCPTW "is dedicated to providing forums for tutors to share and present research at national and international conferences." Regional conferences for tutors or writing center professionals (e.g., the Rocky Mountain Peer Tutoring Conference that started in 1984; the MidAtlantic Writing Centers Association) also provide such forums. These conferences, coupled with the *Writing Lab Newsletter* Tutor's Column, provide outlets for undergraduate scholarship. I would submit that undergraduates who tutor are the most likely authors of scholarly and research essays as they have become, in effect, practitioners who feel compelled to contribute to "the House of Lore" (27). Delli Carpini (2007) shares this opinion when he notes that a course for writing majors on teaching and tutoring writing resulted in a "surprising" increase in "disciplinary scholarship and activity" (29) and the "growth of an inquiry-based community" (30) that approached the faculty postcourse about research projects. In *MKC*, North called for a "re-establishment of Practice as Inquiry" (371) and notes that if there is any core or center to composition studies, it lies in *practice*. It seems that our students have taken up that challenge.

Undergraduate researchers are seemingly less well integrated into professional meetings such as CCCC and the publications of the National Council of Teachers of English (NCTE). What might appear to be a striking example in the affirmative is the Fishman, Lunsford, McGregor, and Otuteye Braddock Award-winning essay (and CCCC presentation), "Performing Writing, Performing Literacy" (2005). The two student coauthors, however, are also subjects of the research project, enrolled in writing-program classes. They exemplify North's notion that the profession was in 1987 moving toward a "gradual authorization of student writing" (11). Likewise, the *CCC* essay "Cross-Curricular Underlife: A Collaborative Report on Ways with Academic Words," authored by five undergraduates in first-year composition and faculty member, Susan Miller, features the student researchers as participant-observers (Anderson et al. 1990). The students are not majors in a degree program but members of lower-division writing courses. In fact, much of the published collaborative work by students and faculty seems to arise from lower-division, general-education writing classes (e.g., Tayko and Tassoni 1997), in which students are more *subjects* than researchers. While students in lower-division writing courses certainly have the capability of contributing knowledge to the profession, as suggested by Downs and Wardle (2001), they are not necessarily our writing majors.

Finding instances of student-faculty collaborative essays or student solo essays in which the student is in a writing-studies degree program is difficult. Grobman undertook such an analysis for her "The Student Scholar" essay and compiled a list of fewer than two dozen titles, several of them derived from sites of research within writing programs (e.g., Fishman et al.; Anderson et al.) rather than writing degrees. And certainly not all of these count as *research*. Glenn Newman offers in the special issue of *Composition Studies* focused on the writing major a reflective note about creating his own degree program in rhetoric and writing studies (2007). While his essay offers a window onto one student's experience, it is not based in inquiry. Grobman ponders the notion of *authorship* and *authority* in "The Student Scholar" (2009). Is it better or not to identify authors when they are students? Although admirable, the notion of "blind" authorship that does not contextualize the writer as student, assistant professor, or director, leaves out crucial information for the reader or any scholar who is trying to determine the participation of undergraduate researchers in the profession.

CHALLENGES AND OBSTACLES TO UNDERGRADUATE RESEARCH IN THE WRITING MAJOR

Assuming that those of us in the profession do feel compelled to work with undergraduates and share our own enthusiasm for research in writing studies, how do we accomplish that? The barriers to increased undergraduate research in composition are real. The relative youth of rhetoric and composition studies, called an "emerging field" by North twenty-five years ago, has worked against establishing a research agenda for students. And certainly the newness of writing studies majors has been a limiting factor.

The research methodology class that should be integral to all writing studies programs, undergraduate and graduate, suffers for several reasons. Many of the faculty who turned to rhetoric and composition as a professional career may have received their training in literature and may be unschooled in appropriate research methodology. North noted that many of us came to composition through literature by "accident, coercion, or choice" (i). The epistemological roots of composition studies bring to the forefront this tension between humanities and social sciences and expose a hierarchical pecking order. Whether voiced or not, there is an elitism among research methodologies. I would argue that the scientific method is at the top of such a hierarchy in higher education. Within an English department, literary criticism has dominance, largely due to longevity. Studies in writing have often been associated with pedagogical or *applied* scholarship, not necessarily viewed as being as valuable as the purer scholarship of literary criticism. As a result, scholars in writing may have invested for the sake of survival in the humanistic traditions to the detriment of the emerging field of composition. Bazerman et al. (2006) write movingly of "What Schools of Education Can Offer the Teaching of Writing"; he is one of the rare persons who crosses the divide between English and education, Applebee and Langer being two who preceded him.

At the time of *MKC*, the picture of scholarship on writing studies was quite hopeful even if North wondered about happy endings in his conclusion. Its approaches were varied—clinical, ethnographic, formalistic, and historical. It was a time of the qualitative-quantitative research debate when the former began its ascendancy and acceptance in the profession. As is so typical in human history, though, the pendulum has perhaps swung too much in the direction of qualitative research or what may *pass* as qualitative. As Richard Haswell argues in his "NCTE/CCCC's War on Scholarship" (2005), support for "RAD scholarship"—scholarship that is replicable, aggregable, and data supported, has largely been withdrawn. Juzwik et al. (2006) find in their overview of research on writing for the six-year period from 1999 to 2004 that the research methodology most often used is "interpretative." Where are today's clinical ground-breaking studies that build upon the benchmark work of Janet Emig and others?

The muddying of research methods does not provide students in writing studies with clear paths to undertaking research. North himself identified methodological mayhem as a threat to the field. The richness of writing studies that draws on traditions of inquiry derived from anthropology, linguistics, sociology, education, cultural studies, and psychology also provides so much complexity that these are not easily shared with students. On the other hand, phenomenological approaches that largely ask students to "see what's out there" are too often used as an end in themselves rather than as a prewriting or invention techniques for framing a study. Descriptive narrative reports have been termed "research," when they have in practice little practicality in their ability to generalize. What is more, such approaches do not contribute to theory. They also fail to help us advance in understanding the learner or the nature of teaching. There are practical reasons as well to wanting answers to these questions. Good communication skills continue to be an imperative for an educated society and workforce.

Adding to this shift in "research" culture is another problem that hobbles research in writing studies, what David Schwalm calls a lack of "corporate culture" (2004). As Schwalm puts it, writing programs, so often the logical site of research, have an inconsistent emphasis on assessment, what could be termed *institutional research*. Writing programs also lack a history of collaborative research. A lack of funding for writing programs has naturally created few people who can undertake research. Schwalm notes that there is not an "army" of staff. Intramural and extramural support for writing research is limited at best, although a hopeful trend is the number of writing and communication programs (e.g., Clemson) that have positioned themselves as endowed centers with the funds to undertake important assessment.

Schwalm, a central administrator who has a big picture view, would probably also cite other obstacles that might add to the plight. Are those in writing studies conversant with the larger institution and the literature of higher education? Are they familiar with offices of institutional research and the standard campus data points on admissions indices, retention figures, and graduation rates? Are they aware of the role of writing in the context of the larger institutional framework, particularly with enrollment and curriculum management? Is there an awareness of first-year experience programs and community-based research (rooted in the intersection of undergraduate research with service learning) and how writing is related to them? Are there connections to development and public relations units that might advance the goals of writing and publicize important literacy issues? Finally, is there an understanding of how writing studies and writing programs may serve a campus-wide goal of responsible conduct of research (RCR) that goes beyond plagiarism issues to a broader understanding of integrity (Kinkead 2007)?

Faculty roles and rewards are integral to either supporting or dissuading faculty involvement in undergraduate research. The mentorship of students—undergraduates and graduates—should *count* in decisions of tenure, promotion, and merit. In the sciences, students may function as worker bees in the lab, providing help to a professor carrying out a project. Can we in composition studies reenvision our work in ways that students may be involved?

The obstacles to undergraduate research in writing studies are significant but not insurmountable. What can we do? First, we should look to the STEM fields as models, not necessarily to replicate them, but to adopt strategies that would serve students in writing studies. A humanistic tradition of inquiry relies on sole authorship; in contrast, scientific and social-sciences research tends to adopt a ladder approach to initiating students into the field of inquiry. Our goal is to move the novice to an apprenticeship through mentorship, helping the naïve student become an expert. This can be done, in part, by establishing research assistantships common in other disciplines. Faculty researchers must learn to break down the parts of the research process into chunks that can be performed by students. For instance, the compilation of a bibliography or a review of literature is a skill that a student can learn fairly easily, and such work may be, in fact, tedious for the faculty member.

Mentoring is a skill in itself, one that should be highly prized by graduate students who are our future faculty.[3] At my own institution, graduate students in the department of English have started in their graduate student association—cleverly called SAGE—a mentoring program for undergraduates.

While STEM research provides models for research, what is notably lacking in the profession is funding to conduct research. While volunteering for "the experience," or receiving credit through an undergraduate research course number is laudatory, nothing can replace money. We have addressed this on our campus in some measure by establishing

3. For more on this, see Entering Mentoring by Handelsman et al. (2005) for a training program as well as Merkel and Baker's How to Mentor (2002).

university-wide undergraduate research fellowships that provide students with an honorarium to engage in research from day one of their undergraduate careers. Incoming students compete for these fellowships at Scholars Day (Kinkead 2008). They are then paired with a faculty mentor once they arrive on campus in the fall. Our research *fellowships* were once scholarships, funds given to the students with no strings. While scholarships are truly helpful, they do not provide the benefits that fellowships in research do: hands-on learning; concrete products in research that make the student more competitive for prestigious scholarships and fellowships; and substantive letters of reference. We also have funded *meaningful academic employment* to help students find jobs on campus within their field of study. These include undergraduate teaching fellows, writing fellows, and supplemental instructors, which provide a foundation for students to work one on one with a faculty mentor. As I have mentioned before, donors tend to like and support programs in which students are practicing and applying what they are learning in the classroom. And communication skills are viewed by many, particularly corporations, as essential skills for the citizen.

Grants for undergraduates to conduct research, undertake scholarly projects, or create art are typical on campuses that have centralized undergraduate research offices. These grant programs could help fund writing majors to conduct research in archives, carry out survey research, or test a new model. Such grants can also be found at the college or department level, particularly if the administrators of those units have made active learning a priority. Might CCCC or The Council of Writing Program Administrators (WPA) investigate the possibility of a national grant competition to spur undergraduate research?

We can learn from the writing center community how to go about enhancing undergraduate research. In North's "House of Lore" (27), there seems to have been a continuous *open house* for students. As I have already suggested, the standard seminar in tutoring naturally results in questions on improving practice, which, in turn, leads to inquiry. The writing center profession has also enacted spaces where students/tutors/researchers may perform or publish their work. The Tutor's Column in *WLN* is one of them; the national and regional conferences on peer tutoring are another. Undergraduate researchers can also join in the more general audience in on-campus celebrations and NCUR. "Making student writing more public is also a way of acknowledging and rewarding the faculty who invest time in student research projects" according to David Chapman, writing in *Peer Review* (2003a). And, it would be very helpful if CCCC provided spaces in its journal and conference for these up-and-coming colleagues. We have done that very well for our graduate students but much less so for our undergraduates. Take for instance, the call from the American Anthropological Association for its 2008 meeting, inviting young scholars into the fold:

> Undergraduates are an increasingly important element in the *production of . . . knowledge* [italics added]. Students, working closely with faculty, build a critical foundation for professional development that is unparalleled in other aspects of their college curricula and academic life. Through these experiences, students develop vital skills and an intimate understanding of . . . processes, research development and execution, and presentation of one's results to a scholarly audience.

That said, it would also be helpful for CCCC to solicit posters for some of its sessions, acknowledging the broader approach to disseminating research, which allows for individualized conversations between researcher and audience.

The rewards for faculty in working with undergraduate researchers are considerable. As Chapman (2003b) notes, it "enhances faculty members' professional lives. . . . [as it] often helps keep faculty members abreast of disciplinary trends and developments. The satisfaction in watching a student present or publish the results of a project can be tremendous" (B5).Chapman continues, "It makes us aware of the solitary hours our students spend in library research and compiling notes, the long conferences in which student and teacher work together to revise a paper, and even the current concerns of researchers beyond our campus. In focusing attention on undergraduate research, we are reinforcing the notion of what we think a university should be" (B5).

North remarks with some cynicism that "it's a lot easier to call for new or more careful inquiry than it is to get it" (135). Will we get more and more visible undergraduate research in our discipline and in our field? The distribution of undergraduate research in writing studies across the nation is difficult to assess; however, a request for proposals issued for a new volume on *Undergraduate Research in/on English Studies* (Grobman and Kinkead 2010) resulted in an encouraging number of responses. Our colleagues nationwide are engaging in curricular innovation in writing program courses to provide a research-based learning environment and also engage the new writing major in research.

North was motivated to write *MKC* as he moved from his initial excitement and fervor for composition to a desire to understand the underpinnings of the field. My own marginalia from *MKC* at the time of its publication recall a similar fervor and excitement. Finally, in one place, a comprehensive volume written with style and humor. (The analogy of the philosophers to a marina still draws a smile.) In the concluding section, "Futures," North ponders whether there will be any happy endings for composition. He is, he admits, rather gloomy about its prospects. The new writing major was certainly not on the horizon at the time, although it might have been anticipated as a natural outgrowth of the new graduate programs in composition. It is also a natural product of North's suggestion that composition break away from traditional departments of English. The excitement and fervor felt for undergraduate research is no doubt evident in this chapter. An appeal for more undergraduate research by our up-and-coming colleagues in composition studies derives from my own experience in learning from students across the breadth of disciplines at my campus and at others of the power of inquiry and hands-on learning in their personal, professional, and intellectual growth. It is an experience that I hope others invite into their academic lives.

REFERENCES

Anderson, Worth, Cynthia Best, Alycia Black, John Hurst, Brandt Miller, and Susan Miller. 1990. Cross-curricular underlife: A collaborative report on ways with academic words. *CCC* 41 (1): 11–36.

Babcock, Matt. 1996. Leggo my ego. *Writing Lab Newsletter* 19 (5): 10.

Bauer, K.W., and Joan S. Bennett. 2003. Alumni perceptions used to assess undergraduate research experience. *The Journal of Higher Education* 74: 210–230.

Bazerman, Charles. 2002. The case for writing studies as a major discipline. In *Rhetoric and composition as intellectual work*, edited by Gary Olson. Carbondale: Southern Illinois University Press.

Bazerman, Charles. 2007. *Handbook of research on writing: History, society, school, individual, text.* New York: Erlbaum.

Bazerman, Charles, Danielle Fouquette, Chris Johnston, Francien Rohrbacher, and Rene Agustin De Los Santos. 2006. What schools of education can offer the teaching of writing. In *Culture shock and the practice of profession: Training the next wave in rhetoric and composition*, edited by Virginia Anderson and Susan Romano. Creskill, NJ: Hampton.

Bost, David. 1992–93. Seven obstacles to undergraduate research in the humanities (and seven solutions). *CUR Newsletter* 13: 35–40.

Boyer Commission on Educating Undergraduates in the Research University. 1998. *Reinventing undergraduate education: A blueprint for America's universities.* Carnegie Foundation for the Advancement of Teaching.

Braddock, Richard, Richard Lloyd-Jones, and Lloyd Schoer. 1963. *Research in written composition.* Urbana, IL: National Council of Teachers of English.

Brown, Renee, Brian Fallon, Jessica Lott, Elizabeth Matthews, and Elizabeth Mintie. 2007. Taking on turnitin: Tutors advocating change. *The Writing Center Journal* 27 (1): 7–28.

Chapman, David W. 2003a. Undergraduate research and the mandate for writing assessment. *Peer Review* 6 (1): 8–11.

———. 2003b. Undergraduate research: Showcasing young scholars. *The Chronicle Review* 50 (3): B5.

Conference on College Composition and Communication Ad-hoc Committee on the Ethical Use of Students and Student Writing in Composition Studies. 2001. *CCC* 52 (3): 458–490.

Conference on College Composition and Communication. 2007. Writing majors at a glance. CCCC Committee on the Major in Rhetoric and Composition. http://www. ncte.org/cccc/gov/committees/majorrhetcomp.

Connors, Robert J. 1981. The rise and fall of the modes of discourse. *CCC* 32: 444–463.

Corroy, Jennifer. 2003. Institutional change and the University of Wisconsin-Madison writing fellows program. *Young Scholars in Writing: Undergraduate Research in Writing and Rhetoric* 1: 20–34.

Council on Undergraduate Research. nd. About the council on undergraduate research. http://www.cur.org/about.html

Council on Undergraduate Research. 2005. Joint statement of principles in support of undergraduate research, scholarship, and creative activities. http://www.cur.org/SummiPosition.html.

Delli Carpini, Dominic F. 2007. Re-writing the humanities: The writing major's effect upon undergraduate studies in English departments. *Composition Studies* 35 (1): 15–36.

DeVries, David N. 2001. Undergraduate research in the humanities: An oxymoron? *Council on Undergraduate Research Quarterly* 21: 153–55.

Dotterer, Ronald. 2002. Student-faculty collaborations, undergraduate research, and collaboration as an administrative model. In *Scholarship in the postmodern era: New venues, new values, new visions*, edited by Kenneth J. Zahorski, 81–89. New Directions for Teaching and Learning 90. San Francisco: Jossey-Bass.

Downs, Douglas, and Elizabeth Wardle. 2007. Teaching about writing, righting misconceptions: (Re)envisioning FYC as intro to writing studies. *CCC* 58 (4): 552–584.

Durst, Russell K. 1991. Promising research: An historical analysis of award-winning inquiry, 1970–1989. *Research in the Teaching of English* 26 (1): 41–70.

Dyson, Anne Haas. 1984. Learning to write/learning to do school: Emergent writers' interpretations of school literacy tasks. *Research in the Teaching of English* 18: 233–64.

Ede, Lisa. 1999. *On writing research: The Braddock essays, 1975–1998*. Boston: Bedford/St. Martin's.

Elgren, Tim, and Nancy Hensel. 2006. Undergraduate research experiences: Synergies between teaching and scholarship. *Peer Review* 8 (1): 4–7.

Emig, Janet. 1971. *The composing processes of twelfth graders*. Urbana, IL: National Council of Teachers of English.

Estrem, Heidi. 2007. Growing pains: The writing major in composition and rhetoric. *Composition Studies* 35 (1): 11–14.

Fishman, Jenn, Andrea Lunsford, Beth McGregor, and Mark Otuteye. 2005. Performing writing, performing literacy. *CCC* 47: 224–252.

Fitzgerald, Kathryn. 2001. A rediscovered tradition: European pedagogy and composition in nineteenth-century midwestern normal schools. *CCC* 53 (2): 224–250.

Flower, Linda, and John Hayes. 1977. Problem solving strategies and the writing process. *College English* 39: 449–461.

Grobman, Laurie. 2009. The student scholar: (Re)negotiating authorship and authority. *CCC* 61: 175-96.

———, and Joyce Kinkead. 2010. *Undergraduate research in English studies*. Urbana, IL: National Council of Teachers of English.

Handelsman, Jo, Christine Pfund, Sarah Miller Lauffer, and Christine Pribbenow. 2005. *Entering mentoring.* Madison: University of Wisconsin Press.

Harris, Muriel.1984. Editor's note. *Writing Lab Newsletter* 8 (10): 1.

Haswell, Richard H. 2005. NCTE/CCCC's recent war on scholarship. *Written Communication* 22: 198–223.

Hathaway, R.S., Nagda, B.A., and Gregerman, S.R. 2002. The relationship of undergraduate research participation to graduate and professional education pursuit: An empirical study. *Journal of College Student Development* 43: 614–631.

Heath, Shirley Brice. 1983. *Ways with words.* New York: Cambridge University Press.

Hillocks, George. 1986. *Research on written communication.* Urbana, IL: National Council of Teachers of English.

Involvement in learning: realizing the potential of American higher education : final report of the Study Group on the Conditions of Excellence in American Higher Education. 1984. National Institute of Education (U.S.). Study Group on the Conditions of Excellence in American Higher Education.

Juzwik, Mary M., Svjetlana Curcic, Kimberly Wolbers, Kathleen D. Moxley, Lisa M. Dimling, and Rebecca K. Shankland. 2006. Writing into the 21st century: An overview of research on writing, 1999–2004. *Written Communication* 23 (4): 451–476.

Kardash, C.M. 2000. Evaluation of an undergraduate research experience: Perceptions of undergraduate interns and their faculty mentors. *Journal of Educational Psychology* 92: 191–201.

Keillor, Garrison. 2005. A prairie home companion, January 15. Washington, DC: National Public Radio.

Kinkead, Joyce A., Nanette Alderman, Brett Baker, Alan Freer, Jon Hertzke, Sonya Mildon Hill, Jennifer Obray, Tiffany Parker, and Maryann Peterson. 1995. Situations and solutions in writing-across-the-curriculum tutoring. *Writing Lab Newsletter* 19 (8): 1–5.

Kinkead, Joyce. 2007. How writing programs support undergraduate research. In *Developing and sustaining a research-supportive curriculum: A compendium of successful practices*, edited by Kerry K. Karukstis and Timothy E. Elgren. Washington, DC: Council on Undergraduate Research.

———. 2008. A successful model of undergraduate research. In *Developing, promoting, and sustaining the undergraduate research experience in psychology*, edited by Richard L. Miller and Robert F. Rycek. Society for Teaching Psychology. http://teachpsych.org/resources/e-books/ur2008/ur2008.php.

Lancy, David F. 1993. *Qualitative research in education: An introduction to the major traditions.* New York: Longman.

Light, Richard. 2004. *Making the most out of college: Students speak their minds.* Boston: Harvard University Press.

Loban, Walter. 1976. Language development: Kindergarten through grade twelve. Urbana, IL: National Council of Teachers of English.

Lowe, Kelly. 2007. Against the writing major. *Composition Studies* 35 (1): 97–98.

MacArthur, Charles A., Steve Graham, and Jill Fitzgerald, eds. 2006. *Handbook of writing research.* New York: Guilford.

MacNealy, Mary Sue. 1998. *Strategies for empirical research in writing.* New York: Longman.

McDorman, Todd. 2004. Promoting undergraduate research in the humanities: Three collaborative approaches. *CUR Quarterly* 25: 39–42.

Merkel, Carolyn Ash, and Shenda M. Baker. 2002. *How to mentor undergraduate researchers.* Washington, DC: Council on Undergraduate Research.

Nagda, B.A., Gregerman, S.R., Jonides, J., von Hippel, W., and Lerner, J.S. 1998. Undergraduate student-faculty partnerships affect student retention. *The Review of Higher Education* 22: 55–72.

National Conference on Peer Tutoring in Writing (NCPTW). nd. What is NCPTW? www.ncptw.org/aboutus

National Conferences on Undergraduate Research. nd. What is NCUR? http://www.ncur. org/ugresearch.htm.

National Conferences on Undergraduate Research. 2005. Joint statement of principles in support of undergraduate research, scholarship, and creative activities. http://www. ncur.org/ugresearch.htm

Newman, Glenn. 2007. Concocting a writing major: A recipe for success. *Composition Studies* 35 (1): 79–80.

North, Stephen M. 1987. *The making of knowledge in composition: Portrait of an emerging field.* Portsmouth: Boynton/Cook.

Pemberton, Michael A. 2003. The *Writing Lab Newsletter* as history: Tracing the growth of a scholarly community. In *The center will hold: Critical perspectives on writing center scholarship,* edited by Michael Pemberton and Joyce Kinkead. Logan: Utah State University Press.

Petrillo, Lauren. 2004. The visible rhetoric and composition of invisible antebellum female seminary students: Clary Seminary, Liberty, Missouri, 1855–1865. *Young Scholars in Writing* 1 (2): 15–24.

Reinvention Center. www7miami.edu/ftp/ricenter

Robillard, Amy. 2006. *Young Scholars* affecting composition: A challenge to disciplinary citation practices. *College English* 68: 253–270.

Rogers, V. Daniel. 2003. Surviving the culture shock of undergraduate research in the humanities. *CUR Quarterly* 23 (3): 132–35.

Schneider, Barbara. 2006. Ethical research and pedagogical gaps. *CCC* 58 (1): 70–88.

Schwalm, David. 2004. Re: undergraduate research & composition studies. WPA-L. https:// lists.asu.edu/cgi-bin/wa?A2=ind0407&L=WPA-L&P=R3379&1=WPA-L&9=A&I=-3&J= on&K=3&d=No+Match%3BMatch%3BMatches&z=4. Smagorinsky, Peter, ed. 2006. *Research on composition: Multiple perspectives on two decades of change.* New York: Teachers College.

Sommers, Nancy. 1980. Revision strategies of student writers and experienced adult writers. *CCC* 31: 378–388.

Steneck, Nicholas H. 2007. *ORI introduction to the responsible conduct of research.* Washington DC: Office of Research Integrity.

Tayko, Gail, and John Tassoni, eds. 1997. *Sharing pedagogies: Students and teachers write about dialogic practices.* Portsmouth, NH: Boynton/Cook.

Uffelman, Larry K. 1995. Victorian periodicals: Research opportunities for faculty-undergraduate research. *CUR Quarterly* 15: 207–208.

University of Missouri-Kansas City. Department of English. *Young Scholars in Writing* mission statement. http://cas.u*MKC*.edu/english/publications/youngscholarsinwriting/ missionstatement.html

Willison, John, and Kerry O'Regan. 2007. Commonly known, commonly not known, totally unknown: A framework for students becoming researchers. *Higher Education Research and Development* 26 (4): 393–409.

Yancey, Kathleen Blake. 2004. Made not only in words: Composition in a new key. *CCC* 56: 297–328.

Young, Richard E., Alton L. Becker, and Kenneth L. Pike. 1970. *Rhetoric: Discovery and change.* New York: Harcourt.

9

PEDAGOGY, LORE, AND THE MAKING OF *BEING*

Matthew Jackson

The first line of the Stephen North's introduction to *The Making of Knowledge in Composition* reads: "This book is about how knowledge is made in the field that has come to be called Composition" (1987, 1). By focusing on *how* people claim to know what they know, North distinguishes what he does from other works about composition that are concerned with *what* people claim to know about writing.

One of the important ways that North talks about the making of knowledge in composition is the everyday "how" of practitioner discourse he calls "lore." For North, lore is defined as, "the accumulated body of traditions, practices, and beliefs in terms of which Practitioners understand how writing is done, learned, and taught" (22). While I use the term *discourse* (which, for many readers, carries a more formal connotation), it is vital to highlight the fact that North feels that lore is primarily a matter of talk, that less formal kinds of talk are the most common, and that this common informal lore represents compositionist [practitioner] knowledge "at its most authentic" (51).

This is the kind of knowledge that is made in a tightly-knit community of neighbors as they talk about some of their most significant issues in a casual, across-the-fence kind of talk. It is what we now call, thanks to *The Office*, "water cooler" ways of knowing. For those of us who have worked outside of academia and shared information over the cubicle wall, it is not surprising that, for North, important types of lore take place informally (24), and yet these bodies of lore are clearly very "rich and powerful bodies of knowledge" (27). In harmony with North's view of lore, phenomenology, as a philosophical way of knowing, holds as one of its tenets that many of the most important ways of knowing are found in the most mundane of our interactions (this will become important below). Also similar to a phenomenological perspective is North's claim that "Lore is embodied in the more usual ways humans embody what they know" (29). As such, lore takes on profound implications for composition pedagogies and philosophies as North, in *MKC,* seeks to elevate lore to a place of respect in the pantheon of composition knowledge. In what follows, I will attempt to reiterate this goal, albeit from a stance that is *otherwise* than North's.

INTUITION AND JUDGMENT FOR COMPOSITION PHILOSOPHERS

I would like to pick up on North's use of the term *embodied* in his discussion of lore for compositionists. Considering compositionist lore as an embodied art in practice captures some of the intersubjective essence of the pedagogical relationship that can really only be studied, evaluated, and considered seriously in terms of the lived moment in which it happens. I say this because of the sense of agreement I have with North when he suggests that a pivotal point in practitioner authority—and, as I am arguing, for composition philosophers—is that we must be willing to take compositionists at their theoretical and pedagogical word concerning what is effective practice. As North puts it, if we cannot be "trusted as the best judges of what works and what doesn't," then we are not the best people to decide what to do pedagogically. For North, the inverse is also true, and to validate and trust practical inquiry and routine practice is to "accept that Practitioners can see or sense or feel signs of change that outsiders, and even students, cannot: that things are happening that require both involvement and an appropriate sensitivity to perceive" (50).

Composition practitioners and philosophers alike may have felt that their sense of personal judgment in their work is somewhat marginalized within the field of composition as well as in academia in general; we often feel that what we have to say, based on personal experience, thoughts, and feelings—even when formalized and published—is marginalized by those in authority. This issue seems to have attained a heightened sense of gravity and a serious degree of consequence as teaching and learning goals, methods, and outcomes have become more rigid and codified in a rubric-ridden environment of high-stakes testing and evaluation that has gained force and legitimacy in the throes of the current recession—particularly as administrators are constrained to make budget cuts based more on the quantity of objective data than on the quality of subjective findings. The knowledge that is being made and, *a fortiori,* the infinitely unique individuals involved in the making of being in composition cannot be reduced to calculated formulae.

Perhaps now—even as we are tempted to go with the economic and administrative flow and make our work seem more concretely valuable by assuming the status of a service industry for student-consumers paying for an education in a corporation-university—perhaps now is the time to dig in our individual and collective heels and stand up and speak out for the legitimacy and validity of our individual and intersubjective communal authority in determining the ways that the "what" and "how" of making knowledge is best taught and learned in the composition classroom.

While North doesn't think that compositionists do know, "in any exact way," what they are looking for in terms of pedagogical approaches and best teaching practices, North feels that "[we] mostly expect to know it when [we] see it. We may know we have found it because it 'feels right'; that is, it makes sense in terms of our experience" (45). I agree with North's claim here and would, based on North's assertions about practitioners, extend the argument to composition philosophers' modes of inquiry—that they are a type of art, most often a "combination of informed intuition and trial and error" (45). Indeed, North's view of practitioner and composition philosopher ways of knowing, from a phenomenological perspective, sounds a lot like the philosophical notion of intuition. North's definition of lore combined with intuition works importantly for my purposes here in arguing for the viability of composition practitioner and philosopher authority.

While I agree with North on the importance of intuition for practitioners and philosophers in composition, I have one point of disagreement with North's assessment of how intuition works for compositionists—particularly concerning the *amount* and *type* of autonomy he grants to the individual. While North admits that communal lore offers compositionists options, resources, and "perhaps some directional pressure" (28), he seems to feel that the individual finally decides—on his or her own—what to teach and how to teach it, including a self-assessment of the effectiveness of the teaching. And though I agree that teachers really do have a sense of what works best in the classroom, I'm neither willing to advocate a teacher-takes-all positionality nor a perspective of free-rei(g)n teaching—even with the additive move of critical self-reflexivity. For North, the individual compositionist grants final say as to what counts as knowledge or *knowing* (28) and, from my reading of North's book, the individual compositionist *ipso facto* also has the ability to say what counts as *being* as well. In my opinion, and this is the argument I will limn in the remainder of this chapter, individuals—and certainly compositionists—are intersubjective beings; the making of knowledge and, now, the making of *being*, are inherently intersubjective processes.

My argument here relies on the assumptions that we are "ourselves" only in that we are in relation to others; and, as infinitely unique as each one of us is, we only have independence and agency as an endowment of the other. My views here are influenced by the philosophy of Emmanuel Levinas; in particular I borrow heavily from his critique of autonomy and the self-interest of the being-for-itself in the world. Autonomy, in my reading of Levinas, is simply too dangerous in its tendency and its capacity to follow its own reason in fulfilling its own agenda, which can result in a good, but has tended historically to lead to the abuse of power. For Levinas, the view of *being* as relational is important for many reasons, the least of which is not the need to guard against being-for-itself. In reconciling the discussion above concerning compositionists following their own intuition, I would add that we can only be trustworthy compositionists as we intersubjectively triangulate our ways of *knowing* and *being*.

KNOWING AND BEING IN COMPOSITION

Levinas is best known as a philosopher of ethics, of ethics as first philosophy after which we constantly seek as a way of being—not an ethics as a moral code of the already known that tells us, categorically, how we should be. In considering Levinas's philosophy as a way to build on North's ideas, I will also try to make plain the ways North helps us to understand and make some practical sense of Levinas's elusive transcendental ethics.

North, in his focus on lore as the knowledge-making discourse of practitioners, implies an inherent aspect of relationality; this aspect is the intersubjectivity of the compositionist within various communities, including colleagues in our disciplines and areas of specialization, along with more literal communities where we live among neighbors and loved ones with whom we share our lives. But most importantly, the relational aspect of knowledge making in composition is the relationality we have with our students—the *pedagogical intersubjectivity* that is at the heart of our work in composition.

And yet, for all of North's concern with practitioner inquiry as a valuable form of knowledge in composition, his discussion is marked by a conspicuous absence of the student. That is, while the student and the pedagogical relationship are mentioned in passing and assumed in the discussion, the intersubjective pedagogical relationship between students and teacher is not discussed directly or in depth; it is more of a presence of an absence. The problem that arises from this absence is that there is neither an allowance for the serious consideration of an intersubjective pedagogical ethic that is necessary for a robust composition philosophy, nor an allowance for an effective practitioner. While North is able to speak of the making of knowledge, *MKC* falls silent on the subject of the making of being. So, even as North sought to uplift lore as the viable knowledge that emerges from pedagogy, it seems to be precisely his inattention to the intersubjectivity of the pedagogy—to the *making of being*—that, in my view, somewhat diminishes his conception of lore and its potential for practitioners and philosophers alike.

From a Levinasian perspective, the ethics of intersubjectivity are *a priori* to the pedagogical relationship, even as the pedagogical automatically brings the dimension of the ethical into question. I suggest that the ethical dimension of pedagogy demands that we ask different questions of North's work in *MKC*: rather than being concerned with the making of *knowledge* in composition, we turn our attention to concerns with the making of *being* in composition. The question of *who is being made by whom* in composition should give us pause. And even as we turn our attention to concerns about *being* rather than *knowing*, it is only right that, in this collection commemorating North's accomplishment in composing a book that helped give shape and meaning to our discipline, we acknowledge North's novel and controversial argument for conceiving of practitioner inquiry as a valuable form and way of *knowing*. And, I will argue, that what is assumed in the making of knowledge in composition is an implicit recognition of the value of the *making of being* in composition. What is pedagogy, after all, if not a contributive force in the making of being?

While questions about *knowing* and those about *being* are not mutually exclusive, there is significance in the apparently simple but profound differences between the two phrases "making *knowledge* in composition," and "making *being* in composition." Concerns about the making of knowledge follow the historical and philosophical primacy of epistemology; the quest and question of knowledge by the cogito has been the primary concern of philosophy, and subsequently of rhetoric and composition, for centuries. The phrase "making *being* in composition," on the other hand, suggests an ontological turn that points toward the notion of intersubjective ethics. (After all, it is in the curvature of intersubjective space that the significance of the making of being can best be explored.) In order to enhance the ethical aspect of lore, of pedagogy itself, and to suggest that ethical intersubjectivity is a *way* for composition practitioners and philosophers to know and to do our work—to *be and become* as compositionists— I draw on the unique and nuanced qualities of Levinas's philosophy.

REFIGURING BEING IN COMPOSITION: BEING AS RELATIONAL AND ETHICAL

In looking to ethical intersubjectivity as the foundation for a philosophy of being in composition, we necessarily turn toward the kinds of "beings" we *are* and the kinds of beings we help "make" as we do our work in composition. My line of argumentation here draws on the phenomenological tradition, particularly the work of Levinas and his radical notion of ethics as first philosophy. Ethics for Levinas is not a pregiven "known," but rather something after which we seek, intersubjectively. In my relationship with the Other, I am always already responsible and have an ethical obligation for the welfare of the Other. And it is here in this *a priori* sense of ethical intersubjectivity in pedagogical relationships that compositionists, *de facto*, are involved in the making of *being*.

Levinas's philosophy necessarily begins with assumptions about humanity that differ radically from conventional Western thinking. He argues that we are not autonomous beings of consciousness; rather, we are beings only because of our face-to-face relationships with others. We are relational beings and as such are inherently responsible for others; responsibility is "the essential, primary, and fundamental structure of subjectivity" (1985, 95). For Levinas, there is no escaping this responsibility, and it is this obligation that gives me my uniqueness as a being— not a being-for-myself, but a being-for-the-other. This responsibility is not grounded in the cognitive structure of my ego—not in my own ability to reason—but rather in the face-to-face relation with the Other. Further, the rupturing of my autonomy by the Other and the overflowing of any knowledge I might have of the Other keeps me from ever being sure about my own self and my own place (1974, 49).

Accordingly, the objection Levinas has with "self-reasoning being" is that there is nothing that the ego does not already know, including the Other; under the rubric of reason, I already have in my mind and can grasp the idea of the Other. My pedagogical (and therefore ethical) relationship with the Other is thus reduced to an objective assessment of what I think it should be. The danger with an ethics of egoism is that it has a tendency to become self-serving in terms of what Levinas calls the *conatus essendi*, the perseverance of "being-for-itself" (1974, 4–5, 118). Pedagogical responsibility, then, is not an objectifying comprehension of the face of the Other. Rather, the uniqueness of the face of the Other is "the way in which the other presents himself, an infinity exceeding *the idea of the other in me*," which opens my being to ways of knowing and being *otherwise*. Thus pedagogy is intersubjective, and knowing and being come from the other and bring me "more than I contain" (1996 50–51; italics added). To be in relation to the infinite in the face of the Other is to receive from the Other, to be taught, to learn (*enseignement*) from the Other; inasmuch as we learn from the Other that which we cannot learn by ourselves, the infinity of the Other puts into question the notion of being as the autonomous reasoning self.

A philosophy of composition pedagogy, grounded in a Levinasian intersubjective ethics, is opposed not only to the traditional "banking" model of pedagogy, in which the expert teacher "deposits" her knowledge in the "vaults" of her students' heads, but it also—in what I assume will be a more controversial move—eschews the notion that pedagogy's primary value is the production, through whatever means, of an assemblage of knowledge(s) that can be put to use in some utilitarian fashion. Instead, pedagogy is grounded in intersubjective ethics and regards the value of the very *process* of pedagogical interaction—of being in the moment of mutual edification—in which teacher and students *are beings-with-and-through-one-another*.

THE SAYING AND THE SAID OF COMMUNICATION IN COMPOSITION

From a phenomenological perspective, lore is the primary discursive means through which compositionists make, share, modify, and validate knowledge as composition practitioners and philosophers. In this perspective, lore has the teacher-student relationship as its primary concern. In recalling North's definition of lore as casual talk that serves to establish the lived, embodied experience of compositionists, it is necessary to make a brief distinction here between Levinas's use of the terms *Saying* and *Said*, where *the Saying* represents the infinity of ethical intersubjectivity and *the Said* represents the necessary discursive modes we use in concrete communication with each other. Considering lore, then, as an embodied "intersubjective saying" presents the difficult paradox wherein both the form and the content of an ethical Saying are necessary but always uncertain as they appear in the Said. In contrast to the Western scholarly tradition that prizes the clarity of a "thematizing consciousness" that produces certainty in language with the tool of comprehension (*to grasp*) in representation and interpretation (e.g., research paper requirements), Levinas creates a discursive discomfort with his premise that we can never be totally certain about meaning in language. Perhaps if we approach the tasks of thinking, writing, and performing intersubjective communication in pedagogy with the kind of hard work, hesitancy, and humility that Levinas requires, we might allow for new ways of being *otherwise* in composition pedagogy.

Communication for Levinas is not the safe assuredness of a universal system of signs used to represent reality as a truth of the intentional consciousness. In other words, communication cannot be represented, as it often is, as the "sender" who gives a "message" to the "receiver" as if through a conduit that ensures mutual understanding.

> Communication with the other can be transcendent only as a dangerous life, a fine risk to be run. These words take on their strong sense when, instead of only designating the lack of certainty, they express the gratuity of sacrifice. In a fine risk to be run, the word "fine" has not been thought about enough. It is as antithetical to certainty, and indeed to consciousness. (1974, 120)

Communication with the Other for Levinas signifies a risky intersubjective adventure; communication with the Other, for whom I am asymmetrically responsible, is necessary and risky because it is the representation of *substitution* where substitution is understood simply yet profoundly as self-sacrifice in my responsibility for the Other. Believing that communication is indispensable to ethical intersubjectivity, Levinas claims that responsibility can only happen when communication is the performative signification of substitution as responsibility of the one-for-the-other, a modality or way of being-for-the-other.

Even as we are thinking about Other(s) for whom we are responsible and deciding how to distribute our responsibility, we are allowing our ego—our consciousness—to slip in and take control of our being. Levinas, in my interpretation, claims that we are always already in an intersubjective positionality—we do not choose whether or not to "communicate" with the other—that happens, *de facto*, in my being-in-the-world. My "choice" is in the *way*—the degree to which—I communicate with the other; and the only way I can communicate responsibly is in *being*-for-the-other. And while responsibility can take the form of some great material deed or sacrifice, more often than not the ethical saying of intersubjective responsibility takes place as a simple kindness (even the little there is) in our greeting of students, getting to know their names, lecturing respectfully, evaluating and responding in our response-ability to their writing, making time to consult with each other face to face, or in the Saying of a kind word at the end of the day.

Levinas submits that the Saying is represented in my *being* responsible for the Other, my substitution for the Other, which is "signification par excellence" (1974, 117). More simply stated, this means that the Saying is made manifest in my very *way* of being responsible in my intersubjectivity, including what I say, have said, and do not say; Saying is said *in the signification of my being*. Saying is the term that Levinas uses to refer to *a priori* responsibility of the one-for-the-other: "The responsibility for another is precisely a saying prior to anything said" (7). Saying is a "pre-original language, the responsibility of one for the other, the substitution of one for the other" (43). Concerning substitution, Saying can be thought of as exposure to an Other; to *say* is to "approach a neighbor" and is "a condition for all communication" (47–48). In terms of an intersubjective pedagogy for compositionists, the notion of Saying puts me in a relationship of responsibility prior to my sense of myself as an ego.

My coming to terms with this responsibility and my approach to Others is the "fine risk of saying" that makes one vulnerable in "the exposure of one to the other" (Levinas 1974, 94). That is, the alterity of the Other ruptures my interiority and I open myself, in passivity, to my obligation for the other. In this sense, "saying is the risky uncovering of oneself" that breaks up the interiority of the self, that exposes the self to traumas, to vulnerability. (48). In this state of being we are open to learning from the Other, from that which is beyond our grasp. Being open to the infinity of the Saying of the ethical is a pedagogical positionality that might be an appropriate approach to the saying of the composition philosopher; as such, Saying should not be thought of in terms of an accessible realm of the infinite as a correlation of the yet-to-be-said. In other words, the relationship between the Saying and the Said should not be thought of as "ethical truths" waiting to be understood through better reasoning and more dialogue: these are not truths that can be discovered, comprehended and written down—captured—in the Said.

A critical point in the remainder of my discussion here is to establish an understanding that while ethics is first philosophy and intersubjectivity is *a priori*, they do not strip us of agency; agency is vital to pedagogical action. The key is that while making the best use of reason and knowledge that I can, I must remain open to the rupturing of the infinite in the alterity of the Other. In doing so, I act as a witness of the infinite uniqueness of the Other, even as I witness my own sense of subjectivity as I am invested with that agency from beyond myself. Levinas describes the intersubjective call of responsibility for the Other as a voice that "comes from the other shore," a voice that interrupts my sense of being-for-myself and forbids the return of the self to itself—giving me a sense of self, but forever putting the autonomy of my being into question (1974, 183).

I take pedagogical action, then, in accordance with what Levinas calls the "ethical voice of conscience" that is "not the simple innateness of an instinct or the intentionality in which the *I think* would continue to have the last word." The inner voice is not one that reverts back to the self—to the intuition of the same and the known of the self—but rather one that is informed by and shaped by the Other. My ethical subjectivity is thus heteronomous and my judgments and actions are informed by a multiplicity of others (1999, 34–35). The "inner voice" of ethical subjectivity is that "sense" that causes people to take action in the name of goodness without "knowing," as in having a certain, reasonable knowledge of what is "right" at the time. The teacher's responsibility for the other is thus a *way* for there to be glory and infinitude in pedagogy and a way for all compositionists to be philosophers of a kind.

In my very responsibility for the Other as a teacher, I am "as a sign given to the other of this very signification"; the "here I am" puts me in the service of others who look at me, see me, hear me in "the sound of my voice, the figure of my gesture—the saying itself." Teaching thus becomes a voice of witnessing, a voice bearing witness to that which is beyond what can be laid out in a theme of the Said as mere words. As a witness I can, in an intersubjective Saying, pronounce peace to the Other and exercise my responsibility to the Other. This is the teacher's ultimate responsibility: to open up pedagogy to the infinite where "glorification is saying, that is, a sign given to the other, peace announced to the other, responsibility for the other, to the extent of substitution" (Levinas 1974, 147–149). In this way, "peace is under my responsibility. . . . I alone am to wage it, running a fine risk, dangerously" (167).

CONCLUSION: A PROLEGOMENA FOR COMPOSITION PHILOSOPHERS AND THE MAKING OF BEING

There is a niggling in my soul urging me to apologize for the moral over-tones of this essay—as if I know what we should do and how we should be in composition. In North's words, my discussion makes it seem as though those who want to do the right thing will simply follow my advice (113). I hope I have made it clear that a Levinasian approach to re-membering ourselves as composition philosophers is a way of being-with-others that would have us face our pedagogical relationships with humility as we con-sider the ethical primacy in the making of knowledge and, *a fortiori*, the making of being. I don't pretend that the set of assumptions and asser-tions I have set forth are any "better" than others; but I do think they are worthy of serious consideration (even as I share North's skepticism about how many people are actually listening to these philosophical exhorta-tions) (92–93).

Inasmuch as composition pedagogy is the professional anchor for most rhetoric and composition faculty in English departments, in order to validate and give credence to our most basic practices for our sake, for our students', and for the sake of the discipline itself, we need to step back and look at the core aspect of what we do: we teach stu-dents by engaging in pedagogical, relational, intersubjective encoun-ters. While many may look down upon composition as an unsophisti-cated service community necessary to higher education, such dismissal recedes if composition is considered *otherwise* than through conven-tional academic lenses that objectify and measure one's worth in terms of market-driven types of knowledge production. The worth and value of compositionists simply cannot be calculated under the dictates of current institutional constraints. The significance of who we are and what we do can be found, somewhat ironically, in the seemingly mun-dane practices of teaching writing if—and this is crucial—if pedagogy is reconsidered as an intersubjective ethical phenomenon; that is, the making of being.

I submit that a Levinasian intersubjective ethics is a way for us to think about being compositionists engaged in the making of being as the merging of pedagogical practices with the pursuit of the philosophically ethical. Such a notion of pedagogical ethics is not a process of applying already known Kantian, Aristotelian, or any other model of ethics to our pedagogies. Rather, the ethical in a Levinasian sense is the intersubjec-tive striving for an ethics that is pursued in human relationships that are never human enough—there are always ways of being-in-the-world with others that are more ethical.[1]

REFERENCES

Levinas, Emmanuel. 1969. *Totality and infinity.* Pittsburgh, PA: Duquesne University Press.

———. 1974. *Otherwise than being or beyond essence.* Translated by Alphonso Lingis. Pittsburgh, PA: Duquesne University Press.

———. 1985. *Ethics and infinity.* Translated by Richard A. Cohen. Pittsburgh, PA: Duquesne University Press.

———. 1996. *Basic philosophical writings.* Edited by Adriaan T. Peperzak, Simon Critchley, and Robert Bernasconi. Bloomington: Indiana University Press.

———. 1999. *Alterity and transcendence.* Translated by Michael B. Smith. New York: Columbia University Press.

North, Stephen M. 1987. *The making knowledge in composition: Portrait of an emerging field.* Portsmouth, NH: Heinemann.

---

1.   I would like to thank Gary Hatch, Brian Jackson, Kristine Hansen, and the editors for their helpful feedback on this chapter.

10

PRACTICE AS INQUIRY, STEPHEN M. NORTH'S TEACHING AND CONTEMPORARY PUBLIC POLICY

Patricia A. Dunn

At a time when policymakers are circling higher education with No-Child-Left-Behind sound bites such as "student learning outcomes" (Spellings 4), one of North's central questions from *The Making of Knowledge in Composition (MKC)* (1987) is more critical than ever: "What *do* people know about the teaching of writing that they didn't know fifty or a hundred years ago, and how do they know it?" (Preface; italics in original). With composition handling much of the writing that goes on in college, that field will be a prime candidate for the same kind of public interrogation K–12 schools are suffering right now in the clutches of No Child Left Behind legislation, interrogations already beginning to play out in accreditation processes in colleges of education and coming soon to a discipline near you. North was correct when he observed in 1987 that writing "tends to be far more vulnerable to non-academic fields than most other fields" (375). No one blames economics departments for students' overextended credit cards, or philosophy departments for students' drunk driving, but everyone blames departments of English and writing for students' perceived problems with composing.

It is only by a conscious effort to sort out the epistemological beliefs influencing our teaching that compositionists today can make informed decisions about best approaches to teaching and assessing writing—and to make the case for such approaches to a skeptical public that will soon be posing unwelcome questions to the professoriate. How *do* we know our students are learning? Can we demonstrate this new knowledge persuasively to those who will ask for such evidence? Answering those and other questions demands that we know what we do and what we value in our teaching. And as this chapter shows, Stephen North—in *MKC* and in his own teaching—exhibits attitudes toward students and employs pedagogical practices that can help composition answer those questions.

Examining those attitudes again in the twenty-first century, when they are sorely needed, can help composition formulate more convincing arguments to influence public policy affecting the teaching of writing.

PRACTICE AS INQUIRY IN NORTH'S RESEARCH

North's key title phrase, "the making of knowledge," already asserts a clear epistemological position: that people make knowledge. More than two decades later, this position is still puzzling to those who, subconsciously perhaps, see knowledge as fixed, something to be known by experts and merely distributed, who see teaching as telling, assessment as reciting. Similarly, North's recommendations for "methodological consciousness" (370) may be incomprehensible to those who see teaching as a simple distributive model, practitioners as incapable of theorizing, and practice as unworthy of analysis.

North's attention to, analysis of, and high expectations for practice are everywhere in *MKC*. He writes early on, "Writing and the teaching of writing are activities as complex as any human beings undertake" (30). On at least five occasions in this text, he refers to teaching as an "art" (23, 29, 35, 36, 45). He acknowledges "a general erosion in Practitioner authority" (50), and he laments a "devaluation of lore," (72). He wishes a higher percentage of teaching were "practice-as-inquiry" (36), though he understands that "the conditions under which most Practitioners work" make that inquiry "very much harder" (36). He criticizes the historians for not using teachers and students as informants for their research (74), and Braddock et al. for not recognizing "practice as knowledge-making at all" (325). He labels as harsh Janet Emig's characterization of composition teaching in the high schools as "essentially a neurotic activity" (326), and he goes on to list many others who have a knee-jerk contempt for high-school teachers and college instructors of writing (325–29).

Although composition is a field, North says, that is "concerned with the ways writing is done, taught, and learned," (364), he points out that "the modern version of the field is founded, really, on the subversion of that practical tradition" (364). Near the end of the book, he argues that practitioners will need "to become methodologically aware" while the scholars, the researchers, and the rest "must treat practice with much greater respect" (372). He argues not only for "methodological pluralism" among all the camps, but writes that the field "with its back turned more firmly than ever on the potential of practice as knowledge-making, promises to be a feeble Composition indeed" (368). Many college administrators and political leaders most distinctly do *not* view teaching as an art, let alone as intellectual inquiry of any kind. North, however, sees instruction, if done consciously, as both an art and as an activity requiring complex epistemological analysis. Over twenty years after *MKC* was published, North's view of teaching still sounds almost radical. The freshness of his view, well into the twenty-first century, is a sad commentary on the still-too-common view of teaching as an enterprise absent of theory.

Throughout *MKC*, North argues for methodological consciousness. That is, whether knowledge makers are doing case studies, think-aloud protocols, ethnographies, philosophies, hermeneutical analysis, or other work, they should be aware that their method is one among many, that it is not the only way to research or make knowledge. In addition, methodological consciousness can and should be extended to practice, which is what North means when he calls for more "practice as inquiry" (33). He devotes pages thirty-three to fifty-five to a discussion of this concept, and he returns to it again and again throughout the text. According to North, for practice to be considered inquiry, it must produce "new" knowledge (33). Practice can be called inquiry only under these conditions:

(a) when the situation cannot be framed in familiar terms, so that any familiar strategies will have to be adapted for use;

(b) when, although the situation is perceived as familiar, standard approaches are no longer satisfactory, and so new approaches are created for it; or

(c) when both situation and approach are non-standard. (33)

North estimates that practice becomes inquiry only about 10 percent of the time, mostly because of "the impossible numbers" most practitioners face. He acknowledges that many times, perhaps most times, teaching is "at best, a craft" since "the time and energy required to respond to practice as inquiry are mostly devoured by the impossible numbers" (34).

In the same way Mina Shaughnessy's *Errors and Expectations* was remembered, according to North, more for its "vision" than for its exercises (48), North's *MKC* should be studied more often than it is for its respectful, theoretically-informed vision regarding practice. Yes, the text is highly prized for its analysis of more conventional makers of knowledge: the historians, the experimentalists, and so on. North's substantial attention to practice, however, is often misinterpreted as negative. But when he critiques teaching lore, he does so because of his high standards for what practice should be, for what writing pedagogy can be, for his dismay at how teaching has been (and still is) discounted and disrespected in the academy.

PRACTICE AS INQUIRY IN NORTH'S TEACHING

As we have seen, in *MKC*, North argues that professionals in composition should be "methodologically aware" (372), including practitioners. In other words, all knowledge makers should be conscious enough of their theoretical assumptions to reflect upon whether their theories are truly consistent with their work, whether it be in a laboratory, a library archive, or a classroom. What if we had a snapshot of North's own teaching circa 1987 and could see if he practiced what he preached? Would Professor North's teaching qualify as "practice-as- inquiry" (36) as Stephen M. North defined that phrase in *MKC?*

I was a doctoral student in North's graduate course, Introduction to Composition Theory, in 1988, just after *MKC* was published. I experienced firsthand North's unconventional pedagogy. Class projects included a complex "jigsaw" of cooperative groups (in which students become experts on a topic and circulated to other groups), major collaborative projects, both written and oral, and intricate, student-created visual representations of the field. I also realized—though not until years later—that the instructor's own deeply held beliefs about writing, learning, and knowledge consistently supported his choices regarding course design.

North's book demonstrates a deep respect for teaching, a call for methodological consciousness regarding all methods of inquiry, including practice. As someone who has seen North teach, I argue that his 1988 course demonstrated the methodological consciousness of its designer *and* that it was an example of practice as inquiry, a claim he has never made, but one I am making here. This serious attention to pedagogy, this alertness regarding what intellectual tasks we ask students to do and how we'll know if they're learning, is still rare, still needed.

Why does it matter that North devotes so much space and passion to practice in *MKC?* So what that he taught a theoretically informed graduate class in composition theory at about the same time as his book came out? To begin with, he was clearly thinking though his pedagogy in the same way he was asking others to think through their modes of inquiry and how those modes meshed with, or departed from, others' ways of making knowledge. Also, North's call for more practice as inquiry is a call for instructors to be more methodologically conscious of why they make the choices they do regarding course content, project design, assessment, and use of students' time. His pedagogy in the course I describe in the next section meets North's definition of practice as inquiry because it fits into his category *b*: "when, although the situation is perceived as familiar, standard approaches are no longer satisfactory, and so new approaches are created for it" (33). Although the situation may have been familiar—he had taught graduate courses in composition theory before—the standard approaches used then (and still used, in many graduate courses) must have been for him "no longer satisfactory": lecturing to new graduate students about course material, having them read reams of material and then attempt to make sense of it in a large, teacher-led class discussion, requiring them to write a conventional research paper on a course-related topic, and so forth. The new approaches he created for this class placed his practice into the category of "inquiry," demonstrated in the carefully-written syllabus and the complex, interrelated projects.

The next section devotes much space and analysis to one class North taught in 1988. I do so for several reasons. Of all the many valuable classes I took at Albany, North's remains the most vivid more than twenty years later. While *MKC* affected many people across the country, comparatively few people know about North's teaching, though it influenced a substantial number of Albany graduates who have since gone on to direct writing programs, writing centers, and writing-across-the-curriculum/writing-in-the-disciplines (WAC/WID) programs; to teach composition and rhetoric all over the country; and to direct dozens of doctoral dissertations. So I hope to provide a glimpse of a graduate course he taught about the time *MKC* was published in order to help others in the field see how North's classroom was an example of methodologically conscious practice. It reflected the connection between theory and practice, as well as the respect for, and the intellectual engagement with, teaching that he advocates in his book. And because both of them are so important for composition—and for more enlightened public policy concerning the teaching of writing in secondary education—I hope to foreground practice as inquiry in this course and to show how well-theorized practice can be transformative.

INTRODUCTION TO COMPOSITION THEORY, SPRING 1988

I have, sitting on my desk in front of me as I write this, the dog-eared and rapidly yellowing syllabus of a graduate course I took with Stephen M. North in the spring of 1988, just after *MKC* was published in 1987. The course was called Introduction to Composition Theory (AEng 508) and took place in Humanities 129 at SUNY Albany (as the University at Albany was known at that time). North's syllabus is extensive for a syllabus even today: six pages, single spaced, in purple ink, a common feature of "dittoes" of that era, documents prepared on typewriters and then run through nostril-clearing mimeograph machines.

The reading list for that graduate course was as varied as it was crushing: nine books and sixteen journal articles, not including substantial background reading required to complete three major oral and written projects, plus an exam. The books were by James Berlin, Robert Connors, Lisa Ede and Andrea Lunsford, Peter Elbow, E.D. Hirsch (juxtaposed to George Dillon's critique of Hirsch), James Moffett, Mike Rose, Mina Shaughnessy, and North's own book. The articles were from *College Composition and Communication*, *College English*, and *Research in the Teaching of English*, all on reserve. We read people whose work North must have admired and people he obviously took issue with, but we could make only educated guesses about his estimations. He posed problems and we worked on them. He was teaching in the traditional way only in that he possessed a vast knowledge of the field, but he shared that knowledge with us not by yammering on for three hours every week, but through challenging, student-centered course design and collaborative, multigenred, multimodal projects. He invited us to make our own knowledge as we read widely, researched further, collaborated in our groups, and completed projects that included writing, presenting, graphing, discussing, circulating among groups, visualizing, and so forth. In that course, our brain cells went to the gym, exercising sets of muscles we didn't know we had.

This focus on students making knowledge instead of the teacher distributing it emerges from theoretical, epistemological concepts still underused in many educational institutions today, from universities on down, where so many assessments try to measure lower-order tasks that can be easily scored by underpaid readers or machines. The projects described in the next several sections were designed with a methodological consciousness regarding practice, in a manner theoretically consistent with epistemological beliefs about what constitutes knowledge, about how people learn, about complex manifestations of that learning. In the last two decades, composition has moved even further away from practice, a direction North warned against in *MKC*; the next sections of this essay point the spotlight back onto practice and the methodological consciousness it deserves.

The "Pick a Theorist" Project

In one project from this class, we were grouped via lottery with two other people. This trio was to research a particular influential figure, a theorist in composition/rhetoric. That is, we were to read a large, representative sample of that person's books, articles, and chapters, dividing the texts among ourselves as we saw fit. The listed theorists were Edward P. J. Corbett, James Kinneavy, James Britton, Ann Berthoff, Linda Flower and John Hayes, Donald Graves, Lee Odell, and George Hillocks. We were to prepare both a written and oral report on our findings, the latter to be a pedagogical experience of the kind that our particular theorist/scholar would be most likely to design, given his or her epistemological views and theories of learning.

The lots we drew for this project landed me happily in a group with Mary Ann Cain and George Kalamaras, friends then and now. The three of us were to research the theories and research of Lee Odell. I still have and still use the articles I read by Odell (one of the most underappreciated researchers in composition). I still use versions of North's teach-in-the-style-of-this-theorist assignment, and I try to emulate the detailed requirements for and description of the project. Here is how a portion of this "Pick a theorist" assignment was described in the syllabus:

> The object of the presentation, remember, is to make the particular writer accessible to an audience that will mostly not have read him or her; and, as far as possible, to fit that writer's work into the material we'll cover in the regular readings. To that end, flat-out lectures—however brilliant—are NOT an option. Use handouts, activities, skits, psycho-drama, video-tapes, overhead projectors, music—anything you can think of—just don't talk at us. I strongly urge you to do at least one full rehearsal.

Dividing up Odell's work among the three of us, we read just about everything he had ever written or cowritten. Nothing at that time was available online. We scoured the library for his coedited books on assessment, haunted the bound-volume section in the bowels of the university library for his older articles, and pestered the interlibrary loan desk for his more obscure articles and book chapters. We drove across the

Hudson River from Albany to Troy to interview Odell in his office at Rensselaer Polytechnic Institute.

Having amassed all this information about Odell, including an audio-tape of the interview, we now had to figure out how to teach Odell's theories to the class who had not read this work, and also to write up a paper that captured his theories and our thoughts about those theories. The three of us met several times at my home or theirs, and we brain-stormed how we could do a presentation without the "straight lecture" North had warned us against. We had to be methodologically conscious of how our forty-five-minute presentation intersected with Odell's theo-ries of teaching writing. We had to extrapolate the practice from the theory, or the theory from the practice, discussed in the articles.

One *English Journal* article Odell had cowritten with junior-high-school teacher Joanne Cohick encapsulated and demonstrated his view (adapted from Young, Becker, and Pike's tagmemic theories) about the importance of perspective change in making writing more sophisticated. To help stu-dents become more aware of the importance of perspective change, Odell and Cohick had students "watch their favorite TV program and count the number of times the camera changed focus (i.e., angle and distance) within a time span of two minutes" (1975, 49). In his chapter, "Measuring Changes…" in the book *Evaluating Writing*, Odell describes a similar exer-cise regarding the "intellectual process" of perspective change (1977, 107). Students take a magazine picture and then isolate different sections of it by blocking out other sections with construction paper. Students can see the effect of isolating a significant piece of the picture such as a face or an eye. This mechanical manipulation of perspective should theoretically help students experiment with perspective change in their writing (128). To demonstrate (not lecture on) this feature of Odell's theory regarding perspective change, we first used a folk tale that demonstrated views from different perspectives and had our classmates discuss shifts in focus and how a camera might move if filming the story. We also played a snippet of the audiotaped interview we had conducted with Odell.

However, the pièce de résistance of our presentation was the now-classic scene from the 1983 film *Risky Business*, in which Tom Cruise, as Joel Goodson living large while his parents are away, dances around in his underwear to "That Old Time Rock and Roll." There are several per-spective changes in that clip. First, in the opening bars of the Bob Seger tune, we see Joel slide into the doorway frame, his socks like skates on the polished wood floors. Then we see him dance all through the living room, air guitar in hand, climbing on the furniture, dropping to his knees, and spinning on his back on the floor. In the very last shot of that scene, however, the perspective switches to the front lawn, where the dancing figure, framed by the window, is now miniscule. The speaker-blasting fantasy was larger than life and completely consuming while the camera was in the living room; from a distance the same scene looks silly and small. Someone describing this same scene from these two different perspectives would be writing about very different events. This clip was a perfect way to teach Odell's theory about the importance of perspective change to people who hadn't read all his work.

This multigenred, collaborative project helped me understand and remember to this day Odell's theories and practices. Not only did this project require substantial research, but we were also placed into an authentic, rhetorical situation, requiring us to translate pages of theoretical readings into an accessible presentation for a particular group of peers who had not read the same material. This project design, a result of practice as inquiry, demonstrates a carefully considered approach that would be an effective way of getting a large class of composition neophytes deeply attuned to the theories and resultant practices representative of a substantial part of the field at that time.

This unusual assignment also exemplifies methodological consciousness: going beyond ruminations about theory to demonstrate how theory might be demonstrated methodologically. Experimenting with theoretically informed practice, which North did with this project, is a more difficult step than many instructors are willing to take, or willing to risk. Attention to classroom practice leaves the teacher/scholar fairly vulnerable, since the concreteness of teaching, especially teaching that challenges widely held assumptions about learning, makes it more open to critique than theorizing alone will allow. Taking the time to be methodologically conscious about practice is also risky because of the low status of teaching in the academy, a point North emphasized in *MKC*.

Graphing the Field

Another intellectual task that illustrated the methodological consciousness of its designer was a classroom activity. Near the end of the semester, after we had read a vast number of books and articles, we were told to chart, graph, or otherwise represent groups or scholars/theorists/researchers in composition, showing where their theories intersected, overlapped, or departed from one another. I found this task excruciatingly difficult.

In that classroom, there were two large blackboards running the length of the wall. At the height of this in-class exercise, a dozen or so graduate students were covering these boards with lines, circles, and arrows. They were arguing with one another, erasing lines, redrawing them, and drawing loops and boxes around and through the names and theories. After the chalk dust settled, they then explained the organized chaos they had produced on the board, and the class heard many insights and analyses regarding the work of Connors, Kinneavy, Shaughnessy, Lunsford, Flower and Hayes, and the rest. We had read all their work, but this chalkboard extravaganza was a way to grapple with their theories and research and practice and to see what they had in common and how they were different, to conceptualize trends, chart problems, connect studies, and juxtapose practices in composition. This challenging, sometime raucous activity was also a way for us to see where we fit, theoretically and pedagogically, into the web on the board. This exercise made us both learners and teachers, playing with concepts, exploring the dialectical potential of composition theories.

This activity too is an example of practice as inquiry as North defines it in *MKC*. That is, it must have been a "new approach" to helping graduate students visualize different geographies of the field, when the usual approaches were "no longer satisfactory" (33). In the humanities, visual representation is often viewed as less intellectually rigorous, less worthy of respect than is syllabically dense prose. Therefore, the newness and messiness of that chalkboard activity, coupled with the initial puzzlement with which its announcement was greeted by doctoral students, speaks to its experimental quality, the risk its designer was willing to take in applying epistemological assumptions to his real classroom.

The Jigsaw Reports

Another major project from that class—this one massive in terms of the amount of work it required—also plunged us deeply into the emerging field of composition. Each group of five was to research a number of composition journals, write a report on our findings, and deliver an oral report, not to the class but to a small group of other students. Then we'd move, jigsaw fashion (with one person giving and gathering information at one group), to another group. For this project, we were to read a large representative sample of articles from a number of years. We were to research how the journal began, who founded it, what it covered, who wrote for it, and how it had changed since its beginning. It was a forum analysis of the kind James Porter (1986) describes—and a huge amount of work. The jigsaw format allowed us to report our findings in a more intimate small group and ask questions in a more civilized fashion than the large group would have provided. By changing groups often, we heard a number of short, interactive accounts of a cross section of journals without hogging endless hours of class time.

Such a design required a leap of faith on the part of the instructor and, again, resulted from a consciousness of method on North's part, a rendering of theory into practice. Because he could not sit in on all the groups, he depended on students to be makers of knowledge. It was well-considered use of class time, built upon substantial research outside of class. By seeing citations of scholars over and over and perusing the Works Cited in these articles, we learned even more about where to turn for further research, who was who in this young field, the variety of issues it addressed, the controversies it debated, and what other research we ought to read. In addition to helping us learn a vast amount of theory and practice, we also learned about the subfields in composition: writing centers, WAC/WID, creative writing, writing in the two-year college, writing in the first-year composition course (FYC), basic writing, workplace writing, community literacy, and so forth. It was a smart design for graduate students, a way to get us up to speed very quickly on the geography of the field, its histories and main researchers, its flagship journals and its more modest, specialized ones. We had to roll up our sleeves and sift through dozens of articles from different publications, to pick up the journals in our hands, to make connections and judgments, to see trends and problems in contemporary journals, and to watch how composition professionals grappled with controversies in the past.

It was a smart design for the professor, too. Having recently finished *MKC*, North could have easily lectured to us every week on the hundreds of books and articles with which he was currently so familiar. However, his methodological consciousness about teaching, his knowledge that people require active engagement to learn higher-order concepts, kept him from simply "delivering" knowledge. We had to solve problems, make connections, analyze, critique, and compare concepts, theories, and practices—all intellectual tasks we would need as compositionists. The results of this student research kept the professor a learner as well. As twenty pairs of eyes read through both archived and current composition journals, he continued to learn about this rapidly expanding field, and he could revisit canonical articles through new eyes.

This theoretically refreshing idea—that teachers can and do learn from students—is absent in contemporary public policy regarding education and curriculum development. This idea is not significantly evident even in the academy, where for over forty years we have known about Paulo Freire's recommendation that learning be "co-intentional," (1973, 56) that is, that it should flow both ways, with teachers also learning from their students.

METHODOLOGICAL CONSCIOUSNESS AND UNCONVENTIONAL PRACTICES

Those who rely primarily on conventional lectures and traditional research papers may not understand the preparation involved in designing a course with such elaborate, multigenred, interrelated projects. They may not be sufficiently aware of their own approach to see it as *an* approach rather than as *the* default way of running a course. The teacher-centered approach is a feature of "banking concept" teaching critiqued by Freire: the professor passes information along, top down, to passive students who supposedly absorb this knowledge, unchanged. If such professors understand and embrace the implications of this transmission model, then perhaps they are being pedagogically self-aware, but they may not be fully conscious of how much or how little their students are learning for the long haul. If learning does not occur at the level they would like it to, assuming their assessments are valid, they may blame the students or the difficulty of the material, but never the design of the course. The intellectual tasks we encountered in North's class, on the other hand, are methodologically consistent with the view that people learn best by being actively involved in research, synthesis, and analysis. They construct new knowledge by working with classmates and with the teacher/scholar in Vygotsky's "zone of proximal development" (1978), an intellectual task above them but not, with the guidance of the instructor, beyond their reach.

In 1988, these collaborative assignments, jigsaw presentations, and nonprint confrontations with theories and models of learning were unusual and new, even to me, and I had gone to school in the 1970s, when it was not unusual to have writing assignments inspired by a Simon and Garfunkel song, a piece of modern art, or long moments of yoga-like silence. I thought North's class reflected great changes in pedagogical method in the years between my college graduation and my return to graduate school. But the courses I've taken and observed since then—with the exception of other excellent classes taught at Albany in that era by Lil Brannon, Judith Fetterley, and C.H. Knoblauch—are still overwhelmingly lecture based. What's wrong with lectures? Maybe nothing, if all students are actively listening. But in the lectures I've heard and observed, the professor is lecturing, the material is being covered, and the chapters are receding into the past. The students, however, are just not all that rapt. They're not learning if they're daydreaming, dozing, or checking their text messages. In all the controversies that occupy people who research pedagogy, there is no disagreement about the importance of students' active engagement in their own learning. If North used these methods in doctoral courses, with students who would most likely pay attention to lectures, then these methods should be used with all students. So why don't more professors use jigsaws, debates, student-led discussion, visual representation, cooperative and collaborative projects? I don't think it's because professors make a conscious decision to reject student-centered teaching. I just don't think they think about teaching very much.

They may think about the reading selections for the class. They may spend many well-intentioned hours marking up papers or meeting with students during office hours. They are good people who no doubt take their teaching seriously. However, their attitude about teaching places it outside the realm of that which can be theorized. *Intellectual inquiry* into how knowledge gets made and whether or not the design of their course is theoretically consistent with their views of how people learn, is just not something they have been educated to consider.

Perhaps they do not think of teaching as something that *can* be theorized. They may theorize the interpretation of the works they use in their class. They may theorize different approaches to the historical documents or other textual artifacts connected with their subject matter. But they do not view their class as itself an artifact worthy of being theorized. As North points out so often in *MKC*, teaching is simply not valued in the academy. He is willing to say what many in higher education would deny:

> Moreover, at the colleges and the universities where class sizes and teaching loads are usually the smallest, institutional priorities—in particular, a low regard, at least in terms of professional advancement, for teaching—undermine the chances that instructors will make the effort required to develop contributions to lore by this means [practice as inquiry]. (35)

Although there are exceptions—institutions that really do value and seriously evaluate teaching, and certainly individuals across disciplines who do take it seriously—teaching in too many institutions still comes in far below scholarship and publication when faculty are evaluated and grants are distributed. For instance, my university recently announced a grant of $5,000 for an interdisciplinary, interinstitutional conference, Conversations in the Disciplines. The guidelines for these Intercampus Scholarly Conferences, funded by the State University of New York, stated: "The emphasis of the program is *scholarly and creative development* [italics in original] rather than administrative, curricular, or instructional matters." The adjectives "scholarly and creative" are clearly juxtaposed to "instructional" matters, which are lumped in with "administrative" and "curricular." So the assumption here is that there can be no scholarship and no creative development on "instructional matters." The writers of the call carefully underlined "scholarly and creative," and just in case readers had any funny ideas about applying that phrase to teaching, they added a clarifying phrase specifically excluding pedagogy. They wanted to make sure they wouldn't find themselves reading any proposals about *that.*

Here's another example of how pedagogy is viewed as a contaminant. In New York State, to get English 7–12 teaching certification, a student needs a certain number of "content" courses and a certain number of "pedagogy" courses. A course in composition theory must be described very carefully in order for it to "count" as a "content" course. If the words *teaching, pedagogy,* or *practice* come in contact with the course title, eyebrows are raised, disinfectant cans are retrieved, and the offender is removed from the vicinity of the "content" (literature) courses.

One of the main arguments in *MKC* is that teaching should get more respect, that it should be grounded in inquiry and done by thinking, reflective practitioners who face challenging situations with serious analysis and methodological self-consciousness, who are aware when learning is not happening and, instead of blaming their students, know how to pose critical questions about their own methodologies. I wish to extend North's larger argument regarding methodological self-consciousness and apply it beyond the conventional borders of the field, as wide as those borders currently are. Yes, we should respect each other's work, encourage inquiry in our practice. We should also share our vast knowledge of invention, critical consciousness, one-on-one tutoring, peer response, and rhetoric with others who are teaching writing. Composition can find its heart again by fully embracing that which its fellow academic fields have been running from: practice.

COMPOSITION, PRACTICE, AND PUBLIC POLICY

Composition needs to be proud of its roots in pedagogy and the teaching of writing. It needs to counter, not be complicit with, the apathetic or negative view of practice that is so pervasive in higher education. In *MKC*, North comments on this attitude: "For Composition Scholars trying to survive in the context of a field like literary studies, practicality can be a liability" (368). If our colleagues down the hall disrespect practice, we should turn our efforts instead to those who do not need to be convinced that teaching is important, those we can collaborate with, those whose students also deserve best practices in the teaching of writing, those who are working in the eye of the No-Child-Left-Behind storm. These colleagues are right down the street or perhaps sitting in our graduate courses. They are high-school teachers of English. Their main interest is practice, not publishing. As public policy begins to turn its probe towards higher education, we need our secondary-school colleagues to share with us their survival strategies. And they need us.

As reported in a June 21, 2008, *Los Angeles Times* article, the graduation rates in Los Angeles have declined for two years in a row, and required exit exams are having "a huge effect on dropouts." UCLA professor John Roberts is quoted in the article: "In 2008, far fewer students will graduate than probably any year in the last 25 years" (Landsberg). Because of inconsistencies in the reporting of dropouts across the United States, it is difficult to accurately measure what No Child Left Behind has done for, or to, high-school students. But with only 48 percent of LA students finishing high school on time, it is clear that their schools and no doubt many others across the country need whatever research composition can show them about best practices in the teaching of writing. Collaboration between professionals in college composition and in the high schools is not high on the agenda of the Conference on College Composition and Communication (CCCCs), partly because of our field's preference for theory and distancing from practice, a trend North critiqued in *MKC*. However, recent public-policy decisions and their detrimental effect on the teaching of writing should lead us to reconsider our role outside colleges and universities.

There is much research we know about, and have known about for decades, that is simply not getting out into the larger world. Older research is deliberately cited here, to make the point that we have had plenty of time to effect change in how writing is taught to vast numbers of students, but that this change is slow at best, nonexistent at worst. There is research that shows that people write more and write better when they know they have at least a chance of succeeding (Parker and Goodkin 1987, 19); we know about the importance of writing in a real rhetorical situation (Crowley and Hawhee 1999) and after having analyzed the forum at which the discourse is aimed (Porter 1986). We know that there are effective invention strategies in addition to free-writing or conventional outlining (Childers, Hobson, and Mullin 1998; Dunn 2001; Hecker 1997), and that peer response *does* work if done intelligently and after having trained students and given them practice responding (Denyer and LaFleur 2001). We know that error is, to a large extent, a phenomenon of power differentials between writer and reader (Williams 1981), and that when asked to rank essays cold, without knowing the authors, without predetermined criteria, readers will give every possible ranking available (Diederich 1974). We know that a reader's knowledge of a writer's authority (or lack thereof) affects that reader's judgment of that writer's work (Knoblauch and Brannon 1984, 161–64). We know that students pay very little attention to the marginal comments and editorial corrections teachers make on those students' texts (Knoblauch and Brannon 1981), and that direct teaching of conventional grammar does not carry over into effective editing strategies for writers (Schuster 2003). We know that "coherence" is a function not simply of the writer's text but of the background knowledge of the person reading the piece (Witte and Faigley 1981, 202), and that previous texts and the concept of intertextuality greatly influence the shape of disciplinary texts and how they are received by readers used to writing in and working with those genres (Bazerman 1988; Porter 1986; Russell 1991). There is research that shows when teachers constantly "correct" students' home language and consistently disrespect students' home language, even implicitly, those students use *less* academic prose and *more* of their home language; we know that when teachers respect students' home language by demonstrating knowledge of the rule-bound, systematic nature of its grammar, that those students use *less* of their home language and *more* academic prose (Hollie 2001; Smitherman 2000, 160–1; Taylor 1989; Wheeler 2005).

This list could go on. The point is that much writing pedagogy continues in the schools as if this is still the middle of the twentieth (or even the nineteenth) century. Readers skeptical that antiquated writing pedagogies are still in use should visit some of the high-school English classes I've visited in my new role as an English educator, where "revising" is simply copying over a handwritten theme and correcting the spelling, where "writing" is still taught as finding errors on a worksheet. There are lectures about "proper English" and "standard English" as if the last fifty years of linguistic research never happened. There are lessons on the five-paragraph theme as if it hasn't been discredited ad nauseum by two generations of composition professionals. There are isolated parts-of-speech drills and "myth rules" (Schuster's term) about not using "I." There are "term papers" assigned with little to no context regarding purpose, constraints of the genre, knowledge of the reader, or where to look for reliable research. Yet teachers are shocked and appalled when students "plagiarize," and blame is distributed to the students, with teachers completely oblivious to Rebecca Moore Howard's research regarding "patchwriting" and scholars' own use of it with impunity (1999).

It's not that there aren't already some excellent books for high-school teachers on the teaching of writing. It's not that there aren't challenging and sophisticated writing courses out there or worthwhile classes that include writing. However, there are still far too many that are just insufferable. And the students who have the furthest to go regarding academic literacy are getting the worst of it: the most low-level tasks, the most rigid and artificial writing assignments, the most insults about the ways they and their families speak. Those students drop out of school out of boredom or disgust long before they reach first-year composition (FYC) classes, where they might first show up on the radar screen of composition professionals. We need to widen that screen *before* FYC as well as *after*.

North argues as much in his book, foregrounding in prominent passages in *MKC* histories of high-school/college collaboration. In the first pages of chapter one, for example, he highlights Arthur Applebee's history of English in secondary schools, pointing out that in the late 1950s, college English professors—then literature scholars—involved themselves in reforming the high-school English curriculum (9–10). We still see their influence in the overwhelming emphasis on literary classics in secondary education and the short shrift given to rhetorically sophisticated writing projects.

In another prominent passage, this one toward the end of his last chapter in *MKC*, North highlights as a possible "important prototype" (373) the National Writing Project (NWP), a collaboration between high-school and college teachers that has been in existence since 1974. North praises the features of the NWP: that it respects teachers' first allegiance to students (as opposed to scholarship); that teachers "are treated with dignity"; that "there is little of the old top-down, theoretician to practitioner hierarchy"; and "the classroom is recognized as the community of first importance" (373).

While most of *MKC* is about the history and future of composition at the college level, it is significant that North begins and ends his book with a focus on how high-school English teachers and the high-school English curriculum intersect with college English professors. In the nearly twenty-five years since *MKC* was published, many composition professionals have themselves become tenured members of their departments. They are now in a position to greatly influence the high-school writing curriculum, should they choose to become involved.

We in CCCCs are already deeply concerned about literacy beyond the FYC class. We write conference papers about the teaching of writing in homeless shelters, refugee camps, and community literacy programs. We concern ourselves with medical rhetoric, the rhetoric of nation building, service learning, and literacy practices all around the world. The 2008 Call for Program Proposals for the 2009 CCCCs draws our attention to "adult education centers, prisons, coffee houses, and areas beyond our borders" (1). It is truly admirable that CCCCs is concerned with writing programs in community centers, homeless shelters, and nursing homes. However, since we are in the business of using our research and theorizing outside the FYC realm of our roots, then we should add high schools to our list of spaces and literacy sites worthy of our attention. We are encouraged to examine programs in coffeehouses, yet high-school classes down the street are invisible to us.

As long as composition has already extended its sphere of interest to the time *after* FYC—up and out to WAC, WID, upper-level college composition, adult and community literacy, workplace writing, service learning, medical rhetoric, and so forth—it should extend its sphere only slightly in the other direction, *before* FYC, to those young people who in a matter of months will be sitting in our FYC class, unless they are among the 30 to 50 percent who drop out before they get there (Bridgeland, Dilulio, and Morison 2006; Dillon 2008; Eckholm 2006).

CONCLUSION

Many public-policy controversies today regarding teaching and testing are really about fundamental differences in epistemological assumptions, and in attitudes about teaching. Exposing, naming, and sorting out those assumptions and attitudes would be a worthwhile first step into gearing up for accountability demands, which are surely coming to higher education. Publicly theorizing these assumptions would also make composition more accountable—and more visible—to the outside world, more able to promote responsible writing pedagogies for students before they come to college, and more invigorated by the thousands of practicing writing teachers in the secondary schools.

North's arguments about teaching in *MKC*, if debated by contemporary compositionists, colleagues across the curriculum, high-school English teachers, and members of the general public, could result in more rhetorically effective public discussions about best practices in teaching writing before, during, and after college composition. North's own pedagogical practices, if discussed more widely, could also promote more responsible and effective teaching of so many young people the school system is currently driving away.

This urging to reform public policy regarding education, a position implied if not stated in *MKC*, has not been taken up by most of its readers. However, if composition as a field is to more effectively practice what it preaches, it needs to take practice as seriously as it takes other forms of inquiry, as seriously as researcher North argues in *MKC* that it should be, as seriously as Professor North took it in that routine graduate class described earlier. Composition professionals need to step up and argue for more rhetorically sophisticated writing pedagogy in all educational venues, even if their university colleagues will not reward them for doing so. Composition has a right to be proud of its historical and ongoing commitment to social justice. It can both continue to work for more democratic educational practices and reinvigorate itself by collaborating with high-school teachers of English and by speaking out about public policy regarding best practices in the teaching of writing. By now, composition should have enough security, courage, and leadership ability to take a more active role in making high-school students' experiences with writing empowering enough to make them want to stay in school. In North's words from the last paragraph of *MKC*, our country's "national preoccupation with literacy" opens the possibility that "anything can happen" (375). Let's set our collective sights on public policy and the ethically responsible teaching of writing in the schools.

REFERENCES

Bazerman, Charles. 1988. *Shaping written knowledge: The genre and activity of the experimental article in science.* Madison: University of Wisconsin Press.

Bridgeland, John M., John J. DiIulio, Jr., and Karen Burke Morison. 2006. The silent epidemic: Perspectives of high school dropouts. http://www.gatesfoundation.org/nr/downloads/ed/TheSilentEpidemic-ExecSum.pdf..

Childers, Pamela B., Eric H. Hobson, and Joan M. Mullin. 1998. *ARTiculating: Teaching writing in a visual world.* Portsmouth, NH: Boynton/Cook Publishers.

Cooper, Charles R., and Lee Odell, eds. 1977. *Evaluating writing: Describing, measuring, judging.* Urbana, IL: National Council of Teachers of English.

Crowley, Sharon, and Debra Hawhee. 1999. *Ancient rhetorics for contemporary students.* 2nd ed. Boston: Allyn and Bacon.

Denyer, Jenny, and Debra La Fleur. 2001. The Eliot conference: An analysis of peer response groups. *Voices from the Middle* 9: 29–39.

Diederich. Paul. 1974. *Measuring growth in English.* Urbana, IL: National Council of Teachers of English.

Dillon, Sam. 2008. States' data obscure how few finish high school. 2008. *New York Times,* March 20. http://www.nytimes.com/2008/03/20/education/20graduation.html?

Dunn, Patricia A. 2001. *Talking, sketching, moving: Multiple literacies in the teaching of writing.* Portsmouth, NH: Boynton/Cook Heinemann.

Eckholm, Erik. 2006. Plight deepens for black men, studies warn. *New York Times,* March 20. http:///www.nytimes.com/2006/03/20/national/.

Freire, Paulo. 1973. *The pedagogy of the oppressed.* Translated by Myra Berman Ramos. New York: The Seabury Press-Continuum.

Hecker, Linda. 1997. Walking, Tinkertoys, and Legos: Using movement and manipulatives to help students write. *English Journal* 86: 46–52.

Hollie, Sharroky. 2001. Acknowledging the language of African American students: instructional strategies. *English Journal* (90):54–59.

Howard, Rebecca Moore. 1999. *Standing in the shadow of giants: Plagiarists, authors, collaborators.* Stamford, CT: Ablex Publishing.

Knoblauch, C.H., and Lil Brannon. 1984. *Rhetorical traditions and the teaching of writing.* Portsmouth, NH: Boynton/Cook.

———. 1981. Teacher commentary on student writing: The state of the art. *Freshman English News* 10 (2): 1–4.

Landsberg, Mitchell. 2008. Graduation rates declining in LA unified despite higher enrollment, study finds. *Los Angeles Times,* June 21. http://www.latimes.com/news/education/la-me-grads21-2008jun21,0,3489530.story.

North, Stephen M. 1987. *The making of knowledge in composition: Portrait of an emerging field.* Upper Montclair, NJ: Boynton/Cook.

Odell, Lee. 1977. Measuring changes in intellectual processes as one dimension of growth in writing. In *Evaluating writing: Describing, measuring, judging,* edited by Charles R. Cooper and Lee Odell. Urbana, IL: National Council of Teachers of English.

———, and Joanne Cohick. 1975. You mean, write it over in ink? *English Journal* 64: 48–53.

Parker, Robert P., and Vera Goodkin. 1987. *The consequences of writing: Enhancing learning in the disciplines.* Upper Montclair, NJ: Boynton/Cook.

Porter, James E. 1986. Intertextuality and the discourse community. *Rhetoric Review* 5:

34–45.

Russell, David R. 1991. *Writing in the academic disciplines, 1870–1990: A curricular history.* Carbondale: Southern Illinois University Press.

Schuster, Edgar. 2003. *Breaking the rules: Liberating writers through innovative grammar instruction.* Portsmouth, NH: Heinemann.

Smitherman, Geneva. 2000. *Talkin that talk: Language, culture and education in African America.* London and New York: Routledge.

Spellings, Margaret. 2006. Secretary Spellings' prepared remarks at the National Press Club: An action plan for higher education. http://www.ed.gov/news/speeches/2006/09/09262006.html.

Taylor, Hanni U. 1989. *Standard English, black English, & bidialectalism: A controversy.* New York: Peter Lang.

Vygotsky, Lev. 1978. *Mind in society: The development of higher psychological processes,* edited by Vera John Steiner, M. Cole, E. Souberman, and S. Scribner. Cambridge and London: MIT Press.

Wheeler, Rebecca. 2005. Code-switch to teach standard English. In Kenneth Lindblom's Teaching English in the World column. *English Journal* 94: 108–112.

Williams, Joseph. 1981. The phenomenology of error. *College Composition and Communication* 32: 152–68.

Witte, Stephen P., and Lester Faigley. 1981. Coherence, cohesion, and writing quality. *College Composition and Communication* 32: 189–204.

11

ON THE PLACE OF WRITING IN HIGHER EDUCATION (AND WHY IT DOESN'T INCLUDE COMPOSITION)[1]

Stephen M. North

Among other things, *The Making of Knowledge in Composition* (*MKC*) was an exploration of the place of writing and writing instruction in U.S. higher education. In the twenty-five years since its publication, the number of such explorations—and, it seems fair to say, the discontentments that drive them—has been on the rise. We have seen it manifested, for example, in proposals for reimagining English studies and/or English departments: James Berlin's *Rhetorics, Poetics and Cultures* (1996); James Seitz's *Motives for Metaphor* (1999); David Downing, Claude Mark Hurlbert, and Paula Mathieu's *Beyond English Inc.: Curricular Reform in a Global Economy* (2002); and so on. In Rhetoric and Composition circles more specifically, we have seen it in the various incarnations of the "abolitionist" movement that has enjoyed considerable visibility, if not necessarily impact, since the late 1980s. Most dramatically, perhaps, we have seen it in a small but striking number of institutional changes whereby writing has been resituated in new, albeit variously conceived, units. And indeed, these impulses are reflected in contributions to this volume (e.g., Smit and Kinkead).

My own take on this debate derives primarily from having had a hand in developing, administering, and especially teaching in an undergraduate writing sequence through the English major at the University of Albany from 1988 to 2000, but also from the ways in which that experience has affected my thinking about developments in Composition. Together, they have led me to hope for, if not exactly predict, the emergence of something that might be called writing studies.

---

1.   Even though the editors have chosen to use lowercase "c" when referring to composition in the other chapters of this collection, I will use the lowercase and uppercase "c" here and elsewhere in this chapter, as appropriate, as I did in *MKC*, to explicitly distinguish between composition as a school subject and Composition as a field.

LESSONS IN RHETORIC AND POETICS

The story of what officially came to be called the Writing Sequence through the English Major: Rhetoric and Poetics begins in 1987, the year *MKC* was published, and the same year I accepted an appointment as my English department's director of writing. The year before, 1986, the department had convinced the university to let it stop offering its longstanding, forty-section-per-term English composition (Eng 100) course. In its place, and with the help of some of the resources that had been devoted to that course, the department, through the agency of the writing center, would help develop a university-wide writing intensive (WI) program that situated the undergraduate writing experience—albeit not instruction in writing per se—in discipline-based courses. Students would be required to take two such courses in order to graduate, at least one at the upper-division level.

The decision to simultaneously eliminate English composition and not, as would surely have been more typical, to treat the WI program as a supplement or complement to it, was based on such things as finances (because English had rightly kept enrollments in English composition at twenty-two, it was consistently rated by the university as over-staffed—that is, not getting a big enough bang for every buck) and the economy of student requirements (if English composition was allowed to fulfill the WI requirement, it would both remain in high demand and discourage the development of WI courses in other disciplines). In any case, the decision had the dramatic effect of leaving the English department, for the first time in its century-long history, without any clearly defined relationship to writing instruction.

It also meant, of course, that the new director of writing—me—had a really slim portfolio. The position had always been pointedly asymmetrical. The department had directors for undergraduate and graduate Studies, with a third for journalism, which was a separate minor. The director of writing, described in the bylaws in language parallel to the others, was to "advise the Chair on all matters pertaining to writing." However, absent the forty-section-per-term behemoth of English composition, not to mention all the attendant staffing headaches that were the writing director's primary *raison d'etre*, there were only a handful of active courses to advise the chair about. And their titles testify eloquently to the inadequacy of the department's (and, to be fair, the larger discipline's) efforts to come to grips with whatever "writing" might be when it wasn't contained as English composition, at one end of the spectrum, and literature, at the other: Introduction to Creative Writing (102); Expository Writing (300); Critical Writing (301); Creative Writing (302); and Practical Writing (309, once but no longer required by the business school). There were also a few 400-level courses in the catalog, but they were distinguished from these others mainly by having "advanced" attached to these other titles, and were in any case rarely offered.

The tenuousness of my new position—and of writing—became apparent by the end of my first month in office, when the chair who had appointed me so that he could take advantage of my writerly wisdom . . . didn't. At all. Thus, when the next spring's schedule appeared in October, it was the first time I had seen it. And whereas in the past writing courses—counting English composition—had represented about half of the department's overall offerings—55 of 110 sections, say—there were now, count 'em, nine: four each in Eng 301 and Eng 300, because English majors were required to take one upper-division writing course; and one in Eng 302, which also technically fulfilled the requirement, but also required permission from the instructor.

Well, I typed the requisite memo by way of protest, of course, notified all the other self-identified writing people in the department, and subsequently met with the chair and the undergraduate director (the latter of whom had done the bulk of the actual scheduling) to express our outrage. A few more writing courses made their way into the schedule that term, and in subsequent semesters I submitted my slate of recommendations early—and then nagged a lot.

In seeking a longer-term, structural solution, though, I also began to lobby for a wholesale revision of the undergraduate curriculum that would make writing courses a more integral and substantive part of it. My arguments were based less on intellectual principles than on personnel. By virtue of a peculiar mix of hiring patterns and retirements, the department had an unusually large contingent of writing people: fully ten out of thirty, including poets, fiction writers, and scholars in Rhetoric and Composition. To be sure, all of us were fully capable of teaching in the extant curriculum's literature and writing courses. But surely, we argued, it would make more sense, most notably for our students, to feature us in ways that played more directly to our professional strengths.

These appeals went nowhere for three years, my entire first term as director of writing. The chair at that time was a self-proclaimed pragmatist, and his position was not, from that perspective, unreasonable. Whatever advantages renegotiating the place of writing might produce, he argued, they almost certainly wouldn't be worth the risks posed by opening the entire curriculum up for the negotiations required to gain them. Nobody knew what conflicts might emerge—around writing or elsewhere—and, more to the point, he simply wasn't willing to find out. Why risk upsetting twenty satisfied people just because ten are unhappy?

At the beginning of my second term, therefore—with the same chair—I took a different tack, and suggested that we develop a separate writing track through the English major. It was definitely not my preference; in most educational systems, separate was almost always unequal. But there was structural precedent for it elsewhere in the college and, perhaps not surprisingly, the chair was happy enough to entertain at least the possibility. Again, I suspect his reasoning was simply pragmatic: if you could make ten people happy—or at least keep them busy—without disturbing the other twenty, why not?

So we set about designing the sequence. As might be expected at a large public institution, this was a complicated process, and as much for bureaucratic as intellectual reasons. The program had to consist of the right number of courses (no more, that is, than its literature counterpart's twelve); be on the right scale given faculty interest (fifty new students per term); produce, on average, the same number of seats per section as the other sequence (we devised a course, required of all writing majors and open to anyone, designed to enroll 150 and so balance out writing classes of 15), and so on. We also discovered, by floating a few trial balloons past university governance, that we would need to foreground its "content" more forcefully. Students couldn't just major in *doing* writing, we were told. They needed to actually *learn* something.

The comment rankled, no question, touching as it did on the kind of licensing debates to which English departments are all too prone. What does a poet or a novelist—or, for that matter, a compositionist, know, after all, as compared to a Victorian scholar, say, or an Emersonian? But it forced us to articulate more fully the disciplinary context out of which we believed the sequence would emerge and into which students would be initiated. Rhetoric and Poetics, we named it, invoking the two traditions we did indeed believe informed our otherwise widely varied modes of expertise; and in particular rhetoric and poetics as those traditions informed text making in a print (and, increasingly, postprint) culture. Like other English majors, then, sequence students would read a good deal—"learn" a lot—in order to study the ways in which writing functioned in culture, and they would write *about* what they read; but they would do so with the specific curricular goal of doing that writing *in* and *from* a range of the forms they studied, as well, and therefore not—like their counterparts—exclusively the argumentative academic prose of the reader/critic.

Eventually, the sequence was approved. Our sometimes high-flying rhetoric notwithstanding, it was a very rudimentary structure, to put it politely. At its core were a scant five courses, and while they provided curricular space for what turned out to be interesting work, that's about all they did. There were the three required fifteen-seat writing courses: Eng 202, Introduction to Rhetoric and Poetics; Eng 303, Rhetoric; and—don't laugh—Eng 304, Poetics. These were, as I noted above, sub-vened by a 150-seat lecture-cum-spectacle course called Contemporary Writers at Work, in which, as per the title, we would aim to feature live guests whenever possible. And the capstone would be Eng 450, a senior-level special topics course appropriate for aspiring writers (e.g., Images of the Writer in U.S. Culture).

Still, while I wish we could have designed a more sophisticated vehicle, and while the ongoing costs of making it function (wrangling with the department's extant apparatus over advisement, scheduling, staffing, etc.) always seemed disproportionately high, participating in the writing sequence turned out to be by far the most rewarding curricular experience of my thirty-year career as a teacher of writing, a dramatic—and most welcome—departure from what I had done, and indeed continued to do, under the aegis of Composition. I learned a lot from teaching in the rhetorics and poetics sequence. Four lessons were most important.

First, I learned that I want to teach in a writing curriculum that is an extension of the faculty's scholarship. Sharon Crowley has pointed out how very anomalous composition is as a mode of postsecondary instruction in that it did not, and still does not, "emanate from some subject matter, discipline, or field of study" (1998, 6). This was certainly true during its first eighty-five years or so—the preComposition era, if you will—when what the students learned was literally considered to be pre-college and, as such, had no basis in the faculty's licensed scholarship. Things have changed a little bit as Composition has become more professionalized, so that at least some faculty earn their academic places on the strength of their research on the writing that composition students do. Nevertheless, while the teaching of composition may be influenced by such research, it can hardly be said to "emanate" from it in the way it does for economics, say, or physics, or sculpture. We don't teach students composition, in other words, to put them on track to becoming compositionists, to join us in what we do.

In the sequence, however, we were doing just that: taking the expertise we had developed through our various, ongoing researches, making it available to students, and inviting them to join us. The invitation was, as I say, a very rough-and-ready one, and lacked the kind of developmental articulation—our equivalents, as it were, of economics calculus, micro, macro, and so on—featured in older enterprises. But that didn't seem to matter. We were happy just to have a space in which to work such patterns out, and the students seemed similarly pleased to join in the process. Perhaps that level of mutual contentment would have worn off over time, but it was great while it lasted.

Second, I learned that I want to teach writing to people who are self-selected. One of the peculiarities the English composition course at U. Albany had come to have—a property shared, I suspect, by most of its counterparts in other institutions—was that it was impossible for a student to actually choose it. In other words, even though in its last few years at Albany, English composition was technically not mandatory for all students, it was required or strongly recommended by so many majors, minors, and subsequent institutions (e.g., medical schools, law schools), and in any case perceived by students and parents as such a standard rite of passage, that the option of choosing it freely, as though it were an elective that might be interesting—that was pretty much gone. So while I had certainly taught plenty of motivated students in English composition, none of them really had had the chance to be self-selected.

In the sequence, however, I taught nothing *but* the self-selected. I don't want to exaggerate the significance of this; even self-selected majors are quite capable of grumbling about one or another course in the curriculum, of being less thrilled about poetics than rhetoric, or vice versa. Even so, self-selection—and especially universal self-selection—does make a real difference. So, for example, each student who self-selects for a given major is likely to have higher individual expectations, in every class, of herself, the other students, and the teacher, than she would when conscripted. And the collective effect is even greater: when every student in a section is thus self-selected, both the mean and the median level of such expectations—again, for everyone involved—is likely to be much higher than in a class in which all the students are enrolled by mandate. A higher percentage of the students are likely to really want to be there, and those who are reluctant, for whatever reason, will likely be less so.

My favorite emblem for the difference I'm trying to describe is not a writing class per se, but from Contemporary Writers at Work, the upper-division lecture-hall course that helped make the sequence financially viable. I had taught courses of comparable size a few times before with reasonable success, but let's face it: amphitheater settings promote monologue over dialogue, anonymity over intimacy. However, teaching a group of self-selected, upper-division writing majors—many of whom knew one another quite well from the small writing courses and such extracurricular events as the sequence's open mic sessions—was more like turning up on the set of *Oprah*, say. The room was always buzzing with conversation when I arrived, and during the sessions, students were always game for interaction: with me, with one another, with our various guests. They understood the importance of the course to the overall enterprise and, since they were members of that enterprise by self-selection, they were committed to making the course the best experience it could be. Again, maybe that effect would have worn off in the sequence's second or third decade, had it gotten there. But I don't see why.

Third, I learned that I want to teach writing in a context where there is both curricular and developmental continuity. From my perspective, the most important line of research to emerge in composition over the past twenty-five years has been that on the development of writing abilities: Richard Haswell's *Gaining Ground in College Writing* (1991), Anne Herrington and Marcia Curtis's *Persons in Process* (2000), Marilyn Sternglass's *Time to Know Them* (1997), and so on. And what those studies, in conjunction with my work in the sequence, brought home, was how precious little instructional exposure I had had to undergraduate development in this sense: how few opportunities I had had even to teach writing at the upper-division level at all, let alone to work with the same writers over their undergraduate careers. It's an occupational hazard for composition teachers: we are so locked into the writing students do in their first year that we rarely get to see what they do later. Unfortunately, this also means—to adapt a phrase from Haswell's wonderful book—that it is hard for us to carry out our "professional obligation" to read that entry-level student writing with "acuity and fairness" (1991, 91), because we have no real, hands-on, instructional, visceral experience with where that writing might be headed.

In the sequence, by contrast, this kind of experience was *de rigueur*. By design, all the teachers, TAs and part-time instructors included, rotated through the three workshop classes; and a number of us also took turns with Contemporary Writers at Work and the senior-level topics course. This meant that all of us not only got to see the writing of our students in general from first year to last, but—because the operation was small enough—that we each got to teach some of the same students in two or three courses over that span. And similarly, of course, our students got to know us, as well: our ways of teaching, reading, responding. I believe these kinds of mutual familiarity benefitted all involved, allowing us all to do a better job of reading one another with acuity and fairness. And I am certain, to offer a more selfish take, that these deeper, long-term teaching relationships the sequence allowed were ultimately my favorite feature of it, an unanticipated but most welcome source of joy.

Last but not least, I learned that I want to teach writing in an enterprise where goals are commensurate with resources. For me, at least, the most maddening feature of work in Composition has always been that these two—goals and resources—were rarely on the same planet; and even when they were, it was never for very long. The litany is familiar: first-year composition programs with shoestring budgets, administered by untenured assistant professors, staffed by TAs and part-time instructors, trying to meet underspecified and/or unrealistic expectations about student composing; writing centers enlisted as extracurricular support in these campaigns, but with institution-wide constituencies that create student-to-staff ratios of five hundred to one, say, or one thousand to one; writing-across-the-curriculum (WAC) programs waxing and waning as grant money comes and goes, charged with effecting serious change in departmental and disciplinary cultures but with no real leverage, gnats negotiating with elephants.

So the sequence was like coming home to a place I'd never been. This was something we could do. Since the sequence qualified as a major, its courses had to be offered, and offered regularly. They had to be staffed either by the core faculty—already in place—or, according to ratios stipulated in the founding legislation, by self-selected TAs, lecturers and/or part-time faculty. Since the teachers, like the students, were self-selected, faculty development could be voluntary, ongoing—meetings every other week—and on a manageable scale. And even when the enterprise was operating at its maximum capacity of two hundred, the ratio of students to full-time, tenure-track faculty would still be a very acceptable twenty to one. In short, we could continue to do our research, engage in the kinds of service that would keep the sequence moving forward, and promise students that we would be there as teachers for them and their writing, year in and year out, until they graduated. And it was a promise we could keep.

Unfortunately, as the framing dates 1988 to 2000 indicate, the sequence did not live happily ever after. A few years after we launched both it and a new, writing-friendly PhD program, tensions in the English department grew to the point where a self-identified writing studies group sought permission from the university to leave English and form its own unit. The request was seriously considered—a year's worth of study by three outside consultants, lots of meetings, and so on—but ultimately denied. Shortly thereafter, the university hired a new chair from another institution who was willing to say, for attribution, that the success of the sequence was problematic: that in a healthy English department, such a program would never thrive. And so a few years after that, when the department renegotiated the undergraduate curriculum, it was no surprise that the new configuration featured courses identified with areas of faculty expertise—including rhetoric and poetics—but none that were linked as tracks or sequences, or offered in any regular rotation. Such arrangements were deemed logistically too complicated and at least potentially divisive. So the writing sequence was gone—a victim, as it were, of reconciliation.

Frankly, though, that painful ending only solidified for me the other lessons I had learned from the sequence, and taught me a fifth: I learned I want to teach writing in a unit that doesn't experience the successes of its writing faculty and students as any sort of a threat. And while I have framed these lessons in individual terms—as representing what I want—I have come to believe that they also represent what would be best for writing instruction in higher education overall. Whenever college writing instruction is offered, in short, I believe it ought to be given by faculty teaching self-selected students in programs grounded in that faculty's research, featuring clear curricular and developmental continuity, and with goals that match up with resources. Truth be told, it's a shame I even have to spell it out.

THE (BOGUS) PROMISE OF COMPOSITION

As you can tell from my consistent use of Composition as a foil so far, my experience in the sequence has significantly altered my view of the enterprise I described in *MKC*—and not for the better. In chapter one of that book, you may recall, I tell the story of how, as part of a broader academic reform movement that was to transform "English-the-school-subject" into "English-the-discipline"—and to make it, not incidentally, part of the U.S. response to the emerging challenges of the Cold War—the "second class academic citizens" who were engaged at their various institutions in the low prestige postsecondary enterprise referred to as *c*omposition found themselves with an opportunity to promote both that enterprise and their own professional standing as its proprietors. Out of this somewhat curious set of circumstances, I argued, *C*omposition was born. And all of this, I implied—and certainly believed—was a good thing.

I no longer believe that. For at least forty years now, Composition has labored mightily to fulfill the promise implicit in composition since the latter, which emerged at Harvard in 1874 as the name for some capacity student applicants lacked, was grudgingly institutionalized a decade later in a required course that has since, as the story goes, spread almost everywhere. And what was that promise? To deliver to higher education's discipline-based faculty undergraduates who could write with such fluency, coherence, and propriety that nothing they submitted would disturb what those faculty imagined ought to be the smooth, uninterrupted flow of their evaluative reading. The idea was then and is now to free such faculty members—the "University," as the Harvard Committee on Composition and Rhetoric put it in their 1897 report—from "rudimentary drill," so that they would be "able thenceforth to devote [their] means and energy to [their] proper function, that of the Advanced Education" (Brereton 1995, 125–6).

Most of our efforts to this end, like those of our less professionalized predecessors, have been curricular. Again and again, and then again and again and again—as close to *ad infinitum* as any pedagogical project in the history of U.S. higher education—we have tried to devise the fifteen- or thirty-week course that would work the necessary transformation. I would say that we have tried it all, but they just keep coming: personal writing, daily writing, research writing, I-search writing, sentence combining, epistolary writing, writing about literature, writing about unsolved murder cases, writing about difficult texts, writing about popular culture, writing grounded in classical rhetoric, writing grounded in the social sciences/hard sciences/humanities, teaching writing by conference, teaching writing by lecture, teaching writing as problem solving, teaching writing by teaching computer programming, teaching the composing process . . . I don't think I'm in disputed territory here. An enormous amount of energy and ingenuity has gone into designing the perfect composition course.

However, we have also undertaken two impressive extracurricular campaigns. In one direction, then, we have developed ways of identifying those students least likely to manage the requisite transformation by ordinary curricular means, and created extra or precurricular spaces—remedial writing, basic writing, and so on—to give them extra time and instruction and, not incidentally, to insulate our faculty clients from their disturbing texts. In the other direction, by way of picking up at least some of the students insufficiently transformed by their allotted fifteen or thirty weeks of instruction, we have developed postcurricular spaces like writing centers and writing labs. We don't generally like to discuss the function of such facilities in these terms—I am certainly on record as opposing such representations—but I guarantee you that our faculty colleagues mostly do, and that their doing so is a key source of the leverage that keeps these facilities in operation.

Last but not least, we have gone so far as to intervene on the faculty side of the composition equation by means of the writing-across-the-curriculum campaign. That is, as it has become clearer and clearer that we couldn't depend on composition courses, even with extracurricular support, to deliver students who could produce texts acceptable by faculty standards, we sought instead to alter that standard. I would be happy to concede, of course, that there is more to the WAC movement, or that there can be. Nevertheless, its otherwise utterly anomalous presence in U.S. higher education—it is the only enterprise, so far as I know, in which one group of faculty actively seeks to alter the teaching of all the rest (Calculating Across the Curriculum? Philosophy Intensive Courses?)—is a function of the same compact that has driven all our other initiatives.

At this point in Composition's history, in fact, I am willing to say that we have done everything we could by way of making good on the promise of composition, except to declare—or at least to act on, since I believe we have known it for quite some time—that the promise is bogus. That it can't be kept. That if a newly admitted student enrolled in a discipline-based course truly cannot produce writing acceptable to that course's sponsoring professor, the odds that a fifteen-week composition course—forty-five hours in class, ninety out—will transform that student into someone who truly can produce acceptable writing for that professor are very slim. Everything we know about the development of writing abilities confirms this: it just doesn't work that way. Moreover, the odds get even slimmer if the writing course does not derive from that sponsoring professor's discipline; if it is conceived as a one-off, inoculatory undertaking; if the student has no choice about taking it; if the instructor is underpaid, overworked, undertrained, inexperienced, or any combination thereof. And they get slimmer still, of course, if—as is likely to be the case—the composition course qualifies in two or three or all of these categories. Mind you, I'm not saying that all sorts of other wonderful things might not happen in such a course. They might, and they do. But judged against the promise of composition, it will almost certainly fail.

I can understand why Composition—we—might be reluctant to embrace this truth or, if we have embraced it, to act on it too rashly. The teaching of composition is a big business, and one that continues to grow. According to the National Center for Education Statistics' listing of the top thirty postsecondary courses (2004), "English composition" has long been the most frequently taken course in U.S. higher education. It accounted for 2.9, 3.1 and 3.2 percent of all undergraduate credits earned in 1972, 1982, and 1992 (the last year for which data is reported), respectively, averaging a full percentage point higher than the courses ranked second (General Biology at 1.9; Introduction to Economics at 2.4; and Introduction to Psychology at 1.8). And since these are percentages of a steadily growing undergraduate population, the franchise has also grown in absolute terms: in 1972, there were just under eight million undergraduates; by 1992, that number was closer to 12.5 million. Under any circumstances, then, setting out to renegotiate the educational and institutional terms of such a juggernaut would be challenging. Doing so when, as in this case, we have capitalized on that business—literally and figuratively—as the centerpiece of our overall franchise . . . well, the prospect is daunting indeed.

And yet I think that is exactly what we ought to do, what we need to do. For as much as Composition has gained by means of its commitment to this promise of composition, that commitment has also long since begun to warp—as false promises will—everything we do. Perhaps the most obvious and best documented has been its effect on working conditions. As plenty of scholars have already pointed out, the primary rationale for the heavy loads and low pay of composition instructors has been, and still is, that they do "rudimentary drillwork," as the Harvard Committee put it. We have worked hard to alter those working conditions over the past twenty-five years and more, but it is clear to me, at any rate, that they are a structural given. In a system where discipline-based departments offering majors are the key units, it is highly unlikely that units offering predisciplinary instruction, especially on the scale that universal composition requires, will ever be staffed with anything like a full complement of faculty lines. It just wouldn't make sense.

In addition, however, I would argue that this bogus promise has also warped our pedagogical deliberations, our discussions of teaching. From its beginnings, Composition has not only been consumed by its search for the perfect composition course, as I suggested above, but constrained to engage that quest as a zero-sum game: to imagine that since we only get one shot at teaching composition, we have to do it either my way or your way, sentence combining or I-search, writing as problem solving or writing about literature. Consider, as a particularly visible example of this phenomenon the series of public, and then published, exchanges between David Bartholomae and Peter Elbow in the late 1980s and early 1990s. In a broad sense, the question they engaged had to do with how we ought to approach writing instruction in the academy and how we ought to situate students therein. Bartholomae argues that the prevailing attitude in such instruction ought to be "skepticism," whereas Elbow would prefer "credulity." And both scholars present their positions quite eloquently. So far, so good.

But notice what happens when the requisite zero-sum framing kicks in, as in David Bartholomae's conclusion to "Writing with Teachers: A Conversation with Peter Elbow":

> I don't think I need to teach sentimental realism, even though I know my students could be better at it than they are. I don't think I need to because I don't think I should. I find it a corrupt, if extraordinarily tempting genre. I don't want my students to celebrate what would then become the natural and inevitable details of their lives. I think the composition course should be part of the general critique of traditional humanism. For all the talk of paradigm shifting, the composition course, as a cultural force, remains fundamentally unchanged from the 19th century. I would rather teach or preside over a critical writing, one where the critique is worked out in practice, and for lack of better terms I would call that writing, "academic writing." (1995, 71)

The argument is perfectly reasonable, but why—instructionally speaking—does it have to be either/or? If the distinction these scholars are exploring is really important, and I think it is, wouldn't it make more sense for students to take courses grounded in *both* approaches— one skeptical, one credulous—so that they could explore this distinction for themselves? I think so, and I am inclined to believe that had that possibility figured as a viable option, both Bartholomae and Elbow would think so, as well. But because of the way the promise of composition constrains our discussions, what's best for students as developing writers in this broader sense isn't really even on the table. And that's just perverse.

Finally, I would argue that the effect of these constraints on Composition's research agenda has been, if anything, even worse. Most obviously, of course, it has led to lots of research on the same perversely framed problem we have tried to solve as teachers, and with the same sort of zero-sum focus: Which use of forty-five hours of instruction is most likely to prompt a heterogeneous group of conscripted students to produce texts of an unspecified type in subsequent but unspecified courses that will be favorably regarded by the unspecified group of faculty readers who teach those courses? Good luck.

Meanwhile, though, this rather hopeless obsession has also both limited the amount of research energy available for other kinds of inquiry and, I think, diminished the perceived value of such work. In other words, the promise of composition has tended not only to narrow Composition research—to hog its energies, as it were—but to also isolate Composition from the larger world of writing and literacy studies: the further a line of inquiry is perceived to be from telling us how to fulfill the promise, the less likely it is that anyone in Composition will even read about it, let alone undertake it. This isolationist tendency is never completely successful, of course. Journals like *Written Communication*, in one direction, and *Writing on the Edge*, in the other, represent consistent efforts to connect to a broader agenda. Nevertheless, my own sense is that over the past twenty-five years, Composition's continued devotion to composition has made it more insular in this sense, not less.

Overall, then, I believe Composition has more than held up its end of the original *c*omposition-becomes-*C*omposition bargain—even, as I have indicated here, to its own detriment and the detriment of the students it seeks to serve. But it was a bum deal from the get-go. Time to renegotiate.

TOWARD DEPARTMENTS OF WRITING STUDIES

So here is where I end up: writing instruction in U.S. higher education ought to be housed in departments of writing or writing studies. These departments should have their own full-fledged, discipline-based faculty; their own staffs; their own budgets; and their own space. The faculty should represent as broad a range of writing backgrounds as is practicable (e.g., novelists and technical writers, poets and journalists, playwrights and rhetoricians). They should develop instructional programs that grow out of their collective research, have curricular and developmental continuity, and invite writing majors to join the enterprise in numbers commensurate with the department's human and fiscal resources. Writing in such departments should be understood as a complex technology of serious cultural significance—along the lines, say, of graphic design or computer science—the serious study of which, therefore, would absolutely not be something for which every undergraduate is suited, either by aptitude or inclination. Degree programs should be more on the scale of a business degree, say—fifty or sixty or even seventy credit hours—than the typical liberal arts major. In such departments, in other words, everybody would agree that learning to write in anything like a serious way is hard, and that it takes a long time.

In keeping with its status as a full-fledged department, writing studies would not be responsible for the literacy of all students on campus, any more than mathematics is for their numeracy or philosophy their ethics. It should therefore not offer the kind of universally required, precurricular course that has traditionally been called composition. If other departments or an institution's administrators express an interest in providing better writing instruction for some set of undergraduate or graduate students, writing studies might well be willing to help, but its four provisos would be very clear and very firm (and worth repeating, as in this chapter): (a) any such course would have to grow out of the knowledge making of whichever full-fledged faculty offered the instruction, and be an invitation for students to join that enterprise; (b) it would have to include the genuine possibility of student self-selection; (c) it would have to have an explicit connection to a longer curricular and developmental trajectory; and (d) the faculty teaching the course would have to articulate goals commensurate with the resources available.

As I suggested at the beginning of this chapter, I do not believe I am alone in my discontentment with the status quo. Indeed, David Smit's chapter in this volume, like some of his other recent publications, is based on related concerns over what I've called here the promise of composition, except that he seems to be less obsessed than I am about giving students the opportunity to make their own writing the centerpiece of their undergraduate educations. In that respect, my position has more in common with the one Joyce Kinkead presents in her chapter, and with some of those she mentions along the way: Charles Bazerman's "The Case for Writing Studies as a Major Discipline," for example; the CCCC Committee on the Writing Major; the Writing Majors at a Glance website.

Indeed, an Internet search for degrees in writing turns up any number of institutions offering not only undergraduate but graduate degrees—the MA, usually, but also a few PhDs—in technical writing, creative writing, editing and publishing, and so on. And while actual departments of writing are still relatively rare, they at least exist, and certainly two—the writing department at Grand Rapids State and the writing program at Syracuse University—go a considerable way toward realizing the kind of impulses that shape my position here. On the one hand, then, the Grand Rapids State department has assembled the kind of diverse writing faculty I believe is so desirable, with members credentialed in poetry, fiction, rhetoric, journalism, and so on. And while Syracuse's faculty is more homogeneous—much more Rhetoric and Composition-centric—their offerings are the most comprehensive I know of, with a major, a minor, and a doctoral program.

Still, while I believe that I am in good company with what I am proposing here, and that there is considerable evidence that the time is right, I know I am asking a lot. The most admirable quality of the Composition community, after all, and certainly the one that drew me into it more than thirty years ago, is its unswerving commitment to the cause we serve. So the kind of shift I am proposing, this radical rethinking of that commitment and the equally radical restructuring of our institutional place—well, it will come hard. It will be a matter of *e*volution more than *r*evolution. By the same token, though, I know that this commitment is not really to Composition as such, but to the students it allows us to serve. For that reason, if the vision of writing studies I am proposing here allows us to serve them more ably—and my experience in the writing sequence utterly convinces me that it will—then I have both hope and faith that the Composition community will do what it takes to get there.

REFERENCES

Bartholomae, David. 1995. Writing with teachers: A conversation with Peter Elbow." *College Composition and Communication* 46. (1): 62–71.

Berlen, James. 1996. *Rhetorics, poetics, and cultures: Refiguring college English studies.* Urbana, IL: NCTE.

Brererton, John. 1995. *The origins of composition studies in the American college, 187–1925.* Pittsburgh, PA: University of Pittsburgh Press.

Crowley, Sharon.1998. *Composition in the university: Historical and polemical essays*. Pittsburgh, PA: University of Pittsburgh Press.

Downing, David B., Claude Mark Hurlbert, and Paula Mathieu. 2002. *Beyond English Inc.: Curricular reform in a global economy*. Boston: Boynton/Cook.

Haswell, Richard. 1991. *Gaining ground in college writing*. Fort Worth, TX: Southern Methodist University Press.

Herrington, Anne J., and Marcia Curtis. 2000. *Persons in process: Four stories of writing and personal development in college*. Urbana, IL: NCTE.

National Center for Education Statistics. 2004. Top 30 Postsecondary Courses. http://nces.ed.gov/programs/coe/2004/section5/indicator30.asp.

North, Stephen M. 1987. *The making of knowledge in composition: Portrait of an emergingfield*. Upper Montclair, NJ: Boynton/Cook.

Seitz, James E. 1999. *Motives for metaphor: Literacy, curriculum reform, and the teaching of English*. Pittsburgh: University of Pittsburgh Press.

Sternglass, Marilyn. 1997. *Time to know them: A longitudinal study of writng and learning at the college level*. Mahwah, NJ: Lawrence Erlbaum.

PART FOUR

Disciplinary Identities, Disciplinary Challenges: Unity, Multiplicity, and Fragmentation

12

STEPHEN NORTH'S *THE MAKING OF KNOWLEDGE IN COMPOSITION* AND THE FUTURE OF COMPOSITION STUDIES "WITHOUT PARADIGM HOPE"

David Smit

Although I admire Stephen North's *The Making of Knowledge in Composition* (*MKC*) a great deal, I find it difficult to evaluate the book's impact and influence. *MKC* came out in 1987, when the field of composition studies was undergoing what has been called the "social turn," a new recognition of the importance of context in discourse, and a concomitant interest in theory and cultural studies. Before the "turn" to context and theory, the field may have had something similar to an established canon in literature. At least we did at the University of Iowa, when I was there in the mid-1980s. The work all of us in composition/rhetoric, professors and graduate students alike, had in common were by the three Jameses—Kinneavy, Moffett, and Britton—Peter Elbow, Linda Flower and John Hayes, Ann Bertoff, and Janet Emig, indeed many of the people North deals with in his book. When large studies appeared adding to our knowledge of writing, even when they were the product of very different methods and offered conflicting prescriptions for how writing should be taught, it was still possible for us to think of them as joining the existing canon. I am thinking primarily of George Hillocks's *Research on Written Composition* and Shirley Brice Heath's *Ways with Words*. But when North's book was published, things were beginning to change. The field was becoming more diverse and the notion of a canon for both practical and theoretical reasons seemed less attractive or perhaps even impossible.

On the one hand, the scope and depth of *MKC* seemed to equal that of its canonical predecessors. A number of the first reviews praised the book in canonical terms (Lloyd-Jones 1989; Raymond 1989), and to this day there is no book that matches it as an overview and analysis of the kinds of research produced by the field of composition studies as a whole.

On the other hand, the tone of the book was sharply critical, and many later reviews, responses, and analyses took issue with North's characterization of practitioners and their kind of knowledge, what North called "lore" (Bartholomae 1988; Rankin 1990). In addition, the social turn and the increased emphasis on theory and cultural studies in the field have made the book seem old fashioned and not quite as relevant as it may have been in earlier times. It is significant that new overviews and taxonomies of the profession do not build or elaborate on North's categories. Indeed, in Mark Wiley, Barbara Gleason, and Louise Wetherbee Phelps's *Composition in Four Keys* (1996), *MKC* is simply one of four alternative "maps" to the profession, not including the "map" of *Four Keys* itself, and in his introduction to the section on "Alternative Maps," Mark Wiley is studiously neutral about the process of conceptualizing the field and gives no prominence to *MKC*.[1] It is also significant that none of what Wiley, Gleason, and Phelps call alternative maps to the profession base their taxonomies on how and what we know about writing. Rather, the four keys of Wiley, Gleason, and Phelps's book are nature, art, science, and politics, which express "communities of interest and difference" (3) among people working in composition studies. Clearly, we are a long way from a set of canonical texts that could help define the field, which may be why my sense is that *MKC* is not widely taught and is not widely cited, except in histories of the field. Composition studies is a different field than it was twenty-five years ago.

As a result, I find it deeply ironic that in the final chapter of *MKC* entitled "Futures," and in a chapter of *Composition in the Twenty-First Century* entitled "The Death of Paradigm Hope, The End of Paradigm Guilt, and the Future of (Research in) Composition" ("DPH"), published nine years after *MKC*, North defined the current state of the profession and looked to the future, providing good reasons why *MKC* may have been less influential than he would have liked it to be. I would argue that in *MKC*, although North got a few things wrong, he was generally right about certain long-term trends in the profession, and that when he followed up his analysis of the future of composition studies in "DPH," he was even more accurate. The field may now be characterized as postmodern, with no dominant theory or narrative, and we may view *MKC* as a transitional book, the last of the canon and the beginning of the postmodern era in the field, which may be characterized as "No More Masterpieces."

---

1.   For more on this, see also Berlin (1982) and Fulkerson (1990).

My argument will begin with a summary and an analysis of North's diagnosis of the prospects of composition studies as a field and then proceed to my own prescription for dealing with that diagnosis. More specifically, I will summarize North's vision of the future for composition studies in *MKC* and "DPH" and provide evidence that, with some glaring exceptions, North's vision has come true and that the fragmentation he predicted can only continue. My prescription will be that, like North, we should embrace this fragmented future, although I will point out some of its unintended political consequences. My main point, however, will focus on one aspect of North's vision that he does not deal with directly: the fragmentation of the field in terms of curriculum. I will argue that because the world outside composition studies has no clear idea of what it means to be a teacher, scholar, researcher, or writing-program administrator in composition studies, and no clear idea of what it means to teach writing, the field is open to criticism from other constituencies in the university, from boards of regents and legislators, and from the public at large that particular forms of instruction or the kinds of writing taught in the university do not prepare students to do the kinds of writing various constituencies want them to.

My prescription is to take North's diagnosis one step further. I suggest that the field should proclaim to the world just how postmodern the teaching of writing really is. Paradoxically, this admission might provide the field with more support because it would acknowledge the very pragmatic and contingent nature of writing in ways that the larger public could understand.

NORTH'S VISION OF THE FUTURE FOR COMPOSITION STUDIES

In the first chapter of *MKC*, "*c*omposition Becomes Composition," North explains why it is so difficult to conceptualize just what composition studies is as a form of inquiry. Because the field came of age in the late 1950s and early 1960s, when the successful launching of Sputnik by the Soviet Union during the height of the Cold War sent shock waves through American higher education, composition as the third leg of the English tripod—literature and language were the other two—became a source for federal funding but only if it was based on "research" that federal agencies could understand as justifying particular reforms in curriculum or pedagogical practices. In a short span of time, traditional teaching practices in composition, what North calls "lore," could no longer be justified simply because they had been used for decades, if not for centuries.

There was a resulting explosion in scholarship and research, all of it loosely associated with writing and writing instruction, but this scholarship and research quickly took on a life of its own, and its relationship to particular curricular or pedagogical practice became more distant and theoretical. It became increasingly difficult to hold, as John C. Gerber had held during his first year as the first president of the Conference on College Composition and Communication (CCCC), that composition studies had a central core of beliefs and values and a common research agenda. In 1950, Gerber complained that teachers of composition and communication "have had no systematic way of exchanging views and information quickly. Certainly we have no means of developing a coordinated research program." Gerber assumed that teachers of writing—and communications more generally—have a common objective and that what they need is more information and a coordinated research program. If CCCC meets these needs, Gerber said, "the standards of the profession will be raised" (12).

But in the decades following the renewed interest in composition as an integral part of English, the notion that composition studies could agree on common objectives and a coordinated research program became increasingly difficult to maintain. By the time of *MKC*, North could argue that as a discipline for "*doing* something," composition has focused on the teaching of writing, but that "the modern version of the field is founded, really, on the subversion of that practical tradition" (364). Thus, by 1987 North seems to think of composition studies not as a coherent academic discipline but as a collection of academic endeavors—of people in different ranks in the academic hierarchy doing very different things, from historical scholarship to empirical work only tangentially relating to writing per se, holding very different philosophies about the nature of writing, and also teaching writing in very different ways—all of them justifying their work by claiming some affiliation with writing instruction or administration.

This strikes me as a fair characterization of composition studies today, although nowadays the field encompasses an even broader notion of rhetoric and "literacies." We now speak of the rhetoric of things that are only metaphorically texts—architecture, film, and other visual media—and of a broad spectrum of literacies—visual literacy, functional literacy, and scientific and technological literacy, to name a few—that go well beyond the traditional essay. Whatever holds composition studies together today, it is something more encompassing and amorphous than simply teaching writing.

In the concluding chapter of *MKC*, North characterizes composition as becoming even more fragmented as time goes by: "Composition as a knowledge-making society is gradually pulling itself apart. Not branching out or expanding, although these might be politically more palatable descriptions, but fragmenting: gathering into communities or clusters of communities among which relations are becoming increasingly tenuous" (364). As this centripetal force increases, North envisions only two possibilities for composition as a field: either it will lose its "autonomous identity altogether," absorbed into fields other than English—education or linguistics or sociology, for example—or it will continue in English departments and lose its ability to preserve the variety of its knowledge-making methods. In the first scenario, practitioners of various research methods will become increasingly unhappy with composition as such a "loose baggy monster," to use a phrase Henry James applied to popular novels. These practitioners would naturally want to associate with people who do work similar to their own, and thus "Formalists concerned with the composing process would go off into cognitive psychology, Experimentalists into experimental psychology or schools of education, Ethnographers into anthropology, and so on" (365).

The alternative scenario is that composition scholars who stay in English departments will find themselves under intense pressure to model their research after the research done by literature faculty, and since, according to North, with the possible exception of the work of David Bleich and other reader-response scholars, literary scholarship has seldom focused on pedagogy, composition scholars will eventually divorce their research from their practice. They may remain what North calls scholars—historians, philosophers, and critics—but their work will become increasingly theoretical and hermeneutic, involved in the interpretation of published texts and divorced from the practicalities of teaching writing or of improving literacy in general.

North summarizes:

> [Composition's] long-term survival, then, will hinge on change of two kinds: First, Composition must break out of its constricting relationship with literary studies, either by taking a larger share of responsibility for knowledge-making in English departments, or by moving outside of such departments altogether. Second, it must find some way to establish an internal, inter-methodological

peace—to bypass or defy, in other words, the effects of Diesing's law [that scholarly cooperation can only occur within a method, not a field], so that the methodological pluralism that was responsible for creating Composition in the first place can remain its vital core. (369)

Interestingly, North does not believe that composition's becoming an independent academic unit would solve the problems inherent in its very nature. Even as a separate academic unit, a department of composition studies or writing studies, composition would face the difficulty of resolving methodological differences and appreciating methodological diversity, especially as it relates to practice (370).

There is a great deal of evidence that the fragmentation of composition studies that North foresaw in *MKC* has indeed taken place, although not in the precise way he described it. First of all, it seems to be true that what North called researchers—experimentalists, clinicians, formalists, or ethnographers—are not associated with English departments proper but with departments of education and psychology. However, this may be not because these researchers have broken off from English but because they were never associated with English departments in the first place. In the two major journals that publish research in composition studies—*Written Communication* and *Research in the Teaching of English*—overwhelmingly the researchers involved are not in English departments. For example, in volume 23 of *Written Communication* for the year 2006, there were thirteen articles about writing by seventeen authors and coauthors. Of those seventeen people, only two were from departments of English, and one was from an Asian department of English and communication. In a bibliographic overview of research in writing from 1999 to 2004, Mary M. Juzwik and her colleagues (2006) surveyed a wide variety of journals to determine the types of research that were being published. Of the sixteen journals the authors surveyed, only three were major journals in composition studies: *Written Communication*, of course, and also *Research in the Teaching of English* and *College Composition and Communication* (*CCC*). Journals such as *Rhetoric Review* and the *Journal of Advanced Composition* (*JAC*) were not surveyed. Clearly most of the research in writing—again, in North's sense of the term—is being done outside of departments of English, and the publication of research in composition studies is limited to basically three journals.

In addition, North thought scholars in composition studies would increasingly produce scholarship modeled after literary scholarship. But while it is true that a significant number of composition scholars do interpretive and theoretical work related to literary scholarship, there has not been a major movement in that direction. Only one of our major journals, *JAC*, regularly publishes theoretical work that parallels work done by literary scholars, and the major books devoted to the relationship of composition theory to literary theory are not numerous: John Schilb's *Between the Lines* (1996) and Schilb and John Clifford's *Writing Theory and Critical Theory* (1994) come to mind. Of course, there are also scholars such as Sidney Dobrin (1997) and Raul Sanchez (2005) working in the area of *theory*, who could be considered analogous to the similar interest among literary scholars. And many scholars in composition studies, such as Lynn Worsham and Gary Olson (1998), share an interest with literary scholars in the issues of gender, race, class, and sexuality. There is a host of books on these topics in composition studies. But despite the theoretical underpinnings of these books and articles in cultural studies, the focus of the work in composition studies is much different from that in literary studies. Most of the work in composition studies is rooted in the practice of using gender, race, class, and sexuality to understand and promote literacy. As a result, I don't think it is fair to say that scholars in composition studies have modeled their work along the lines of literary scholars. If anything both composition and literary scholars share an interest in cultural studies, which is common to the humanities in general.

Finally, North predicted that composition scholars would have to establish their own knowledge-making methodologies in English departments in order to survive, but he was skeptical that this was possible. However, *College Composition and Communication* (*CCC*), our most comprehensive journal, publishes work from scholars in English, which suggests that that there is a unique kind of scholarship in composition studies that is accepted in English departments. In volume 58, September 2006 to June 2007, the journal published sixteen major articles. Seven of them dealt with teaching issues, five were primarily historical, and one dealt with theoretical issues in research. Only three were what North would call "research": two were case studies, and one was a historical study with a great deal of empirical data on the relationship of labor markets and literacy.

Many of those seven *CCC* articles about teaching cited student texts as evidence, but these texts were not part of an in-depth case study of the students as writers. Rather, the student texts provided examples of how students responded to certain kinds of instruction or of the effects of the curriculum being discussed in the article. Both the case studies and the articles on teaching entertained a tentative hypothesis about a certain kind of instruction and offered a very subjective interpretation of student texts in support of that hypothesis. They offered insightful, personal interpretations of texts that might help other teachers think through similar problems or inspire researchers to study their conclusions more rigorously. These articles on student writing did not worry about validity and reliability or attempt to document the effectiveness of instruction using the rigorous research methods North categorized as experimental, clinical, formalist, or ethnographic. What these articles exemplify may be less a distinctively scholarly method than a continuation of the essayistic scholarly tradition applied to student texts. Such work is distinctively different from literary scholarship, and it is my sense is that this scholarly analysis of student writing is indeed accepted for tenure and promotion in a large number, if not most, of English departments with programs in composition and rhetoric. Thus, I think we can say that the field *has* carved out its own domain of knowledge making, or at least a way of applying scholarly analysis to student texts that distinguishes scholarly work in composition/rhetoric from literary studies.

There is also a certain amount of evidence that in response to the pressures North noted, composition has to some extent "[broken] out of its constricting relationship with literary studies" (369) by forming new academic units, be they writing courses or tracks within departments, interdisciplinary units such as writing across the curriculum, or independent writing programs.

As early as 1989, Donald Stewart reported that of 197 English departments, 74 offered a "block of courses" or track other than literature, either in creative writing or "practical or applied composition." Fifty-three additional departments offered individual courses in "practical or applied composition," such courses as "professional and technical writing," "writing and editing," or "career writing" (190–91). Seven years later, Bettina Huber reported that the percentage of four-year English programs with a concentration in "writing (e.g., professional, technical)" increased from 29.2 percent in a 1984–85 survey to 45.9 percent in a 1991–92 survey (1996, 66). Clearly, the broad trend is toward more undergraduate tracks and concentrations in writing, and Carl Lovitt (2005) reports that these writing tracks and concentrations are gradually becoming more focused on writing and requiring less literature.

The latest survey of bachelor's degrees in English by the United States Department of Education also indicates an increasing number of students graduating with BAs in "English composition," "Creative writing," and "Technical and business writing," although it is not clear if the larger numbers reflect an increased number of programs or simply more graduates in existing programs (Laurence 2007, 5). In either case, undergraduate writing programs seem to be thriving.

Also in the mid-1980s, the Modern Language Association found that more than a third of the 194 four-year colleges and universities responding to a survey had some form of writing instruction across the curriculum; that is, in those institutions writing was taught in discipline-specific or particular content courses in addition to those courses designated as writing courses (Survey 1985). A later and more extensive survey by Susan McLeod and Susan Shirley published about the same time, confirmed these results: of 1,112 institutions that included two-year community colleges, 38 percent had some form of writing across the curriculum (1988, 103).

In addition, there has been a recent increase in the number of writing programs independent of English departments. Seven of them, as well as Harvard University's long-established independent program, are described in Peggy O'Neill, Angela Crow, and Larry Burton's *A Field of Dreams: Independent Writing Programs and the Future of Composition Studies* (2002). Most of these programs, plus the free-standing multidisciplinary program at Duke University, headed by Joseph Harris, are newly established, often less than five years old, so it is too soon to know how much of a trend they indicate.

Clearly, then, composition studies has developed a distinctive form of scholarship—the close reading of student texts in support of pedagogical practices or cultural analysis—that English studies as a whole accepts as the equivalent to literary scholarship. And composition studies has separated itself from literary studies in a variety of ways institutionally, either by offering separate tracks in BA and MA programs, by working in writing-across-the-curriculum programs, or by establishing separate academic units. All this may reflect the pedagogical and theoretical diversity in the profession, or it may be an indication that the fragmentation North predicted is proceeding apace. It may be too early to tell.

By 1996, the year "DPH" was published, North had come to accept the fragmentation of the field as a good thing. According to North, because of our postmodern, critical, and historicizing attitude toward all knowledge, "paradigm hope," the myth of pure scientific research, of "'genuine contributions to knowledge' untainted by the apparatus of institutional life" is dead (200).

North does not mourn the death of paradigm hope, the death of Gerber's vision of common objectives and a coordinated research program for the profession. In fact, he finds it liberating. A belief in any central paradigm, North argues, is ultimately stultifying: such a belief fixes a set of pedagogical practices "internally" so that they can be studied in a disciplined way over time, which in effect inhibits true experimentation and change; and such a belief tends to preserve a set of institutional practices "externally," by providing a powerful incentive to maintain the current organizational and curricular status of writing instruction in colleges and universities (200–01).

North has an alternative vision of research in composition studies. In his vision, research will be "tied closely to our increasingly diversified instructional efforts": "Instead of leading an orderly march toward a perfected practice, research will find itself hurrying to keep up, serving as a companion—perhaps a commentator—trying to engage those practices in what will very often be a breathless dialogue" (203).

This breathless dialogue of pedagogical practice and research will eventually promote, North speculates, a broader range of research interests, a "wider range of issues [explored and reported] in a wider variety of forms," resulting in a greater quantity of research produced ever more quickly, which will in turn make that research "both far less transportable and—though the term may seem unpleasant—far more disposable," less and less applicable to any time or place other than a few related sites and practices and less and less capable of being generalized over time (205). Indeed, North's vision of composition research seems to be an apotheosis of postmodernist theories of knowledge: composition pedagogy and the research based on that pedagogy are now and will become increasingly local, historicized, contingent. According to North, composition studies will continue to focus on pedagogical issues, but as our pedagogical practices and our writing curricula continue to diversify and fragment, the research based on these practices will become increasingly "less transportable" and "more disposable."

In "DPH," North seems to have reconceptualized his earlier idea of composition in some interesting ways. First, he has focused only on the research in composition studies that is directly related to instructional practice. He seems to be less concerned with the kind of research he labeled as "scholarly" in *MKC*—rhetorical history, philosophy, and crit-icism—that is not directly related to particular pedagogies; he is more concerned with research that effects instruction. As a result, he implies more obviously than he did in *MKC* that the pedagogies of composition studies are incoherent and contradictory. This too, I think, is a fair char-acterization of the field.

The range of pedagogies in composition studies is well summarized in Gary Tate, Amy Rupiper, and Kurt Schick's collection of essays on the profession, *A Guide to Composition Pedagogies* (2001). The book contains chapters on process pedagogy, expressive pedagogy, rhetorical peda-gogy, collaborative pedagogy, cultural studies pedagogy, critical peda-gogy, feminist pedagogy, writing across the curriculum, writing centers, basic writing, and pedagogy based on technology. As I have argued else-where, the essays in Tate, Rupiper, and Schick's collection clearly dem-onstrate that the various theories, methods, and pedagogies in the field have no common theoretical basis, no shared assumptions about the nature and value of writing, and no communal sense of what kinds of writing should be taught and learned (Smit 2004, 137–38).

Moreover, the primary way scholars and researchers devoted to one form of pedagogy interact with scholars and researchers devoted to other forms of pedagogy seems to consist primarily of border raids, in which the researchers and scholars in one area point out the problems in the assumptions and points of view of those in other areas. For exam-ple, in the September 2006 *CCC*, there was a bitter exchange between Russell Durst and William Thelin on the value of critical pedagogy. And in the February 2007 issue, there was a spirited exchange between Phillip Marzluf and his critics on ways to teach diversity and the kinds of writing to incorporate into that instruction.

This radical fragmentation about the very nature of writing research and instruction is perhaps best illustrated in the response in 1995 to an article in *CCC* by Denise David, Barbara Gordon, and Rita Pollard. These scholars surveyed the very different ways that writing is taught in American colleges and universities: as a form of personal expression, as an introduction to the discourse of various disciplines, as a means of transforming social inequities, and as a way to talk about multicultur-alism, literature, or other topics. In order to bring some coherence to these divergent views, David, Gordon, and Pollard proposed that com-position studies get back to basics and rethink the fundamental ques-tion, what do we mean when we call a course a writing course? (524).

To promote such reflection, the group suggested that all writing courses should have the following characteristics:

1. The development of writing ability and metacognitive awareness is the primary objective of a writing course.

2. The students' writing is the privileged text in a writing course.

3. The subject of a writing course is writing. (525–26)

That is, what the students should spend most of their time thinking about and talking about is how they go about understanding themselves as writers, how they get ideas, how they compose in relation to various subjects, genres, and audiences, and how they respond to criticism of their work.

But David, Gordon, and Pollard's proposal prompted two major critiques in *CCC* a year later. Katherine Gottschalk (1995) noted that in their list of characteristics for a good writing course, David, Gordon, and Pollard confused an objective ("the development of writing ability and metacognitive awareness") with the means of achieving that objective (student writing being the text and the subject of the course). Gottschalk had no problem accepting the development of writing ability and metacognitive awareness as the goal of a writing course, but she wondered what it meant to make student writing the text and subject of the course. Obviously, she said, students have to write about something. Shouldn't writing instructors then devote class time to extensive discussion of what the students are writing about so that the students will have a better grasp of their subject matter? And when students write persuasively from a certain position, they need to know the consequences of that position and its effect on others. Shouldn't then writing instructors devote class time to exploring various points of view and their implications? In short, to Gottschalk it was not at all clear how we can distinguish between the teaching of a subject matter and teaching how to write about it.

Phyllis Mentzell Ryder also responded to David, Gordon, and Pollard, but from another perspective. Ryder notes that writing is socially conditioned and "blends together social, linguistic, and political analysis as well. Rhetorical analysis goes far beyond determining what "choices" the authors have made; rather, it examines what choices were made for the authors by the larger cultural contexts. Further, it examines the intended and unintended effects—the ways that language hides one meaning even as it offers another" (601). As a result, Ryder suggests, if writers need to be metacognitively aware of how language works, shouldn't writing instructors also spend considerable class time offering students "useful theoretical insights about language so that they can critically engage with the world around them?" (1996, 601).

In many ways this exchange of views epitomizes the fragmentation of instruction with the rise of theory and the cultural turn in English studies. Each of the participants in the conversation I have just summarized represents a particular theory or philosophy of instruction. David, Gordon, and Pollard represent the process approach, or perhaps expressivism, because they insist that a writing class ought to focus on helping the students work through writing process and the primary texts of the course ought to be the students' own work. Gottschalk represents a writing-across-the-curriculum approach, perhaps even service-learning programs and professional writing courses, because she insists that instructors teach writing in the context of particular subject matter. And Ryder represents critical pedagogy because she is concerned that students learn about the social and political implications of writing so that they can be trained to critique social and political systems and work to change them. Just what these various composition pedagogies have in common is not at all clear, if they have anything in common at all.

In short, after forty-five years as an academic field—if we accept North's argument that 1963 is the year the field came of age—composition studies, as North predicted, is still arguing fundamental principles: what to study about writing and how to do it, what to teach about writing and how to do it. As a result, because writing is taught by people with such radically different methodologies for studying writing and such radically different ideologies about what writing is, how writing should be taught, and indeed, what writing instruction should accomplish, composition studies has no central vision of what it means to teach writing. Indeed, composition studies has no means for even talking about the differences that divide the profession.

THE POLITICAL IMPLICATIONS OF NORTH'S VISION

In "DPH," North is more sanguine about the fragmentation of composition studies than he was in *MKC* because he has come to be suspicious of all totalizing schemes, all universals. He seems to have in mind a competition among the pedagogy-research groups in the field. Over time the scholars and researchers in these groups will experiment with new pedagogical practices and develop theories and research methods in order to study these practices. Gradually the publication of these theories and research studies will have some sort of impact on the field as a whole.

But the irony of North's position is that it too, like the pure research paradigm he disparages, promotes an overpowering conservatism in which every researcher and scholar can diligently work in her own pedagogy-research specialty and comfortably ignore everything outside the narrow confines of that specialty, and every classroom teacher can comfortably continue to teach the way she always has because there is no consensus about how writing ought to be taught or even what constitutes knowledge in the field. If all forms of research and pedagogical practice can be critiqued from any number of theoretical and pedagogical points of view, then all of them wind up dying the slow death of a thousand cuts. There are no common warrants upon which to base persuasive strategies and there is no acceptable way to reach consensus, except within each local research or teaching community.

To his credit, North sees the problem and offers two warrants by which all of us can judge the relevance and importance of any research project: plausibility and utility (1996, 205). But of course this begs the question, for if we have no common vision of what constitutes knowledge in the field, then we have no common sense of what is plausible and useful. North says that he is indebted to Patricia Harkin's "The Postdisciplinary Politics of Lore" (1991), so I assume that he would approve of the way Harkin deals with the problem of competing theoretical and pedagogical practices: Harkin envisions "a series of conferences that ask us to work up from the practice of lore, not down from a theory of writing" (156). Each conference would deal with a certain problem in the field, and featured guest teachers would be presented on videotape showing how they deal with the problem. Then a panel of "representatives of disciplinary ways of knowing, experienced in thinking through the implications of a practice," would meet to discuss the implications of the various pedagogical strategies illustrated on videotape. The purpose of the panel discussion would not be for teachers to take away ideas that work from the theorists, but for theorists to provide a philosophical and theoretical justification for the practices on the tape which already do work and to comment on the strengths and weaknesses of each practice from a variety of perspectives. Such a conference, Harkin hopes, would not be characterized by either/or logic but by a dialogue in which the difficulties of particular pedagogies will be honestly explored. And by extending the conference through a telecommunication system to allow callers nationwide to question the participants—the theorists and the teachers and students demonstrating a particular practice—that dialogue might have the potential to truly create knowledge for a broad constituency (137–38).[2]

I appreciate Harkin's vision, and I definitely think it is worth trying. However, Harkin assumes that there is enough consensus in composition studies for a group of conference planners to agree on what good practice is. It is significant that her example is of a tutor and a single student in a writing lab rather than in a classroom with, say, twenty students. Tutorials strike me as much less controversial than a pedagogy for a "regular" classroom, whatever that might be. Harkin also assumes that a range of commentary from such disparate points of view as those of "a Carnegie Mellon empiricist, a Marxian, an Elbow-oriented 'romanticist,' a linguist, a classical rhetorician, a phenomenologist" could actually interact in such a way as to produce something called knowledge. Harkin herself does not hold out the possibility that this knowledge would be a consensus, only that it would demarcate "persons and problems that it thinks important" (1991, 138). In other words, even with her brilliant strategy for emphasizing pedagogy in the profession, Harkin agrees with North that there is little hope that knowledge in composition studies will ever be anything more than the equivalent of what a conglomeration of pedagogical and research interest groups do in their own unique and peculiar ways.

There are other more political implications to North's vision. First of all, the theoretical fragmentation of the profession naturally carries over to pedagogical practice. As a result, the field presents a very confused picture of what it means to be a "professional" writing teacher. Because composition studies has no common research tradition, no common research methodology, no common teaching practices, it has no common view of what it means to be a professional except an institutional one: a professional in composition studies is someone in a tenure-track line at a college or university who does something related to writing or someone who regularly teaches writing as an instructor. But just what a professional *does*—just what a professional in composition studies researches and how she researches it and just how a professional in

---

2.   For more on this, see Schilb (1991).

composition studies teaches writing, if she teaches writing at all—is not at all clear, especially since many other people at a university where a professional in composition studies works may be involved in the teaching of writing and rely on certain kinds of scholarship and research, on certain methods of teaching writing, that have little or nothing to do with the scholarship, research, and teaching of the professional. I am speaking, of course, of the adjuncts, part timers, and graduate students who do most of the teaching of writing at our colleges and universities.

The adjuncts, part timers, and graduate students who are involved in the teaching of writing are not professionals in the same sense as the tenure-track professionals in composition studies or full-time instructors, but the reason they are not professionals in the same sense may have nothing to do with scholarship, research, and teaching. Many adjuncts, part timers, and graduate students read professional journals and are aware of what is going on in the field; many of them actually publish in the field; many of them are the best teachers of writing at their respective colleges and universities. But it is also true that many others of these adjuncts, part timers, and graduate students have little professional preparation to teach writing. They have little or no graduate training in composition and rhetoric and only the broadest sense of what constitutes good writing and how to teach writing.

Without a common vision of what it means to do research in composition studies or a common vision of what writing is, how writing is learned, and how writing ought to be taught, the term *professional* in composition studies becomes almost meaningless. And if being a professional in composition studies only reflects institutional standing, it is no wonder that the professional study and teaching of writing causes confusion and does not inherently command respect. If the professional at University X encourages students to write short personal essays critiquing society from the perspective of cultural studies, and her primary teaching strategy is the analysis of theoretical texts, and an adjunct at the same university invites his students to write personal narratives, informative magazine profiles, and persuasive editorials for the campus paper, and his primary teaching strategy is the analysis of his own students' writing in response to the assignments, on what basis does the public decide what being a professional in composition studies means? On what basis do they decide that being an institutionalized professional, a member of the professoriate or a "regularized instructor," is more advantageous to the promotion of literacy than being a part-time adjunct?

But the most serious implication of the fragmentation of composition studies is that it suggests another reason for the profession's continued ambivalent standing: it is not organized to promote a common vision before the public. Other professions—most obviously the medical and legal professions—often present blurred and troubled images to the public. Newspapers regularly run stories about possible malpractice on the part of doctors and the contradictory results of yet another study of the effects of certain diets in preventing cancer or what a person's ideal weight should be. The image of lawyers as social parasites is almost at the level of folk legend. And yet most members of the general public have a clear sense of what these professionals *do*, at least when they make appointments to see them. That sense may be simple and even naïve but it is the basis of a relationship, perhaps only a grudging respect, between the public and these professions.

Most professions also have central organizations such as the American Medical Association or the American Bar Association, which claim to speak for their constituents. The public knows that these organizations do not speak with one voice for the profession. They read editorials by doctors arguing the merits of various plans for healthcare, and they see lawyers on the television news shows protesting the nominees approved by the ABA for the supreme court. But despite all of these complex messages and mixed signals, the public can separate the activities of most professionals from their political stances and accept them for their performances as professionals despite their views on national health insurance or the qualities of Joseph Alito as a supreme court nominee. They know enough about what these professionals do to form opinions about what constitutes a good doctor or lawyer, about what constitutes appropriate medical care or effective legal representation, and they can distinguish a professional's activities from her political stance.

There is a great deal of evidence that the public often cannot distinguish between what a composition studies professional does and her political stances, as the great furor over the proposed course in writing at the University of Texas in 1990 demonstrated. In the public uproar over English 306 at the University of Texas, the obvious question was Why should writing be taught through case studies of discrimination law? (Brodkey 1995). The content of the course seemed to many people to be totally arbitrary and unconnected to any generally accepted sense of what it means to be able to write. This is just one indication that the public has no clear idea of what it means to be a teacher, scholar, researcher, or writing program administrator in composition studies.

Perhaps even more damning in the eyes of the public is that the field seems defensive when its representatives talk about the effectiveness or ineffectiveness, the success and failure, of various forms of instruction. Composition scholars are well known for objecting to standardized multiple-choice tests as measures of writing ability, for opposing timed essay tests as a measure of how well students write or how successful writing programs have been, for pointing out the difficulties of validity and reliability in forms of portfolio assessment. As a result, the public at large could easily infer that writing professionals believe that they are beyond criticism and evaluation, that there are no ways of assessing writing and measuring the effectiveness of writing instruction. The reasonable question, of course, is, why should the public pay for instructional programs that cannot demonstrate their effectiveness?

If the problem of research in composition studies is as North diagnoses it—that the field has no dominant pedagogy or research paradigm—and if there is no consensus in the field about what writing is, how writing should be taught, or how it ought to be evaluated; indeed, just the opposite, if the field is now truly postmodern, and every position is so historicized and so critiqued that no research paradigm can ever *hope* to dominate, that no forms of instruction or methods of evaluation can ever *hope* to demonstrate their superiority over others, then the question is whether the field will ever have more influence and power than it has now, whether it can ever make more of a difference than it does now in helping people learn to write.

PRESCRIPTION

It seems to me that there is a way for the profession to capitalize on the fact that it is now localized, historicized, and contingent, both theoretically and pedagogically, and that such a move would be the logical extension of what North—and Harkin—have suggested. That strategy would be to acknowledge to the world that writing research is without paradigm hope so that writing must of necessity be taught from some particular theoretical point of view using a particular method of instruction—that the writing curriculum must reflect the diversity of writing itself. In fact, I would go beyond North and argue that writing can only be effectively taught in genre-specific and context-specific ways, that what students learn about writing in one context may not transfer to other contexts, that the way we study writing instruction in one context may not apply to writing instruction in other contexts, and that to teach writing in particular courses is to teach a very narrow and limited sense of what "writing" is because there is no such thing as generic writing. There is only writing for particular purposes in particular contexts using particular genres. Or to put it in terms of the medieval realist-nominalist controversy, there is no such thing as "tree-ness"; there are only particular trees. In this countervision, composition studies would acknowledge that the field has a limited ability to affect the teaching of writing through traditional writing courses.

Such a countervision would also entail admitting that there can be no dominant forms of instruction or evaluation because there is no such thing as writing in general, that all instruction and evaluation must be geared to much more limited questions: Can certain kinds of instruction help students learn some limited aspects of writing? Can certain forms of evaluation demonstrate that some group of students learned some limited aspect of writing or that certain writing programs foster certain aspects of writing? Given this point of view, the field could cheerfully admit the wide range of what students learn in writing classes. It could cheerfully admit that in Professor X's writing course, students learn to write dense social analyses from the point of view of cultural studies, while in Instructor Y's class, students learn to write personal narratives, informative magazine profiles, and persuasive editorials for the campus paper. It could cheerfully admit that in writing-across-the-curriculum programs students learn to write essays about topics in particular academic disciplines, and in service-learning programs they learn to write about and for a variety of service organizations.

We as members of the profession may find the admission of our diverse theories, methods, and practices difficult to accept because such an admission would make it clear for all to see that the emperor has no clothes, that we have been at best misguided and at worst misleading and evasive when we claim to teach writing in some broad way. Such an admission would open our courses and writing curricula to intense scrutiny from all our constituents and stakeholders to what exactly we teach, why we teach it, and how. We could no longer disguise our course content and methods behind the vague phrase, "Well, I am just teaching writing."

Nevertheless, I think that admitting the truth would be broadly accepted by the public at large. Listen to students talk to one another about their writing courses. They know without being able to articulate it very well that they are not learning the same things in their different writing classes. Pay attention to the dialogue between your own composition-program administrators and the admissions officers at your college and university as they negotiate the acceptance of transfer credits from other institutions. They know from experience that students who transfer credits in a literature-based writing course did not learn the same things about writing as the students at your university who are required to take a writing course in argument and persuasion. Listen to faculty members as they talk about how their students can't write in their upper-level courses, even though the students have taken Composition I and II. Our colleagues know without being able to articulate it very well that what students learn in Comp I and II does not prepare them to write in ways that faculty outside of writing programs expect them to. It is time as a profession to admit all this. In some deep sense, our constituencies and stakeholders already know it. We simply have to be honest and face up to the implications of what we and they know is true. Writing has to be learned and taught course by course, genre by genre, discourse community by discourse community, context by context. Introductory writing classes are simply that: introductions to the great adventure of becoming literate in a wide variety of genres in a number of different discourse communities.

If we as a profession wanted to implement this vision, we would face a number of difficulties. First and foremost, of course, is the practical matter, given the diversity of the field, of how to promote such conflicting views of pedagogy and research. The two entities that could promote the diversity of theory and practice in composition studies to both the university community and the larger world are the Conference on College Composition and Communication (CCCC) and its parent organization, the National Council of Teachers of English (NCTE). Both organizations work to articulate broad policies on such matters as class size and the use of part-time nontenure-track faculty, but neither group has ever indicated, or indeed shown any apparent interest in determining, whether any particular pedagogical theories and practices are more appropriate than any other. Perhaps this is as it should be. But it is not so large a step from being neutral in the theory wars to promoting the notion that writing ability is complex and difficult to achieve and that particular theories and methods promote different aspects of writing; that to be broadly literate, students need to be exposed to a broad range of writing in a variety of contexts; and that to be competent in particular genres about particular subject matter, students need intense exposure to those genres in the contexts in which those genres are used.

CCCC and NCTE will change their focus and promote a postmodern view of writing only over time, and only as the postmodern view of writing becomes more widespread, and as change agents at particular institutions begin to modify their curricula to provide more writing using particular genres in particular contexts. The process will be evolutionary, but as I have argued before, the fragmentation of the field is an indication that the process is well under way (Smit 2004, 215–23).

Another difficulty would be dealing with the intensely political issues raised by an admission that there is no such thing as generic writing. Admitting the diversity of writing practice and research might open the writing curriculum to criticism from those who want to go "back to the basics" or who think much of higher education is too liberal, as in the Students for Academic Freedom movement. Such an admission could open a new front in the culture wars. Some constituencies and stakeholders might be outraged at how "political" some forms of writing instruction are. Others might want students to avoid learning how to write expressive and essayistic genres as part of a broad literate tradition and focus only on those genres appropriate for their careers in a profession or in corporate or bureaucratic life. Such constituencies can be powerful and can lobby state legislatures and local administrators to cut those courses they find offensive or inappropriate.

However, it strikes me that this is a political struggle worth starting. I think it is wrong to hide our practices in anonymity. We need to be open and honest about the methods we use and the genres we actually teach in our writing classes. We need the hard discipline of justifying our courses in the fire of political give and take. And most of all, we need to give our students the chance to choose the kinds of instruction and genres that would best suit their needs and interests.

And that leads to one final difficulty: the writing courses offered by certain faculty might suffer if the larger community learned what they were really promoting as "writing." Of course, if we were open and honest about the ways we teach writing, promoting our content and methods in catalogue course descriptions, there would be competition among different contents and pedagogies, and a gradual sorting out. We would have to face the fact that given such truth in advertising, some kinds of writing classes would be more popular than others because they would meet more directly our students' needs and interests. But the argument for truth in advertising is compelling: If our writing courses are not meeting our students' needs and interests, what are we offering them for?

Such a countervision would also entail admitting that evaluating writing is difficult and that as a result our methods of evaluation are extremely limited. They are often limited to how well students can write particular genres in particular contexts. Portfolio evaluation may have problems with validity and reliability, but portfolios can demonstrate that with a certain amount of help students can write certain genres with something approximating generally recognized standards for those genres. The profession could also cheerfully admit that even timed essay tests on particular topics tell us something about how students write: they tell us how well students write timed essay tests on those topics.

Stephen North's *The Making of Knowledge in Composition* may have had an uncertain impact on the field of composition studies, and its influence may be in dispute. But about the major historical trends in the profession, I think North was basically right. It is time we as a profession embraced his vision as the most accurate portrayal of who we really are and what we really do. As a profession we have an ethical obligation to be open and honest about what we know about writing, how we conduct research in writing, and how we teach writing. And in thinking about our obligations, in contemplating who we are as a profession, and in deciding what we ought to do in the future, we have no better model of thoughtfulness and vision than Stephen North.

REFERENCES

Bartholomae, David. 1988. Review of *The making of knowledge in composition: Portrait of an emerging field* by Stephen M. North. *Rhetoric Review* 6: 224–28.

Berlin, James. 1982. Contemporary composition: The major pedagogical theories. *College English* 44: 765–77.

Brodkey, Linda. 1995. Writing permitted in designated areas only. In *Higher education under fire: Politics, economics, and the crisis of the humanities,* edited by Michael Berube and Cary Nelson. New York: Routledge.

David, Denise, Barbara Gordon, and Rita Pollard. 1995. Seeking common ground: Guiding assumptions for writing courses. *College Composition and Communication* 44 (6): 522–32.

Dobrin, Sidney. 1997. *Constructing knowledges: The politics of theory building and pedagogy in composition studies.* Albany: State University of New York Press.

Fulkerson, Richard. 1990. Composition theory in the eighties: Axiological consensus and paradigmatic diversity. *College Composition and Communication* 41: 409–29.

Gerber, John C. 1950. The conference on college composition and communication. *College Composition and Communication* 1: 12.

Gottschalk, Katherine K. 1996. Uncommon grounds: What are the primary traits of a writing course. *College Composition and Communication* 47 (4): 59–99.

Harkin, Patricia. 1991. Postdisciplinary politics of lore. In *Contending with words: Composition and rhetoric in a post-modern age*, edited by Patricia Harkin and John Schilb. New York: Modern Language Association.

Huber, Bettina J. 1996. Undergraduate English programs: Findings from an MLA survey of the 1991–1992 academic year. *ADE Bulletin* 115: 34–73.

Juzwik, Mary M., et al. 2006. Writing into the 21st century: An Overview of research in writing, 1999–2004. *Written Communication* 23: 451–76.

Lloyd-Jones, Richard. 1989. Review of *The making of knowledge in composition: Portrait of an emerging field*, by Stephen M. North. *College Composition and Communication* 40: 98–100.

Laurence, David. 2007. Trends in bachelor's degree awards, 1989–90 to 2005–06. *ADE Bulletin* 143: 3–7.

Lovitt, Carl R. 2005. Literature requirements in the curricula of writing degrees and concentrations. *Writing Program Administration* 29: 11–29.

McLeod, Susan, and Susan Shirley. 1988. National survey of writing across the curriculum programs. In *Strengthening programs for writing across the curriculum*, edited by Susan H. McLeod. New Directions for Teaching and Learning 36. San Francisco: Jossey-Bass.

North, Stephen. 1987. *The making of knowledge in composition*. Upper Montclair, NJ. Boynton/Cook.

_____. 1996. The death of paradigm hope, the end of paradigm guilt, and the future of (research in) composition. In *Composition in the twenty-first century: Crisis and change*, edited by Lynn Z. Bloom, Donald A. Daiker, and Edward M. White. Carbondale: Southern Illinois University Press.

O'Neill, Peggy, Angela Crow, and Larry Burton. 2002. *A field of dreams: Independent writing programs and the future of composition studies*. Logan: Utah State University Press.

Rankin, Elizabeth. 1990. Taking practitioner inquiry seriously: An argument with Stephen North. *Rhetoric Review* 8: 260–67.

Raymond, James C. 1989. Review of *The making of knowledge in composition: Portrait of an emerging field*, by Stephen M. North. *College Composition and Communication* 40: 93–95.

Ryder, Phyllis Mentzell. 1996. Will your disciplinary umbrella cover me? *College Composition and Communication* 47 (4): 599–602.

Sanchez, Raul. 2005. *The function of theory in composition studies*. Albany: State University of New York Press.

Schilb, John. 1991. What's at stake in the conflict between "theory" and "practice" in composition? *Rhetoric Review* 10: 91–97.

_____. 1996. *Between the lines: Relating composition and literary theory*. Portsmouth, NH: Heinemann-Boynton/Cook.

_____, and John Clifford, eds. 1994. *Writing theory and critical theory*. New York: Modern Language Association.

Smit, David W. 2004. *The end of composition studies*. Carbondale: Southern Illinois University Press.

Stewart, Donald C. 1989. What is an English major, and what should it be? *College Composition and Communication* 40: 188–202

Survey of the Profession. 1985. New York: MLA Commission on Writing and Literature.

Tate, Gary, Amy Rupiper, and Kurt Schick, eds. 2001. *A guide to composition pedagogies*. New York: Oxford University Press.

Wiley, Mark. 1996. Map making. In Wiley, Gleason, and Phelps.

Wiley, Mark, Barbara Gleason, and Louise Wetherbee Phelps, eds. 1996. *Composition in four keys: Inquiring into the field*. Mountain View, CA: Mayfield.

Worsham, Lynn, and Gary Olson. 1998. *Race, rhetoric, and the postcolonial*. Albany: State University of New York Press.

13

ARE WE THERE YET?
The Making of a Discipline in Composition

Kristine Hansen

A frequently debated question among composition scholars during the 1980s, 1990s, and even beyond, was whether the field was a discipline or not. For years, many respected figures in the field have spoken of it as such (e.g., Connors 1999; Goggin 2000; Lauer 2006; Phelps 1988; Slevin 2001), but there are some who firmly disagree or at least express doubt (e.g., Crowley 1998; Harris 2005; Haswell 2005; Miller 2003; Smit 2004). Stephen North's own answer in 1987 was that composition was not a discipline and could become one only if five criteria were met. First, either it must escape the strangulating domination of literary studies in English departments by founding autonomous departments, or it must establish knowledge-making parity with literary studies in English departments by creating, accumulating, and disseminating knowledge "in ways that would meet with academic approval" (1987, 370). North found the latter possibility unlikely, so he thought autonomy was needed, where, he hoped, the second criterion might be met: establishment of "inter-methodological peace" so that the methodological pluralism that brought composition into being might remain its "vital core" (369). In such spaces, he believed, a new discipline might emerge if the final three criteria were to combine and form a methodologically coherent enterprise: first, "heightened methodological consciousness"; second, "a spirit of methodological egalitarianism," making respectful understanding the norm for all methods of inquiry; and, third, the reestablishment of practice as inquiry—that is, an acceptance and appreciation of what lore is and how it "can usefully interact" with other kinds of knowledge (370–71).

In this essay, I use North's five criteria to judge whether composition might, nearly twenty-five years after the publication of *MKC*, be called a fully formed discipline, and I evaluate North's criteria by examining how the field has developed and how his own published positions changed since he made his predictions. The evidence to be considered in making this judgment is vast, varied, and always changing. It's impossible to survey it all, and like anyone looking at the records of the past and present, I interpret the evidence in light of my own experience and biases. I must take the reader down a meandering road, starting with a consideration of composition's location and status. The end of the journey may be disappointing since I conclude we haven't arrived yet.

AUTONOMOUS DEPARTMENTS OR KNOWLEDGE-MAKING PARITY IN ENGLISH

At the outset, it's critical to note that by "Composition," North meant the teaching of writing. In 1987 he viewed the invention of the term "composition studies" as a "subversion of that practical [pedagogical] tradition," and he saw the direction in which composition studies was heading as "taking the long way around" to establishing a discipline. As he said, "Training in a discipline ordinarily implies preparation for *doing* something, and in Composition, that something has been and in practice largely remains teaching writing" (364; italics in original). Interestingly, North did allow that composition was a profession, but one with "relatively limited control over the training, licensing, and review of its members" when compared with professions like law and medicine—which are also disciplines (364). Curiously, however, in *MKC* North did not comment on the material conditions in which composition programs were supposed to professionalize their members, though it was certainly the case in 1987 that graduate students, part-time teachers, and untenured full-time teachers were sizeable percentages—in some places likely the majority—of the staff teaching composition courses.[1] How the few PhD-holding compositionists at that time were supposed to take these lowliest members of the academy and form independent departments was not explained any more than the shape of these departments was outlined. Were they to offer only typical general-education courses in first-year writing, perhaps basic writing, and maybe an advanced writing course or two? Would they offer a major? Would there be undergraduate as well as graduate courses in the teaching of writing? Would there

---

1.   According to data derived from the U.S. Department of Education, IPEDS Fall Staff Survey, in 1989 (two years after the publication of *MKC*) faculty in all degree-granting institutions were composed of 36.4 percent part-time faculty and 16.9 percent full-time faculty not on a tenure track. In other words 53.3 percent of college faculty in 1989 were not tenured or on a tenure track.

be courses in writing for the workplace? To be fair, it was not North's purpose to undertake such explanations in the last chapter of *MKC*; still, it would be interesting to know what he envisioned at the time.

Nearly twenty years later, it's clear that the favored path North laid out in his first criterion—escaping the domination of literary studies and establishing autonomous composition departments—has not yet happened in any widespread way. In fact, I am aware of no department in a North American university or college that calls itself a "department of composition," though we are now starting to see autonomous departments that focus on writing and rhetoric. Deborah Balzhiser and Susan McLeod (2010), members of the Conference on College Composition and Communication (CCCC) Committee on the Major in Rhetoric and Composition, indicate that as of 2008 there were at least sixty-eight majors in writing offered at sixty-five different institutions. Of these sixty-eight majors, Balzhiser and McLeod conclude that twenty-three were offered in autonomous departments having the words *rhetoric, writing, language* and/or *communication* as the most prominent terms in their various titles. Judging from the website where the CCCC Committee on the Major reports data, it appears that none of these majors take the teaching of composition as their main purpose; in fact, all of them seem to prepare students to be not teachers but practicing writers who address largely nonacademic audiences in various genres, including journalism, business writing, public relations, science writing, technical writing, writing for the Web, and essays, fiction, and poetry. Yet at this writing in 2010, even if the number of writing majors were twice what it was in 2008, with over four thousand postsecondary institutions in the United States, it would still not amount to one percent of the total. Although an emerging national trajectory promises increasing numbers of academic departments devoted to writing, it also seems that the education of writing teachers will not be their principal object.

But North did suggest that composition might become responsible for a greater share of knowledge making within English departments, thus an equal partner in those domains. An indication of emerging equality comes, again, from the data analyzed by Balzhiser and McLeod (2010), who identify forty-five writing majors located within departments of English, literature, or humanities—good evidence that a few departments are willing to expand their curriculum to include more courses offered by rhetoric and writing specialists. However, like the twenty-three independent writing majors, the forty-five majors offered in

English and humanities departments comprise a broad range of courses preparing students to produce, rather than teach, various kinds of writing. By my count, only six list a course in the teaching of writing—and these are all elective courses at that.

Still, though the numbers are small, it is significant that there are now at least sixty-five campuses where students can major in the production of writing, if not its teaching. But what does this trend signify? First, the names of these new units and majors suggest that, as North defined it, composition may be too slender a thing to sustain an entire academic department. Perhaps many of these new entities are responsible for the teaching of required general education courses in composition; but, if so, such courses don't seem to play a large role for their majors, since only fifteen of the sixty-eight majors on the CCCC committee's list even use the word *composition* in any course titles. *Rhetoric*, however, with related words like *persuasion* and *argument*, figures prominently in how these new majors conceive of their offerings, appearing in the title of at least one or more courses offered by fifty-six of the sixty-eight majors. Perhaps *composition* smacks too much of the outmoded belief that writing skills could be taught once and for all in a single first-year course. If so, what North said at the 1993 Writing Program Adminstrators (WPA) Conference on Composition in the Twenty-First Century, only six years after the publication of *MKC*, is strikingly prescient. There he suggested that the "set of practices" we call "composition" should no longer be served or conserved by an active research enterprise, not only because of composition's "troubled genealogy as a particularly limited mode of literacy instruction, the institutional residue of a disenfranchised rhetoric" but also because of "the no less problematic labor practices by which it has been maintained" (1996, 201). Further, he predicted the word *composition* would disappear from college catalogs along with the disappearance of "traditional composition programs and their constituent courses from college campuses." He foresaw that "composition, creative writing, expository writing, and the like—all those 'kinds' of writing that the English curriculum has tended to consign to a pre- or extradisciplinary role—will come together in 'writing'" (202). So the majors emerging now may be the start of the fulfillment of North's 1993 vision.

This new trend could also signify that some English departments are trying to recruit and/or retain students by offering other professional tracks besides certification in secondary teaching. They are adding to their venerable creative writing courses other kinds of writing that students can major in. The study and teaching of multiple kinds of writing may be a sign of the success of composition programs and the scholarly work performed in and for them. In the introduction to his *Handbook of Research on Writing*, Bazerman (2008) asserts, "There is clearly a global renaissance in writing studies at all levels on every continent" and notes that "in the United States, the one robust and pervasive pedagogic site for the teaching of writing, as well as research and scholarship on writing, has been in the first-year university course, out of which the field of composition has arisen" (2). That the word *composition* does not appear in the title of his handbook suggests that Bazerman also finds *writing* a more inclusive and positive term.

The upshot here is that the first half of North's first criterion, the emergence of departments devoted to the teaching of composition, has not materialized. But perhaps something even more significant is beginning to arise. It is not yet a new discipline of writing studies, for as Bazerman says, "No single discipline is fully committed to studying writing in its full range." Perhaps a single discipline could not encompass all that Bazerman's handbook includes: multidisciplinary research drawing on "archaeology, anthropology, technology studies, typography, cultural history, intellectual history, religious studies, sociology, political science, law, gender studies, economics, psychology, neurology, and medicine, as well as . . . linguistics, education, and composition studies." But what is emerging is a new appreciation of the interdisciplinarity of writing, which leads to a clearer view of writing as "part of the infrastructure of society and a medium of participation" in it. That appreciation in turn has led to a better understanding of the need to support writing education (2008, 3). Perhaps the new writing majors are the leading edge of more enlightened institutional support than has typically been given to composition.

But I'm getting ahead of myself. So far, fewer than one hundred institutions have begun to make writing a significant, multifaceted object of study by establishing departments and/or special curricula for students who want to major in writing. What is happening in the other more than 3,900 postsecondary institutions where composition is still merely composition, still just a program, a few general-education courses, in an English department? Are these spaces in which the other half of North's first criterion—knowledge-making parity with literary studies—is being realized? Goggin's portrait of the field's growth, *Authoring a Discipline*, gives impressive evidence that such parity is being established. Goggin argues that the number and diversity of scholarly journals created since the end of World War II "have helped to establish a strong disciplinary identity for those who claim [rhetoric and composition] as their primary professional and scholarly area" (2000, 187) by giving them an intellectual and social space in which to conduct their conversations. Yet another kind of evidence for parity is the number of PhD-holding members of English departments who call their field composition and rhetoric. Between 2000 and 2006, about 30 percent of the ads in the MLA Job Information List called for people with such credentials, a higher percentage than for any other job category; an average of 455 such jobs were advertised in each of those seven years (Association 2006, 9). Presumably, most of the people who took these jobs are expected to be active researchers, and since fewer tales are told today of specialists in rhetoric and composition being denied tenure on grounds of scholarship, perhaps their literary colleagues are more inclined to accept their publications as legitimate than in the 1980s. It seems apparent that rhetoric and composition scholars have been creating and disseminating knowledge that meets with academic approval, particularly in English departments, where most of them are located.

But North also stipulated that the knowledge made by research in the field should "accumulate." It is debatable that this is happening in the sense that a coherent body of knowledge is systematically being formed. Articles and books accumulate, but more in the sense of accretion. Haswell has voiced strong concern about the field's unsystematic knowledge making, saying that composition research generally "has an air of bricolage, with researchers taking up whatever methods, theories, and participants lie readily at hand. There are few large-scale research projects, few extended research lines, few replication studies, even few systematic reviews of research" (2008, 332). Further, Haswell sternly condemns the two "flagstaff organizations," NCTE and CCCC, for failing to foster the accumulation of knowledge by not sponsoring RAD research, that is, research that is "replicable, aggregable, and data-supported" (2005, 201). Such research is critical for the maintenance and growth of a discipline, he contends, citing Carr and Kemmis's dictum that "no profession can exist without a body of systematically produced knowledge" (quoted in Haswell 2005, 198). Haswell graphically depicts how research in NCTE/CCCC-sponsored journals on three traditional concerns in composition—the library research paper, student gain in writing courses, and peer critique—has drastically decreased over the fifty-year period from 1940 to 1990. He further faults NCTE/CCCC for failing to sustain sponsorship of an annual bibliography that would allow easy access to the state of knowledge on a given topic. "Bibliography and RAD scholarship are connected," Haswell states. "Scholarship cannot grow without a knowledge of what has gone before" (2005, 206).[2]

I explain below why I agree with Haswell's censure of the field for not paying sufficient attention to these dimensions of discipline formation. But I think North in 1993 would likely not have agreed with him. When North addressed the WPA conference goers in Oxford, Ohio, he announced the death of "paradigm hope," a phrase he coined to describe the "myth" characterizing research as a noble enterprise in which selfless scholars, guided by seasoned advisors and editors, inform themselves of all previous research on a topic, ask the questions still needing answers, design careful investigations by conducting pilot studies to validate and refine their instruments, then collect data and conduct follow-up studies—with the result that a new nugget of understanding is neatly added to an existing body of knowledge, and the collective good of the field is advanced. In effect, North said, the myth of paradigm hope promises to make composition teaching a science. The trouble with paradigm hope, however, is that it "suppresses the material and political conditions that shape the scene" (1996, 198), and it acts to fix the set of institutional practices we call composition *as* composition, to constitute them as the object of inquiry in such a way that "change in those practices should only come as the result of, or failing that, only with certification by, research findings" (200). We have already seen North's doubt that an intellectually impoverished composition supported by unfair labor practices ought to be conserved in this way. So he absolved the field of "paradigm guilt" by renouncing the castigation that often follows when we realize that all of our research is not adding up coherently or improving the status of composition programs.

North did not, however, renounce research or predict its disappearance in his 1993 address. Instead, he predicted that the range of research interests would expand, that research would be reported in a wider variety of forms, that the rhythm of research and publication

---

2.   To fill the gaps in our knowledge of completed research, Haswell and Glenn Blalock, to their great credit, have taken upon themselves the enormous chore of cataloging in CompPile, a Web database, any and all composition research they can find. According to an email from Blalock to the author on September 21, 2008, they had identified well over 95,000 studies.

would be speeded up, and that although research would be more accessible, it would also be less transportable and more "disposable" or short-lived (1996, 203–205). These predictions—which I think are now being validated—do not, to me, indicate North believed research means "anything goes," because he apparently still upheld the ideal of methodological integrity so evident in *MKC*. But that integrity would no longer stem from "a researcher's commitment to other researchers or the demands of a cumulative system"; rather, it would come from a commitment to end users of the research. Instead of seeking scientifically "proven" or "true" findings, the field would look for "plausibility and utility" (205). It seems that in 1993 North had not given up on the need for research investigating writing in the larger sense. So even though his remarks express doubts about a research enterprise supporting composition as such—and, by implication, doubts that composition should become a discipline—I proceed to examine how the North of *MKC* thought research methods would have to be regarded and employed in a discipline-building enterprise and whether his stipulations have been satisfied.

METHODOLOGICAL CONSCIOUSNESS, PLURALISM, AND EGALITARIANISM

North's second, third, and fourth criteria for disciplinarity all have to do with methodology. A discipline could be formed, he believed, only if its members continued to be methodological pluralists, conscious of the variety of methods, respectful of the strengths of each, and willing for all of them to be employed equally in the creation of new knowledge. "Inter-methodological peace" would be the key to sustaining the vitality of composition research. Just how peaceful and pluralist is the field today with respect to methods? As a group do we possess "heightened methodological consciousness" and enact a "spirit of methodological egalitarianism"? More to the point here, is there a way to answer these questions empirically, not just impressionistically? What follows is my attempt to give such an answer.

First, however, the reader must remember that in *MKC*, North divided composition knowledge makers into three basic groups, each group using one or more methods. The first group were practitioners, whose goals were pragmatic and whose method for making knowledge was their practice in the classroom, where they tested solutions to problems in order to determine their validity, then disseminated their findings largely through conference presentations and other oral forms, but also in such print genres as textbooks, essays, and notes in forums such as *CCC*'s Staffroom Exchange. The second group were scholars—historians, philosophers, and critics—who were comfortable using the humanistic methods of textual dialectic, the "seeking of knowledge via the deliberate confrontation of opposing points of view" (60). North explains that he did not call this second group "Rhetoricians," the label many of them would have chosen for themselves, because he did not believe there was "any inherently Rhetorical mode of inquiry" (64). The third group were researchers, North's umbrella term for those using empirical methods: experimentalists, clinicians, formalists, and ethnographers. North saw the first three kinds of researchers as sharing "the positivist tradition's fundamental faith in the describable orderliness of the universe" (137) and the ethnographers as belonging to the phenomenological tradition, which celebrates "the individual consciousness as the source of meaning" (139). In these three groups—practitioners, scholars, and researchers—he found a total of eight research methods.

North fashioned his taxonomy of eight methods following the lead of Paul Diesing, whose 1971 book describing research methods in the social sciences is cited throughout *MKC*. Like Diesing among his tribes of social scientists, North claimed to be a participant-observer among "the people of Composition" and to have identified eight research "communities" that had identifiable patterns of knowledge making. These communities were not well-organized groups, but rather, in Diesing's phrase, "prominent locations" in the terrain of the field (6–8). In North's view, the borders of these communities were open to immigration, and people could (perhaps should) be members of more than one. Oddly enough, however, he could find only a few members in some of them; for example, in his chapter on the critics, who practice the hermeneutical method, he identified only Kinneavy and himself as scholars working to establish and interpret "a Composition-based canon" (117). Likewise, the formalists, researchers intent on building models "whose internal logic in some specifiable ways resembles that of the phenomenon under study" (239), were few, their most noted members being Flower and Hayes. Yet "formalist" is not a name Flower and Hayes used to describe themselves or their research based on cognitive protocols. Neither did those using case study methods call themselves "Clinicians," the way North did, nor is it clear they saw themselves as building a canon of idiographic portraits, as he described their work. North's reliance on Diesing may have led him to see some communities in composition and to give them names that just don't hold up under scrutiny and over time.

Despite the flaws of his taxonomy, I have summarized North's eight methods at some length because I propose to use them as a template for assessing the field's methodological consciousness, pluralism, and egalitarianism since 1987. One way to take the methodological measure of the field is to consider its textbooks for introducing graduate students to research methods. The field has an array of such books, many now dated, but still worth having on the shelf. As someone who has regularly taught a graduate research methods course since 1988, I count in addition to North's book four other texts that give students an overview of a range of methods with enough detail about each that students could use the descriptions to plan and conduct their own research: Lauer and Asher's *Composition Research* (1988); Hayes et al.'s *Reading Empirical Research Studies* (1992); Kirsch and Sullivan's *Methods and Methodology in Composition Research* (1992); and MacNealy's *Strategies for Empirical Research in Writing* (1999). Table 1 lists these four books alongside North's text and indicates whether or not they have a chapter on each of North's eight methods; but Table 1 also lists other methods these books include that North didn't. I have sometimes translated between the terminology used in North's taxonomy and that used in the other volumes. For example, if a book has a chapter on teacher research, I consider that it treats what North calls "practitioner inquiry"; if the book treats the case study method, I call it the same as North's "clinical" method. Likewise, I think what North calls "philosophical" inquiry would be called "theoretical" by most compositionists today. So my translations or equivalencies are listed alongside North's terms in Table 1. I have also collapsed some categories; for example, Lauer and Asher's two chapters on experiments and quasiexperiments are treated as one.

From Table 1, the reader will see that none of the other four books treats all of North's eight methods, and each of them discusses one or more methods he didn't include. None of them discusses his "Critical" method, but two discuss a method called "discourse analysis," a difference that points to an important distinction. For North, critical or hermeneutic inquiry begins with the researcher identifying a problem; finding, assembling, and validating relevant texts that have some bearing on the problem; then seeking patterns in the texts that support an interpretation, which is entered into the communal dialectic. Likewise, discourse analysis (also called text analysis) seeks to solve a problem or

TABLE 1

Research Methods Explained in Five Composition and Rhetoric Textbooks

Method	North	Lauer & Asher	Hayes et al.	Kirsch & Sullivan	MacNealy
Practitioner / Teacher research	x			x	x
Historical	x		x	x	
Philosophical / Theoretical	x			x	x
Critical	x				
Experimental	x	x	x	x	x
Clinical / Case study	x	x	x	x	x
Formalist / Cognitive Studies	x		x	x	
Ethnographic	x	x	x	x	x
Survey		x	x		x
Interview / Focus group					x
Discourse or Text Analysis				x	x
Meta-analysis		x			x

answer a question, and it includes finding, assembling, and validating relevant texts to analyze. But discourse analysis considers texts as empirical data, so care is taken to ensure the texts are systematically chosen to be representative and reliable. Frequently, certain textual features are counted in order to present valid descriptions, but discourse analysis also has qualitative dimensions. As Huckin (1992) points out, context is very important in discourse analysis, and discourse analysts are now more attuned than in earlier years to sociological and cultural factors as they analyze and interpret textual data. While Kinneavy's *A Theory of Discourse* (1971) is an example of North's critical method, Connors and Lunsford's study of the frequency of formal errors in student writing is an example of discourse analysis (1988). Although discourse analysis is a method that has been used in composition since 1963 (think of Hunt's research on T-units or Christensen's on the sentence), North didn't pay it due consideration in *MKC*.

Likewise, North slights the methods of surveying, interviewing, and meta-analysis in *MKC*. He acknowledges the survey method in his introduction to empirical methods, noting some two hundred survey studies between 1963 and 1987. But he quickly dismisses it as a mode of inquiry used more often to "gain political leverage" than to make knowledge, and he finds no community of inquirers "united by their loyalty to this methodology" (140). Similarly, he barely notices the interview as a tool of the clinical method for collecting case study data. Meta-analysis, or the method of reviewing a number of empirical studies and statistically summarizing a great deal of quantifiable data in order to produce widely general conclusions—such as Hillocks did in *Research on Written Composition* (1986)—doesn't even come up in North's book. Thus, in a sense, North himself could be criticized for not being entirely methodologically conscious, pluralistic, and egalitarian. Perhaps no one book could be. Three of the comparison texts—Lauer and Asher, Hayes et al., and MacNealy—are biased in favor of empirical methods; and although Kirsch and Sullivan's book is more evenhanded, it is not comprehensive.

In addition to the books listed in Table 1, compositionists have authored other useful texts that reflect on and describe how to use a single research method or a group of related methods. Here I count Ray's (1993) and Fleischer's (1995) books on teacher research, Smagorinsky's (1994) collection on think-aloud methods, Bishop's (1999) book on ethnography, and Mortensen and Kirsch's (1996) anthology of reflections on the ethical practice of qualitative research methods. We now have a new generation of books about writing research, not how-to books, but wide-ranging surveys of the present state of knowledge on issues that include composition teaching but go beyond it. Along with Bazerman's *Handbook of Research on Writing* (2008), we have Smagorinsky's *Research on Composition* (2006) and MacArthur, Graham, and Fitzgerald's (2006) *Handbook of Writing Research*. These handbooks present concise summaries of the results of more than four decades of writing research created by many methods. Contributors of various chapters in these handbooks appear to be methodologically pluralistic and egalitarian, reporting knowledge created by any credible means. A notable exception would be Haswell in Bazerman's volume, who again shows his preference for "RAD" research by prefacing his contribution, "The Teaching of Writing in Higher Education," with the caveat that he limited his survey to "formal research," or "any study whose method of investigation and data collection is systematic and exact enough that the study can be tested, replicated, and extended" (2008, 331). Even so, Haswell's bibliography compares favorably to that of other chapters, with over ninety entries.

Given this array of books, the field should rate high for methodological consciousness. Because there are many other useful texts on research methods by people outside the field, it's fair to say if someone isn't conscious of the variety of methods available to use in composition research, it's not for want of books. But books are only as good as the uses they are put to, so we need to take the methodological measure of the field in other ways, such as by asking whether graduate students are being taught about research methods. The evidence available to answer this question is rather sketchy and partly dated. In 2008, Brown et al. repeated a 2007 survey of the field's PhD programs in rhetoric and composition, reporting that they collected data from sixty-seven programs. However, apparently only forty-eight of those responded to questions about their curriculum. Of those, only twenty-two, or 46 percent, offered at least one course in research methods. A similar (but admittedly very flawed) survey in 2004 of fifty-five MA programs found that only twenty-eight programs, or 51 percent, offered such a course (Brown et al. 2005). Pierce and Enos in 2006 obtained survey data from 127 faculty members in rhetoric and composition (a return rate equal to only 21 percent of the population queried) indicating that courses in research methods were the fifth most common kind of core course in graduate programs, with twenty-four respondents stating the course is required at their institutions. Pierce and Enos also found that MacNealy's book was the "most often listed" for the research methods course (they give no precise figure). Taken together, these results do not inspire confidence that professors in the field place a high priority on instilling methodological consciousness in new members. But in the absence of more reliable data, we don't know the present state of the field. Even if all graduate programs required a course entitled Research Methods, we wouldn't know what was taught in those courses or whether they are required or elective without asking more detailed questions. Despite North's misgivings about survey research, it's obviously an important method to know and use, particularly so that we can take regular snapshots of who we are and what we do collectively. It's hard to imagine a national discipline—whether of composition or of writing studies—forming itself effectively in ignorance of the practices followed at various sites engaged in its work, yet we lack sufficiently comprehensive survey data to help us even understand ourselves. The money and expertise required to do reliable surveys are no doubt factors in this neglect; the neglect is nonetheless evidence of a shortcoming in the field's methodological awareness.

Yet another way to determine whether North's criteria of methodological consciousness and pluralism are being met is to examine what research methods have been used to create the knowledge published in our journals. An exhaustive examination of this kind is beyond the scope of this essay, so I conducted a limited analysis of articles in two major journals, *College Composition and Communication* (*CCC*) and *Research on the Teaching of English* (*RTE*). I believe the results are adequate to begin to draw valid conclusions about methodological consciousness, pluralism, and egalitarianism. First, however, a note about my own method: I randomly chose one issue of *CCC* from each volume of the journal between 1987 and 2007. I ignored editors' notes, book reviews, speeches, and comment-and-response exchanges to examine only the articles reporting new research. I used North's eight methods and the others listed in Table 1 to classify the articles according to the kind of research method the authors used to create the content. I had to add *multimodal* to the list because it became clear that some articles were based on a combination of methods, each of which played a primary and equal role in creating the knowledge discussed. (I also had to add *other* to account for articles that could not be categorized otherwise.) At first I planned also to randomly choose one issue of *RTE* from each volume over the twenty-year span, but I quickly saw that there are inherent problems in comparing the two journals. *CCC* publishes mainly articles about college composition, though it is starting to include other topics such as adult literacy in communities and various ethnic groups. *RTE*, in contrast, publishes a good deal about the reading and writing of students in elementary and secondary schools, much of it by people from schools of education. So I decided to analyze only the articles in *RTE* that were about either college composition or adults' writing. But in order to get an adequate sample of such articles roughly comparable to the number examined in *CCC*, I looked at every issue of *RTE* between 1987 and 2007. The results of my analysis are in Table 2.

What conclusions can be drawn from Table 2? First, it's obvious that the two journals generally publish different kinds of research. *RTE* has remained largely true to the purpose for which it was created in 1967, to be a venue for empirical research (Herrington 1989, 118–19; North

TABLE 2

Research Methods Used to Create Articles
for CCC and RTE, 1987–2007

Method	CCC[1]	RTE[2]
Practitioner / Teacher Research	18/11[3]	0
Historical	13	2
Philosophical / Theoretical	20	9
Critical	27	0
Experimental	1	24
Clinical / Case Study	5	11
Formalist / Cognitive Studies	0	1
Ethnographic	1	7
Survey	0	1
Interview / Focus Group	3	1
Discourse or Text Analysis	1	10
Meta-analysis	0	1
Multi-modal	3	7
Other	4	3
Total	107	77

[1] Figures in this column are based on analysis of a random selection of one issue per volume over the twenty-year period.
[2] Figures in this column are based on a review of the entire contents of each issue over the twenty-year period.
[3] The first tally, 18, refers to the number of brief Practitioner contributions in the Staffroom Interchange section that was a part of *CCC* from 1987 through 1991. The second tally, 11, refers to Practitioner articles published after the Staffroom Interchange disappeared in 1992.

1987, 135). Between 1987 and 2007, three research methods—the experiment, case study, and discourse analysis—were most frequently used to make knowledge, although ethnographic and multimodal research were also relatively frequent. Interestingly, the experimental method has decreased in frequency over time, with only three experiments being reported in the pages of *RTE* since 1998; this statistic may either substantiate North's judgment that the method is not the giant it was thought to be in 1967 (1987, 146), or it may indicate that criticism of this method has caused people to stop thinking about questions that can be answered experimentally. The relatively high number of philosophical articles in *RTE* is an anomaly, not an indication the journal is losing its focus: seven of nine articles in that category appeared in a single 1993 issue for which the editor specifically invited theoretical arguments. The scarcity of research in *RTE* conducted by survey, interview, and meta-analytic methods suggests, perhaps, that researchers lack expertise, funds, or time to use these methods; or they lack pressing and interesting questions these methods might answer. Or if those suppositions aren't true, and researchers *are* doing these kinds of research, perhaps they are publishing the results elsewhere. That only one article in the past twenty years of *RTE* used North's "formalist" method may indicate how thoroughly the social turn in composition has dried up research based on cognitive protocols.

Leaving aside practitioner inquiry, which I will discuss below, Table 2 also reveals—and this will not surprise regular readers of the journal— that there is in the pages of *CCC* a definite slant toward critical and theoretical/philosophical methods, with a respectable number of articles created by historical methods. (But the reader must bear in mind here that I looked at only one of every four issues, so the number of articles produced by each of these methods over the twenty-year span may be about four times larger.) Researchers may be partial to these types of inquiry not only because of their intrinsic value but also because they are relatively easy to use and familiar to people who have matured academically in English departments. The top three methods generally require little or no funding; and they don't require the careful planning or expertise in design, controls, and statistics that empirical methods sometimes do. Moreover, they are understood and valued by the literary scholars who dominate the English departments where most compositionists are employed. I believe there is some truth to Hairston's (1992) contention that compositionists who use the theories currently in vogue with literary critics are more likely to earn the approval of their colleagues, so the dominance of these methods is unsurprising.

The few studies using empirical methods show a clear bias toward the qualitative techniques used in case studies and interviews. The two *CCC* articles I found that used quantitative empirical methods were a quasiexperiment by Peterson (1991), "Gender and the Autobiographical Essay," and a discourse analysis of student papers by Connors and Lunsford (1988), "Frequency of Formal Errors in Current College Writing." Intriguingly, the authors of both articles make rhetorical moves that seem to show they don't want to be too closely identified with the kind of research they are reporting. Peterson, in describing the two groups of students she studied, states, "I do not pretend that my sample was perfectly chosen (whatever that might mean)" (171), suggesting that she doesn't understand random sample selection, doesn't care about it, or disbelieves in one of the essential premises underlying much experimental research. Similarly, Connors and Lunsford adopt the folksy ethos of Ma and Pa Kettle as they report their research, perhaps to underscore their admitted unfamiliarity with the method or to suggest there is something amusing about employing it. One wonders if Peterson's article could have been published in *CCC* if it hadn't tapped into feminist concerns of the time, or if Connors and Lunsford's article would have been as welcome if they had adopted a more straightforward scientific ethos.

The diffidence of these scholars, together with the preponderance of theoretical, critical, and historical research in *CCC*, does not necessarily prove the field lacks methodological consciousness and pluralism, if pluralism means a climate that allows multiple methods to exist. To prove such a lack, I would have to survey all composition journals and books published from 1987 forward. The fact that most people publishing in *CCC* choose most of the time to use one of only two or three methods to invent their articles needs not equate with ignorance or intolerance. But it does tend to raise questions about egalitarianism, if egalitarianism means equal respect for and valuing of all methods. Ironically, despite his insistence that the field needs all methods to retain its vitality, in *MKC* North himself exhibits some misgivings about the experimental method, questioning whether it is a sleeping or a dying giant— "or maybe not a giant after all" (146). He was neither the first nor the last to question the utility or even the presence of certain methods of research in the field; others include Berlin (1988), Bizzell (1982), Connors (1983), Flynn (1995), and Foster (1990). When Joseph Harris edited *CCC*, he wrote that he usually rejected articles taking "the form of empirical research reports on writing," finding them "better suited for other journals" (1994, 303), although it's not clear that the mandate of *CCC* forbids publishing empirical research. The stance of such critics has been strongly challenged, most notably by Charney, who in three separate articles (1996, 1997, 1998) has carefully analyzed the occasional antiempirical polemics. McLeod (2006) has also scolded the field for continuing to bicker about the place of empirical methods, "with some among us equating empirical research with positivism, a reductive approach that is not worthy of us" (531). In a similar vein, Barton has pled for an end to negative arguments that question the ethics of empirical research. She worries that graduate students may naively and falsely believe that empirical studies are unethical, and that, as a result, they will not be taught "what *ethical* means in the context of an empirical investigation" or when an empirical method is the right choice for a given question. Consequently, they will be unable to contribute fully to interdisciplinary teams that "expect members to be conversant with the full continuum of ways to ask questions, investigate problems, interpret results, and formulate new questions" (2000, 409).

A refreshing and novel argument in favor of greater methodological egalitarianism is Johanek's in *Composing Research* (2000). She painstakingly lays out the justification for a "contextualist research paradigm" to help the field escape the trap of dichotomous thinking and debate about quantitative and qualitative methods, a trap that "keeps us locked in the past and divided against ourselves" (7). All research methods have both limits and potential, she argues, depending on the contexts in which we ask our research questions, so we need to embrace them and use as many as needed to seek answers (186). We need to stop thinking of statistics as antithetical to our purposes and embrace numbers as the natural phenomena that they are (190). Charney notes that if we disparage the very idea of objectivity, an idea based in using public, shared methods that "allow truth claims to be assessed and understood by others," all we can hope to produce are "numerous individual subjective studies." The result of that is "a broad shallow array of information in which one study may touch loosely on another but in which no deep or complex networks of inferences and hypotheses are forged or tested." Our situation then is one in which the authority of any research rests mainly on the ethos of the researcher, because

> without the means to contest and refine our methods and our data directly— through shared use and critique—all we can do is fight over which authority to valorize: the author, the critic, the experimenter, the trendiest theorist or philosopher, the political activist, or the participants whose interests we claim to define and promote. (1996, 590)

All of these arguments support Haswell's contention that composition (or writing studies) is not yet a discipline because we have not developed a systematic, deeply textured, and easily searched body of knowledge (2005). Database searching requires, after all, descriptors based on established categories and widely accepted terminology. We have developed some promising starting points for such a body of knowledge,

since many excellent studies in composition have laid a strong foundation for further research. Rather than building on them, however, we've
repeatedly abandoned them for something new. Part of the answer to
why our research is so often a mile wide but only an inch deep can be
found in Connors's (2000) "The Erasure of the Sentence," in which he
describes how promising the 1970s research on sentence combining
was until, for a convergence of reasons, no one continued the research,
so the pedagogy largely disappeared after 1983, despite its demonstra-
ble success. Three lines of criticism—antiformalism, antibehaviorism,
and antiempiricism—converged and torpedoed both the research and
the pedagogy. "The sentence was erased by the gradual but inevitable
hardening" of "the field of composition studies as a subfield of English
studies" (121). Because compositionists mainly reside where first-year
composition does, in English departments, they adopted attitudes about
"textuality, holism, stratification by status, theory-desire, [and] distrust
of scientism" that characterize literary studies, and they began cutting
ties to education, speech, communications, psychology, and quantitative research that had begun to inform composition in the 1950s (121).
"Distrust of scientific empiricism has left us with few proofs or certainties
not ideologically based," says Connors, adding, "More has been lost than
sentence-combining here" (122).

I find Connors' argument persuasive since my time in the field is coex-
tensive with the rise and then the erasure of not only the sentence but
of other research lines that have been replaced by what seems an almost
exclusive focus on criticism and theories. MacDonald (2007) corrobo-
rates my sense of the past two decades with "The Erasure of Language,"
in which she documents how the field has stopped paying attention
not just to the sentence, but to language in general. As a result, today's
new writing teachers are ignorant of what they will need to know at a
time when our students are coming from more diverse language backgrounds and need more solid instruction in the structure and the use
of the English language than ever before.[3] "Academic professionals benefit from standing on the shoulders of their predecessors," MacDonald
states, "so that they do not have to continually reinvent knowledge, but
if we do not cultivate and pay attention to the storehouse of knowledge
we already have, we will eventually have to do that reinventing" (619).
Because the premium placed on novelty in scholarship pushes people

---

3.   For more on this, see Preto-Bay and Hansen (2006).

to keep looking for something entirely new to write about, I believe we are witnessing the fulfillment of North's 1993 prediction that writing research would become more "disposable" and less transportable, something to be judged by its "plausibility and utility" rather than by its fidelity to methodological rules or its goodness of fit with what we already know. But I don't think this vision is something we should welcome or accept as the inevitable new order of scholarship.

MacDonald characterizes the constant preference for originality over deeper research in established categories of inquiry as "a sort of professional attention deficit disorder that keeps us from sustaining a conversation long enough to work on and improve" our understanding (2007, 619). Her solution, which I endorse, is to encourage many more graduate students and professionals to take on the less prestigious and possibly more difficult task of researching, reviewing, replicating, and refining investigations that would deepen and reticulate, and therefore strengthen, our knowledge. I am not calling here for theoretical or critical inquiry to go away; I am simply calling for equal respect for empirical inquiry and its impulse toward systematic knowledge construction, an impulse not incompatible with theorizing and criticizing. As Charney has emphasized to empiricism's detractors, there is nothing about empirical research methods or their users that is inherently "sexist, or racist, or stuck in retrograde ontologies, or implicated in social injustice" (1997, 565).

As I turn next to examining the status of practitioner inquiry, I can't help noting the irony that this method is the most empirical of all, based as it is in experience, the very meaning of the Greek *empeiria*, from which *empiricism* descends. In 1987, North thought that composition could not be a discipline without the reestablishment of practice as inquiry—an acceptance and appreciation of what lore is and how it "can usefully interact" with other kinds of knowledge (371). How has composition fared in that respect?

PRACTICE AS INQUIRY

Twenty-some years after *MKC*, it seems obvious that lore is still alive, generally accepted and appreciated—and probably most in evidence today on the listservs where compositionists seek and give advice, trade tried-and-true ideas and practices, and critique or tweak new ones. But whether lore is interacting usefully with other kinds of knowledge is more difficult to determine. Part of my answer is based on what I found by examining *CCC* and *RTE*. The reader will note that Table 2 shows no instances of a practitioner article in the *RTE* column, but there are two tallies in the *CCC* column. The first tally, eighteen, refers to the number of brief (usually two or three pages set in small type) practitioner contributions in the Staffroom Interchange section that was a part of the journals I examined from 1987 through 1991. The second tally, eleven, refers to all the practitioner articles I found between 1992 and 2007, published after the Staffroom Interchange disappeared in 1992, when editor Rick Gebhardt initiated the practice of publishing practitioner inquiry under the heading Articles. In two issues he edited, I found four articles that formerly would have been in the Staffroom Interchange because they were like the pieces previously published in that section—short, personal reports of successful teaching ideas, almost all devoid of references to other publications. Their placement with articles made by other methods suggests Gebhardt valued them equally as valid knowledge. This attitude persisted with subsequent *CCC* editors Joseph Harris, Marilyn Cooper, and Deborah Holdstein, who also published practitioner articles. I found seven articles published after Gebhardt's editorship that were clearly invented in the way North describes practitioner inquiry as proceeding. Like the earlier pieces, they are largely experiential in their logic, pragmatic in their aim, narrative in structure and personal in tone, bearing the marks of testimonial and advice. However, they are far more substantial, and they tend to cite secondary sources that create a context for the practice-based argument, suggesting that practitioner inquiry can usefully interact with knowledge made in other ways. In some cases, the secondary sources ratify the practice—not that it needs anointing—just to make the point that a particular idea has been realized empirically. In other cases, secondary sources are cited because the practice disproves a theory or counters an argument they make.

To take one example, Royer and Gilles's (1998) "Directed Self-Placement: An Attitude of Orientation" is most persuasive when the authors argue directly from their experience and the program data they collected to validate their then-new and unusual practice of letting students place themselves in an appropriate first-year course. It's obvious Royer and Gilles know the strength of their position. Nevertheless, they cite William James, John Dewey, and Peter Elbow to demonstrate how their experience realizes ideals articulated by these thinkers. They also cite Brian Huot and Edward White, quibbling a little with their positions on the most desirable placement procedures. The authors' authority rests in their successful practice, which allows them to claim the validation of some experts and to challenge the authority of others. Other practitioner articles make similar moves.

Seven articles don't make a trend (remember, there may be more practitioner articles in the issues of *CCC* I didn't examine), but I see signs here that North's final criterion is not a vain hope. Unfortunately, my enthusiasm for *CCC* editors' willingness to publish practitioner knowledge in the journal is dampened when I consider that probably most practitioners in composition are overworked adjuncts and green graduate students. How much inquiry is going on their classrooms? Even when these practitioners develop interesting lore by seeking and finding novel solutions to problems, are their working conditions such that they have the leisure, the support, and the opportunity to communicate their knowledge usefully to others? The conditions under which many composition teachers labor and the high turnover in their ranks militate against the fruitful development of practice as inquiry and usually make the exchange of lore little more than oral recipe swapping among desperate, harried teachers.

In fact, Vandenberg (1998) has argued that the ability of PhD-holding compositionists to produce the favored texts we call "research" rests on the fact that the very function of the "vast majority of writing teachers" is not to research and write but "to sustain the privilege of publishing professionals." In a cruelly ironic way, the very people most responsible for promoting literacy "*are prevented by conditions of their employment from fully utilizing it*" (28–29; italics in original). Vandenberg argues that if the working conditions of writing teachers are to change, the change will not come from the publication of more research texts like his; instead it must come from "physical and symbolic action *outside* the order of academic publishing" (29; italics in original). Likewise, Goggin (2000) acknowledges that we "continue to struggle on numerous fronts against marginalization" because political and material conditions for teaching composition have scarcely improved in the last fifty years (187), and she argues for reconceiving the teaching of writing "on a systemic level" (203). The systemic change we need would fully enfranchise all practitioners by making them members of a real discipline. A real discipline, in Richard Ohmann's (2002) words, is aimed "at the professional goal of winning and sustaining privileged conditions of labor, at control over its content and procedures, regulation of the market for it, exclusion of the uncertified from practice, control over admission of new members, public respect for authority, good pay, and so on" (215). It takes only a few moments' consideration of Ohmann's criteria to realize we aren't there yet.

CONCLUSIONS

I have argued that composition in the last twenty-plus years has had only mixed success in meeting the five criteria North set out in 1987: very few independent departments have been created—though the promise of more departments, or at least more majors, seems likely, as books like *What We Are Becoming: Developments in Undergraduate Writing Majors* attest (Giberson and Moriarty 2010). Continuing MLA Job List ads for rhetoric and composition scholars and the existence of writing majors within a few English departments suggest that some knowledge-making parity has probably been established between literature and composition. However, much of that parity seems to have come at a price, since a good deal of the knowledge currently being made is only of the theoretical, critical, or historical kind, the traditional methods of inquiry practiced and valued in English departments. There is little evidence that, on the whole, individual members of the field have much interest in using a wide spectrum of methods, and even less evidence of widespread expertise in using empirical methods. In that sense scholars in writing studies do not measure up to North's call for methodological pluralists, and an active or latent suspicion of empiricism seems to hinder the achievement of methodological egalitarianism. Practitioner inquiry appears to be thriving, at least for some members of the field, in the informal venues that North claimed it was wont to inhabit. It can also sometimes be published and interact with other forms of knowledge, if it has a certain novelty and timeliness, with clear implications for larger issues current in the field. But lore is not likely to be published by most of the practitioners now laboring in the field because they lack time and incentives. So, using North's criteria, I have to say that composition— or writing studies, if that is the best new name for what composition has become—is not yet a discipline, despite the gains made since 1987. (Interestingly, Balzhiser and McLeod confirm this judgment by noting that the National Research Council classifies the field as an "emerging discipline" [2010, 429]).

Still I tip my hat to North for foreseeing over twenty years ago that independent departments would be the most likely place for a discipline to develop. The increasing numbers of departments and majors in writing augur well for a better future, but there is still much work to do. All the disciplines I am aware of have autonomy, and they meet Ohmann's conditions for a profession. Most important, they have a curriculum with both undergraduate and graduate courses for educating those who would claim to have mastered the knowledge and practices of that discipline. In contrast, we generally have, as Fleming says, a curriculum with "at one end, a fifteen-week course on writing for incoming freshmen; at the other, a multi-year program of advanced study for PhD students. Between the two, there is little or nothing" (1998, 173). We are now seeing more courses filling up the vast middle, but there is often a strained coherence in the courses offered as an undergraduate curriculum and, as Balzhiser and McLeod note, there is "little consensus about what a writing major should look like" (2010, 422). This muddled picture may stem from the fact that many campuses offering a major in writing must, from political necessity, at first cobble together a curriculum out of existing courses and a few others invented by the faculty they already have. When most campuses have a sensible sequence of courses in writing that students can major and minor in, and when most campuses can hire people to teach writing who have taken those courses and who are experts in the discourse of writing studies, we will have the beginnings of a discipline. When most campuses have a critical mass of professionals, not just one or two administrators, using a whole range of methods to make knowledge about writing and teaching writing, and when people in writing studies can apply for grants from major national foundations and list their own names as the principal investigator in a study (something they currently cannot do because the field is not recognized, according to Johnson [2010]), we will have gone a good way down the road toward disciplinarity. And when the knowledge those scholars create is categorized in libraries, bibliographies, and databases under headings that make it easily retrievable, and when all of that knowledge is taught, respected, and used, then we will have a discipline.

In the meantime, let us cheer the further development of strong writing-across-the-curriculum (WAC) and writing-in-the-disciplines (WID) programs, for out of those may grow the courses that will lead to more majors and minors. Let us test the various proposals made to teach students to be writers in more meaningful and enduring ways than the heretofore required jump through a generic first-year hoop. These include the intriguing plans put forward by Fleming (1998), who has sketched out a new rhetorical paideia; by Jackson (2007), who offers Dewey's ideas as a way to update the Athenian paideia and teach rhetoric for civic responsibility; by Spellmeyer (2002), who calls on writing specialists to form interdisciplinary alliances with fields currently getting the most academic capital, such as science and engineering; and by Smit (2004), who calls for a three-stage curriculum in writing taught by people who are specialists in various discourses and expert writing teachers—and who are rewarded for being such. Let's thoroughly discuss the proposals put forward in 1993 by Parker and Campbell and in 2010 by Johnson, who urge us to think of writing studies as an "interdiscipline." Parker and Campbell propose more cross training of writing teachers in applied linguistics so they can apply linguistic theory to understanding and teaching writing. Johnson's more comprehensive proposal outlines an "economy and heuristic of craft knowledge" (684) that includes the ways writing makes products, processes, selves, and cultures, thus inviting the field to think far beyond the narrow limits of the first-year writing course. As we note the ubiquity and importance of writing in our culture and study the multifaceted processes that produce, in multiple media, all the varied genres of writing that surround us, we can't help but see the need for more and better ways of understanding and teaching others to participate in what Bazerman (2008) calls the "infrastructure of society" (3). As we conduct more and better research to build a stronger body of knowledge and as we develop and successfully teach a greater variety of writing courses, the closer we will come to establishing a bona fide discipline. On the other hand, the more we continue to do business as usual, the more we perpetuate the naïve notion that a universal ability to write is easily acquired once and for all by the average eighteen-year-old student taught by teachers who don't really belong to a profession. Disciplinarity never has been and never will be at the end of that road.

REFERENCES

Association of Departments of English (ADE). 2006. From the editor. *ADE Bulletin* 140: 3–10.
Balzhiser, Deborah, and Susan H. McLeod. 2010. The undergraduate writing major: What is it? What should it be? *CCC* 61: 415–433.
Barton, Ellen. 2000. More methodological matters: Against negative argumentation. *CCC* 51: 399–416.
Bazerman, Charles, ed. 2008. *Handbook of research on writing: History, society, individual, school, text.* New York: Lawrence Erlbaum Associates.
———. 2008. Introduction to Bazerman, 1–4.
Berlin, James. 1988. Rhetoric and ideology in the writing class. *College English* 50: 477–494.
Bishop, Wendy. 1999. *Ethnographic writing research: Writing it down, writing it up, and reading*

it. Portsmouth, NH: Heinemann Boynton/Cook.

Bizzell, Patricia. 1982. Cognition, convention, and certainty: What we need to know about writing. *Pre/Text* 3: 213–243.

Brown, Stuart C., Monica F. Torres, Theresa Enos, and Erik Juergensmeyer. 2005. Mapping a landscape: The 2004 survey of MA programs in rhetoric and composition studies. *Rhetoric Review* 24: 5–127.

Brown, Stuart C., Theresa Enos, David Reamer, and Jason Thompson. 2008. Portrait of the profession: The 2007 survey of doctoral programs in rhetoric and composition. *Rhetoric Review* 27: 331–340.

Charney, Davida. 1996. Empiricism is not a four-letter word. *CCC* 47: 567–593.

———. 1997. Paradigm and punish. *CCC* 48: 562–565.

———. 1998. From logocentrism to ethnocentrism: Historicizing critiques of writing research. *Technical Communication Quarterly* 7: 9–32.

Conference on College Composition and Communication. 2009. Writing majors at a glance. CCCC Committee on the Major in Rhetoric and Composition. http://www.ncte.org/cccc/gov/committees/majorrhetcomp.

Connors, Robert. 1983. Composition studies and science. *College English* 45:1–20.

———. 1999. Composition history and disciplinarity. In *History, reflection, and narrative: The professionalization of composition, 1963–1983*, edited by Mary Rosner, Beth Boehm, and Debra Journet, 3–21. Stamford, CT: Ablex.

———. 2000. The Erasure of the sentence. *CCC* 52: 96–128.

Connors, Robert, and Andrea Lunsford. 1988. Frequency of formal errors in current college writing, or Ma and Pa Kettle do research. *CCC* 39: 395–409.

Crowley, Sharon. 1998. *Composition in the university: Historical and polemical essays.* Pittsburgh, PA: University of Pittsburgh Press.

Fleischer, Cathy. 1995. *Composing teacher-research: A prosaic history.* Albany: State University of New York Press.

Fleming, David. 1998. Rhetoric as a course of study. *College English* 61: 169–191.

Flynn, Elizabeth. 1995. Feminism and scientism. *CCC* 46: 353–69.

Foster, David. 1990. Hurling epithets at the devils you know: A response to Carol Berkenkotter. *Journal of Advanced Composition* 10: 149–152.

Giberson, Greg A., and Thomas A. Moriarty. 2010. *What we are becoming: Developments in undergradaute writing majors.* Logan: Utah State University Press.

Goggin, Maureen Daly. 2000. *Authoring a discipline: Scholarly journals and the post-World War II emergence of rhetoric and composition.* Mahwah, NJ: Lawrence Erlbaum Associates.

Hairston, Maxine. 1992. Diversity, ideology, and teaching writing. *CCC* 43: 179–93.

Harris, Joseph. 1994. The *CCC* review process. *CCC* 45: 303–306.

———. 2005. Déjà vu all over again. *CCC* 57: 535–541.

Haswell, Richard H. 2005. NCTE/CCCC's recent war on scholarship. *Written Communication* 22: 198–223.

———. 2008. Teaching of writing in higher education. In Bazerman, 331–346.

Hayes, John R., Richard E. Young, Michele L. Matchett, Maggie McCaffrey, Cynthia Cochran, and Thomas Hajduk. 1992. *Reading empirical research studies: The rhetoric of research.* Hillsdale, NJ: Lawrence Erlbaum Associates.

Herrington, Anne. 1989. The first twenty years of *Research in the Teaching of English* and the growth of a research community in composition studies. *RTE* 23: 117–137

Hillocks, George. 1986. *Research on written composition.* Urbana, IL: National Council of Teachers of English.

Huckin, Thomas N. 1992. Context-sensitive text analysis. In Kirsch and Sullivan, 84–104.

Jackson, Brian. 2007. Cultivating paideweyan pedagogy: Rhetoric education in English and communication studies. *Rhetoric Society Quarterly* 37: 181–201.

Johanek, Cindy. 2000. *Composing research: A contextualist paradigm for rhetoric and composition.*

Logan: Utah State University Press.

Johnson, Robert. 2010. Craft knowledge: Of disciplinarity in writing studies. *CCC* 61: 673–690.

Kinneavy, James. 1971. *A theory of discourse*. New York: Norton.

Kirsch, Gesa, and Patricia Sullivan, eds. 1992. *Methods and methodology in composition research*. Carbondale: Southern Illinois University Press.

Lauer, Janice. 2006. Rhetoric and composition. In *English studies: An introduction to the discipline(s)*, edited by Bruce McComiskey, 106–152. Urbana, IL: National Council of Teachers of English. .

Lauer, Janice, and J. William Asher. 1988. *Composition research: Empirical designs*. New York: Oxford.

MacArthur, Charles A., Steve Graham, and Jill Fitzgerald, eds. 2006. *Handbook of writing research*. New York: Guilford.

MacDonald, Susan Peck. 2007. The erasure of language. *CCC* 58: 585–625.

MacNealy, Mary Sue. 1999. *Strategies for empirical research in writing*. Boston: Allyn & Bacon.

McLeod, Susan. 2006. "Breaking our bonds and reaffirming our connections" twenty years later. *CCC* 57: 525–533.

Miller, Susan. 2003. Why composition studies disappeared and what happened then. In *Composition studies in the new millennium: Rereading the past, rewriting the future*, edited by Lynn Z. Bloom, Donald A. Daiker, and Edward M. White. Carbondale: Southern Illinois University Press.

Mortensen, Peter, and Gesa E. Kirsch. 1996. *Ethics and representation in qualitative studies of literacy*. Urbana, IL: National Council of Teachers of English.

North, Stephen. 1987. *The making of knowledge in composition: Portrait of an emerging field*. Upper Montclair, NJ: Boynton/Cook.

———. 1996. The death of paradigm hope, the end of paradigm guilt, and the future of (research in) composition. In *Composition in the twenty-first century: Crisis and change*, edited by Lynn Z. Bloom, Donald A. Daiker, Edward M. White. Carbondale: Southern Illinois University Press.

Ohmann, Richard. 2002. Afterword to *Disciplining English: Alternative histories, Critical Perspectives*, edited by David R. Shumway and Craig Dionne, Albany: State University of New York Press. 213–219.

Parker, Frank, and Kim Sydow Campbell. 1993. Linguistics and writing: A reassessment. *CCC* 44: 295–314.

Peterson, Jane. 1991. Gender and the autobiographical essay. *CCC* 42: 170–183.

Phelps, Louise. 1988. *Composition as a human science: Contributions to the self-understanding of a discipline*. New York: Oxford.

Pierce, Karen P., and Theresa J. Enos. 2006. How seriously are we taking professionalization? A report on graduate curricula in rhetoric and composition. *Rhetoric Review* 25: 204–210.

Preto-Bay, Ana, and Kristine Hansen. 2006. Preparing for the tipping point: Designing writing programs to meet the needs of the changing population. *WPA Journal* 3: 37–57.

Ray, Ruth E. 1993. *The practice of theory: Teacher research in composition*. Urbana, IL: National Council of Teachers of English.

Royer, Daniel J., and Roger Gilles. 1998. Directed self-placement. *CCC* 50: 54–70.

Slevin, James. 2001. Inventing and reinventing the discipline of composition. In *Introducing English: Essays in the intellectual work of composition*, edited by James Slevin, 37–56. Pittsburgh, PA: University of Pittsburgh Press..

Smagorinsky, Peter, ed.1994. *Speaking about writing: Reflections on research methodology*. Sage Series in Written Communication 8. Thousand Oaks, CA: Sage.

———. 2006. *Research on composition: Multiple perspectives on two decades of change*. New York:

Teachers College Press.

Smit, David W. 2004. *The end of composition studies.* Carbondale: Southern Illinois University Press.

Spellmeyer, Kurt. 2002. Bigger than a discipline? In *A field of dreams,* edited by Peggy O'Neill, Angela Crow, and Larry W. Burton. Logan: Utah State University Press.

U.S. Department of Education. 1989. IPEDS fall staff survey. www.aaup.org/NR/rdonlyres/9218E731-A68E-4E98-A378-12251FFD3802/0/Facstatustrend7505.pdf.

Vandenberg, Peter. 1998. Composing composition studies. In *Under construction: Working at the intersections of composition theory, research, and practice,* edited by Christine Farris and Chris M. Anson. Logan: Utah State University Press.

14

COORDINATING CITATIONS AND THE CARTOGRAPHY OF KNOWLEDGE
Finding True North in Five Scholarly Journals

Brad E. Lucas
Drew M. Loewe

With *The Making of Knowledge in Composition: Portrait of an Emerging Field* (*MKC*), published in 1987, Stephen North took on a daring effort to map complex sets of investigations and practices under the big umbrella of composition, studying disparate sites of research on their own terms. Within a year, *MKC* had gained enough attention to warrant three separate reviews (by James C. Raymond, Richard L. Larson, and Richard Lloyd-Jones) in the February 1989 issue of the field's flagship journal, *College Composition and Communication* (*CCC*). For over two decades, *MKC* flourished as a publication central to the field's debates about history, research, and disciplinary practices. According to SUNY-Albany, North's home institution, *MKC* "is required reading in virtually every graduate writing program in the country" (Excellence Awards). Moreover, as this very collection attests, North's work has become a part of the field's collective consciousness: regardless of one's opinions about *MKC*, North's book is a part of the intellectual landscape and has generated conversations that continue to influence our work as scholars and teachers.

Of course, it is easy to support claims that a book is important to a field. However, when considering importance, questions of kind and of degree draw our attention. In other words, how important is *MKC* to the field we call rhetoric and composition, and how has it shaped our scholarly conversations? As a means of invoking the crucial role of citation in scholarship, we offer a familiar passage from Kenneth Burke:

> Imagine that you enter a parlor. You come late. When you arrive, others have long preceded you, and they are engaged in a heated discussion, a discussion

too heated for them to pause and tell you exactly what it is about. In fact, the discussion had already begun long before any of them got there, so that no one present is qualified to retrace for you all the steps that had gone before. You listen for a while, until you decide that you have caught the tenor of the argument; then you put in your oar. Someone answers; you answer him; another comes to your defense; another aligns himself against you, to either the embarrassment or gratification of your opponent, depending upon the quality of your ally's assistance. However, the discussion is interminable. The hour grows late, you must depart. And you do depart, with the discussion still vigorously in progress. (1974, 110–11)

Burke's metaphor of the parlor debate is perhaps one of the most frequently cited passages from his work, and it highlights the ongoing "conversation" that we all entered late and learned to understand while the arguments raged on.[1] Our particular aim in this chapter is to explore how *MKC* has played a role in composition's parlor and how it has shaped the conversation in the decades since its publication. Through citation analysis, we reveal both the erratic peaks of scholarly engagement with *MKC* and how those trends were to some extent shaped by publications in *CCC*. While we discover patterns of our collective scholarly behavior, we also conclude that most of our field's academic "moves" are unique. Moreover, through our bibliometric analysis, we also illustrate an underemployed method for assessing the circulation and impact of scholarship on the field, providing a quantitative dimension to the complex qualitative discussions that have shaped the discipline's thinking about its history and its publishing practices.

Rather than mustering an argument about North's impact on the field or tracing how his ideas gained importance, we wanted instead to identify scholarship that cited *MKC* and to gain a better sense of how *MKC* was used and positioned in composition scholarship from 1987 to 2006. Given unlimited time and resources, we could have collected citations from every publication that referenced *MKC*; instead, we decided to work with a set of five academic journals to provide data for bibliometric analysis. Our decision was not simply one of convenience. We wanted to have a sufficient number of publications and authors to conduct our analysis, and we were interested in tracing citations with some temporal regularity. For our purposes, however, we wanted to use a sample of journals that reflected the broad foundations of the discipline. After all,

---

1.   For more on this, see Graff and Hoberek (1999).

peer-reviewed journals remain a central forum for any field's conversations. They are one of the best—if not *the* best—places to look for examining how the conversation is taking shape and what impact any particular contribution to it makes.

First, we chose *CCC* and *College English* (*CE*) because they are National Council of Teachers of English (NCTE) publications that focus explicitly on rhetoric and composition and English studies, respectively. We also chose three others for contrast: *Rhetoric Review* (*RR*), *JAC: A Quarterly Journal for the Interdisciplinary Study of Rhetoric, Writing, Multiple Literacies, and Politics* (formerly, *JAC: Journal of Composition Theory*, and before that, *JAC: Journal of Advanced Composition*), and *Composition Studies* (*CS*) (formerly, *Freshman English News*). We chose these particular journals because their blend of quantity of citations of *MKC* and differing editorial aims and audiences yields a broad yet deep picture of how scholars have engaged *MKC* over the past twenty years. As we will discuss later, scholars could—and indeed, should—conduct studies similar to ours with scholarly books and editions or other academic journals.

We document the patterns of citation across these five journals over twenty years, noting not only the number and frequency of references to *MKC*, but also the types of engagement with *MKC*. In short, our study provides some empirical evidence of the exigence from which this collection arises. The types of engagement in these five journals range from superficial "scholarly nods" to frequent citations. Some articles engage only North's concept of practitioner "lore" or his nomination of 1963 as the birth date of the discipline, whereas others take on sustained challenges to North's methods and conclusions. We evaluate the spectrum of critical responses to *MKC* from over 130 articles that cite it in these journals over a two-decade span, composing an aggregate evaluation of the book's influence from the published work of scholars who used North's work and shaped the conversations of our discipline.

Researchers can conduct such work not just for historical aims, but also for more immediate concerns. By measuring the circulation of *MKC*, we are also calling attention to a way of seeing our current scholarship as it unfolds—recognizing that even the most influential books make limited and erratic appearances in composition scholarship. In other words, our analysis of *MKC* not only sheds light on the impact of North's publication, but it also illustrates the methodological benefits of bibliometric analysis, especially for a discipline that has only recently moved beyond its status as an "emerging field."

BACKGROUND FOR MAPPING NORTH'S INFLUENCE

Our study is in the tradition of bibliometrics; that is, the quantitative study of published scholarly work intended to reveal evolving patterns, trends, and values in any given discipline or field. Bibliometrics has been a useful practice in the sciences for over a century (Pritchard and Witting 1981), but gained disciplinary interest in other fields in the 1960s, including psychology (Garvey and Griffith 1964), sociology (Crane 1967), and communication (Parker and Paisley 1966). Communication scholars, in particular, took great interest in bibliometrics in the mid-1980s, conducting several studies and even dedicating a special issue of *Communication Research* to bibliometrics in 1989. As L. Miles Raisig explained in 1962, bibliometrics is used "to demonstrate historical movements, to determine the national or universal research use of books and journals, and to ascertain in many local situations the general use of books and journals" (450). Bibliometrics can be used to measure differing characteristics of scholarship during a particular period (Reinsch and Lewis 1993), a discipline's interaction with other fields (Forman 1993), or the circulation of particular ideas or concepts and their "impact rating" (Funkhouser 1996). Emerging from decades of research in information science, bibliometrics offers tools useful for asking different questions than composition scholarship usually asks, thereby providing new avenues for historical and transdisciplinary research.

As Éric Archambault and Étienne Vignola Gagné explain, bibliometric methods particularly relevant to social sciences and humanities can be classified along three broad sets of indicators—that is, along three particular types of criteria around which analysis clusters. The first of these types of indicators is *publication count*, which, as the name suggests, involves counting publications to examine trends in research areas or patterns of specialization. The second type of indicator, *citations and impact factor*, aims to measure citations in terms of influence and circulation, which involves making judgments about the impact of a particular scholarly contribution by examining citations to that contribution. Finally, the third type of indicator is *cocitation and coword analysis*, which examines relationships between authors and selected terms (2004, 2). Cocitation maps evolve when an author cites two other authors together (Andrews 2003, 47), while coword analysis examines texts in which pairs of selected terms occur together (Qin 1999, 133). These bibliometric methods can be blended to, as Archambault and Gagné put it, "build multifaceted representations of research fields, linkages among them, and the actors who are shaping them" (2004, 2). In a Burkean sense, bibliometric analyses aim to observe, trace, and map the published conversations after they occurred, and as they moved from parlor to parlor.

Our approach follows closely a line of bibliometric inquiry that traces the impact of one scholarly work, an approach similar to Katherine W. McCain and Laura J. Salvucci's study of Frederick P. Brooks's *The Mythical Man-Month* (2006). Their project—famously, in bibliometrics circles—analyzed 497 articles (1975–1999) that cited Brooks's collection of essays about the development of the first large-scale computer operating system. Similarly, Eugene Garfield (1985) traces citations to Derek John de Solla Price's book *Little Science, Big Science*, mapping the surge of interest in and circulation of de Solla Price's ideas throughout the scientific community. Our project, though smaller in scale, takes on a similar aim: it traces *MKC* over two decades of scholarship in academic journals, and ours is one of the few studies in rhetoric and composition to take this approach.

North was, of course, interested in a variety of research methods, yet rhetoric and composition scholarship has too often foregone the benefits of examining its own scholarly conversations using the tools of bibliometrics. In one of the very few bibliometric studies in rhetoric and composition, Christopher G. Hayes (1988) examined four years' worth (1971–72 and 1976–77) of *CCC* and *CE*, two of the journals we examine in our own study. Hayes's aim was to determine whether articles published in those journals during those years used a core of canonical works or concepts to define and argue about the relationships between composition and literary studies and composition and psychology (4–5). However, Hayes's project is a *CCC* presentation, necessarily limited in its scope, and available only through the ERIC database. Other scholars (notably Sue Hum [1994] and Maureen Daly Goggin [2000]) have traced the history and development of ideas in academic journals, but our aim is less to comment on the discipline during a historical period and more to document the path of a book that is clearly central to the history of the discipline.

Probably more familiar, and certainly more readily available, to readers of this collection is Charles Bazerman's *Shaping Written Knowledge: The Genre and Activity of the Experimental Article in Science*. In one chapter, Bazerman uses bibliometrics to analyze eighty-seven years' worth of scientific articles about spectroscopy published in the venerable journal

Physical Review (*PR*). Bazerman shows how *PR* authors positioned themselves relative to one another's arguments and traces changes in argumentative and generic moves across a broad sample, concluding that *PR* authors cited previous work to establish a tradition and eventually used more references, resulting in longer and more complex articles (1988, 165–67). Bazerman argues that such citation trends reflect a "traditional view that science is a rational, cumulative, corporate enterprise," but more importantly, that citation practices reveal patterns reflecting the making of knowledge "through linguistic, rhetorical, and social choices" (183). In another context, Carol Berkenkotter and Thomas N. Huckin explain,

> The use of citations is intrinsic to scientists' [and we would add, all scholars'] story making because it contextualizes local (laboratory) knowledge within an ongoing history of disciplinary knowledge making. Such contextualization is essential because it is only when the scientist places his or her . . . findings within a framework of accepted knowledge that a claim to have made a scientific discovery—and thereby to have contributed to the field's body of knowledge—can be made. (1993, 111)

Examining the use of citations helps illuminate the linguistic, rhetorical, and social contexts of how scholars put particular works (in this case, *MKC*) to use in shaping ongoing conversations.

To put it another way, bibliometric methods offer ways to examine what Howard D. White and Katherine W. McCain call "the patterned behavior of human beings—the authors, editors, and indexers on the production side of learned publication" (1989, 123). As Burke's parlor metaphor suggests, different actors will make different moves in citing a source, such as aligning themselves with or against a premise, marking out the scope of a claim, or connecting themselves to those who have also "put in their oar" on a particular issue. Indeed, Shirley K. Rose calls scholarly citation "a courtship ritual designed to enhance a writer's standing in a scholarly discourse community" (1996, 34). We examine five journals of our field for evidence of the different communities' courtship—and other—rituals centering on *MKC*.

CITATIONS OF *MKC*, 1987–2006

Selecting (or blending) particular types of bibliometric indicators involves making choices about what one wishes to find out. In this case, we wanted to know how *MKC* has been used—and how frequently—in *CCC*, *CE*, *RR*, *JAC*, and *CS* over the last twenty years. We began by searching the journals for any references to *MKC* and compiled a data set of citations from 131 articles. Based on our initial reading of the citations, we each worked independently to determine a coding scheme to classify the articles according to what particular *MKC* content was used. We then compared our classification codes, finding them quite similar, and we synthesized them into the six categories for Indicator 3 (listed below). We then determined it would be useful to include two other indicators—to note how *MKC* was used (Indicator 2), and to what extent it appeared in the article (Indicator 1).

For *Indicator 1 (Attention Given to MKC)*, we decided to use a variation of Blaise Cronin's (1994) "tiered citation" typology, in which citations are categorized by *Oeuvre* (complete works of North); *Motif* (North and other writers like him); *Opus* (*MKC*); *Chunk* (section/paragraph/chapter); and *Quantum* (formula/phrase). For our purposes, however, the categories of *Oeuvre* and *Motif* went beyond the scope of our study, so we decided to break down *Chunk* and *Quantum* into four categories, ranging from summary to extended engagement.

For *Indicator 2 (How MKC Used)*, we borrowed an annotation scheme from Simone Teufel, Advaith Siddharthan, and Dan Tidhar (2006), who used categories based on "contrast, weaknesses of other work, similarities between work, and usage of other work." Our use of the category "lateral citation" for Indicator 2 comes from David Franke's study of the essays published in the collection *Feminine Principles and Women's Experience in American Composition and Rhetoric*. Franke examined how the contributors positioned themselves relative to the scholars whose work they were engaging. Franke reported being "surprised" by "the way that the writers identified their antecedents. . . [using] a particular rhetoric of attribution" that he found to be "less hierarchical" and which centered on "collaboration and connection over argument and defense." To draw the distinction between agonistic and collaborative citation practices, Franke dubbed these practices *vertical* and *lateral*, respectively (1995, 376). *Lateral citation* does not involve abdicating the scholar's role in evaluating or critiquing the work of others; however, a lateral citation foregrounds citation as conversation, with participants in the conversation "borrowing from others who have gone before . . . and extending the discourse beyond" the individual (381). In short, we use the *lateral citation* category to identify articles that make a citation connection to *MKC*, but not for any particular argumentative aim or purpose beyond identifying the article with North's work.

Thus, we used these bibliometric indicators:

Indicator 1. Attention Given to MKC (that is, the extent of each particular article's engagement with *MKC*, ranging from cursory to extended), with the following categories:

> *MKC* listed in Works Cited but not cited in text
>
> *MKC* referenced as a whole
>
> Term(s)/concept(s) summarized or paraphrased
>
> A passage from *MKC* cited
>
> A sentence or more from *MKC* cited
>
> Extended use/engagement with *MKC*

Indicator 2. How MKC Used (this characterizes the primary uses to which an article puts *MKC*; for example, to show contrast or to connect rather than to critique), with these categories:

> *MKC* cited to show contrast
>
> *MKC* cited to show similarity
>
> *MKC* cited to critique
>
> Lateral citation (to connect)
>
> Perfunctory (only in Works Cited)

Indicator 3. Content from MKC (this characterizes the subject matter of the citation), with these categories:

> Historical
>
> Status of composition as a discipline
>
> Mapping composition's research sites
>
> Lore/practitioners
>
> Research methods defined/explained
>
> North's contribution to the field

Working independently, we each reread the 131 citations to *MKC* in *CE*, *RR*, *JAC*, and *CS* from the years 1988 through 2006, using the coding scheme and placing each article into one of the categories for each of the three indicators. For example, in her 2005 article for *JAC*, Margaret M. Strain summarizes North's historical content, specifically North's dubbing of the Braddock report as composition's "charter," which she uses for purposes of showing similarity (coded as 1C, 2B, 3A using the indicators above):

> Not a few of our disciplinary histories have identified the 1960s as a period of foment and growth, noting the power of research to authorize writing studies as an intellectual pursuit. Stephen North calls Richard Braddock, Richard Lloyd-Jones, and Lowell Schoer's *Research in Written Composition* the field's "charter" (135). James Berlin credits the authors along with the editors of NCTE publications such as *Research in the Teaching of English* as contributing to the "creation of a discipline" (131). (2005, 514)

Other articles invoke a term from *MKC* for support, as in this passage from James N. Laditka's 1991 *RR* article:

> But why ask of theory what might be its implications for changes in our practice? Why, indeed, should we not rather interrogate theory from the perspective of our daily experience as teachers, celebrating what Stephen M. North has called our Practitioner's "lore," our private knowledge of what seems to work in the day-to-day of our classrooms? (1991, 298)

Often (about one in five instances), however, only the title and author invoke *MKC* in its entirety. Consider Russell K. Durst's 1990 article in *CCC*:

> Research on composition is a growing and seldom-charted terrain. In recent years, several studies have begun to chart that terrain. Anne Herrington's "The First Twenty Years of Research in the Teaching of English" looks at the growth of a research community in composition by analyzing the articles on writing which appeared in *RTE* from 1967 to 1986. George Hillocks's *Research on Written Composition* examines the research on writing instruction appearing between 1963 and 1983. And Stephen North's *The Making of Knowledge in Composition* examines composition studies as a whole, categorizing different types of inquiry and discussing the theoretical and methodological frameworks of the various approaches. (394)

Here, Durst refers to *MKC* as a whole as a means of showing similarity and signifying North's contribution to the field (scored as 1B, 2B, 3F). A 1989 *RR* article by Lester Faigley also invokes *MKC* as a whole, but with a more critical angle, and regarding disciplinary mapping (scored as 1B, 2C, 3C):

> The study of writing must be at some level the study of written language. Yet some recent overviews of the field suggest otherwise. One apparently

noncontroversial aspect of Stephen North's controversial survey of writing research, *The Making of Knowledge in Composition*, is the omission of linguistics as an important disciplinary subfield. North does not even include language or linguistics in the index. (240)

Conversely, many of the other articles (again, about one in five) make extensive use of *MKC* (code 1F), citing lengthy passages and summarizing vast portions of *MKC*, so they are too lengthy to include here.

TABLE 1

Number of articles citing MKC in the journals Rhetoric Review,
College Composition and Communication, College English,
Composition Studies, and JAC (1988–2006)

	RR	CCC	CE	CS	JAC	Total
1988	3	1	0	0	1	5
1989	4	9	1	1	1	16
1990	1	4	0	1	3	9
1991	4	1	5	2	2	14
1992	2	0	0	2	5	9
1993	1	7	2	1	2	13
1994	2	1	0	0	2	5
1995	4	2	2	1	4	13
1996	1	1	0	0	0	2
1997	2	3	2	1	0	8
1998	0	4	0	2	0	6
1999	0	4	1	0	2	7
2000	0	3	2	1	1	7
2001	0	0	1	2	3	6
2002	0	0	0	0	1	1
2003	0	0	1	0	1	2
2004	0	0	1	0	0	1
2005	0	1	0	1	1	3
2006	0	1	0	1	0	2

Examining each of the 131 articles for our bibliometric indicators yielded 393 scores (three per article), of which our separate coding of the data resulted in only twenty-three discrepant readings, a 99 percent inter-rater reliability rate. (We adjudicated the discrepant readings to provide the findings we present below.) We attribute this extraordinarily high rate not to our reading prowess but instead to the ease of using the categories we created together. Ultimately, we believe the coding scheme was reliable because the indicators of attention, use, and content were easy to iden-tify, and this facility makes bibliometric analysis particularly well suited for compositionists. After all, compositionists are the faculty who are the most thoroughly well versed in the teaching, critical reading, and evaluation of citation practices and academic argumentation, so we are confident that other scholars could carry out similar work for other purposes.

The number of articles with citations (see figure 1) to *MKC* is itself revealing. Not surprisingly, *MKC* is cited frequently in the years immedi-ately after publication, but there is an erratic pattern of appearance with peaks in 1989, 1991, 1993, and 1995. In the individual journals, a similar pattern is discernible, with some years registering multiple citations and other years carrying no references at all to *MKC*. (Interestingly—and perhaps because of North's attention more toward composition than rhetoric—there are no references to *MKC* in *Rhetoric Review* after 1997.) It might be tempting to make claims about the causes behind these ebbs and flows, and we could speculate that the pattern is due to trends in research or the dialogic nature of scholarly publishing, but such conclu-sions are difficult to support.

What can be gained, however, is the straightforward—but nonethe-less significant—understanding that an influential work, even one as canonical as *MKC*, will most likely circulate differently at different times in different journals. If this understanding holds true for other works across other publications in our field, then we can begin to imagine its practical impact on our considerations of current scholarship, especially if motivated by tenure and promotion decisions. In other words, a schol-ar's output cannot easily—or validly—be summed up by measuring cita-tions in a journal or two for only a few years. We believe, instead, that a more expansive view that crosses multiple publications reveals a rich portrait of a work's circulation and longevity and, thus, of a scholar's contributions to particular conversations.

The need for an expansive view is even more pressing for scholarship in new media environments, such as electronic portfolios, blogs, digital films, websites, and podcasts. Many compositionists' home departments

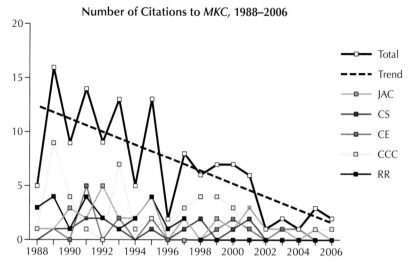

Figure 1. Number of articles citing MKC in the journals Rhetoric Review, College Composition and Communication, College English, Composition Studies, and JAC (1988–2006). Total number of citations and trendline included.

are ill equipped to evaluate such scholarship (Modern 2007, 11, 41–45). What's more, new media tools make possible new ways of measuring the influence of a scholar's work. Such tools include online archives, materials digitized by commercial entities such as Google, online syllabi, tracking of website visits and downloads, archives of meaningful contributions to discussion forums (such as the writing program administrators' listserv, WPA-L), and "peer-evaluated online communities" such as Slashdot, The Pool, and others (Blais et al. 2007).

The aggregate data from the five journals also provides us with an overall trajectory that enables us to test some hypotheses about scholarly publishing. According to one study of twelve journals in information science over two decades (White and McCain 1989), citation data "generally take the form of a negative exponential distribution" in which there is a peak period during years two and three (for most articles, but up to six for very influential ones) and then there is a steady decline (perhaps 10 percent annually for science, less for arts and humanities) (155–56). We can see these trends with *MKC* as well, and by this reasoning, it qualifies as an influential work for sustaining an overall increase in citations for the first six years after publication, as seen in figure 2.

Citations of *MKC* in these five journals show an overall decline of roughly 10 percent a year from 1994 to 2006, as depicted in figure 3.

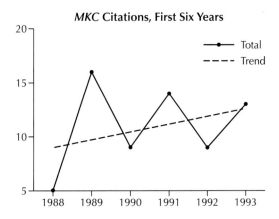

Figure 2. Trendline for articles citing MKC 1988–1993.

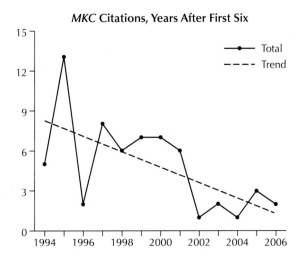

Figure 3. Trendline for articles citing MKC 1994–2006.

Other studies using bibliometric approaches like ours may allow the field to assess whether other assuredly influential works follow similar patterns of circulation and use. There is also a predictive component of this analysis that might hold promise to counterbalance the subjective evaluations of peer reviewers, many of whom have a stake in the subject matter. For example, in most tenure and promotion decisions, external reviewers play a vital role in evaluating to what extent a scholar

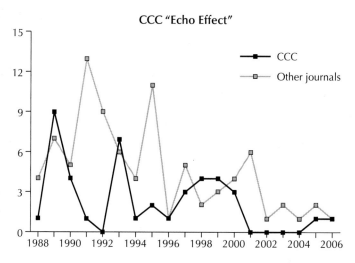

Figure 4. Influence of CCC on other publications.

contributes to the field. While these evaluations are necessary and useful, a bibliometric analysis *demonstrating* how a work is influential could also be brought to bear on such decisions. Of course, like any evaluative measure, such quantification has the potential to be abused, but we think that such metrics could give us an additional way to evaluate the impact of scholarship on our work. After all, with further studies to determine the reliability of this pattern, or evidence of other patterns, it could be possible to assess a book's status as influential in the field—and have citation evidence to support it. Furthermore, such research could be useful for academic publishing decisions, in which sales alone may not reflect a book's influence.

Another compelling pattern that warrants further study is what we call the "*CCC* echo effect": our data suggest that the rise and fall of citations to *MKC* in *CCC* articles precedes a similar rise and fall in the other four journals (as a whole). Two discernible periods, 1988 to 1992 and 1992 to 1996 (see fig. 4), show an almost identical two-year lag time between the peak of citations to *MKC* and a similar peak of citations in the other journals.

Such a pattern suggests that the discipline's flagship publication, *CCC*, drives—to some extent—what scholarship is produced and published in other venues. If this echo effect holds true for other citation data sets, then the leadership role of the *CCC* editorial board may not be just to influence what *CCC* publishes but also what is published in the field more generally.

Finally, and perhaps most importantly, the data regarding the citations of *MKC* confirmed our initial expectations and provided some surprises, as Table 2 sets out.

TABLE 2
Content and usage frequencies

Indicator #1: Attention Given to *MKC*	#	%
A. *MKC* listed in Works Cited but not cited in text	5	3.82
B. *MKC* referenced as a whole	25	19.08
C. Term(s)/concept(s) summarized or paraphrased	48	36.64
D. A passage from *MKC* cited	10	7.63
E. A sentence or more from *MKC* cited	16	12.21
F. Extended use/engagement with *MKC*	27	20.61
No score	0	0.00
Total	131	100

Indicator #2: How *MKC* Used	#	%
A. *MKC* cited to show contrast	8	5.97
B. *MKC* cited to show similarity	69	51.49
C. *MKC* cited to critique	28	20.90
D. Lateral citation (to connect)	23	17.16
E. Perfunctory use (only in Works Cited)	5	3.73
No score	1	0.75
Total	134	100

Indicator #3: Content from *MKC*	#	%
A. Historical	40	18.26
B. Status of composition as a discipline	31	14.16
C. Mapping composition's research	34	15.53
D. Lore / practitioners	52	23.74
E. Research methods defined / explained	33	15.07
F. *MKC*'s contribution to the field	25	11.42
No score	4	1.83
Total	219	100

Citations summarized there show that *MKC* has been used most often in this way: a term or a concept from North's book is summarized or paraphrased (37 percent) to show similarity to—or support for—an author's position (51 percent), and it is usually about lore or practitioners (24 percent). These aggregate numbers indicate how *MKC* has most commonly been used, but they should not be understood to indicate that there are perfunctory gestures simply repeated in our scholarship—what North in *MKC* imagines as "strictly ceremonial" "ritual salutation[s]" (340). Of the 131 articles, only eleven (8.4 percent) demonstrated the three traits exclusively, suggesting that even though our scholarly conversations might demonstrate collective patterns, they are generally unique in their individual motives and structures.

CONCLUSIONS

After collecting the citations from the journals, we had anticipated data that would show an emphasis on lore-practitioners, but we did not expect that the remaining content categories would be so evenly distributed: historical (18 percent), status of composition as a discipline (14 percent), mapping composition's research (16 percent), research methods defined/explained (15 percent), and *MKC*'s contribution to the field (11 percent). The distribution suggests that *MKC*'s primary influence might be in articulating a perspective about practitioner knowledge making, but the other concepts in the book hold substantial—and similar—importance.

Ultimately, bibliometric studies like this one can generate empirical evidence to support (or challenge) our thinking about the circulation, influence, and impact of scholarship, even extending to fundamental questions about, for example, which scholarship is crucial for graduate students in their coursework and exam preparation. With the continued growth of rhetoric and composition as a discipline, and an increasing worldwide interest in research on writing, we should embrace bibliometric approaches for the historical insights they provide—as well as the empirical support that can augment personal perspectives or "common knowledge" about scholarship in the field. As Robert Connors argued, the "rhetoric of citation systems" has "silently undergirded the enterprise of Western intellectual activity" but has "largely gone unremarked," and our "citation choices have always seemed *so* formalized that they have remained submerged, little discussed" (1999, 242; italics in original). Robust analyses of the complexity of citation practices in rhetoric and composition can infuse the field with empirical support for theoretical claims about importance, influence, and longevity—and to what extent the field coheres.

Critiques of bibliometrics are to be expected: after all, quantitative measures of complex discussions in the Burkean parlor are bound to be reductive. We do not aspire to create a perfect model with predictive capabilities, but we do hope to bring additional tools to our discussions of the history and scholarly activity of the discipline. For example, a more expansive study of *MKC* that included citations from our scholarly books and edited collections, and from additional journals, might reveal different patterns or provide additional support for the findings we have shared here. Furthermore, we might benefit from similar studies of other decidedly influential books in the field. For example, did the use of Shirley Brice Heath's *Ways with Words* follow a pattern similar to *MKC*? Did Peter Elbow's *Writing without Teachers* or James Kinneavy's *A Theory of Discourse* circulate through our scholarship in similar ways?

Providing methodologically sound maps of scholarship would enable us to examine, with greater precision and transparency than is typical, how the knowledge we produce takes life in the pages of our publications. Richard Haswell, for example, has already made a compelling case that NCTE/CCCC has systematically excluded research that is "replicable, aggregate, and data supported" (2005, 201). Haswell cautions that when composition's influential professional organizations show a wholesale aversion to a fundamental approach to making knowledge, such an aversion may be the field's undoing: "When college composition as a whole treats the data-gathering, data-validating, and data-aggregating part of itself as alien, then the whole may be doomed. Even now, the profession's immune system—its ability to deflect outside criticism with solid and ever-strengthening data—is on shaky pins" (219). Just as North startled readers in 1987 by asserting that there had been no replication studies in the field (159), Haswell urges us to rethink our research energies, and he does so by providing evidence that our research energies are misdirected, or at the very least, severely imbalanced. Bibliometric studies certainly are one tool that can provide us with depictions of our publishing practices—the ways in which knowledge is inscribed, impressed, negotiated, resisted, and often assimilated in the Burkean parlors of a field. Such portraits may be invaluable as we leave our "emerging field" status behind and continue moving forward into our disciplinary future.

REFERENCES

Andrews, James E. 2003. An author co-citation analysis of medical informatics. *Journal of the Medical Library Association* 91 (1): 47–56.

Archambault, Éric, and Étienne Vignola Gagné. 2004. The use of bibliometrics in the social sciences and humanities. *Science-Metrix.* http://www.science-metrix.com/eng/reports_2004_t.htm.

Bazerman, Charles. 1988. *Shaping written communication: The genre and activity of the experimental article in science.* Madison: University of Wisconsin Press.

Berkenkotter, Carol, and Thomas N. Huckin. 1993. You are what you cite: Novelty and intertextuality in a biologist's experimental article. *Professional Communication: The*

Social Perspective, edited by Nancy Roundy Blyler and Charlotte Thralls, 109–27. Newbury Park: Sage.

Blais, Jolene, Jon Ippolito, Owen Smith, Steve Evans, and Nate Stormer. 2007. Promotion and tenure guidelines addendum: Rationale for redefined criteria—new criteria for new media. *Version 2* (2). http://newmedia.umaine.edu/interarchive/new_criteria_for_new_media.html.

Burke, Kenneth. 1974. *Philosophy of literary form: Studies in symbolic action.* 3rd ed. Berkeley: University of California Press.

Connors, Robert J. 1999. The rhetoric of citation systems, part II: Competing epistemic values in citation. *Rhetoric Review* 17 (2): 219–45.

Crane, Diana. 1967. The gatekeepers of science: Some factors affecting the selection of articles for scientific journals." *American Sociologist* 2 (4): 195–201.

Cronin, Blaise. 1994. Tiered citation and measures of document similarity. *Journal of the American Society for Information Science* 45 (7): 537–38.

Durst, Russel K. 1990. The mongoose and the rat in composition research: Insights from the *RTE* annotated bibliography. *College Composition and Communication* 41 (1): 393–408.

The Excellence Awards 2001. Excellence in teaching, Stephen North. 2001. State University of New York-Albany. http://www.albany.edu/feature2001/excellence_awards/stephen_north.html.

Faigley, Lester. 1989. The study of writing and the study of language. *Rhetoric Review* 7 (2): 240–56.

Forman, Janis. 1993. Business communication and composition: The writing connection and beyond. *Journal of Business Communication* 30: 333–52.

Franke, David. 1995. Writing the unmapped territory: The practice of lateral citation. *Feminine principles and women's experience in American composition and rhetoric*, edited by Louise Wetherbee Phelps and Janet Emig, 375–84. Pittsburgh, PA: University of Pittsburgh Press.

Funkhouser, Edward Truman. 1996. The evaluative use of citation analysis for communication journals. *Human Communication Research* 22 (4): 563–74.

Garfield, Eugene. 1985. In tribute to Derek John de Solla Price: A citation analysis of *Little science, big science. Scientometrics* 7: 487–503.

Garvey, William D., and Belver C. Griffith. 1964. Scientific information exchange in psychology. *Science* 146: 1655–59.

Goggin, Maureen Daly. 2000. *Authoring a discipline: Scholarly journals and the post-World War II emergence of rhetoric and composition.* Mahwah: Lawrence Erlbaum Associates.

Graff, Gerald, and Andrew Hoberek. 1999. Hiding it from the kids (with apologies to Simon and Garfunkel). *College English* 62 (2): 242–254.

Haswell, Richard H. 2005. NCTE/CCCC's recent war on scholarship. *Written Communication* 22 (2): 198–223.

Hayes, Christopher G. 1988. Defining composition: Evidence from the citations, years 1971–72 and 1976–77. Paper presented at the CCCC, St. Louis, MO, March 17–19. ERIC Document Reproduction Service, ED 294 235.

Hum, Sue Yin. 1994. *Mapping disciplinary territory through professional journals: Composition and rhetoric Scholarship in the 1970s.* PhD diss., Texas Christian University.

Laditka, James N. 1991. Language, power, and play: The dance of deconstruction and practical wisdom. *Rhetoric Review* 9 (2): 298–311.

McCain, Katherine W., and Laura J. Salvucci. 2006. How influential is Brooks' Law?: A Longitudinal citation context analysis of Frederick Brooks' *The mythical man-month*." *Journal of Information Science* 32 (3): 277–95.

Modern Language Association (MLA). 2007. Report of the MLA Task Force on evaluating scholarship for tenure and promotion. *Profession 2007*: 9–71.

North, Stephen M. 1987. *The making of knowledge in composition: Portrait of an emerging field.* Upper Montclair, NJ: Boynton/Cook.

Parker, Edwin B., and William J. Paisley. 1966. Research for psychologists at the interface of the scientist and his information system. *American Psychologist* 21: 1061–72.

Pritchard, Alan, and Glenn R. Witting. 1981. *Bibliometrics: A bibliography and index, 1874–1959.* Watford, England: ALLM Books.

Qin He. 1999. Knowledge discovery through co-word analysis. *Library Trends* Summer: 133–59.

Raisig, L. Miles. 1962. Statistical bibliography in the health sciences. *Bulletin of the Medical Library Association* 50: 450–61.

Reinsch, N. L., Jr., and Phillip V. Lewis. 1993. Author and citation patterns for *The Journal of Business Communication. Journal of Business Communication* 30: 435–62.

Rose, Shirley K. 1996. What's love got to do with it? Scholarly citation practices as courtship rituals. *Language and Learning Across the Disciplines* 1 (3): 34–48.

Strain, Margaret M. 2005. In defense of a nation: The National Defense Education Act, Project English, and the origins of empirical research in composition." *JAC: A Quarterly Journal for the Interdisciplinary Study of Rhetoric, Writing, Multiple Literacies, and Politics* 25 (3): 513–42.

Teufel, Simone, Advaith Siddharthan, and Dan Tidhar. 2006. An annotation scheme for citation function. Proceedings of the 7th SIGdial Workshop on Discourse and Dialogue, Sydney, Australia. http://www.cl.cam.ac.uk/~as372/sigdial-final.pdf.

White, Howard D., and Katherine W. McCain. 1989. Bibliometrics. *Annual Review of Information Science and Technology* 24: 119–86.

15

MAKING SPACE IN COMPOSITION STUDIES
Discursive Ecologies as Inquiry

Patricia Webb Boyd

In the final chapter of *The Making of Knowledge in Composition* (*MKC*), published in 1987, Stephen North asks a question that has provoked much discussion within our field: "Is there any chance then for an academically full-fledged, autonomous, multi-methodological, knowledge-making Composition?" (369). This question surfaced at a time when composition was trying to make a place for itself in the university. In 1987, composition did not have a clearly delineated identity as a discipline and was widely seen as a service arm of the university. Composition was the sad woman in the basement (Miller 1991), overshadowed by the resurgent interest in literary studies and its adoption of postmodern theories. Primarily viewed as practice—that is, the teaching of writing—rather than a coherent group of practitioners, researchers, and scholars, composition's image in the university was not a shiny one.

It is not surprising, then, that a key trend in composition at the time was for researchers and scholars to separate themselves from practice as inquiry. In order to validate their work in institutions that privileged scientific inquiry and departments that privileged literary theory, composition researchers and scholars insisted that the work they did produced the knowledge and that practitioners then applied the knowledge. When those outside the field of composition critiqued students' writing abilities, those within blamed practitioners for not effectively using the knowledge that researchers and scholars had transmitted to them. Scholars and researchers did not consider the limits of their own research; rather, they argued that "practitioner inquiry had failed to produce knowledge adequate for the demands of teaching writing," thus allowing scholars and researchers to shift the emphasis away from "the shortage of adequate knowledge toward the problem of dissemination, of getting the Practitioners to use it, and use it properly" (North, 329). Thus, in a time when "power, prestige, professional recognition and advancement" (363) in the university were gained through scientific legitimation, composition scholars and researchers separated themselves so much so that we were "largely unaccustomed to entertaining the notion of practice as a mode of inquiry at all" (21).

More than twenty years later, practice as a valued form of inquiry is, unfortunately, still challenged. In fact, "lore," which North defines as "the accumulated body of traditions, practices, and beliefs in terms of which Practitioners understand how writing is done, learned, and taught" (22), has been increasingly devalued by the field as "what to do on Monday" kinds of information—not knowledge. North predicted that if practice as inquiry was not once again valued, the field of composition would be subsumed into either literary theory within the English department or into other disciplines like linguistics, psychology, or education. While composition has not dissolved, those in the field are still not comfortable with their identity within and outside the university, so much so that a good deal of our research has not moved beyond the questions North asked in 1987: "What exactly is this field called Composition? Where does it come from? How does it work? Where is it going?" (Preface). For North, the answer lies in the field's valuing of multidisciplinary research methods—most importantly, the valuing of practice as inquiry.

Some areas of composition studies have begun to recoup practice as inquiry in a way that shows its value to the field, the university, and the surrounding community. At the heart of ecocomposition and other place-based research is an embracing of practice as inquiry, but not to the exclusion of other methodologies. The kinds of research questions posed by ecocompositionists require significant interaction across the methodological communities within composition as well as across various disciplines like ecology, biology, cultural studies, and environmental rhetoric. The approaches to research that this community of inquirers takes combine methods of practitioners, scholars, and researchers. Through its multimethodological pluralism, ecocomposition research begins to achieve the goals North lays out for effective knowledge making in composition: "*heightened methodological consciousness*"; "*methodological egalitarianism*"; *and increased recognition of and reestablishment of the validity of practice as inquiry* (370–1; italics added).

Studying the ways that ecocomposition and place-based research both enact and critique these principles provides us with a way of locating composition in the university as a valid, valuable discipline that is multidisciplinary. Further, a study of ecocomposition and other place-based studies helps us see how composition can actually move beyond anxiety over its identity to positioning itself as an engine of significant change both within and outside the university. To demonstrate both those important points about the development and future of composition, this chapter begins with North's arguments for the importance of practitioner inquiry as a complement to scholars' and researchers' inquiry. Then it considers the evolving research paradigm represented in several core texts in ecocomposition.

NORTH'S HOUSE OF LORE

In *MKC*, North lays out the key methodological approaches that compositionists have taken in their research on writing, explaining and analyzing three key communities of inquirers: practitioners, scholars, and researchers. According to North, these methodological communities comprise "groups of inquirers more or less united by their allegiance to one such mode, to an agreed-upon set of rules for gathering, testing, validating, accumulating, and distributing what they regard as knowledge" (1). As he sees it, the problem that plagues composition is a lack of understanding about and respect for different methodological communities. Particularly attacked is practitioner inquiry because of its constructed image as technical application rather than knowledge construction. Lore, which is the primary knowledge made by practitioner inquiry, came under attack because, as a collection of teaching practices that are shared primarily orally and validated through individual use, it is seen as a collection of decontextualized, disconnected, undertheorized recipes or "how to" guides. Objections to lore, then, came mostly from the difficulties of *validating* the solutions/practices.[1]

However, North argues that as a research method, practice as inquiry has produced important knowledge that brings coherence to the field. Even as it has been critiqued by scholars and researchers, lore has been remarkably durable, due in part to its permeability and flexibility. North actively resists the view that practitioners merely apply knowledge that is constructed by scholars and researchers; he argues that practitioners have

---

1.   See Fulkerson, this volume.

created useful knowledge that results from "shared institutional experience, knowledge that is thus "formed under conditions and circumstances that are widely shared" (28). However, North asserts that is it is important to recognize not all practice is inquiry. In order for it to become inquiry that produces knowledge, practice responds to three circumstances:

> when the situation cannot be framed in familiar terms, so that any familiar strategies will have to be adapted for use;
>
> when, although the situation is perceived as familiar, standard approaches are no longer satisfactory, and so new approaches are created for it; or
>
> when both situation and approach are non-standard. (33)

According to North, then, practitioner knowledge is constructed through clearly defined parameters of inquiry; it is not a random meshing together of disparate practices.

North's description of the "House of Lore" paints a particularly apt picture of how practitioners create and validate their knowledge:

> A rambling, to my mind delightful old manse, wing branching off from wing, addition tacked to addition, in all sorts of materials—brick, wood, canvas, sheet metal, cardboard—with turrets and gables, minarets and spires, spiral staircases, rope ladders, pitons, dungeons, secret passageways—all seemingly random, yet all connected. (27)

As a metaphor, this house highlights the multidisciplinary nature of practitioner inquiry. It draws on studies and methods from a variety of fields and predilections (i.e., the brick, wood, canvas, etc.). The branches of the house illustrate that there is not a central core to practitioner knowledge—or lore—because many different types of research questions and study areas are valued in the house. And, yet, there is still a connection between the diverse studies that bind them together into a community of inquirers who share similar commitments and goals.

North argues that these kinds of methods must be embraced alongside the more centralized scholar and researcher methodologies: "What is required here . . . as the basis for a transformed composition, is a full recognition of and appreciation for lore: an understanding of what it is and how it works such that other kinds of knowledge can usefully interact with it" (371). He warns that unless lore is valued as inquiry, the entire field of composition is destined to be a feeble mirror of its original methodological pluralist identity. Yet, practitioners must also learn about researchers' and scholars' methods, because practitioners are prone to borrowing methods decontextually, thus overlooking the important ideological implications of methodologies. Further, validation and legitimation of lore is based on individuals' evaluation of the knowledge. While North argues that lore is communal, "the individual, finally, decides what to do and whether (or how) it has worked—decides, in short, what counts as knowledge" (28). The lack of communal validation of knowledge is problematic because it overlooks the social contexts in which knowledge is constructed and negotiated.

Both of these aspects of practitioner inquiry are problematic, but North argues that they can be solved through methodological diversity within composition. In his eyes, three changes needed to be made:

> First, there would have to be heightened methodological consciousness. Members of each methodological community would have to come to understand not only their own, but each others' mode of inquiry. (370)
>
> Second, there would have to be a spirit of methodological egalitarianism. Understanding one's own method, and then other methods, is an important first step, but it is not enough. All methods, and all kinds of knowledge, would have to be assumed to be created equal (371).
>
> Third, it would require the re-establishment of Practice as inquiry. . . . Practitioners have been responsible for Composition holding together as long as it has. But they have been, and remain, just that: at the center of the field's knowledge-making explosion, exerting a sort of epistemological gravitational pull, there has always been the enormous inertial mass of lore. (371)

Ultimately, what must happen, North insists, is for all three groups—practitioners, scholars, and researchers—to become familiar with and to value each other's methods and knowledge. Since practice as inquiry has suffered greatly in the field, North emphasizes that the composition community must particularly focus on studying and valuing—and reinventing—practitioner inquiry. Thus, a revised version of/use of/ creation of lore needs to be one of the field's key foci. This revisioning could lead to a stronger position for composition both within and outside the university.

ECOCOMPOSITION: PRACTICE, CRITIQUE, AND CHANGE

Turf battles still rage in the field of composition. Practitioner inquiry is still viewed by some (perhaps too many?) in suspect ways for many of the same reasons North described. However, since North wrote about this in

1987, important strides toward valuing practitioner inquiry as a knowledge-making activity have been made, and important revisions to validation and legitimation of lore have also been made. Ecocomposition is a
key area within composition that is embracing methodological pluralism
and thus provides strong examples of how various inquiry communities
can learn about each other's methods, how they can begin to value multiple methods, and how they can use this understanding to strengthen,
and perhaps even reinvent, practice as inquiry.

Put quite simply by Christian Weisser and Sidney Dobrin, "Ecocomposition is the study of the relationships between environments (and
by that we mean natural, constructed, and even imagined places) and
discourse (speaking, writing, and thinking)" (2001, 6). Ecocomposition
is invested in studying how *place* impacts discursive practices and how
our discursive actions impact the places within which we live. While
some ecocompositionists do study "natural" places, many focus on constructed and imagined places, thus highlighting that ecocomposition
is not nature writing, but rather a critical investigation of the myriad
places we inhabit and create. Ecocompositionists analyze both the ways
composition places itself institutionally as well as the ways it incorporates the study of place into the classroom and research. As Christopher
Keller and Christian Weisser explain in the introduction of their edited
collection, *The Locations of Composition*, "We hope to emphasize places
and their meanings for the discipline, with particular emphasis upon
how those places lead to new spaces, new activities, and new instances of
making room in the discipline." In ecocomposition, though, the reason
to study the place is to understand the relationships constructed there—
"to emphasize how those places and activities constantly shift and move
in relation to one another" (2007, 5). Studying place, then, is also about
studying movement and modification.

Ecocompositionists focus on experience, living texts, and interactive
relationships as the central features of knowing, knowledge construction, and legitimation of knowledge. Ecocomposition values lore, but a
lore that is situated within a larger ecological context than North imagined, one that looks at systems of interactions.

THE NEW RESEARCH PARADIGM OF ECOCOMPOSITION

As a basis for both pedagogy and research, ecocomposition privileges
practice as inquiry in a way that values methodological pluralism. As I
will show through an analysis of core texts that have defined this new

research paradigm, the boundaries between practitioner, researcher, and scholar blur in ecocomposition as the focus shifts from a common methodology to a common set of questions and orientations that invite, indeed require, multimodal investigations of the problems facing the discipline, the university, and the world today.

"The Ecology of Writing": Groundwork

In her highly influential 1986 *College English* article "The Ecology of Writing," Marilyn Cooper proposes an ecological view of writing as a corrective to the dominant image of the writer as solitary individual. To construct this new model, she draws on the field of ecology because its primary focus is on systems, not on the individual, and thus it encourages us to study how individuals operate in systems, not as isolated entities. In this ecological view, writing encompasses much more than the individual writer and her immediate context. An ecologist explores how writers interact to form systems: all the characteristics of any individual writer or piece of writing both determine and are determined by the characteristics of all the other writers and writings in the systems (368).

These concrete, observable systems are not predetermined containers/places into which writers insert themselves; instead, they are constructed through interactions with both places and other individuals within those places.

In order to participate within these systems, writers must draw on their own experiences and knowledge of the complex system that already exists/is continually being constructed around ideas: "One does not even begin to have ideas about a topic, even a relatively simple one, until a considerable body of already structured observations has been mastered" (Cooper 1986, 369). Interacting with other people, ideas, and cultural norms that dominate within these systems is at the heart of any writing project. By extension, then, it makes sense that knowledge would be constructed and validated through interactions in these complex systems rather than by isolated, individual writers. The knowledge produced, then, is validated by members of a community who are collaboratively producing knowledge.

Ecocomposition: Theoretical and Pedagogical Approaches

While Cooper's article lays important ground for ecocomposition scholarship, her focus is limited to studying interactions between readers and writers. As Christian Weisser and Sidney Dobrin point out in the introduction to their edited collection, *Ecocomposition: Theoretical and Pedagogical Approaches*, ecocomposition focuses on all social relationships, "not just those with writers and readers." Since "ecocomposition posits that writing is an activity that affects not only other writers and readers, but the total relations of discourse both to its organic and inorganic environment," Weisser and Dobrin argue that ecocomposition must "examine relationships with other texts, discourses, other organisms, environments, and locations" (2001, 20).

Identifying a need for spatial analysis to complement the prevailing temporal analyses that tend to dominate composition, the authors in this edited collection lay out a crucial foundation for studying place in new ways. All the authors are located in the humanities in the university, but they begin to draw on interdisciplinary work—such as ecology, biology, and architecture—in addition to using more conventional humanities-based resources—such as feminist theory, literary theory, environmental rhetoric, and rhetoric/composition studies. The articles in this collection provide examples of practitioner-based inquiry that begins with a common problem—redefining "the discipline's boundaries in order to provide more contextual, holistic, and useful ways of examining the world of discourse" (Weisser and Dobrin 2001, 1). Their research questions and studies work to develop a "theoretical perspective for perceiving the self and the social as recursively at work on one another, as engaged in an ecologically symbiotic relationship" (Bawarshi 2001, 70). Through reading the articles, it becomes clear that ecocomposition is useful because it can help "us recognize that a writer and his or her rhetorical environment are always in the process of reproducing one another, so that 'environment' is not some vague backdrop against which writers enact their rhetorical actions; instead, the environment becomes in critical ways part of the very rhetorical action that writers enact. We create our environments—our rhetorical situations—as we write within them; that is, we create our contexts as we create our texts" (70).

The writing classroom has always been an important environment for compositionists. While it will continue to be a crucial place to study, it is important for compositionists to critically analyze and move beyond the limits of a purely classroom-based focus. In "The Politics of Place: Student Travelers and Pedagogical Maps," Julie Drew (2001) argues that our teaching and research methods must change because we too often ignore the fact that students have lives outside the composition classroom. When our research focuses purely on students in the *classroom*, we are not truly studying the multiple places in which their ideas, values, and writing are produced. To fully study the systems in which students are located and act, she argues, we must realize that "students pass through, and only pause briefly within, classrooms; they dwell within and visit various locations, locations whose politics and discourse conventions both construct and identify them" (60). Therefore, we need to change our view of students, seeing them as *travelers* and not as *students*:

> Modifying our notions of what students are and do to include traveling may create opportunities for students to acknowledge and use the power relations that exist in the often conflicting discourse communities they traverse, and for Compositionists to improve pedagogical practices in ways that have positive material consequences for writers. (60)

Students are only in our classes for a small portion of their lives, yet we try to draw conclusions about their writing and their social realities based on our analyses of their time there. If we are going to study social relationships, we need to make sure we look beyond our usual sites of study.

In addition to encouraging readers to expand our conceptions of students' locatedness, the authors in the collection argue that we must likewise expand our conceptions of methodology in order to include interdisciplinary approaches. This emphasis on the need for interdisciplinary research that extends beyond the humanities is a key theme woven throughout the book. In his article, "Sustainable Composition," Derek Owens argues that, given the complexity of the problems facing our world, universities must take up the issue of sustainability as one of their core goals across disciplines. He argues:

> Disciplines can no longer afford to situate themselves "outside" the need to envision a sustainable culture; sustainability can no longer be a trope associated only with "specialized" programs of environmental studies, planning, architecture, economics and ecology. (2001, 29)

Since composition tends to approach research and teaching from a more holistic view, Owens says, it should play a central role in creating new environments within the new American university as it advances sustainable goals. "Because thinking sustainably requires a shift from compartmentalized to holistic thinking, and because the disciplinary permeability of the field of composition studies already implies a challenge to the culture of academic specialization, composition offers a logical working space for the promotion of sustainable pedagogies" (2001, 29). In an effort to map out what pedagogies like this might entail, Owens describes his first-year composition curriculum in which he asks students to be vigilant and critical participant-observers in the spaces they already inhabit and move through. He teaches them to use writing to analyze and evaluate those spaces and, if students identify problems in those spaces, he encourages them to draw on interdisciplinary research to develop a fuller understanding of the problems as well as pose potential solutions. He offers his class as one example of how we might engage students in a more holistic approach to knowledge construction, but he does not claim that his is the only way to do so.

While Owens does not specifically label his research "practice as inquiry," he enacts the key principles and core strategies North outlines in his definition of practitioner inquiry. As North highlights, practitioner work tends to be reactive in that the practitioner "needs to decide what to do as a means to an end determined by someone or something else" (37). In Owens's case, the "someone or something else" is the cultural need for creating and enacting sustainable practices in the university. The reaction then is based on "something in a situation" that "creates a discomfiture and seems to demand a non-routine reaction: an ordinary situation seems extraordinary, or to demand extraordinary treatment, or both" (North, 37). Owens argues that the "ordinary situation" of the university structure no longer works and therefore demands extraordinary treatment. Owens's work proceeds clearly through the six steps that North lays out as the practitioner's process for research: "identifying a problem, searching for cause(s), searching for possible solutions, testing solutions in practice, validation, and dissemination" (36). Throughout his work, he searches for causes (an overemphasis on disciplinary specialization), offers a possible solution (place-based, interdisciplinary assignments), tests the solution (teaching the assignment sequence that he created), and then disseminates his research to an audience of compositionists by publishing the work in the collection.

As North argues, one of the key critiques of practice as inquiry is that it lacks credibility and validity. Other methodological communities have accused practitioners of being "consistently undiscriminating, illogical, and sloppy" (27). Because of the pressures they are under in terms of institutional evaluation of their work, "when Practitioners report on their inquiry in writing, they tend to misrepresent both its nature and authority, moving farther and farther from their pragmatic and experiential power base" (54). Instead of owning and capitalizing on the strength of their practical knowledge, practitioners begin to "look more and more like bad Scholars or inadequate Researchers, and further undermine the public perception of Practitioner authority" (54–5). Facing a consistent devaluing of practitioner knowledge, practitioners "need to be more methodologically self-conscious than any of the other communities: to know the limits of the authority the other modes of inquiry can claim, on the one hand; but to know the limits of their own, as well, and work within them" (55). Therefore, it is crucial, in North's eyes, for practitioners to emphasize what their work contributes without trying to masquerade as researchers or scholars.

While it is clear that Owens and the other authors in *Ecocomposition* embrace multiple methodologies and value practice as inquiry, is it also the case that they are methodologically self-conscious so as to not make grandiose claims about the extent of the knowledge they produce. Balancing authority with openness, Owens and the other authors in the collection create claims of tentative authority. Insisting that their research is only preliminary, they invite readers to further research concepts and practice the strategies described throughout the collection. The authors acknowledge that since they are working with complex systems, determining the exact impact of their work is complex as well. As a result, the authors are quite frank about the limitations of their work. Owens writes: "Will these writing sequences lead my students toward more sustainable habits of living? I have no idea" (2001, 34). While this may seem to be a defeatist and/or nonauthoritative stance, he goes on to say that even if we do not know what the outcome will be, it is incumbent upon us to at least try to encourage our students to critically reflect on their environments (both made and "natural"). Owens vociferously argues that even if we are unsure of the impact we will have on students' lives, we *must* make important headway in changing universities' emphasis on specialization. Taking some step—*any* critically informed step— toward changing our view of place is in itself a success at this point, he suggests. Publishing this work means that a larger community of people can be invited into the discussions and thus the research can be retested, expanded, changed.

Other representative examples of this tentative authority abound in the collection. Christian Weisser: "If we make efforts toward a greener conception of the relations between identity, ecology, and discourse, we *move a step closer toward* a more accurate view of who and where we are" (2001, 93–4; italics added); Julie Drew: "Shifting human geographies, if mapped by those whose travels constitute discursive challenges for them, *may lend themselves* to the formulation of a transgressive and productive pedagogy that builds on student travelers' knowledge and the experience of the politics of place for writing" (67; italics added); Annie Merrill Ingram: "The results and implications of service learning in ecocomposition are limited only by the imaginations and efforts of those who participate. I would like to think that a combination of eco-composition and service learning *begins a quiet revolution* in one group of students' thinking, a process that continues after they finish the course" (222; italics added). Instead of being a limitation, however, I would argue that these moves illustrate that this is, in fact, a community of inquirers who are inviting each other into the process of evaluating and validating the knowledge constructed through practitioner inquiry. As such, this tentative authority illustrates an important corrective to one of the key problems of practice as inquiry: individual validation. As North writes,

> Whereas in other communities the greatest authority over what constitutes knowledge resides with the community—lies, in effect, with *public* knowledge—here it lies with the individual Practitioner, and *private* knowledge. The communal lore offers options, resources, and perhaps some directional pressure: but the individual, finally, decides what to do and whether (or how) it has worked—decides, in short, what counts as knowledge. (28; italics in original)

The knowledge constructed through these authors' research, though, is definitely not private; in fact, the core of ecocomposition is a public view of writing and a study of the complex relationships involved in discursive practices. Weisser and Dobrin insist that "hearing from a range of scholars from a range of places is crucial to ecocomposition scholarship. Ecocomposition must be a biodiverse discipline. The essays in this collection move toward such a diversity" (2001, 2)—and a public diversity at that.

Ultimately, this collection illustrates how compositionists can critically reevaluate our research practices/assumptions and revise them by drawing on interdisciplinary methodologies that make our research more holistic and sustainable. It shows that instead of a pile of unexamined, individual practices, knowledge produced through practice as inquiry is critically informed. These authors actively engage in critical reframings/

rethinkings of previous research findings and therefore challenge a problematic property of lore. North argues that once something is considered lore, it can never be dropped from practitioner knowledge: "There is simply no mechanism for it. Lore's various elements are not pitted against one another within the framework of lore-specific dialectic, or checked and re-checked by Practitioner experiments, so that the weakest or least useful are eliminated" (24). Based on the arguments made in *Ecocomposition*, however, it is clear that the authors do critique previous pedagogies, do retest and invite others to retest their own theories, and that the knowledge found lacking is, indeed, questioned, discounted, and discarded. This revisioning, to my mind, is crucial, if practitioner knowledge is to be valued by other communities of inquiry.

Geographies of Writing: Critical Reworking and Relocating of the Field

"What exactly is this field called Composition? Where does it come from? How does it work? Where is it going?" (North, Preface). In *Geographies of Writing: Inhabiting Places and Encountering Difference*, Nedra Reynolds answers those questions through metaphors. Composition began on the *frontier*, developed into a postmodern, cosmopolitan *city*, and is now constructing itself as a *cyberspace*. According to Reynolds, these three spatial metaphors that represent "imagined geographies" (2004, 27) have played and continue to play a significant role in the construction of composition's disciplinary identity. Rich though these metaphors may be, though, they obscure the material conditions under which compositionists labor and thus limit the changes we can make and the roles we can play in the university and surrounding communities. Although she recognizes that it is disheartening to study the material conditions composition is mired in, Reynolds insists that it is only through studying "spatial practices of the everyday—those habitual movements through space that are often taken for granted or ignored" (45) that we can better the disciplinary status of composition and achieve the democratic goals compositionists have established for their classrooms. In order to do so, Reynolds argues that we must draw on multiple methodologies. She locates her work along multiple matrices:

> This study of writing as spatial practices, informed by postmodern and cultural geography and parallel to so much work in ecocomposition, continues a tradition in composition studies of foraging in other disciplines for theories and approaches that help us to understand writing. (176)

While she does not identify her work as "ecocomposition," her research is invested in many of the same spatial questions that ecocompositionists take up.

Instead of discarding metaphors in favor of studying physical conditions, Reynolds develops one that helps us analyze the ways identities are constructed in material and embodied spaces. For Reynolds, cultural geography is "a rich source for investigating people's relationships to place, and how subjectivity is shaped by ordinary and mundane landscapes, by ubiquitous visual images, and by habitual pathways." Cultural geography's methods help us "to recognize how metaphor and the material are interrelated, contributing to a complex production of space and spatial practices" (2004, 43). She offers the metaphor of the *flaneur*, or rambler, to replace the earlier images of frontier, city, and cyberspace in large part because it emphasizes the necessity for fluid definitions of our field and our goals for writing. The *flaneur* constructs knowledge by moving, walking in particular:

> The *flaneur* embodies the spatial practices of walking as writing, writing as walking; his main focus is to absorb and render the city through writing. . . . The rambler is a figure worth habilitating for material rhetorics and geographies of writing not because he solves something in our dilemmas about visual culture but because he embodies method. Forms of *flanerie* stand for an approach to street life, a way of moving through the world, collecting, arranging, and remembering, dependent on seeing. (70)

What is important about the *flaneur*, then, is that he moves in and out of spaces, across boundaries, through various environments. Reynolds argues that the *flaneur* is "a writer, artist, and journalist who collects as he saunters, sketches as he watches . . . organizes and juxtaposes material in various ways" (2004, 70). The material for his writing comes from the pathways the *flaneur* takes and the landscapes through which he moves: "Misunderstood as an idler, the *flaneur* is a writer, a chronicler, a collector, who uses fragments of consumer culture to make meaning" (71).

Described primarily in Charles Baudelaire's and Walter Benjamin's work, the *flaneur* emerged out of the architecture and capitalism of the modern city (this accounts for Reynolds's deliberate use of "he" to describe the *flaneur*). He is a fascinating and dynamic figure because his movement through the modern city, which was allowed by the structure of the city, actually changed the possible uses of those places along with the identities made available in those places. The *flaneur*, then, is "a figure that offers one model for forms of movement in certain environments, illustrates the connection between place and identity, and emphasizes the importance of learning to see through walking and mapping" (Reynolds 2004, 75). By moving, the *flaneur* changes and is changed. As a model for compositionists, then, the *flaneur* teaches us that studying writing cannot be limited to the physical place where writing occurs, but must encompass the movements through spaces and the encounters writers have in those spaces. Likewise, a discipline should be viewed as an ongoing construction, not a fixed endeavor; we should not strive to map the field (and thereby fix it), but instead to map movements and changes across the field. By studying these movements through the lens of the *flaneur*, we can analyze the ways that metaphorical representations of space shape our material conditions and thus identify ways to better the material conditions through movement. The *flaneur* is, thus, a postmodern emblem of kinetic methodology.

Just as the *flaneur* crosses boundaries in order to engage difference, so must the researcher. In addition to using the modern *flanerie* theories of Baudelaire and Benjamin, Reynolds adopts cultural geography's concept of streetwork to rethink ethnographic fieldwork, draws on postmodern theories of thirdspace to challenge public/private distinctions, and weaves in border theories to investigate the best ways to help students encounter differences. Like the image of the *flaneur*, then, Reynolds models *researcher-as-rambler*, one who moves in and out of places and analyzes what that movement between/among multiple places can tell us about "how people construct and reproduce a sense of place" that helps us "account for and analyze the implications of different senses of place—what does it matter and what does it mean" (2004, 117). The goal for research, then, is not to find *the* answer, but to explore multiple *whys*. What Reynolds shows us through her work is that there are always multiple, competing rules for meaning making in any sphere and that materiality is an important aspect to consider/focus on in order to figure out what is happening in that sphere and, more importantly, why it is happening and what impact it has. As Reynolds summarizes, "Writers, as they construct identities through discourse, are enacting their own lived experiences in the sociospatial world. Words on the page, the visual image, the map, the built object—all reflect a series of moves made for habitual, intentional, or accidental reasons. Keeping track of these moves might give glimpses into the social production of space, embodied in the moves a writer makes and the products of a writer's work" (176–77). This emphasis on tracking movements adds an important dimension to the concept of disciplinarity and research. In order to accomplish these goals, we must draw on multiple methods.

As Reynolds's work shows, composition is not "stripped of its methodological pluralism" (North, 368). In parts of her book where she provides explanations of assignments she gave to her students, she enacts practice as inquiry. In her evaluation of the assignments' impacts, she both uses and critiques ethnographic fieldwork. In her analysis of metaphors that shape composition, she is an historian. At points and times, she is the philosopher, the critic, the practitioner, the ethnographer, the historian . . . the *flaneur.* Instead of a fragmented, incoherent argument, though, Reynolds's work is an example of what truly interdisciplinary research in composition studies can/should look like.

The Locations of Composition: Spatial Disruptions

You are boarding an airplane on your way to a conference. Ticket stub in hand, you walk gingerly up the narrow aisle until you find your seat. Yours is the middle seat and this flight is full. Before you maneuver yourself into your seat, you decide where to put your two carry-on items, trying to figure out what you are going to read during the flight and how much preparation on your paper you need to do. You juggle through your bags, pulling out the necessary items, and then shove your carry-on into the overhead bin along with the two other bags that have been haphazardly thrown into it. You debate about taking one of the square blue pillows that are stowed in the overhead next to your suitcase, weighing the possible comfort offered by the pillow against the potential germ count on the fabric. You opt to leave the pillow and take your suit coat instead, planning to use it as a pillow or a blanket, depending on how the flight goes. Once these negotiations are completed (and twenty passengers are all backed up behind you in the row, waiting for you to get finished so they can make the same decisions and maneuvers once they find their seats), you begin the physical negotiation of climbing over the passenger in 27C and settling into 27B without squashing the passenger in 27A. Seated, you try to find the two parts of the seat belt while balancing your papers and suit coat precariously on your lap. Passenger 27A shifts a little and helps you look for your seat belt because, as it turns out, your seat belt is tangled with hers; passenger 27C is trying to read the *New York Times* but you accidentally bump her arm as you work to untangle your seat belt from 27A's. A small child is obviously in the seat directly behind yours because you can feel the "tap, tap, tap" of a swinging foot against your lower back. You sigh, finish buckling yourself in, and realize that you've forgotten your pen in your carry-on. Knowing that you do not want to go through the hassle of getting up, you resign yourself to reading the *Air Mall Catalog* and dealing with the constant jabbing of a small foot on the back of your seat. You can't wait until the plane takes off so that you can put your seat back.

We have all experienced something similar when we have flown, no doubt. A simple enough scenario. Yet, as Christopher Keller and Christian Weisser emphasize in the introduction to *The Locations of Composition*, this experience serves as a metaphor for the ways we make space for ourselves, our ideas, and our things in physical places. Instead of empty containers waiting for us to insert ourselves into them, the spaces we move through are "products of human activity: the activity of making room" (2007, 4). As we do in our airplane seat, we adjust ourselves in space. In doing so, we also shape/limit/impact how others will be able to make room for themselves and their things. As Keller and Weisser argue, "Making room . . . adjusts locations. I may wish to make room for my body by reclining the seat back as much as possible; however, doing so also adjusts the relationship between my seat and the seat behind me, therein reworking the relationship—the location—between them." Studying location, then, allows us not only to study places and activities, but also "to emphasize how those places and activities constantly shift and move in relation to one another" (5).

Whether or not we keep our seat back up or recline it does not, in the whole of life, make a huge difference (except to the person who sits behind us for the duration of the four-hour flight) in the shape of the world. However, this simple analogy highlights an important contribution/redirection to compositionists' spatial studies. The articles in Keller and Weisser's collection foreground the idea of accommodation—of the ways that relationships within places are constantly shaped through the continual movement of those within the places. Keller and Weisser introduce the concept of *location* to the mix because "locations tell us about relationships, but they also imply adjustment and modification." They argue that mapping the discipline of composition is actually a problematic move because "mapping is to fix the ground rather than to show how the ground is made to seem fixed; it is to chart grounds already made rather than to explore how the grounds are made in the first place, how the grounds are remade, and how the grounds could have been made differently" (2007, 5). Instead of a fixed map of where the field is, then, the goal of this collection is to study composition's movements within the university and throughout various communities. Like Reynolds, the authors in this collection argue that it is crucial to study movements within and across boundaries and spaces in order to see how meaning is made and given to those spaces and the activities therein.

Spatial analysis involves transgressing boundaries, studying why boundaries exist, determining how to study multiplicity, movement, and the visual in ways that highlight the changing dynamics and fluidity of spaces across and through time. The articles in the Keller and Weisser collection actively analyze and challenge the ground upon which previous spatial studies have been based. One of the key arguments/practices posed by earlier ecocompositionists is the need to move beyond the classroom in order to have students engage in public writing. While this goal is certainly a useful one, in "Composition and the Gentrification of 'Public Literacy,'" Elizabeth Ervin asks us to critically analyze the community engagement work we have been advocating and enacting. She encourages us to question not only our methodologies (i.e., how we study the communities, what kind of work we have our students do in them, etc.) but also to question and interrogate the ideological assumptions underlying our methodologies. When assigning public discourse projects for our students, she encourages us to consider whether "our work represents public discourse, public spheres, and public writers in pat, one-dimensional ways. If so, then we might be domesticating our subjects, glossing over their complexities in order to document them more easily" (2007, 50). She argues that our desire for democratic ideals and our drive to create composition as a valid discipline can present us with competing agendas. Too often, our public discourse projects are defined through our institutional needs rather than the community's needs and actually hinder the achievement of the goals for public discourse engagement that we set up for ourselves and our students; our democratic ideals, Ervin argues, then get waylaid by professional drives.

Instead of discarding public discourse projects, she argues that we need an intellectual work document "that articulates how we might work in and with the public in ways that are academically rigorous but that minimize exploitation and displacement (whether unintentional or merely rationalized) and maximize reciprocity" (Ervin 2007, 49). Such a document would shift our focus to studying place as a container for political action and require us to consider the ways that our interactions with the community will change the flows and movements within the community. Thus, instead of inserting ourselves and our students into the community, we should be aware of how the community adjusts/ makes accommodations for different literacy practices. We would actually ask students to study the flows across boundaries, instead of positioning the boundaries as the norm. These kinds of projects, then, would focus on the movement between community and university.

Tom Deans also acknowledges the problematic nature of moving between the university and the community, and he offers us another solution/vision to deal with what Ervin calls the "gentrification" of composition. In "Shifting Locations, Genres, and Motives: An Activity Theory Analysis of Service-Learning Writing Pedagogies," he argues that we need to shift our thinking about community projects from analyzing "how each location shapes written discourse" to analyzing "what happens when we imagine the locations for writing less as places and more as systems of activity" (2007, 290). He argues that if we see a community as a discourse community, then we enter into it, as if it were a fixed entity/place that an outsider could go into. Activity theory, however, "discourages us from seeing contexts as specific locations or as containers of behavior and encourages us to explore the dynamic relations between social contexts and the actions of individuals" (292). He argues that an activity-theory approach (which is drawn from an interdisciplinary focus) emphasizes components that discourse community theories do not: tools ("especially written genres as tools writers use"); motives ("both personal and institutional"); and contradictions ("both within systems and between systems") (294). He argues that we must approach writing with and for the community from these critical frameworks and that service-learning projects can help our students learn more about genres and literacy practices precisely because of the contradictions and problems that service learning presents. Studying the movement across locations and its impact on literacy practices in those locations can help students more fully understand the complexity of literacies.

These and the other articles in the Keller and Weisser collection challenge a basic assumption that guides North's definition of disciplines: coherence. In the conclusion of *MKC*, North asks, "Can Composition really muster enough coherence to justify an autonomous academic existence, or is that just wishful thinking?" (374). Through his study of methodological communities in composition, he concludes that instead of building itself into a discipline,

> Composition as a knowledge-making society is gradually pulling itself apart. Not branching out or expanding, although these might be politically more palatable descriptions, but fragmenting: gathering into communities or clusters of communities among which relations are becoming increasingly tenuous. (364)

However, if we revisit these claims through the lens of the articles in *The Locations of Composition,* we see an argument for a changed definition of disciplinarity, one that would embrace a field being pulled into multiple directions, a field mired in multiple and radically different projects. Instead of trying to provide a coherent picture of where the field is now, the authors here work to analyze how the ground of composition has been constructed to appear this way and how we might use placed-based pedagogies and research to create new uses of space within and outside of the university.

In "The Occupation of Composition," Sidney Dobrin (2007) argues that "composition must become attuned not to spatial metaphors as a method for speaking about its work, but rather to the very dynamics of the production and occupation of spaces in order to elucidate the complexity of composition's (ever-shifting) position(s): historically, institutionally, territorially" (29). Instead of trying to solidify its place within the university, composition must move beyond the places it has been made to/has chosen to occupy already:

> Composition's places can no longer afford to rest in the safety of recirculated conversations of temporal/historical identity, of imposed subjectivities, of self-validation. Composition must move to occupy other places that can—á la Bhabha—move beyond its simulacra safety, its artificial safety, to explore its contingent frontiers in order to produce its own counterhegemonies, in order to not accept the natural boundaries of composition's field. (31)

The task that lies ahead of us, then, should be a process of intense questioning, of interrogating our core assumptions about what a discipline is, what research should be, and what composition means and should mean. Trying to stay within the safe boundaries of older conceptions of disciplinarity will not serve us; we must adjust our movements through space, move into new spaces, and rethink where we want to go.

AND THE ANSWER IS . . .

"Is there any chance, then, for an academically full-fledged, autonomous, multi-methodological, knowledge-making Composition?" (North, 369). And if so, does it rest on heightened consciousness of multiple methodologies; cooperation and collaboration across methodological communities; and increased recognition of and reestablishment of the validity of practice as inquiry? If autonomy is required in order for composition to be a full-fledged field, then, my answer is no—there is not a chance for an autonomous composition because, as ecocomposition shows, knowledge is always produced within dynamic, ever-changing, multidimensional, multidisciplinary systems. Autonomy, then, is not an option, nor should it be, according to the thinkers I've analyzed here.

Further, while it's clear from studying ecocompositionists that composition is drawing on multiple methodologies from multiple disciplines and has a heightened awareness and understanding of various methodologies, researchers in this area do not embrace methodological egalitarianism. Some methodologies work better than others; some are mired in problematic assumptions about students, writing, and community. Some methods simply aren't useful. The authors I've analyzed here do not embrace all methods equally; instead, they encourage us to turn a critical eye not only on the methods but on the long-term implications of those methods and the underlying ideologies that drive those methods. So, if composition is not a full-fledged field unless it embraces all methods equally, then it is not a field.

And yet . . . from studying ecocomposition and other place-based research, we can clearly see that composition is a dynamic, methodologically rich field that is producing significant knowledge about writing and literacy practices in multiple environments. What we see from studying ecocomposition and other place-based research is that composition has adopted a multimethodological understanding of/approach to research. While it is still working to carve a place for itself within the university, its sense of what the goal should be is shifting as disciplinary identities shift. No longer do we see writing as a "fixed" task; rather, ecocomposition and place-based studies encourage us to study the complex ecological systems in which writing is constructed and reconstructed as well as to study how writing constructs and reconstructs those systems. Ecocompositionists encourage us to look beyond our usual assumptions about dissemination and to ask ourselves if there might be better arenas for our work than solely relying on academic journals. And ecocomposition encourages us to rethink the kinds of research questions we think are valuable to ask—to think outside the methodological box and to realize that our questions will require a multidisciplinary, extradisciplinary approach.

Where we research, how we research, what we research, what we do with our research, and who values our research are all shifting. It is precisely the instability of place and the possibilities for changes within place that make this kind of research so fruitful and exciting. As Sidney Dobrin argues, "Composition is in need of spatial disruption" (2007, 31) and disruption and solidification of boundaries are antithetical. Thus, our goals for composition research and teaching are changing, and thus our definitions of what makes composition a discipline are likewise shifting. While there are certainly still valuable connections to North's *MKC* categories and they are particularly useful for newcomers to the field, they no longer adequately paint a picture of what composition is—and, for North, this is a good thing, because we are creating ourselves as a diverse, multimethodological field that makes a difference.

REFERENCES

Bawarshi, Anis. The ecology of genre. In Weisser and Dobrin, 69–80. Cooper, Marilyn M. 1986. The ecology of writing. *College English* 48 ( ): 364–75.

Deans, Tom. 2007. Shifting locations, genres, and motives: An activity theory analysis of service-learning writing pedagogies. In Keller and Weisser, 289–306.

Dobrin, Sidney. 2007. The occupation of composition. In Keller and Weisser, 15–36.

Drew, Julie. 2001. The politics of place: Student travelers and pedagogical maps. In Weisser and Dobrin, 57–68.

Ervin, Elizabeth. 2007. Composition and the gentrification of "public literacy." In Keller and Weisser, 37–54.

Ingram, Annie Merrill. 2001. Service learning and ecocomposition: Developing sustainable practices through inter- and extradisciplinarity. In Weisser and Dobrin, 209–34.

Keller, Christopher J., and Christian R. Weisser. 2007. Introduction. Keller and Weisser, 15–36.

Keller, Christopher J., and Christian R. Weisser, eds. 2007. *The locations of composition.* Albany: State University of New York Press.

Miller, Susan. 1991. *Textual carnivals: The politics of composition.* Carbondale: Southern Illinois University Press.

North, Stephen M. 1987. *The making of knowledge in composition: Portrait of an emerging field.* Upper Montclair, NJ: Boynton/Cook.

Owens, Derek. 2001. Sustainable composition. In Weisser and Dobrin, 27–8. Reynolds, Nedra. 2004. *Geographies of writing: Inhabiting places and encountering differences.* Carbondale: Southern Illinois University Press.

Weisser, Christian R. 2001. Ecocomposition and the greening of identity. In Weisser and Dobrin, 81–96.

Weisser, Christian R., and Sidney I. Dobrin. 2001. Breaking New Ground in Ecocomposition: An introduction. In Weisser and Dobrin, 1–10.

Weisser, Christian R., and Sidney I. Dobrin, eds. 2001. *Ecocomposition: Theoretical and pedagogical approaches.* Albany: State University of New York Press.

16

THE (DIS)ORDER OF COMPOSITION
Insights from the Rhetoric and Reception of The Making of Knowledge in Composition

Lance Massey

The measure of success for this book will be the extent to which readers, reassured at recognizing in some particular chapter their own perspectives—their own communal identity—will then be able, via the juxtaposition provided here, to see the field from other perspectives as well, and fashion for themselves a new vision of Composition.

North

In the introduction to *The Making of Knowledge in Composition* (*MKC*), Stephen North adopts—only partially metaphorically—the stance of participant-observer, offering his sweeping map of composition's knowledge-making communities as an attempt "to make sense of what I have seen and done in my ten years of 'living among' the people of Composition" (1987, 4). In doing so, North partially aligns his project with Paul Diesing's *Patterns of Discovery in the Social Sciences*, and therefore with what North calls "Diesing's law," or the principle that methodology trumps subject matter in establishing professional relationships: "It is easier for an Experimentalist concerned with revision to get along with an Experimentalist studying reading instruction than with a Practitioner or a Philosopher studying revision" (365). This "law," moreover, leads North to predict that composition is "pulling itself apart. Not branching out or expanding, although these might be more politically palatable descriptions, but fragmenting" (364).

Now, almost twenty-five years later, this disciplinary centrifuge would appear to be spinning faster than ever. Noting that "composition studies is a less unified field than it was a decade ago," Richard Fulkerson ups the ante on North: the basis of this disunity, he says, "is now not just methodological, but axiological, pedagogical, and processual" (2005, 680–81). David Smit paints a similar portrait, asserting that composition "has become increasingly divided into narrow areas of concern with little indication that scholars and researchers in one area read, respect, or deal substantively with the work of those in other areas" (2004, 7).[1] And Christine Farris ponders the tensions inherent in and the possibilities presented by composition's "inability to agree on a unified theory" (2003, 58).

Even sanguine portraits of composition's rich methodological diversity still point to a field that, however you slice it, is not unified. (It's just that unity is more important to some than to others.) Gesa Kirsch, for example, writes, "I agree with North; he is correct to observe that we have evolved into a field that" is characterized by both methodological diversity and a growing number of studies that claim only to apply to extremely localized research sites. She goes on to disagree with North, however, that such developments make research "more disposable." "In contrast to North," she says, "I take the position that as scholarship in composition expands and diversifies, it becomes more insightful and valuable" (2003, 133).[2] For better or worse, composition is a remarkably heterogeneous network of practices, attitudes, and interests.

It would seem, then, that we still face something like a disciplinary identity crisis all these years after North set out to map the field, to find order in its seemingly "chaotic and patternless" development since its birth in 1963. At the very least, who we are and what we do remain fuzzy, contestable categories. This chapter, while it is not a map in the sense that *MKC* was (and is), does aim to shed light on the tangle of disciplinary discourses and traditions—modernism and postmodernism, the humanities and social sciences—that have influenced and defined the discipline in fundamental ways and that are largely responsible for that fuzzy multiplicity some of us lament and others of us celebrate. To do so, moreover, I turn my attention in the following section to the reception *MKC* received in book reviews and other published work following its release, and I do so precisely because *MKC* made its appearance at a moment of profound transition in composition—what was coming to be known as composition's "social turn" (a term generally attributed to John Schilb but that was also used by Kenneth Bruffee in 1987, the same year as the publication of *MKC*). My analysis of published responses to *MKC* shows, as expected, a discipline in a state of seeming chaos, teetering back and forth between what might be called modern and postmodern versions of composition. But, as I "pull back" in a later section from my close examination of these responses to a more longitudinal look at some basic citation patterns, my

<hr>

1.   See also Smit, this volume.
2.   See also Taylor (2003) and McLeod (2003).

analysis also reveals a relative stability at a higher scale of disciplinary activity in composition, in which a more or less cohesive social-scientific body of inquiry would seem to be running a parallel rather than intersecting or intertwined course with the equally cohesive, humanistic-hermeneutic tradition in which *MKC*, despite its pretension to ethnographic fieldwork, is ultimately rooted. Finally, as I make clear in the conclusion, these analyses are offered not for their own sake, but as efforts at clarifying our own vision of ourselves and the work we do so that we might better, and more self-consciously, define and redefine the discipline of composition in what are no doubt destined to be years, if not decades, of economic crises and public resistance to a great deal of the work we do.

THE DISORDER OF COMPOSITION: THE RECEPTION OF *MKC*

The release of *MKC* was marked by considerable controversy. Eric Branscomb recalls that "[owing] to its downbeat tone, when *The Making of Knowledge in Composition* was first published, it was almost immediately controversial. One colleague told me, in all seriousness, that upon reaching the final page, she put down the book and seriously considered quitting teaching. The book was undeniably on everybody's mind in the months following its publication" (1997, 2). Similarly, Lester Faigley's observation that "a noncontroversial aspect of Stephen North's controversial survey of writing research, *The Making of Knowledge in Composition*, is the omission of linguistics as an important disciplinary subfield" (1992, 80) implicitly affirms, by using the marked term *noncontroversial*, the book's status as controversial.

Indeed, while there were some lukewarm reviews of and responses to *MKC* (Branscomb 1997, 2), there are a notable number of others that were either glowing or scathing. For example, on the glowing end, both Patricia Harkin and Richard Lloyd-Jones enthusiastically endorse *MKC*. Harkin (1993) adopts North's position on the value of lore wholesale, devoting six full paragraphs of "The Postdisciplinary Politics of Lore" to explicating it, and Lloyd-Jones (1989) refers to *MKC* at various times in his *CCC* review as *thoughtful, challenging, open, astonishing, useful, engaging, modest, detailed, thoughtful, fair,* and *broadly inclusive.* On the scathing end, however, scholars like Richard Larson and David Bartholomae light into North with uncommon fervor (though they might respond that their fervor was occasioned by that of North himself). Larson likens North to a "propaganda analyst," calling North's "scrutiny of individual studies . . . witheringly intense" (1989, 96). "North," he writes, "is not content

with analyses of the substance of others' writings, he has to derogate, collectively and with little supporting evidence, their motives and attitudes"
(97). Bartholomae accuses North of employing a "tired and corrupt
'anthropological' way of speaking" (1988, 225) and of having a "ruthless
critical spirit" (226), even calling the logic of the book "paranoid" (228).

Further complicating the portrait of *MKC*'s controversial reception
is the fact that there is even disagreement within the glowing and scathing camps about precisely what makes the book so monumental and
so insidious, respectively. Some of those who received *MKC* favorably
seemed to see the book as a deeply *modern* work, while others seemed
to interpret it as a virtual *postmodern* manifesto. Likewise, those who
received *MKC* unfavorably saw the book in equally antithetical lights.

Much of *MKC*'s praise is based on its postmodern aspects. Probably
North's strongest advocate, Patricia Harkin, is attracted to his work for
its treatment of "practitioner lore" as a "very rich and powerful [body]
of knowledge" (North 27). Harkin seizes on practitioner lore as a key
mode for working through the Fishian problem of "theory hope," and
in so doing ascribes to lore a postmodern (or, at least, antifoundational)
status. Echoing advocates of postmodern theory in her celebration of
lore, Harkin says that lore "can help us see that disciplinary inquiries
can be strategies of containment; these strategies achieve their coherence by shutting out or repressing . . . contradictions" (1993, 135). The
lore that North describes in *MKC*, then, is, as Harkin characterizes it at
various places in her article, *concrete, pragmatic, contradictory, irregular, ad
hoc, unconstrained, nonreductive, antiessential,* and *postdisciplinary.* In fact,
were I to supply an opposing term for each element in this list, I could
produce a table that could as easily bear the headings "Postmodern" and
"Modern" as "Lore" and "Disciplinary Inquiry."

Lore (Postmodern)	Disciplinary Inquiry (Modern)
concrete	abstract
pragmatic	theoretical
contradictory	consistent
irregular	regular
ad hoc	generalized
unconstrained	constrained
nonreductive	reductive
antiessential	essential
postdisciplinary	disciplinary

Judging by Harkin's reception of it, *MKC* would seem indeed to be a postmodern manifesto *par excellence*, and a welcome one at that.

This reading of *MKC* as a postmodern work—minus, of course, the cele- bratory attitude—is supported by at least one of *MKC*'s negative reviewers. Throughout Larson's review, he seems uneasy with the proposition that knowledge is a social construct. Larson's liberal use of quotation marks in the following passage signals his incredulity toward and even resistance to the concepts that, in his view, drive *MKC*: "North [reviews] the 'con- ceptual tools' used by a variety of scholars (including 'Researchers') to 'make knowledge' about composition and its teaching. (Knowledge is not 'discovered,' it is 'made.')" (1989, 95). Perhaps, in Larson's mind, it is *MKC*'s postmodern theoretical apparatus that is responsible for the relativism of which he accuses it when he asserts that North's "censure" of compositionists "is almost invariably based upon definitions and criteria of North's own devising. North writes the 'laws' that govern each group of studies he looks at" (96). Coming to the defense of Flower and Hayes, for example, Larson says that "North censures Flower and Hayes for failing to meet the criteria North specifies for studies that bear a label he (and not the authors) assigns to their work. A reader may be forgiven for doubting the fairness of this gambit" (96). If I am right, and Larson suspects post- modern theory of enabling this kind of relativism, then *MKC* would, itself, have to be a postmodern work.

But is it? Just as Lauer celebrated, and Larson critiqued, *MKC* based on its postmodern ideas and discursive features, others celebrated, and still others critiqued, *MKC* based on its modernist ideas and discursive features. In those places where he praises the book, for example, James Raymond does so for reasons that are consonant with what we have come to understand as a modernist epistemology. For Raymond, *MKC* is "a welcome map of a sprawling territory" (1989, 93), which suggests that Raymond shares North's valuing of breadth in disciplinary knowl- edge production. Raymond further says that *MKC* is "a portrait, not a prescription," and that, as such, it is "a just and fair reflection of our own omissions and failures" as a field (95). That there are such things as portraits—as purely descriptive analyses, divested of rhetorical inter- estedness—is an inherently modernist notion, as is the notion that any representation, much less that of such a "sprawling territory," can be unbiased in its completeness and objectivity.

Finally, there are those who see *MKC* as an essentially modernist work and critique it for that reason. By far North's most strident critic,

Bartholomae states his fundamental problem with *MKC*: "[In] telling the story of power, North turns to a politics beyond or outside of language" (1988, 228). In his subsequent exchange with North in *Pre/Text*, Bartholomae expands on this position: "What authorized *The Making of Knowledge in Composition*, I argued in my review, was the figure of a 'Stephen North' who stood outside disciplinary boundaries, self-created, a new-Adam (I said in my letter), part of a powerful tradition in American letters, one whose temptations I think we should resist" (1990, 123). As a result of this vantage, North, according to Bartholomae, is unable to see how work that is "political" is so because of the subtle, even invisible ways language and power commingle and produce one another, not because there "are people in 'key positions' pulling the strings" (1988, 227). In a similar critique, Patricia Sullivan argues that North's "positivist" methodology "functions . . . to suppress the underlying issues of gender" in his story (in *MKC*) of a woman struggling to pass her M.A. comprehensive exams. "North," she writes, "does not consider gender as a possible source of the graduate student's difficulty, nor, in the positivist terms in which he casts his notions of causality, can he" (1992, 130). This critical attitude toward positivism is indicative of a postmodern perspective: positivism, for Sullivan, holds much the same place as does modernism for Faigley—or, for that matter, Lyotard, who writes that "science, far from successfully obscuring the problem of its legitimacy, cannot avoid raising it with all of its implications, which are no less sociopolitical than epistemological" (1984, 18). (For Lyotard, positivism is not equated with science, but, rather, with science's attempt to mask its need for a narrative that lies outside of scientific discourse for legitimation [27].)

What this analysis reveals is a field in what appears to be a state of considerable disorder. Just as North did in 1987, I have tried here to present a portrait, though in a more limited way and on a much smaller scale, of composition as it struggled to find and establish a disciplinary identity at the time of and in the years following *MKC*'s publication. As portraits go, however, the one I have just painted is quite different from North's. North's is a realist landscape. In my portrait, however, colors and borders blend. Blues mutate imperceptibly into successively redder grades of purple, which slide again back into blues. Lines that take your eye one way suddenly reverse direction. All this—and only *two* basic categories, modernism and postmodernism, to work with. Is composition in the late 1980s and early 1990s a modern or a postmodern discipline?

Both? Neither? Is North a modernist or a postmodernist, or both, or neither? What about Raymond? Lloyd-Jones? Even my least ambiguous example, Bartholomae—who seems firmly rooted in a postmodern perspective—has been critiqued for positing discourse communities that, while certainly social constructs, are unrealistically monolithic and static and that, therefore, reify existing social inequities (Worsham 1991, 100). Even Bartholomae's devotion to difference, it would seem, is not without its ambivalences. I can only imagine what levels of disorder would reveal themselves were I to mobilize even one more analytical category, much less two or three.

Just as the late 1980s was marked by conflicting notions of what "composition" ought to be (and just as those notions were rooted in conflicting discourses that I have identified as modernism and postmodernism), *MKC*, too, bears the stamp of this transitional quality, simultaneously deploying discourses of modernism and postmodernism. Theoretically, *MKC* is fully immersed in postmodernism, in which knowledge is conceived of as something made, not found (the book's title is a pretty strong indicator of this position). North opens his introduction by describing *MKC* as "a book about how knowledge is made in the field that has come to be called Composition." North goes on to write, in fine postmodern fashion, that *MKC* "is concerned with what I shall be calling the *modes of inquiry* . . . as they operate within *methodological communities*," which are "groups of inquirers more or less united by their allegiance to one such mode, to an agreed-upon set of rules for gathering, testing, validating, accumulating and distributing what they regard as knowledge" (1; italics in original). A note attached to this sentence positions *MKC* even more explicitly within a postmodern sensibility: "[This] approach obviously requires a conception of knowledge . . . in which knowledge is conceived as a social construct, the truth value of which is a function of a given community's commitment to it" (377). In the closing paragraph of the introduction, moreover, a reflective and reflexive narrative voice enacts North's gestures to postmodern theory by acknowledging the situatedness of *MKC* as well as the inevitably partial character of any study designed to render the dynamism of disciplinary activity in the static pages of a book. North writes that the "modes of inquiry I will describe here are not *the* eight modes in the field, with neat and measurable boundaries that will look the same to any investigator. If this study supplies a kind of map, it is of an ever-shifting, ever-moving terrain, whose shape . . . is a function of where you happen to be standing" (6; italics in original). *MKC*, then, would seem to be a thoroughly postmodern work.

Though postmodern in letter, however, *MKC* often seems much more closely aligned with modernism in spirit, particularly in its narrative voice, as well as in the politics of representation and interpretation enabled by that voice. Despite North's gestures to the partiality of all knowledge claims, his is a study driven by the desire to tell the story of everything, to offer, if not *the*, then *a* totalizing vision of composition studies. Rather than "invite individual essays from an 'expert' member of each [methodological] community," North chooses to "provide that image of the whole myself. . . . Whatever the disadvantages of such a method in loss of expertise—no one moving through eight methods is likely to be the leading authority on any one—they seemed to me easily outweighed by the advantages gained in *coherence and breadth of vision*" (5; italics added). Coherence and breadth—these are precisely the kinds of difference-suppressing categories that postmodern theory was designed to resist. And what guarantees this coherence and breadth? By telling the story of composition based on his own "experience" as a member of composition, North guarantees us that this "portrait of Composition *as a whole* is the product of a single consciousness" (5; italics in original). "This image of the larger whole," North writes, can "therefore take shape within a single frame of reference" (6). Such claims, of course, rely on the existence of a unified, coherent self—which postmodern theory explicitly and unambiguously rejects. As might be expected, once North moves from the introduction into the body chapters on composition's methodological communities, the reflexive narrator of the preface and introduction gives way to one more akin to the transcendental subject, whose "view from nowhere" authorizes him (yes, *him*—this transcendental ego has almost always been conceived as a man) to be master of all that he sees; and what he sees is *all*.

This positioning of *MKC*'s narrator above the methodological fray of composition reveals itself most tellingly in the book's implicit politics of interpretation. Steven Mailloux warns us against theories of interpretation that invoke "neutral principles," which "posit rules for guaranteeing correct interpretations" in any situation (1998, 48). Rather, Mailloux argues, interpretation "functions . . . as a politically-interested act of persuasion" (50). Prefatory remarks notwithstanding, North's narrative voice in *MKC* ultimately effaces the interestedness of his own interpretations of others' works in composition, proceeding instead from an assumption of neutral interpretive principles. For example, North devotes more than half of chapter eleven of *MKC* to a microscopic critique of Stephen Witte's essay "Topical Structure and Revision: An Exploratory Study." The crux of North's critique is that Witte overlooks serious methodological differences among compositionists who have studied revision so that he can present their work as a unified body of knowledge. North writes that "what concerns" him in Witte's literature review "is the methodological mix . . . Witte feels able to claim— on the basis of four Clinical studies (Emig, Sommers, Beach, Faigley and Witte), one quasi-Experimental study (Bridwell), two Formalist-based studies (Flower, Flower and Hayes), and the ruminations of a Practitioner (Murray)—that 'recent research' has established that revision is a recursive process performed differently by different groups of writers, and rendered explicable by classification systems." (341)

According to North, then, Witte, having "strung" these studies "together," "is able to overlook not only the less than direct connection between what these studies actually offer . . . but to duck as well the issue of methodological fit" (346). North's critique relies on the assumption that there is such a thing as "right reading"—that interpretation is "capable of being applied in a disinterested manner safe from personal idiosyncrasy or political bias" (Mailloux 1998, 48). In North's reading, it is not possible that Witte's interpretive frame simply differs from North's. How else could he claim to know "what these studies actually offer"? This assumption, then, reveals what seems to be more of a modern than a postmodern attitude toward interpretation.

Such an attitude ultimately leaves North unable to move into a fully postmodern discursive space—though, at the same time, we cannot summarily dismiss North as a modernist in postmodern clothing, either. North imagines Witte scheming to deceive compositionists, cynically "excluding from consideration those approaches to [revision] most inimical to his own needs" and "ignoring or passing lightly over the contradictory features, and at the same time emphasizing the compatible features, of the approaches he does name" (352). "The forces we see at work here, then," North concludes, "are political forces" (351). This claim that Witte's work is political seems to be a postmodern gesture, but it keeps one foot in a modernist world view. I imagine North sees himself enacting the postmodern call to render knowledge political; at the very least, his treatment of Witte's text carries traces of this aspect of postmodern theory. The very next sentence, in fact, taken out of context, might easily have come from one of the era's formative works in the social turn: "[Just] as it has been useful to understand the revolutionary growth of Composition in essentially political terms, so here Witte's construction and deployment of an investigative context is best understood as a political act" (351). This sentence carries the air of a conclusion, as if demonstrating, based on Witte's example, that—don't you see?—knowledge really *is* political. Yet, for North, knowledge only seems to be politicized in its impure form, when it is the product of machination rather than good-faith inquiry. This sense that only tainted knowledge is political and the pure kind is not betrays shades of modernism lurking in North's postmodern gesture. It is precisely this discursive ambivalence—as both an indicator and facilitator of a similar ambivalence in the larger discipline—that, to return to my earlier question, "accounts for such radically different readings" of *MKC* as those offered by its reviewers and other respondents.

THE ORDER OF COMPOSITION: THE NON-RECEPTION OF *MKC*

I have argued that the rhetoric and reception of *MKC* reveal a discipline in a state of relative chaos. My "portrait" of this small slice of composition fifteen to twenty years ago, then, works well with visions of disciplines and disciplinarity like Sheryl I. Fontaine and Susan Hunter's "celebration of the potential openness or incompleteness of the discipline" (1992, 396), Ann Ruggles Gere's characterization of composition as a diverse "complex of forces" (1993, 4), and Paul Prior's metaphorical representation of "disciplines, sub-disciplines, and interdisciplines" as "a dense jungle of texts, technical objects, practices, and encultured persons" (1998, xii). That is, while my analysis of the rhetoric and reception of *MKC* restricts itself to published texts (and, as such, is not "situated" in that term's now dominantly understood sense), even in that stripped-down form the immense heterogeneity and irregularity of disciplinary forces begins to reveal itself.

As one might expect, however, this irregularity is a function of perspective rather than essence. Until now, I have had my analytic microscope set to a fairly high degree of magnification, looking at a relatively small set of texts published within a few years of *MKC*'s publication. It is this microscopic analysis, moreover, that enables me to reveal the complexities—the disorder—lurking within *MKC*'s reception. A broader, more longitudinal analysis could not support the scrutiny I have brought to bear on this little, albeit telling, corner of composition (in much the same way that nobody would or could use, say, a map of Illinois that was itself the size of Chicago.) As I decrease the magnification of my analysis in this section (which means that I move *up* a level of scale), however, the wild tangle of discourses of the previous section suddenly coalesces into a relatively smooth node. That is, the struggle among the various agents of *MKC*'s reception, themselves belonging to clusters of (very) broadly like-minded compositionists, emerges as one distinct part of a larger system of disciplinary activity.

To explore this disciplinary activity, this section surveys the citations of *MKC* in ten years' worth of articles, from 1988 to 1998, in *College Composition and Communication (CCC)*, the *Journal of Advanced Composition (JAC)*, *Rhetoric Review*, *Written Communication*, and *Research in the Teaching of English (RTE)*, and relates this citation to editorial preferences of those journals.

Of the journals devoted exclusively or primarily to composition (first year or advanced), *MKC* was cited twenty-six times in *College Composition and Communication* and fifteen times in the *Journal of Advanced Composition*. Of those journals that publish research and scholarship on composition as well as other topics, such as literature, English studies, rhetoric, literacy, teaching/pedagogy, or written communication (generally conceived), *MKC* was cited nine times in *College English*, thirteen times in *Rhetoric Review*, two times in *Written Communication*, and three times in *Research in the Teaching of English*. Even as I have them grouped here, the numbers immediately reveal a disparity between the number of times *MKC* was cited in *CCC*, *JAC*, and *Rhetoric Review* and the number of times it was cited in *Written Communication* and *Research in the Teaching of English*. Even the next highest number of citations—nine in *College English*—is three times that of *RTE*, and more than four times that of *Written Communication*.

The groups into which I divided the journals above—those that are and those that are not devoted exclusively or primarily to composition—would seem to call for a different pattern of numerical distribution than the one these data reveal. We would expect, naturally, that *CCC* and *JAC* would have a relatively high number of citations, because *MKC* is focused entirely on the discipline of composition, as are (in theory, anyway) *CCC* and *JAC*. We might also reasonably expect that the journals that publish many articles whose primary domain lies outside of composition would contain not only consistently lower numbers of *MKC* citations than do *CCC* and *JAC*, but also similar numbers when compared to each other. Yet *Rhetoric Review* contains more than six times the number of citations in *Written Communication*, at thirteen. And *College English* also contains significantly more citations of *MKC* than does *Written Communication* or *RTE*, even though they all publish work from outside the discipline of composition. As I look at these numbers, then, a new mode of organization suggests itself. Belonging to one group are *CCC, JAC, Rhetoric Review*, and *College English*: these journals all contain a notable number of references to *MKC* from 1988 to 1998. Belonging to another are *Written Communication* and *RTE*: *MKC* is almost never mentioned in them during that time. Whatever the terms of these new associations are, it seems clear that in some formal, public forums in composition, *MKC* has been an object of notable attention, while in others it has gone almost totally unmentioned. Despite compositionists' deep disagreements about *MKC*, then, those who reviewed and responded to *MKC* must have had enough in common to find the same kind of book worthy of so much personal and professional energy. That is, the very fact that some people paid attention to *MKC*, while others did not (at least, not in their published work), suggests that, in a larger sense, the disagreements and angry exchanges—that is, the *disorder*—that made up *MKC*'s initial public reception contribute to a certain *order* at the next higher level of scale.

What is it, then, that holds these texts and authors together, even within what Gary Olson calls composition's "hegemonic struggle," in which "one group of like-minded individuals attempts to further *its* vision of the field, while other groups do the same" (2002, 29; italics in original)? To answer this question, I need to turn from the modern/postmodern binary opposition to another one that will be familiar to compositionists, that of humanism versus social science.

But I need to be clear about how I am using these terms, because my use of them differs slightly from conventional wisdom. For many, postmodernism was primarily a challenge to the humanist assumption that the self is a stable and knowable entity. As such, postmodern theory stands in direct opposition to humanism. At the same time, it stands in opposition to positivist science as well. In short, postmodern theory is against any systematic, totalizing, or otherwise absolutist way of knowing. But it is possible to read postmodern theory in a different light—as an extension of the humanist project—if humanism is understood not as an essential category but, rather, a mode of social and epistemological inquiry and organization. And, by "mode of social and epistemological inquiry and organization," I mean an essentially methodological guide for how to make, disseminate, and understand knowledge. The parameters of this mode then, are this: that humans (and the human) are the ultimate object and locus of knowledge production. As definitions of what it means to be human change, then, so must the specific instantiations of this mode as well as the kinds of knowledge that are produced by them. Postmodern theory holds that the known cannot exist independently of the knower, and that the knower is both producer and product of the known. So, postmodern humanist work will be a mainly deductive process of trying to theorize phenomena like writing—even if, paradoxically, that theorization leads to the conclusion that theory itself is an undesirable goal. By this definition, furthermore, *writing* that is postmodernist can also be humanist if this egocentric orientation to the subject matter is encoded in the text—if the source of its coherence is constructed as the subjectivity of its author rather than the objectivity of its referent. Social-scientific writing, by contrast, is writing in which observation of the external (social) world (irrespective of how much or how little such work acknowledges the fundamentally interpretive nature of such research) is encoded as the primary mode of inquiry.

This distinction between humanistic and social-scientific writing may explain why *MKC* was heavily cited in some journals and almost totally ignored in others. *JAC* and *Rhetoric Review* in particular reflect a humanist orientation in the essays they publish and in their editorial staff, while *Written Communication* has a strong social scientific ethos. By way of comparison (and contrast) I offer the following editorial policies (first two sentences only) of *JAC, Rhetoric Review,* and *Written Communication*:

- *JAC* provides a forum for scholars interested in theoretical approaches to the study of rhetoric, writing, multiple literacies, and the politics of difference. As a forum for interdisciplinary inquiry, the journal features articles that explore intersections between theoretical work in rhetoric and writing studies, broadly conceived, and theoretical work in other fields.

- *Rhetoric Review* is a scholarly interdisciplinary journal publishing in all areas of rhetoric and writing and providing a professional forum for its readers to consider and discuss current topics and issues. The journal publishes manuscripts that explore the breadth and depth of the discipline, including history, theory, writing, praxis, technical/professional communication,

philosophy, rhetorical criticism, cultural studies, multiple literacies, technology, public address, graduate education, and professional issues.

• In the last decade, research on the written word has grown out
of the realization in linguistics, psychology and the cognitive sciences that discourse and language production represent cutting-
edge issues in the these disciplines. Understanding the nature of
written communication has defined an essential nexus of intellectual inquiry into these fields.

The editorial policies of *JAC* and *Rhetoric Review* reflect the properties
of humanist writing that I outline above. *JAC*'s statement immediately
establishes its theoretical orientation, where "theoretical" refers to a mode
of inquiry that conceives of itself as an essentially rational, deductive process. Even more telling, however, is the feel of the language. *JAC* and
Rhetoric Review both call for essays that "explore" their topics, signaling a
decidedly essayist mentality. *Rhetoric Review*, moreover, wants its contributors to "consider" and "discuss" their subjects, calling to mind the reflective attitude that Olson finds in humanism. And *JAC*'s editorial policy
privileges scholars' interests as a reason for publishing the kind of work it
does: what compels it is not only a search for truth but also (and maybe
even foremost) human desire. These policies stand in stark contrast to
that of *Written Communication*, whose first word that explicitly reflects the
type of work it seeks is "research." Work in *Written Communication* is "cutting edge"—a subtle but not unremarkable nod to the narrative of scientific progress. Even the idea that written communication has a "nature"
that can be "understood"—these are linguistic cues that suggest a view of
knowledge as something that, no matter how mediated, is ultimately based
in the external world. The areas of inquiry *Written Communication* lists as
contributing to its interdisciplinarity also differ from those of *JAC* and
Written Communication: the first two mentioned by both *JAC* and *Written
Communication* are rhetoric and writing, while *Written Communication*
opens with linguistics, psychology, and the cognitive sciences.

CONCLUSION: TOWARD A KAIROTIC TACTICS
OF INTERDISCIPLINARITY

The intellectual and professional preferences of these and other journals that publish work in composition merit such close and public attention because doing so helps us understand our disciplinary past and

present. And it is more important than ever to have a firm grasp of our past and present, because our future is on the line. I realize that the "now more than ever" move is a suspect one: when *hasn't* composition, or the humanities more generally, faced a crisis that threatens our place in the academy? As John Muckelbauer and Tim Donovan write, "There have consistently been voices within various fields that have portrayed the moment, *this* moment, as a crucial one, a decisive point for humanistic inquiry" (2004, 851; italics in original). That is, our future is *always* (and by definition) on the line. But rather than dampen the present sense of urgency, this realization simply reminds us that, while we may never *not* be responding to a crisis of one sort or another, one of our jobs is always to try to understand *this* critical moment as clearly as possible. And our moment, from my own vantage as an assistant professor at an underfunded state university, seems especially challenging. States' budgets are being slashed, and universities continue to model policies and management practices after those of the for-profit private sector, placing greater burden than ever on individual units to generate their own revenues rather than rely on "deficit" spending for their continued existence (as if a liberal-arts education were worth only as much as one can turn around and sell it for on the open market). The current economic crisis has not only helped to intensify such practices, but it may also be helping to naturalize them—to render them not the intellectually poisonous administrative *choices* they are but, rather, to make them seem like the unalterable facts of life in contemporary higher education. And if we are indeed inching, as I suspect we are (and as North advocates in his contribution to this volume), ever closer to a nonservice-oriented academic discipline housed in its own departments rather than predominantly in English, with its own textbooks, and with a rich, field-specific program of theoretical and empirical research, then it will not be long before our long-time benefactor, the (nearly) universal first-year writing requirement, will no longer be able—or willing—to sustain us. Such change, moreover, rarely happens smoothly, and the process seems likely, for a time at least, to further entrench and energize the various constituents of what Gary Olson has infamously called the "new theory wars" (2002, 25).

As we face these challenges, it will be necessary to have as clear a sense as possible of our disciplinary identity (or identities, depending on how disposed toward pluralism you are), particularly in terms of the methodological and theoretical currents that inform our work. If, that is, we are to survive the slash-and-burn tactics of the corporate university (note my perhaps naïve hope: I don't want us to survive *in* the corporate university; I want us to survive *it*), we will certainly need to be staunch in our resistance to the oppressive policies and sly tactics of university administrations as well as state and federal legislatures. But, just as surely, we will need to devote ourselves to nourishing at least the potential to develop our own tactical academic alignments and realignments with colleagues of all methodological stripes, both within and outside of composition—to developing a kind of flexible, mobile, *kairotic* interdisciplinarity as a way to navigate the constantly-shifting, unpredictable terrain of contemporary university life.

It is ironic that a study of *MKC* and its reception helps to support this conclusion, since by definition it necessitates somehow getting over our tendency to let methodology trump other potential terms of identification in the forging of our professional associations—methodology being a force of attraction strong enough for North, via Diesing, to have dubbed it (albeit with tongue partially in cheek) a "law." Yet breaking laws is easy when the fabric of the universe in which they operate is altered in some fundamental way. That is, much as Jack Ryan's character in *The Hunt for Red October* realizes that *he* doesn't need to figure out how to get the enlisted sailors off of the Red October (because the Soviet captain would need to have solved that problem himself), we don't have to figure out how to break Diesing's law: it is already being broken for us. When we can no longer take for granted that our individual units and programs will survive the next budget cut—when we are routinely scrambling for solutions to keep our educational missions, our research agendas, and our working situations healthy—then our identities as members of a local university community necessarily become much more important than they may have been for many of us before. That is, the balance of professional exigencies for many compositionists and, indeed, many academics generally, has shifted toward maintaining (forget about improving, for now) our home spaces—our enrollments, our staff, our salaries, our workloads, our jobs. Because, for most of us, such concerns are rooted in a specific locale (or two, or three, for the "freeway fliers" among us), we will be much more likely to work closely and intensely with faculty across the curriculum to try to solve pressing local problems. (Of course this happens anyway, on college- and university-wide committees and in faculty senates, but not often on the scale or with the intensity resulting from the budget crises now facing public and private colleges and universities across the country.) In the process, our professional senses of ourselves cannot help but be changed, as we begin to identify with colleagues in math, or political science, or business. And while the terms of such an identification may still not be based on disciplinary content (North's experimentalist, practitioner, and philosopher, who all study revision), stemming rather from common geography and institutional status, we will still need to do the work of the discipline—publishing, going to conferences, holding office, and the like. If, in the meantime, we are rubbing elbows with sociologists and economists and biologists while we try to bring our creativity and, inevitably, our disciplinary expertise to bear on solving important problems "at home," then whatever new potential professional alignments may emerge from those efforts are bound to manifest themselves in our larger, more dispersed, disciplinary work.

In short, new exigencies require new alignments. But the inevitability that, in the short term at least, many of us will be forced to rethink our professional identities as we work closely with faculty in other programs in our departments as well as faculty in other departments, does not mean that we should simply ride the wave without trying to steer our boards. We need to know—or to be ready to learn—how our work with revision can be linked with work in psychology, sociology, anthropology, biology, economics, or any other discipline whose work touches in any way on processes that affect human behavior and society. We need to understand the relationships between what appears, at this early stage, to be the social-scientific bent of our move toward writing studies and away from composition and the hermeneutic work of the humanities that has driven expressivism and social constructionism alike (and has formed, for so long, the affective core of our discipline). By tracing the dynamics of composition's transition into a postmodern discipline, and by mapping the parallel trajectories of humanistic and social-scientific research within its disciplinary bounds, this project constitutes one small step toward such a self-conscious, and consciously rhetorical, tactics of interdisciplinarity.

REFERENCES

Bartholomae, David. 1988. Review of *The making of knowledge in composition: Portrait of an emerging field*, by Stephen M. North. *Rhetoric Review* 6: 224–28.
———. 1990. A reply to Stephen North. *Pre/Text* 11: 122–30.
Bloom, Lynn Z., Donald A. Daiker, and Edward M. White, eds. 2003. *Composition studies in*

the new millennium: Rereading the past, rewriting the future. Carbondale: Southern Illinois University Press.

Branscomb, Eric. 1997. North northwest: Ethnography and the making of knowledge in composition. In *Voices and visions: Refiguring ethnography in composition*, edited by Christina Kirklighter, Cloe Vincent, and Joseph M. Moxley. Portsmouth, NH: Boynton/Cook.

Faigley, Lester. 1992. *Fragments of rationality: Postmodernity and the subject of composition.* Pittsburgh, PA: University of Pittsburgh Press.

Farris, Christine. 2003. No discipline? Composition's professional identity crisis. In Bloom, Daiker, and White, 57–61.

Fontaine, Sheryl I., and Susan Hunter. 1992. Rendering the "Text" of composition. *Journal of Advanced Composition* 12: 395–406.

Fulkerson, Richard. 2005. Composition at the turn of the twenty-first century. *College Composition and Communication* 56: 654–87.

Gere, Ann Ruggles. 1993. Introduction to *Into the field: Sites of composition studies*, edited by Ann Ruggles Gere, 1–6. New York: Modern Language Association.

Harkin, Patricia. 1993. The postdisciplinary politics of lore. In Harkin and Schilb, 124–38.

Harkin, Patricia, and John Schilb, eds. 1991. *Contending with words: Composition and rhetoric in a postmodern age.* New York: Modern Language Association.

Kirsch, Gesa E. 2003. Ethics and the future of composition research. In Bloom, Daiker, and White, 129–41.

Larson, Richard L. 1989. Review of *The making of knowledge in composition: Portrait of an emerging field*, by Stephen M. North. *College Composition and Communication* 40: 95–98.

Lloyd-Jones, Richard. 1989. Review of *The making of knowledge in composition: Portrait of an emerging field*, by Stephen M. North. *College Composition and Communication* 40: 98–100.

Lyotard, Jean-François. 1984. *The postmodern condition: A report on knowledge.* Translated by Geoff Bennington and Brian Massumi. Minneapolis: University of Minnesota Press.

Mailloux, Steven. 1998. *Reception histories: Rhetoric, pragmatism, and American cultural politics.* Ithaca, NY: Cornell University Press.

McLeod, Susan H. 2003. Celebrating diversity (in methodology). In Bloom, Daiker, and White, 151–54.

Mucklebauer, John, and Tim Donovan. 2004. To do justice to *this* moment: Between exhaustion and totality. *JAC* 24: 851–70.

North, Stephen M. 1987. *The making of knowledge in composition: Portrait of an emerging field.* Upper Montclair, NJ: Boynton/Cook.

Olson, Gary. 2002. The death of composition as an intellectual discipline. In *Rhetoric and composition as intellectual work*, edited by Gary Olson, 23–31. Carbondale: Southern Illinois University Press.

Prior, Paul. 1998. *Writing/disciplinarity: A sociohistoric account of literate activity in the academy.* Mahwah, NJ: Erlbaum.

Raymond, James C. 1989. Review of *The making of knowledge in composition: Portrait of an emerging field*, by Stephen M. North. *College Composition and Communication* 40: 93–95.

Sullivan, Patricia. 1992. Feminism and methodology in composition studies. In *Methods and methodology in composition research*, edited by Gesa Kirsch and Patricia A. Sullivan. Carbondale: Southern Illinois University Press.

Taylor, Todd. 2003. "A Methodology of Our Own." In Bloom, Daiker, and White, 142–50.

Worsham, Lynn. 1991. "Writing against writing: The predicament of *ecriture féminine* in composition studies." In Harkin and Schilb, 82-104.

AFTERWORD

Stephen M. North

I want to begin this afterword by expressing my appreciation to this book's editors, Lance Massey and Richard Gebhardt, for undertaking the project in the first place—editing a volume of this kind is always hard work—and then for inviting me to participate. I don't know that I would have become involved otherwise, and that would have been a shame: I'd have missed what has turned out to be a really interesting opportunity.

As a writer, I found reading the chapters assembled here to be a kind of blessing. For all that might have been good or bad, insightful or wrongheaded, constructive or destructive about *MKC*—and this volume has surely contributed to my continuing education on those fronts—it really was my way of demonstrating my commitment to our collective enterprise by taking the writings of my fellow compositionists as seriously as I could. So not only was it terrific that so many strong scholars should be willing to engage the book all these years later, but that they should do so in such a reciprocally serious and, if I may say so, *MKC*-esque way: their readings, that is, go where they damn well go. Thus, as much fun as it was to read Ed White's account of my narrator as a guide for graduate students (who *wouldn't* want to be that guy?), there was at least as much truth, however unpalatably prepared, in Lynn Bloom's critique of that narrator's dubious patriarchal ties (who'd want to be *that* guy?). And while I felt a little swell of pride when Brad Lucas and Drew Loewe offered bibliometric evidence, as it were, that *MKC* really did have some impact, it was more than matched by Victor Villanueva's deflation-inducingly correct contention that the book's resolute focus on epistemological analysis, so entirely uninflected by ideological concerns, rendered race utterly invisible—along with, though Villanueva kindly doesn't rub it in by saying so, gender, class, sexual orientation, labor practices and so on. In short, reading wasn't always fun, but it felt consistently real.

In the rest of this response, though, I want to focus more on the present than the past—on the rendering of composition offered in this volume, not in *MKC*. And I want to begin by saying that I was struck, more than anything, by the catalog of threats this volume suggests composition is facing. So, for example, Richard Fulkerson and Patricia Dunn—to one of whom I am indebted for a deeply insightful reading of my tortured chapter on practice as inquiry, the other for her generous portrayal of my own teaching—are somewhere between fury and despair about the status of teacher knowledge in two different spheres: within composition, where Fulkerson fears we have abandoned the search for generalizability in favor of ever-more-carefully wrought lore; and between composition and the schools, in which context Dunn believes we have all mostly failed to use whatever it is we do know to affect public policy. Moreover, and despite the more upbeat tone of Matthew Jackson's terrific essay, I came away from it, too, with a sense of foreboding. For as sympathetic as I am toward his account of teaching as an intersubjective ethical phenomenon, his insistence that "the worth and value of compositionists simply cannot be calculated under the dictates of current institutional constraints" bespeaks a potentially fatal lack of fit in still a third sphere, that between composition and its host institutions of higher education. Or let's put it this way: it would be best if the chair of Jackson's department doesn't begin her letter regarding his tenure with that line.

Nor is this anywhere near the darkest of the dark stuff. David Smit's chapter, after all, comes pretty close to declaring composition, at least in its current form, fraudulent. Kristine Hansen's argues not only that the enterprise has had, at best, "mixed success" in moving toward the kind of disciplinary status outlined in *MKC*, but—worse—has demonstrated a disturbing lack of principle along even its limited way, not least by colluding in the systematic exploitation of the labor of its own members. And while, like Matthew Jackson, Lance Massey is at some pains to generate at least a hopeful, if not exactly upbeat, tone, what he nevertheless aims to offer is a way for composition to "survive . . . the slash-and-burn tactics of the corporate university," to resist the "oppressive policies and sly tactics of university administrations as well as state and federal legislatures." Apocalyptic stuff, indeed.

To be sure, the volume sounds some positive notes, too. Even the most pessimistic of the writers I have mentioned so far offer, at least implicitly, some vision, some path—however utopian or systemically wrenching—whereby a morally, pedagogically, and intellectually defensible form of writing instruction might survive, if not thrive, in higher education and beyond. Moreover, I think it fair to say that Joyce Kinkead and Patricia Boyd offer such visions in a more sustained way, or at least a more sustainedly positive way, with the former offering an extended account of and rationale for the writing studies major, and the latter showing how ecocomposition and other place-based research might offer a workable paradigm for a composition enterprise that is still "working to carve a place for itself within the university." And in some sense, surely, it is a positive that at least some contributors are less concerned about whether or how composition might survive than with working in it, and doing so with an impressive level of acumen, intelligence, and energy: the aforementioned Lucas and Loewe; Kelly Pender on philosophical inquiry; Erica Frisicaro-Pawlowski on historical inquiry; and the team of Sarah Liggett, Kerri Jordan, and Steve Price on the intermethodological dynamics of the writing center.

Frankly, though, while I would love to move from the genuine promise of these few bright spots to a dutifully upbeat ending, I can't quite do it. I know I said much the same sort of thing twenty-five years ago at the end of *MKC*, but my worries then—about intramethodological conflict and inhospitable English departments—seem like pretty small potatoes here. I'm not saying there is no hope. If I thought that, I wouldn't have agreed to write an afterword at all; and in fact my involvement with this project has left me inspired by the deep engagement and fierce intelligence of the scholars, young and old, included in this volume. On that score, I will say unequivocally, composition—or rhetoric and composition, or composition studies, or writing studies, or literacy studies, or whatever name or names we end up giving to whatever versions of this cause I believe we share—is far better off now than it was in 1987. But the forces arrayed against that cause and, more to the point, against the people it seeks to serve, strike me, as they seem to strike so many of the contributors, as far more daunting, too. So, as they used to say on *Hill Street Blues*, be careful out there.

INDEX

Teufel, Simone 270
Thaiss, Christopher 42
Thelin, William 223
Tidhar, Dan 270
Tompkins, Jane 36, 43
Trollope, Frances 30, 43

Undergraduate research 7, 9, 137–57

Vandenberg, Peter 257
Varnado, Beverly Bratton 62
Varnum, Robin 95, 101
Vicinus, Martha 38, 43
Villanueva, Victor 7, 8, 121, 133, 323
Vitanza, Victor 72–73, 78, 82, 83
Vygotsky, Lev 184

Wardle, Elizabeth 2, 10, 151, 158
Weisser, Christian 288, 289, 290, 293,
    294, 299, 300, 301
White, Edward M. 6, 10, 17, 27, 29, 30,
    38, 41, 43, 235, 256, 262, 282, 321,
    322, 323
White, Howard D. 269

Wiley, Mark 214
Williams,Jean C. 101, 127, 132
Willison, John 146
Witte, Stephen P. 19, 27, 193, 313–14,
    325
Wolfe, Tom 37, 43
Worsham, Lynn 70–71, 72, 77, 80, 83,
    219, 235, 322
Writing center 7, 8, 9, 12, 13, 37, 92n,
    102–119, 139, 144, 150, 155, 177,
    183, 195, 201, 204, 223, 325
Writing major/minor/emphasis 5, 7, 9,
    137–57, 196–202, 208, 209, 238, 239,
    240, 258, 259, 325
Writing studies 1, 2, 7, 56, 137, 139–146,
    148, 149, 151–154, 156–157, 194,
    202, 207–209, 218, 240, 248, 253,
    258–260, 262, 272, 317, 321, 325

Yood, Jessica 98–99, 101
Young, Morris, 128
Young, Richard 64, 69–70, 71, 72, 83,
    148, 160, 180, 261

ABOUT THE AUTHORS

LANCE MASSEY is an assistant professor of English at Bowling Green State University, where he teaches courses on the profession and on the rhetoric of written discourse in the rhetoric and writing PhD program. He also teaches undergraduate courses on writing and grammar for future language-arts teachers. Lance has authored or coauthored book chapters on the ethics of ad hominem argumentation and ethnographic research methods, and he is coeditor of *Feminism and Composition: A Critical Sourcebook* (2003). Lance's current work problematizes conventional definitions of "personal writing," offering in the process a new ethics of professional reading and writing.

RICHARD C. GEBHARDT is professor emeritus of English at Bowling Green State University where he chaired the department and later directed the rhetoric and writing PhD program. Rick's publications include articles in *CCC, College English, Rhetoric Review, JAC, ADE Bulletin* and other journals, and the collection *Academic Advancement in Composition Studies: Scholarship, Publication, Promotion, Tenure* (edited with Barbara Genelle Smith Gebhardt). In 1977, Rick won the Richard Braddock Award, and from 1986 to 1993 he edited *College Composition and Communication*. Much of Rick's work over the past fifteen years has emphasized the nature and evaluation of rhetoric and composition scholarship, most recently the scholarship of engagement.

LYNN Z. BLOOM is Board of Trustees Distinguished Professor and Aetna Chair of Writing at the University of Connecticut. Her most recent books are *The Seven Deadly Virtues and Other Lively Essays* (2008) and *Writers Without Borders: Writing and Teaching Writing in Troubled Times* (2008). Her current work on *The Essay Canon*, analyzing the fall and rise of the ubiquitous and now "hot"genre—the essay—(after a century of second-class citizenship) that is the foundational material for 150 years of composition teaching and creative nonfiction, led to this critique of North. The overview, "The Essay Canon," was published in *College English* (1999).

PATRICIA WEBB BOYD is an associate professor in the rhetoric and composition PhD program/English department at Arizona State University, where she teaches courses on new media and writing, feminism and composition, and sustainability and literacy practices. She also teaches undergraduate courses in business communication and first-year writing. Patricia's articles have been published in *Kairos, Computers and Composition*, and *College English*, among other places. She is currently working on an extensive project that analyzes the literacy practices of members of online weight-loss discussion boards.

PATRICIA A. DUNN is an associate professor of English at Stony Brook University, where she teaches courses in rhetoric, composition, and English education. She has published two books: *Learning Re-Abled: The Learning Disability Controversy and Composition Studies* (1995) and *Talking, Sketching, Moving: Multiple Literacies in the Teaching of Writing* (2001). Her articles and book chapters, some cowritten, explore intersections of theory and practice, especially regarding multiple literacies and language-related disabilities. Her work has appeared in *CCC, Rhetoric Review, English Journal,* and *Kairos*. With Ken Lindblom, she has written a book which critiques unspoken assumptions in grammar rants.

Erica Frisicaro-Pawlowski is an assistant professor of English at Daemen College, where she serves as writing coordinator and teaches basic, first-year, and advanced composition. She has written and presented research on the rhetoric of disciplinary history, and her interest in *MKC* stems from her dissertation, *Constructing Composition: History, Disciplinarity, and Ideology* (2003). Her recent work (with Margaret Artman and Robert Monge) explores the influence of information literacy instruction on students' research practices.

Richard Fulkerson is a professor emeritus of English at Texas A&M University-Commerce, where he served as director of English graduate studies for over twenty years. He served on the CCCC Executive Committee and wrote numerous articles and book chapters, primarily on argument and on composition theory. His work appeared in *CCC, Rhetoric Review, JAC, Journal of Teaching Writing, ADE Bulletin, Quarterly Journal of Speech, Argumentation and Advocacy,* and *Informal Logic.* He is best known for three *CCC* articles, published at decade intervals, on theories of composition, and for his NCTE monograph *Teaching the Argument in Writing.*

Kristine Hansen is professor of English at Brigham Young University, where she has directed both the composition program and WAC program. She teaches advanced writing, history of rhetoric, composition theory and pedagogy, and research methods. Her most recent book, *College Credit for Writing in High School* (coedited with Christine Farris), explores the high school-to-college transition and the granting of credit for writing done in high-school advanced placement, international baccalaureate, and concurrent enrollment programs. With Joseph Janangelo she coedited *Resituating Writing: Constructing and Administering Writing Programs.* She has published a textbook, *Writing in the Social Sciences,* and articles in journals and edited volumes.

Matthew Jackson, a graduate of the department of education, culture and society at the University of Utah, teaches at Utah Valley University. An interdisciplinary scholar, he belongs to the Philosophy of Education Society, the Rhetoric Society of America, and the Conference on College Composition and Communication. He is interested in the philosophical frameworks of rhetoric and composition, especially concerning ethics and pedagogy. His recent works include "Unsaying the Said as Rhetorical Responsibility" (*JAC* 2009) and "Bordering on Violence: A Levinasian Critique of Ontology and Ethics in Giroux's Critical Pedagogy" (*Philosophy of Education* 2006).

Kerri Jordan is associate professor of English at Mississippi College, where she directs the writing program and teaches courses in writing and writing pedagogy. Formerly a writing center director, she serves as secretary of the International Writing Center Association. Her dissertation, *Power and Empowerment in Writing Center Conferences* (2003), was supported by a grant from the International Writing Centers Association, and her research interests continue to include writing center theory, practice, and assessment.

Joyce Kinkead is a professor of English and Associate Vice President for Research at Utah State University, where she previously directed both the writing program and the writing center. She is a founding member of the National Writing Centers Association and served as its executive secretary for eight years and as coeditor of *The Writing Center Journal* (1985–1991) following Lil Brannon and Steve North. Her publications include *Undergraduate Research in English Studies, Valuing and Supporting Undergraduate Research, The Center Will Hold: Critical Perspectives on Writing Center Scholarship, Writing Centers in Context, A Schoolmarm All My Life,* and *Literary Utah.*

SARAH LIGGETT is professor of English and director of the communication across the curriculum program at Louisiana State University where she teaches in the rhetoric, writing and culture concentration. She is former director of the LSU Writing Center and the first year writing program. She has presented numerous papers at conferences and has published articles on program assessment, technical writing, and teacher education. Her most recent book, a coedited collection of essays, is *Preparing College Teachers of Writing: Histories, Theories, Programs, Practices* (2002). Her current work investigates research methodologies appropriate to writing center contexts, especially program assessment.

DREW M. LOEWE is an assistant professor of English Writing & Rhetoric at St. Edward's University in Austin, Texas. His research and teaching interests include composition theory and pedagogy, twentieth-century rhetorical theory and criticism (particularly Kenneth Burke), online rhetoric, and legal writing. He has published a chapter in the collection *Refiguring Prose Style: Possibilities for Writing Pedagogy* and has published reviews in *KB Journal, Composition Studies,* and *Issues in Writing.* His current projects examine online social movement rhetoric.

BRAD LUCAS is an associate professor of English at Texas Christian University, where he serves as chair of the English department. He teaches courses in composition, document design, argument and persuasion, and professional and technical writing. Brad is the former editor of *Composition Studies.* He is the author of *Radicals, Rhetoric, and the War* (2006), and his work has also appeared in *Issues in Writing* and *Rhetoric Review.*

STEPHEN M. NORTH is a distinguished teaching professor of English at the University at Albany, State University of New York, where he has served as director of the writing center (1981–86, 1998–99) and director of writing (1987–94, 1995–96). He is founding coeditor (with Lil Brannon) of *The Writing Center Journal* and creator of the NCTE book series, Refiguring English Studies. He is the author of *The Making of Knowledge in Composition* (1987), *Refiguring the Ph.D. in English Studies* (with Barbara A. Chepaitis, David Coogan, Lale Davidson, Ron Maclean, Cindy L. Parrish, Jonathan Post, and Beth Weatherby 2000), and articles in journals ranging from *College English* to *Writing on the Edge.* His current work is on mystery and detective fiction.

KELLY PENDER is an assistant professor of English at Virginia Tech where she teaches classical rhetoric for the rhetoric and writing PhD program, as well as courses in editing and issues in public and professional discourse for the undergraduate professional writing program. Her work has appeared in *Postmodern Culture, Composition Studies,* and *Rhetoric Society Quarterly.* And she has published *Techne, From Neoclassicism to Postmodernism: Understanding Writing as a Useful, Teachable Art* (2011), which explains how the concept of techne has shaped the theory, pedagogy, and disciplinary identity of rhetoric and composition since the mid-twentieth century.

STEVE PRICE is associate professor of English at Mississippi College, where he directs the writing center and teaches courses in writing and writing pedagogy. He previously directed the communication-across-the-curriculum program at Monmouth College. Steve has presented papers and workshops on motivating first-year writers, writing center research strategies, and tutor training, and is a founding member of the Mississippi Writing Centers Association. His current work investigates writing center pedagogies, institutional research strategies, and first-year composition course design.

DAVID W. SMIT is a professor of English at Kansas State University, where he directed the expository writing program for ten years. He served as president of the Kansas Association